TURNER PUBLISHING COMPANY
Paducah, Kentucky

TURNER PUBLISHING COMPANY
412 Broadway, P.O. Box 3101
Paducah, KY 42002-3101
Phone: (502) 443-0121

Copyright © 1996. Turner Publishing Company.
All rights reserved.
Additional copies may be purchased directly from
Turner Publishing Company.

This book or any part thereof may not be reproduced
without the written consent of Turner Publishing Company.

This publication was produced using available material.
The publisher regrets it cannot assume liability for errors or
omissions.

Military Chaplains Association Staff:
Executive Director: G. William Dando

Turner Publishing Company Staff:
Publishing Consultant: Douglas W. Sikes
Project Coordinator: Pamela Wood
Designer: Herbert C. Banks II

Library of Congress Catalog Card Number: 96-60185
ISBN 978-1-63026-944-9

Additional copies may be purchased directly from
Turner Publishing Company.

Limited Edition.

Title page: Easter Sunrise Service on Christmas Island, April 1962, Joint Task Force 8 Operation Dominic Atomic Test, led by the only Protestant Chaplain assigned to the operation, Robert L. Maase, USAF. (Courtesy of Robert Maase) This page: Chaplain Arthur E. Lyons, Jr., conducting a field service at Ft. Leonard Wood, MO in 1968 or 1969. An hour of discretionary time was used during the basic training cycle to explain and demonstrate to the trainees what they could expect from chaplains in Vietnam and other combat situations. The first part of the hour was a general description of Chaplain activitives and services in the context of combat. In the second part of the hour, for those who wished to remain, simultaneous field services were conducted by a Catholic and a Protestant and if available, a Jewish Chaplain.

Table of Contents

Introduction 4
Publisher' Message 5
Military Chaplains Association History 6
Special Stories 20
Biographies 40
Index 104

Introduction

Chaplain Herbert Cleveland

Webster's Dictionary says that history is a chronicle, a written record of events. General George Patton said, "The history of war is the history of warriors; few in number, mighty in influence..." As this book comes together we see hundreds and hundreds of warriors of the Lord and placed in the hands of scholars is the written record of events of the most exciting century of the second millennium. Never before have chaplains assumed the influence that they have in the lives of the military fighting force as in the 20th Century.

Several times in the 20th Century, the Chaplains Corps were down to bare bone, but as soon as the trumpet sounded, the faithful men and women of God responded with sacrifice and dedication. That sacrifice and dedication is best memorialized by the heroic action of the forever famous gift of The Four Chaplains as they gave their life for others when their troop ship, the SS *Dorchester* was torpedoed and sunk in the North Atlantic, thus living out the scriptural teaching "Greater love hath no man than this that he lay down his life for his brother."

History of the Military Chaplains Association of the United States of America is the history of the chaplains and their families in the 20th Century. This is not a definitive history, rather it preserves for posterity a chronicle of lives given for God and Country... "Pro Deo et Patria."

Although the MCA belongs to the 20th Century, it receives its strength from as far back in history as the books of Moses when it is recorded in Deuteronomy 20:1-4. "When thou goest out to battle against thine enemies, and seest horses and chariots and a people more than thou, be not afraid of them; for the Lord thy God is with thee, which brought thee up out of the Land of Egypt, And it shall be, when ye are come nigh unto battle, that the priest shall approach and speak unto the people and shall say to them, Hear, O Israel, ye approach this day unto battle against your enemies; let not your hearts faint, fear not, and do not tremble, neither be terrified because of them; for the Lord your God is he that goeth with you, to fight for you against your enemies, to save you."

The Military Chaplains Association was originally conceived of by a group of U.S. Army chaplains sensing a need for a professional organization that would promote the highest ideal of service and sacrifice for God and Country. They were soon joined by the Navy chaplains and as the armed forces matured the Air Force chaplains, the Veterans Affairs chaplains and Civil Air Patrol chaplains were added to the membership. The Military Chaplains Association of the United States of America is here to serve all chaplains in their professional education and development, to uphold the ideals of Faith, Hope and Love and to serve the patriotic needs of our nation.

As we put this book together, we look to a new millennium and a new challenge of serving the Armed Forces of the only remaining super power of the world. Our chaplains are all over the world with the men and women who make the finest Armed Forces in history. Our vision for the future is peace, our method is through service, and our gift is God's mercy.

Publisher's Message

Dave Turner, President

It is indeed a pleasure to present to you the Military Chaplains Association History Book to serve as a reminder of their selfless service to our men and women in the uniformed services and our country. Though meek, they were no less military; though not on the front lines of the conflict, they fought a battle no less noble.

Their enemies were perhaps more diabolical and armed with an even deadlier arsenal of hate, greed, destruction, stress, despair, loneliness, injury, and death. The Chaplains struggled to keep their own spirits high amid overwhelming circumstances in order to provide the strength and support the other military needed. This book is a tribute to their sacrifices and tireless efforts on behalf of the human spirit.

We wish to thank Herbert Cleveland whose loyalty to the MCA helped make this book possible and G. William Dando, Executive Director, who directed the final stages of book production to ensure a quality product. We especially thank those individuals who submitted their personal accounts of service during wartime, yours is a story often untold by history books.

It was a privilege to work with such a distinguished association and document their rightful place in the annals of history. It is our hope that this book will serve as a vivid reminder of these faithful men and women of service.

Dave Turner, President

Chaplain John H. Craven, USN, prays for the dedication of the Fourth Marine Division Cemetery on Iwo Jima, March 1945. (Courtesy of John H. Craven)

Military Chaplains Association History

A BRIEF HISTORY OF THE MILITARY CHAPLAINS ASSOCIATION

The Early Years
1925-1962

As with many associations existing today, both great and small, the Military Chaplains Association evolved from the gathering of an informal group, whose early history, consequently, is only sparsely documented. The initial group of chaplains, all from within the U.S. Army, convened on April 25, 1925, as an outgrowth of an informal council of chaplains convened by the first Army Chief of Chaplains, John Thomas Axton (1920-1928) and became known by the name, the Army Chaplains Association. Chaplain Axton was an efficient and meticulous administrator. He gathered the small group of chaplains around him, welcoming the counsel of fellow colleagues. The Association continued as the instrument of the Army Chief's Edmund P. Esterbrook (1928-1929) and John Julian Yates (1929-1933), unfortunately no minutes or records from this era exist today.

In 1930, the fifth "Convention" was held, resulting in the initial publication in July of *The Army Chaplain* magazine, the forerunner of *The Military Chaplain*. All meetings to that date had been held in Washington, DC. Bishop Brent, the first President of the Association, served from 1925 to 1929 and was succeeded by five others over the following nine years. Army Chaplain Nils Ylvisaker was elected President in 1938 and served until 1946. The Editor of *The Army Chaplain* publication through this term was former Army Chief of Chaplains, Julian Yates, followed by Army Chaplain Alva Brasted, another former Chief of Chaplains. Brasted then presided from 1940 to 1945. There was no formal headquarters for the organization in those days, only the home of the magazine's editor serving as such.

Conventions were held in the 1930s in Washington, DC, Baltimore, New York, Cleveland, Louisville, St. Louis, Chicago, Cincinnati and New York, all with substantial attendance. Because of WWII, there were no conventions held 1940-1945.

In 1940 a representative group of U.S. Navy chaplains accepted an invitation to join the Association and it then became known as the Army and Navy Chaplains Association. In 1946 a convention of the new Association was held in Washington, DC. Since 1948, an annual meeting has been held every year at various locations across the nation, in more than 25 different cities and states. Also following the cessation of the hostilities of WWII, the Association headquarters was located in a number of different locations including the offices of the General Commission for Chaplains and Armed Forces Personnel. To the present time, as far as records are able to indicate, the headquarters have been located in 11 different sites since 1946.

After a decade as the Army and Navy Chaplains Association, the organization was to expand again with the creation of the U.S. Air Force. At the annual convention of the Chaplains Association of the Army and Navy held in New York, May 10-13, 1948, the name of the Association was formally changed to The Military Chaplains Association to embrace all three branches of the military service and the Veterans' Administration because so many chaplains being appointed in the Veterans Administration were former military chaplains.

Commencing with the July-August issue 1948, the magazine of the Association, *Army and Navy Chaplain*, was replaced by *The Military Chaplain*. Chaplain A.J. Brasted served as editor of the forerunner magazine but resigned in the spring of 1945, and Navy Chaplain Clifford M. Drury, a historian who wrote the two volume set of the Navy Chaplain Corps History, was named as his successor. Chaplain Drury wrote in the *Navy Chaplain Corps History* (Vol. II, pg. 258):

"*The Military Chaplain* is unique in the history of journalism for it is the only publication which is supported by chaplains from

three branches of the Armed Services and the Veterans' Administration, Reserves and Regulars, and of all faiths. Indeed, the Military Chaplains Association of the United States brings together in one voluntary paid-membership association more clergymen of the three major faiths than may be found in any other similar organization."

The New York convention raised the annual dues in the organization from $2 to $3 and that included a year's subscription to the magazine. According to what meager records there are, the paid membership of the Association reached 2,443 as of Jan. 1, 1949 of whom 571 were listed as Navy.

Navy Chaplain R. J. White, USNR, was elected the first Navy President of the 16th annual convention of the Association in Washington, DC, Oct. 23-25, 1946. He was reelected in 1948 leading the transition from an Army-Navy organization to a tri-service association and the renaming of the organization. The Association was rechartered on Sept. 20, 1950 by the 81st U.S. Congress as The Military Chaplains Association of the United States of America (public law 792) to include all chaplains of the military service and Veterans' Administration including former chaplains. From 1961-1966, Army Chief of Chaplains Patrick J. Ryan served as President. His zeal, generosity and untiring efforts brought a new era for the MCA.

THE JUSTUS YEARS
1962-1978

Karl B. Justus was installed as the first full-time executive director of the MCA on Aug. 1, 1962. His initial affiliation with the organization, however, dates back to 1951 at which time he served as executive director of the San Francisco office of the National Office of Christians and Jews. His reputation as an excellent fund raiser had been made known to Chaplain Colonel Patrick J. Ryan, U.S. Army, who was the sixth Army Chaplain at the Presidio under General Mark Clark, Commanding Officer. Monsignor "Pat" Ryan requested the aid of Karl B. Justus in raising money for the MCA National Convention which was held at the St. Francis Hotel in San Francisco in May 1951. Visits were made to L.P. Grannini, President of the Bank of America and other generous organizations, and a very successful fundraising effort resulted in a collection of $15,000.00 for the convention. When the convention was over, the excess funds were sent to the MCA office at 1710 16th ST NW in Washington, DC, one mile from the White House.

Karl Justus joined the MCA for $5.00 in 1951, but was not contacted to renew his membership or keep up his dues payments. It was 1961 before he heard from the MCA again. In a surprise call from Monsignor Ryan, he was given an invitation to become the Executive Director of The Military Chaplains Association. Army Chief of Chaplains Patrick J. Ryan had assumed the Presidency of the MCA in 1961 and saw the need for an organized and conscientious director who could raise money and renew interest in the Association. After much consideration, Justus agreed to be interviewed by Monsignor Ryan and a group of Army and Air Force Chaplains from the Washington area. After a considerable interview with many questions, they offered the position to Justus at an annual salary of $10,000.00 and no contract. He accepted the job and moved his family back east from San Francisco in July of 1962. His first order of business involved contacting association members and all chaplains whose names were in the rolls, but who had not been contacted for many years. With practically no money on hand, his job seemed enormous, but with the help of generous business associates, such as James D. Zellerback of the Crown Zellerback Corp., Ted Peterson of Standard Oil of California, Jim Black, President of Pacific Gas and Electric, and Cyril Magnum of Joseph Magnum and Company and chaplains eager to renew their contact with MCA, money started to pour in.

Karl B Justus.

Record keeping was in the hands of Robert Rice, an elderly gentleman who kept a safe and the combination number of that safe quite confidential. After six or seven weeks of dealing with a flood of mail and telephone calls, Mr. Rice suffered a heart attack. The rapid response on the part of the membership overwhelmed him, and he lived only a new weeks following his illness at home. Fortunately, Justus was able to learn the combination number, and upon resuming work at the office, opened the safe and found over 100 dues envelopes which had been sitting there for as long as two to three years. The envelopes contained $5.00 bills and checks, dues from members who had not been recorded or acknowledged. The backlog of work was enormous as none of these donors had received membership cards. Justus secured permission from Monsignor Ryan to hire his wife, Eileen, as a part-time secretary to help with the workload. In addition to updating membership records, he was also writing and editing *The Military Chaplain*.

The first convention that Justus attended was in May of 1963 at the Huntington Sheraton Palace Hotel in Pasadena, CA. His post-convention report, entitled "Convention Afterglow" reflected his success as executive director since the income of the association exceeded the expenses by $512.00. The trust fund was at its highest level since the beginning of the organization's history. As stated in the bylaws, the interest in the trust fund was transferred to the operating fund with the approval of three trustees, Ivan Bennett, Ray Parker and Augustus Goodyear.

With the assistance of Major General (Chaplain) Charlie E. Brown, who was Chief of Army Chaplains, appeals were made to the Chaplains Funds for collections for MCA, and the income rose steadily. As a reserve was built up beyond the operating expense, investments in such stocks as IBM and C & P created additional growth in the trust fund.

The second convention that Justus attended was held in May of 1964 at the Sherman House in Chicago. This convention was chaired by Charlie Murphy, 5th Army Chaplain at Fort Sheridan, and Cloma Huffman. The vice president, the late C. Pardee Erdman, was a golfing friend of Bob Hope, and Pardee convinced the celebrity to come to Chicago to receive the National Citizenship Award for 1964. Seven hundred and fifty people attended the closing banquet festivities at which Mr. Hope received the citation.

During the Viet Nam War years, membership in the MCA grew as the organization was always willing to defend the chaplaincy.

The 1970 convention was also held at the Sherman House in Chicago and was another success. Melvin Laird of the Defense Department received the National Citizenship Award. At that time, protesters of the Vietnam War were in abundance, and Mr. Laird had to be brought into the convention building through the kitchen from a back alley. The American Civil Liberties Union had sent a threat to Melvin Laird that they were going to test the constitutionality of the Military Chaplaincy. A resolution against it was immediately passed. The chaplaincy had to be defended two or three times under Justus' directorship.

At the end of the Karl B. Justus' directorship the trust fund was at its highest point. With the help of Major General Will Hyatt, who was a Missouri Synod Lutheran and Chief of Army Chaplains, the MCA received an extremely generous grant of $50,000.00 from the Aid Association for Lutherans. The money was used to set up professional workshops for chaplains. Under Justus' tenure, several of these were organized including two or three in Germany in 1977, the year before Karl Justus retired.

Justus still considers his 16 years with MCA among the finest in his life. Upon his retirement from the organization on Dec. 6, 1978, he was made Executive Director Emeritus. He will be remembered for his fine work in building up the financial resources of the organization as well as restoring interest in membership.

THE KINGSLEY YEARS
1979-1983

Chaplain, Col, Earl James Kingsley, USAF (Ret.), became the second full-time executive director of the MCA with the retirement of Karl Justus. He began his service at a time of decline in the Association. The glory days of the large membership of those serving during the Vietnam War were over and support from chapel funds and the Chief of Chaplain offices was low. So, not only were finances a problem, but a debate within the leadership as to the direction the Association should go ensued. Divided were opinions as to whether the focus should be on the membership and their needs and desires, or on the active duty younger chaplains as their professional association.

The January/February 1979 issue of *The Military Chaplain* shows that discounts for the National Institute were to be given to MCA members only and no attempt seemed to be made to attract non-members. A big push was made at this time to sign up life members, and much of the control of the Association was in the hands of older retired chaplains with only token support from the active duty. Chapel Fund donations held fairly steady for a while, but soon began to decline.

Emphasis, during this time, was on the development of support for the National Institute. Money had been left by Chaplain Ryan, a strong supporter of MCA, in his will and this had been designated as an endowment for a workshop at each convention. Additional funds were raised to add to the original amount. During this time the Liberty Bell Chapter started a fund to match the Ryan Fund in honor of one of their past presidents, Rabbi Bertram Korn, RADM, CHC, USNR. Finally, by the end of Chaplain Kingley's time, the idea had been generated for a third fund made up of donations from Life Members.

While there was much struggle during these years, there were also bright spots to be remembered. Chaplain Kingsley was able to bring about some stability in membership as well as continue both excellent programming for the National Institute and high quality in *The Military Chaplain* magazine.

Trust funds were turned over to a professional manager at a time when the stock market went through a steep decline. The Trustees were forced to use some of the funds to maintain the program of the Association when current revenues would not support the Association at the level of the past. Additionally, inflation grew at a rapid rate and forced a decrease in what could be done with current dollars.

Annual Command Chaplain and Indorsing Agency Representatives Luncheon held at Patton Hall, North Area, Ft. Myer, VA Host for the ceremony is Major General Francis L. Sampson, Chief of Chaplains, United States Army. Guest speaker is the Honorable Stanley R. Resor, Secretary of the Army.

MCA was at a low point when Jim Kingsley finished his administration and talk became earnest about what future there was for the Association. Old divisions over the directions in which to go became more pronounced and the period that followed was to become a time of floundering, while looking for direction and a sound base upon which the Association could build its future.

The Emery Years
January 1984 - April 1990

After a month of transitional collaboration with his predecessor, Chaplain (COL) E. James Kingsley, Chaplain (LTC) William F. "Bill" Emery, USAR (Ret.), took over the reins as executive director of MCA. He was an experienced MCA member. He had been a founder, an officer and mentor of the Liberty Bell Chapter in Philadelphia, and had served in numerous national offices including President of MCA from 1980 to 1982.

Although he had not had extended active duty as a chaplain, he had faithfully pursued the Inactive Reserve training program until retirement eligibility. Additionally, he had been a line officer, first lieutenant, during the Korean War. He was pastor of Centre Presbyterian Church in New Park, PA, located on the Mason-Dixon line, for approximately 30 years and was well-known throughout the Presbyterian denomination.

Chaplain Emery's home chapter, the Liberty Bell, where he provided so much initiative and energy as founding secretary (1970-1973) and as third president (1973-1976), is an unusually active chapter. Its meetings have always been well attended. During the period 1970-1989, over 100 chaplains were members. Furthermore, six of Philadelphia's Liberty Bell Chapter members have served as National president, and three have served as National Secretary. That chapter is a pioneer in chapter-sponsored local workshops. Liberty Bell also takes pride in having initiated and created the Bertram W. Korn Memorial Fund of over $6,000 specifically to underwrite convention expenses and to provide an annual lectureship. The late Rear Admiral Bertram W. Korn, Chaplain Corps, USNR, was a very popular Rabbi in one of the major synagogues in Philadelphia. Liberty Bell was granted a charter on Jan. 27, 1970 by James Roy Smith, National President (1968-1970).

Chaplain Emery was succeeded as National President by Chaplain (COL) Simon H. Scott, USAF (Ret.), who was dubbed "Mr. MCA". At the first convention during Chaplain Emery's tenure, Chaplain Scott couldn't attend because of illness. Captain Marlin D. "Smokey" Seiders, Chaplain Corps. USN (Ret.), the senior vice-president, presided. This first convention, coordinated by Chaplain Emery, was held April 24 to April 27, 1984 in Cape May, NJ. The coast guard base chaplain was the host.

At that time the national headquarters of MCA was located at 7758 Wisconsin Avenue in Bethesda, MD in the Washington, DC metropolitan area.

One of Executive Director Emery's first projects was to send out a four page questionnaire to every member of MCA which asked the questions: "For you, what is the MCA?, What should the MCA be? In order to achieve what it should be which of the below list of items do you choose or favor, and what additional ones might you suggest?" This was a sort of "taking the temperature" of MCA's *raison d'etre* and future at this point in the summer and fall of 1984. Responses to the questionnaires showed overwhelmingly that the members perceived the MCA to be a professional organization and that the emphasis at future conventions should be professional growth. Strengthening and developing of chapters was perceived as critical for the continued life and growth of MCA. Also perceived as critical to MCA growth was the introduction to MCA of newly recruited reserves and initial active duty chaplains in training. National President Seiders proposed that one year of free membership be given routinely to every Chaplain School Basic Trainee in all three armed services and in the Department of Veterans Affairs (VA). This was approved and that program was began early in Chaplain Emery's tenure.

In April 1985, at Tacoma, WA, the National Institute celebrated the 60th anniversary of the founding of MCA. In April 1983 it had been agreed to establish three National Lectureships... The Patrick J. Ryan Memorial Workshop, the Bertram W. Korn Memorial Workshop and the Life Members Lectureship. These three endowment funds would underwrite costs of speakers and workshop leaders at the annual conventions. Each chapter, associate member, regular member and life member was encouraged to send contributions. This has since proven to be one of the finer steps taken in the MCA program. It has been used actively and has benefited every annual institute, beginning with the one in Tacoma in 1985.

A very sad event that occurred in the early days of Executive Director Emery's tenure was the untimely death, in late 1984, of Chaplain Scott who was then the National President of MCA (1982-1984). A funeral service was held in the Bolling Air Force Base Chapel, Washington, DC with past and present national officers participating in the liturgy. Chaplain Scott, a recipient of the Distinguished Service Medal (DSM), was buried with full military honors in Arlington National Cemetery, Washington, DC.

Chaplain Emery's emphasis was on chapters and individual members and both their growth in contribution and increase in influence in the MCA. These ideas were supported and promoted by both Chaplain Seiders and Chaplain (COL) James E. Shaw, USA (Ret.), who followed him as national president in 1986. Captain Emery contacted the Chief of Chaplains Offices of the three armed services and the Veterans Administration. In February 1985, he was assured that Major General Patrick J. Hessian, Major General John A. Collins, and Rear Admiral Neil M. Stevenson, in newsletters to all Army, Air Force and Navy Chaplains respectively, had requested support for the MCA and recommended that all chaplains give very serious consideration to joining MCA and supporting its local activities wherever chaplains are home ported or assigned. This was philosophically and practically a good way to move forward.

Chapter reports were given a more prominent place and greater importance at the annual conventions and a verbal report of "up to five minutes" on their year's program was requested from each of the active local chapters. Convention attendees looked forward to entertaining reports from some chapters, especially from the Chicago and the Dallas chapters.

Chaplain Emery traveled a great deal, throughout the country, contacting flourishing chapters and aggressively attempting to revive lapsed chapters. Within a few months after his assumption of office, it became very apparent that, due to the restricted and diminishing finances, it would be necessary to give up the headquarters in Bethesda, MD. He found an affordable office at 6216 Baltimore Ave. in Riverdale, MD, near the University of Maryland main campus.

Another innovation which was briefly attempted in the mid-

1980s, but didn't catch on widely, was mini-conferences. This project was prompted, in part, by past experience in the mid-1970s when the Aid Association for Lutherans donated $50,000 to the MCA for the professional development of active duty and inactive reserve chaplains. A number of one-day training sessions, utilizing regional or national expertise for leadership, were held. This project was not continued after exhaustion of the Lutheran's generous gift. The proposed mini-conferences were to be on the order of a seminar or workshop with high caliber leadership by a skilled resource person, often a chaplain detailed to that duty or a chaplain with some expertise who resided in the area. There were several of them held and younger chaplains were especially encouraged to attend.

The initial mini-conference, a "trial balloon" of the proposed program, was held at Fort Snelling, MN on Oct. 9, 1984. Some 30 chaplains gathered for a day of learning, fellowship and briefing on current trends in the Armed Forces and VA chaplaincies. National Secretary, Chaplain (COL) Frank H. Ebner, USAF (Ret.), coordinated the program. He contacted over 100 chaplains, retired, reserve and active duty, in a five state area. Chaplain Emery attended to bring greetings and a briefing on the MCA. While there, he welcomed to MCA its newest chapter, also known as the "Hittites", comprised of chaplains from Minnesota, Wisconsin, Iowa, North Dakota and South Dakota. Officers were elected for the period through 1985. The Hittite chapter was organized on Oct. 9, 1984.

An invitation went out to Department of Veteran's Affairs chaplains in the various VA hospitals across the country encouraging them to enter full and equal membership in MCA. This had been intended since the founding of the Veteran's Administration Chaplaincy, and they began to become members, some even life members. Captain James B. Martin, Chaplain Corps, USN (Ret.), a Roman Catholic chaplain who was the director of all VA chaplains in the mid-1980s, became a national trustee and very actively interested. He was succeeded by Chaplain Herbert B. Cleveland as national trustee. By the 1990 Convention and the end of Chaplain Emery's tenure, the first VA chaplain would be nominated to the line of succession as a national officer. Once again it was Cleveland, who was at that time the Chief of Veteran's Administration Chaplains. He was nominated and filled the place of Rear Admiral Mark R. Thompson, Chaplain Corps, USN (Ret.). He had vacated as vice-president due to physical inability to continue. Thus, the vice-president in 1990-1992 to the National President, Captain S. David Chambers, Chaplain Corps, USNR (Ret.) was Herbert B. Cleveland of the VA branch.

At the institute in 1985 in Tacoma, WA, National Vice-President Shaw began a two-year effort, as Chairman of the National Committee on Chapters and Membership, to attract to the ranks of the MCA an increased proportion of active duty chaplains. Mentioned above were the concurrence and assistance of the four incumbent Chiefs of Chaplains. The Committee on Chapters and Membership was determined to gain new members, start new chapters and revitalize old ones. It sought also to foster an image of the MCA as a professional, fraternal and service organization meriting involvement by every active and reserve military, Veteran's Affairs, Civil Air Patrol and retired chaplain.

That same issue of *The Military Chaplain*, in which Chaplain Shaw outlined his goals and objectives, carried on its last page a sample of a church bulletin-folder that had been developed for Military Chaplains Day. It was suggested for use around July 29, because that was the date when the first Chaplain Corps, the Army Chaplain Corps, was authorized by the Continental Congress in 1775. Included was an order form to MCA distributors for Military Chaplains Day bulletins at $4.00 per 100, Military Chaplains Day inserts at $3.00 per 100. This was, apparently, a "one time" venture which was discontinued.

The 1986 convention in Nashville, TN approved several changes in MCA's Constitution. The first, which didn't require major change, defined the basic categories of membership: full active membership, associate membership and honorary membership. Another major proposal that was acted upon approved full membership on the National Executive Committee for all three members of the Board of Trustees of whom each one shall be from a different Chaplain Service. It was proposed that the number of elected members be reduced from nine to six. That constitutes a voting membership of the four officers, the six elected members and the three trustees for a total of 13 national Executive Committee members who must be active members of MCA National. This was accomplished by attrition and the new terms of the six remaining elected members began in April 1986 at the convention.

The composition of the National Executive Committee of the three trustees and six elected members were to be representative of different geographical areas. Those areas were determined in 1984 by the former Army Command areas, to which they were identical. It was hoped to have a broad, balanced representation from the areas. This worked as long as it was feasible. It was decided that the three trustees should reside in the immediate Washington, DC area because of the need for them to confer. Thus, there would be two check signers available, expediting the investment and supervision or trust funds.

In his inaugural address on April 11, 1986, incoming President James Shaw said, "There is a unique dimension which MCA can and does afford. I call it "Inter-Chaplaincy Fraternalism", and he goes on to say, "I have been a member of MCA since I entered the Army Chaplaincy. I was told that MCA was our organization, chartered by Congress for us. I saw MCA as an organization to which every military and paramilitary chaplain should belong and I still do."

As many other institutions and organizations were beginning to do in this time period, MCA began emphasizing and soliciting bequests. Individual potential givers were encouraged to pledge the transfer of an established trust, an insurance policy, or to designate a direct inheritance which MCA would then receive upon their death. Also in this period, roughly 1986-1988, the National Executive Committee, Trustees and some informed persons in the general membership again began asking the question: "Is MCA viable? Is it feasible to continue?" This was prompted by some difficulty in raising funds and by on-going difficulty in soliciting new members for the organization. The national presidents, from time to time, particularly President Shaw, appointed committees to study these dilemmas and to report their findings periodically to the Executive Committee. Reports indicated that MCA was viable, and that it was feasible to continue MCA. The earlier successful fund drive which raised $36,000 and some additional bequests were endowing lectureships fairly adequately, but more attention to the operating fund was required.

It might be mentioned that in this period two chaplains who were in succession to assume national office were unable to do so because of diminished health. In the first instance at the 1982 convention, a very popular Lutheran Chaplain, Captain Alfred R. Seager, Chaplain Corps, USN (Ret.), living in Newport, RI, was unable to continue his duties as national secretary and assume the office of national vice-president. At that time, Chaplain Seiders became vice-president to Chaplain Scott. The second instance occured in 1990. Rear Admiral Mark R. Thompson, Chaplain Corps, USNR (Ret.) was unable to "fleet up" to the duties of president. Captain S. David Chambers, Chaplain Corps, USNR (Ret.), was installed briefly as vice-president and assumed the presidency in 1990 when the Navy succession came round. He followed Chaplain Ebner who was at that time National Chief of Civil Air Patrol (CAP) Chaplains and the first CAP chaplain to hold the office.

At the April 1987 MCA Institute, Karl Justus, Executive Director Emeritus, and National President Shaw signed a certificate of appreciation for Chaplain (Lieutenant Colonel) William F. Emery, USAR (Ret.). The citation reads in part... *"His dedication to MCA for two decades has been inspiring. As life member, chapter president, national secretary, vice-president and president and every assigned or elected role, his tireless energy and contagious enthusiasm has spear-headed success at local, regional and national levels. His long time faithful leadership helped to broaden and strengthen the Association's image as a professional organization for military, VA and CAP Chaplains. We note his optimistic spirit, his ability to find a way when none is apparent, his sense of money management and his willingness to try alternative ways to achieve goals if principles are not sacrificed. All these have helped to revive declining membership, establish new chapters, bring life to some chapters that were inactive and to improve the level and integrity of MCA's finances. All this he has done in his role as Executive Director of MCA and often at considerable personal sacrifice. It must be stated that in addition to securing the support of the Chiefs of all the military and VA Chaplains in encouraging and even soliciting members for MCA, in this time period we began the first few instances of having one of the Chief of Chaplains appear personally and keynote the convention or institute. You've done that, rotating among the four Chiefs of Chaplains, including the Veteran's Administration and have continued that."*

Upon assuming the office at the convention in Colorado Springs in 1988, President Ebner, at the request of the Association, outlined a course of procedure leading to the report of the Long Range Study Committee, which would seek detailed information as to the status of "futuring" ...that is, of plans and changes being considered or implemented by a number of organizations analogous to MCA. To quote President Ebner: *"The MCA is unique. It is the only organization of Military Chaplains. There are major differences between MCA and other professional organizations. Significant interpretation is required before adopting plans or programs from other entities which share some, but not all, of our concerns. This is in response to some members who are asking, and asking quite seriously - Is there a future for MCA?"*

In late 1988 and early 1989, it was suggested that MCA might provide leadership and service to the Military and VA Chaplaincies by implementing a scholarship program for committed chaplain candidates. This proposal created wide interest. It was proposed that nominations for such scholarships be sought from a wide spectrum of individuals and organizations, ecclesiastical, academic and military, and the selection of recipients and administration of the program be performed by the Association members. MCA is uniquely representative of all faith groups and draws on a wealth of chaplaincy experience. It seems the ideal agency to administer this program. The Scholarship Program has since caught hold and is an attractive professional feature of the MCA.

During this period in MCA's history (1984-1990), finances were a persistent problem, especially in the area of operating expenses. The problem was solved somewhat by a financial campaign which was launched in the fall of 1986 and concluded on Dec. 31, 1988. That campaign realized a total of $36,000 for the Association's trust fund. Around the same time, the National Executive Committee decided to allocate of life membership fees differently. A life membership was then roughly in the $200-$400 range, depending on the age of the applicant. For the first time, the operating fund (working fund) of the Association would be given $25 of each life member fee and the remainder would be put into a trust fund. The reasoning was that if the new life member had now paid all of her/his dues for life, it was important to earn a few dollars interest on the fully paid fee, rather than expend it for current operations. Thus, some very stringent, visionary and intelligent financial management decisions were made. Those decisions have built up the trust funds for endowing professional lecturers, encouraging scholarships and enriching MCA's professional institutes. At the same time, careful attention is continued to remaining financially solvent in the operating funds.

Affiliation of the Military Chaplains Association with the Council on Military Organizations (COMO), an umbrella entity in the Washington, DC area was conceived by the National Executive Committee at its fall meeting in 1988. It was first presented to the Convention held at College Park, MD in April 1989. It was presented by the Committee on Long Range Study. The measure was then approved by the April 1990 Institute in Tampa, FL, and is a very valuable link with, and representation of, the Military Chaplains at the Washington level.

At the April 1989 National Institute, Chaplain Emery was again elected National Secretary of the MCA. He served in this capacity actually less than one term at the same time that he was executive director of the Association. He resigned from both positions, the elected position and the employed position, as of April 30, 1990, after serving approximately one year, for the second time, as secretary of the National Organization.

Chaplain Emery's focused efforts as executive director continued, and after a few years the annual convention workshops caught on. He began inviting the chief of each armed service and the VA Chaplaincy to the Chief of Chaplains workshops to brief the men and women on current trends and events in their Chaplain Corps. By that time as well, the three endowed lectureships... Ryan, Korn and Life Members ... had the resources to feature some top ranking scholars in each geographical area where the national conventions were held. This proved to be a very professional upturn in the overall quality of institutes and are still conducted every year.

Note that Chaplain Emery, who himself had served as National President of MCA from 1980 to 1982, then proceeded to serve as executive director for the next four presidents: Simon H. Scott (1982-1984), Marlin D. Seiders (1984-1986), James E. Shaw (1986-1988) and Frank H. Ebner (1988-1990).

A review of the record indicates that *The Military Chaplain*, Issue #3, May/June 1990 was the last one with the heading address of MCA National Headquarters, P.O. Box 645, Riverdale,

MD, 20737-0645. *The Military Chaplain*, Issue #4, July/August 1990, the first issue under the editorial responsibility of Executive Director G. William Dando, has the address as National Headquarters, P.O. Box 42660, Washington, DC, 20015-0660. It is difficult to determine the exact closing out date of the Headquarters at 6281 Baltimore Street in Riverdale. We may assume that it occurred sometime late in Chaplain Emery's tenure. The office on Baltimore Street, Riverdale was surrendered well before the date of Chaplain Dando's relieving him, because of lack of funds. Chaplain Emery first moved the office into his home in suburban Washington, DC and then to his new home in Dover, DE just shortly before turnover to the incoming executive director.

In the March/April 1990 issue of the magazine *The Military Chaplain* under the heading Pipe Him Aboard!, Bill Emery announced that... *"Chaplain G. William 'Bill" Dando, United States Navy Retired, will assume the duties of Executive Director of the MCA on May 1, 1990. He is not stranger to leadership of MCA. He has served on the National Executive Committee and chaired the MCA convention at Cape May, New Jersey in 1984."* By resolution, the 1990 National Convention held in Tampa, FL, expressed... *"gratitude to William and Mary Helen Emery for their service as MCA paid staff for 42 months, from January 1984 to June 1987 and for continuing without pay for 34 additional months from July 1987 to April 1990."* They had served 76 months altogether, which is slightly in excess of six years. That sacrificial service on Emery's part didn't seem to diminish his activity or his wide ranging interest in promotion of MCA but because of his unpaid service, the treasury became more healthy and finances were on an upward turn at the time of his resignation.

Chaplain Emery encouraged in his last editorial in *The Military Chaplain*, Issue #2, March/April 1990, from St. Luke, the 12th chapter, verse 48: "Everyone to whom much is given, of him much will be required. And of him to whom men commit much, they will demand more." He goes on: "Therefore we can never protest, complain or lament that too much has been or is being required of us and if our fellow citizens who have committed all this to us demand more from us than from others is it not just and fair that they do so?" H spoke as a true soldier and citizen of his country.

Chaplain Emery died in Dover, DE in late 1994. *Contributed by Chaplain M.D. Seiders.*

THE DANDO YEARS
1990-PRESENT

At its fall meeting in 1988, the National Executive Committee appointed a Search Committee of three persons to commence the difficult task of initiating a search for a new executive director with the mandate to make nomination of a candidate for the position to the Executive Committee meeting in November 1989. Five persons submitted an application for the position. After reviewing each dossier, noting references and conducting personal interviews with the three primary applicants, the Search Committee made nomination to the National Executive Committee that Chaplain Dando, a retired Navy Chaplain, was the choice to be appointed to the office. The Executive Committee voted in unanimous concurrence. Chaplain Dando was installed as executive director of the MCA at the National Institute in Tampa, FL, April 1990, to commence work May 1. The National Institute in plenary session received the appointment and also elected a new president, Chaplain S. David Chambers, and vice-president, Chaplain Herbert B. Cleveland, to their respective offices. Because of the financial condition of the Association, the appointment of the executive director was on a part-time basis of 20 hours per week.

Chaplain Dando, USN (Ret.), was no stranger to the leadership ranks of MCA, having previously served on the National Executive Committee and other subcommittees for many years. He chaired the 1984 National Institute in Cape May, NJ, and was fully involved in the 1977 Institute in Winter Park, FL, while stationed at the Naval Training Center, Orlando.

Chaplain Dando is a graduate of West Nottingham Academy, Colora, MD, of Baylor University and Pittsburgh Theological Seminary. Following his Army enlisted service, he completed theological training and took a pastorate in Iowa. Duty with the Navy during his career included a tour with Operation Deepfreeze in the Antarctic, the Marines, Vietnam, Guam, the USS *Proteus*, and the Coast Guard Training Station, Cape May, NJ. He is a native of Baltimore, MD. In order to reduce overhead expenses, it was decided to establish the new Office Headquarters for MCA in his residence near Emmetsburg, MD.

A front page article by the new executive director in the next issue of *The Military Chaplain*, May/June 1990, reflected the supportive sentiment among the membership present at the Tampa Institute. It was entitled: "A New Day in MCA". While the office of MCA would be in the home of the executive director outside of Washington, DC, the National Executive Committee instructed him "to maintain an active presence at all appropriate chaplain and military functions and offices there". A District of Columbia mail address and phone number were obtained. Through the previous years, the visibility of MCA in the active duty community and the participation of the Association in chaplaincy and veteran functions had diminished noticeably: therefore, one of the priority efforts was to reestablish the presence of MCA.

The executive director and the president immediately embarked upon an effort to carry the message of MCA to the Chiefs of Chaplains by personal visitation to their offices and to solicit from them their observations as to what the Association should do to enhance the ministry and training of active duty and reserve chaplains. Significant recommendations were made and these themes were incorporated into the planning for future National Conventions. Although the theme for the forthcoming National Convention in San Antonio, TX, "A New Day in Pastoral Counseling", had already been selected and fit very well the desire to speak to the professional ministry needs of the active duty, reserve and veteran chaplaincies, it was the subject of the 1992 National Institute that grew directly out of the concern expressed by the Chiefs of Chaplains that the annual conference of MCA be a professional experience relevant to chaplain ministry. The theme for the 67th National Institute in April 1992 at Hampton, VA, therefore, was "Ministry to the Military - Pluralistic Issues" with Dr. Martin Marty as Resource Leader.

While it was recognized that the membership was comprised largely of life and retired members, the president challenged the Association with the words: "Those of us from the past must find our primary purpose in creating an Association in the present for the sake of the future."

An excellent new pamphlet, *Why Should A Chaplain Belong*

G. William Dando.

to MCA?, was designed for each military and VA service by the executive director with an introductory paragraph from each Chief of Chaplains for that service; and printing and dissemination of this was heartily approved by the Executive Committee. It affirmed the commitment of the NEC to a significant mission for the Association and answered the question by stating the goals that MCA:

    *Represents the military chaplaincy in various forums

    *Conducts an Annual National Institute

    *Provides workshops for professional growth

    *Interprets the mood and movements of the times in reference to the role of the military chaplain

    *Publishes *The Military Chaplain* six times a year

    *Maintains communication and liaison with the Chiefs of Chaplains, the AFCB, and the faith groups endorsing military chaplains

    *Establishes and provides guidance and resources to local Chapters throughout the nation.

Membership in the Association had been declining for more than two decades from a membership of more than 2,200 in 1970 to a low of approximately 1,200 in 1990. At the fall meeting of the NEC in October 1991, a goal was established for a 25 percent increase in paid membership for the ensuing year. The number of paid-up memberships for the previous year had been 379. The Association had a substantially larger number of Life Members, viz 820, but it was recognized that they were non-contributory, paid-up members, providing no income to the annual operating budget yet receiving every issue of *The Military Chaplain* without additional subscription cost.

Therefore, the executive director in the first year concentrated upon increasing the dues-paying new memberships and was able to report to the plenary session of the business meeting at the 1992 National Convention that the Association had already had an increase of five percent as of April 1. He expressed every reason to believe that the organization would exceed the growth goal and that by fall paid membership would exceed 500. In 1993 total membership increased by seven percent and dues-paying membership by 11 percent, noting also that most of the new members came from the active duty chaplains. This, therefore, became the first year since 1985 that there was any increase in paid membership recorded and the downward trend of well over a decade was reversed. In 1994, membership continued to increase with dues-paying members now numbering 600, marking the highest point in membership since the mid-1980s. Because there had been no change in the Association's dues structure, the NEC increased the cost of life membership to $350 for those under age 55; $300 for those 55 to 65; and $250 for those over age 65.

Still the financial condition of the Association required immediate attention. The trust funds had been depleted through the previous decade and the operating fund was functioning at a minimum. In 1990, there was an end of the year balance of $146,144. This provided little opportunity for travel to the service chaplain schools or outreach to the MCA chapters.

The executive director immediately sought membership for the Association in the Independent Charities of America Inc., and in the spring of 1992 qualification was granted to MCA to participate in the Combined Federal Campaign during the fall of the year. While it was not until the spring of 1993 that the results of the effort would bear fruit, it was envisioned that additional revenue would be forthcoming. A concerted effort, therefore, was initiated to apprise chaplains of all commands of the opportunity to contribute to the ministry of MCA through one-base fund drives. The annual report of the Association notes that "Pledges were received from the 1992 program in the amount of $27,000, of which approximately half was paid in 1993." The dire financial condition of MCA received a timely transfusion.

Three significant initiatives were undertaken in the first year from the 1990 Tampa Convention to the 1991 San Antonio Convention:

1. The Military Chaplains Association became a member of The Council of Military Organizations, Ad Hoc Committee and The Military Coalition. Three years earlier the chairman of the Long Range Study Committee had become aware of The Coalition which was comprised at that time of 16 military-related organizations whose purpose was to provide on behalf of their collective memberships strong advocacy to Capitol Hill and the Department of Defense on important issues affecting their own retirees, reservists and active duty members. There were no membership dues or fees. The Coalition had come into existence in 1985 and quickly was recognized as The Voice of the Military Associations.

The executive director and the president of MCA, therefore, on Feb. 7, 1991, appeared before The Coalition meeting in the National Non-Commissioned Officers Association Headquarters in Alexandria, VA. Chaplain Dando presented a brief history of MCA, the Association's Charter and purpose, and expressed the reasons for desiring affiliation with The Coalition. That day the MCA was voted to be a part of The Coalition as the 24th organization. In this new relationship with The Coalition, the MCA became an independent participant in all matters that affect the military community and a recognized and valued contributor to the agenda of The Coalition. The Coalition worked to develop positions relative to issues before Congress and to testify before the committees of the House and Senate that were working on Bills which affect military people. The Coalition was "The Voice of military and veterans groups". In the Coalition, the executive director of MCA was "The Voice of the Chaplaincy".

MCA now worked in a relationship with other military associations of like commitment. Most important of all, this relationship provided to the Association an opportunity to speak on behalf of the chaplain-membership to issues of concern to MCA and the military in a forum where no other group of chaplains, including the Chiefs of Chaplains or representatives of chaplains like the endorsing agencies, had a voice.

By its participation in The Coalition, the Military Chaplains Association, through the executive director, has addressed such issues as The Survivor Benefits Plan, the COLA for military personnel, health benefits for active duty, reservists and retirees, the draw-down of facilities and personnel, family service and counseling needs and many other people-related matters. Furthermore, Chaplain Dando was asked to co-chair the Coalition's Subcommittee on Military Construction which reviewed the proposals for the 1993 Department of Defense budget. Throughout the year, the president of MCA participated in discussions at three White House briefings by the President of the United States, the Secretary of Defense, the Secretary of the Department of Veterans Affairs and the Chairman of the Joint Chiefs of Staff of the Armed Forces on matters that pertained to the Persian Gulf War as well as military facilities and families. The executive director was invited to participate in the National Foreign Policy Conference for leaders of non-governmental organizations at the State Department with several hundred others from across the country in briefings and discussions with State Department leaders. And in 1994, the executive director was asked to serve as a delegate to the White House Conference on the Aging.

2. The National Veterans Day Committee of the Department of Veterans Affairs was reincorporated into the immediate concern of Chaplain Dando after MCA had been a non-participant for a number of years. The National Veterans Day Committee formed in response to an act of Congress and a Presidential Proclamation, acts to advise the Secretary of Veterans Affairs primarily on the National Observance of Veterans Day but also on any issues upon which he chooses to consult the Committee. *The Military Chaplain* announced in the 1990 September/October issue of the magazine that The Military Chaplains Association had been elected to the Executive Committee of the National Veterans Day Committee, granting Chaplain Dando on behalf of MCA a full vote in the Committee and enabling the Association to share equally with all of the other congressionally chartered national organizations that are involved with veterans. This also enables MCA to host the National Celebration on Veteran's Day, November 11, in the year 2009 and every 20th year thereafter. The president of MCA was now accorded a place of honor on the platform of the annual Veterans Day ceremony in Arlington National Cemetery.

Commencing on July 29, 1988, the local National Capitol Area Chapter of MCA had conducted an annual Wreath Laying Ceremony at the time of the of the changing of the guard at the Tomb of the Unknown Soldier to honor the memory of the first chaplain appointed by the Continental Congress on that date in 1775. The local chapter has also placed a plaque in the Arlington Cemetery Amphitheater Rotunda Museum in commemoration of all chaplains.

3. In the fall meeting of 1991, the National Executive Committee considered establishing a Seminary Scholarship Program for theological students in financial need who were anticipating entering the chaplaincy following graduation. The proposal was referred to a committee-of-three to prepare appropriate guidelines, and the first draft of the guidelines for the Seminary Scholarship Program was submitted to the NEC meeting in San Antonio for tentative approval. The initial concept for a scholarship program and fund of some significant kind was a proposal of Associate Member John Daniel at the National Executive Committee meeting in 1988 on the campus of the University of Maryland.

The fall meeting of the NEC brought the MCA Seminarian Scholarship Program to reality. A board of seven directors was elected and announcement was made that more than $2,000.00 had already been donated to the Scholarship Fund. Furthermore, the Executive Committee voted to provide $10,000.00 as additional seed money for the first year. The first scholarships were presented in the fall to three Chaplain Candidates who had been selected by the Board of Directors to receive the scholarships of $2,000.00 each. The need and interest of students was found to be exceedingly great. However, the July/August 1993 issue of *The Military Chaplain* states, "Less than 15 percent of the candidates who completed an application will receive a scholarship....." because of lack of supporting funds. By the fall semester of 1994, eleven Chaplain Candidates had received scholarship support.

The program was designed: to provide financial assistance through the Seminarian Scholarship Fund for those:

(a) who are enrolled as full-time seminary students in an accredited institution of higher learning,

(b) who have been ecclesiastically approved by their faith group for participation in a Chaplain Candidate Program of the Armed Forces, and

(c) who have been accepted into one of the Chaplain Candidate Programs of the military services.

The enthusiasm of "The New Day in MCA" generated the incubation of other programs and initiatives.

The National Executive Committee in its fall meeting of 1991 created the Emerson Foundation Award, named after the first military chaplain of the United States, Chaplain William Emerson, grandfather of Ralph Waldo Emerson. As Pastor of the "fighting congregation" at Concord, MA, when the alarm was sounded that the British were afoot, Chaplain Emerson was the first to arrive. While the Continental Congress did not take official action to establish the chaplaincy within the Continental Army until July 29, 1775, Chaplain Emerson is recognized and honored as the first chaplain in the Revolution.

The concept for the fund was first proposed by Chaplain Alva R. Appel when he was president of the Board of Trustees. To become a member of the Foundation one must donate $1,000.00 or be honored by a donation in one's name. Membership can only be granted by the trustees and the donations are deposited in the Trust Fund to support the work of MCA. Each newly-inducted member receives a medal suitable to be worn on formal occasions, a shadow box holder with engraved presentation plaque and a special recognition ribbon to be worn annually at the National Convention. At the 1995 National Convention at Atlantic Beach, FL, 20 Emerson Foundation Members had been inducted into the program.

At the National Convention in San Antonio, the Distinguished Service Award Program was established to recognize and promote "excellence in the practice of the chaplaincy and professionalism in ministry." A chaplain from each of the military and veteran services, nominated by the Chief of Chaplains, was selected for the award and presented with a plaque. The name of each awardee was also inscribed on a plaque to be retained in the office of the Chief of Chaplains. Annually, the name of the new recipient of the award would be added to the plaque. By the 1995 National Institute, 15 chaplains had been so honored.

Whereas it had been the practice to present the National Citizenship Award annually at the time of the National Convention, it was decided in 1995 by the National Executive Committee to make the presentation on Capitol Hill. A congressional reception was held in the Senate office building with many representatives from Congress and the Armed Forces present. The recipient of the National Citizenship Award, Senator Sam Nunn, Chairman of the Senate Armed Forces Committee, addressed those present.

During this one-half decade, the National Convention in plenary session considered and issued a number of very significant resolutions on matters of national and service-related policy such as Resolution on the Department of Veterans Affairs, Resolution on Military Retirement Pay, Resolution on Enlisted Earned income Credit, Resolution on Homosexuals in the Military to name only a few. The 1993 National Institute Resolution on Military Health Care was made a part of the material approved by the Department of Defense working group on health care and was forwarded to Mrs. Hillary Rodham Clinton and the full Health Care Committee. The executive director has received responses to MCA Convention resolutions from the President, the Office of the Secretary of Defense, the Chairman of the Joint Chiefs of Staff, the Secretary of Veterans Affairs and from numerous members of Congress.

The 1995 National Convention in Atlantic Beach, FL witnessed the presentation of the first award in the final program established in this period, The Ellen Elvira Gibson Award. According to the best records, Gibson was the first female chaplain to serve in the military service of the country when the governor of Wisconsin and other officials of that state recommended her to be a chaplain of the 1st Wisconsin Heavy Artillery, to which post she was elected. She served at Fort Lyon, VA and performed the duties of a chaplain even though the Secretary of War refused to have her mustered. On Nov. 10, 1864 the matter came to the attention of President Lincoln and he wrote the following: "This lady says she would be appointed chaplain of the 1st Wisconsin Heavy Artillery, only that she is a female. The President has not legally anything to do with such a question, but he has no objection to her appointment." A. Lincoln.

The United States Congress passed a bill on Aug. 5, 1868 granting her chaplain's pay for the time of service, but the $1,210.56 was not paid until March 7, 1876 when she was fully paid from the U.S. Treasury.

The Ellen Elvira Gibson Award is given to a member of MCA chosen by the officers for outstanding service as a volunteer in or out of the Association. Nominations have been made by chapters or individual members.

On April 25, during the 1995 National Convention in Florida, The Military Chaplains Association celebrated its 70th anniversary. From the meager beginning of seven regular and 13 reserve Army Chaplains, the Association now is the most pluralistically-diverse and service-inclusive of any organization for chaplains of the United States Armed Forces and the Department of Veterans Affairs. Its membership is open to all clergy persons who at any time have served the men and women of the Army, Navy, Air Force, Marines, Coast Guard, Civil Air Patrol and Department of Veteran Affairs and is also open to members of the ecclesiastical endorsing community who provide the chaplains from their religious bodies to these services.

The Association formally recognizes the professional excellence in ministry of active duty and full-time chaplains as well as those in the reserve with The Distinguished Service Award. It has presented its National Citizenship Award annually to an eminent American whose life and work exemplify leadership in public service, courage in moral conviction and loyalty in personal faith while serving God and country. It provides theological seminary scholarship assistance to the next generation of chaplains. Its local chapters are spread throughout the country. *The Military Chaplain* has grown from a 6-page news sheet in 1989 to a 16-page magazine with significant articles and information. The Association represents the interests of chaplains in the United States Congress and other forums through the Military Coalition and in the Department of Veteran Affairs through the National Veterans Day Committee.

For 70 years it has bound together chaplains, as its Constitution expresses:

(a) To safeguard and strengthen the forces of faith and morality of our Nation;

(b) To perpetuate and deepen the bonds of understanding and friendship of our military service;

(c) To preserve our spiritual influence and interest in all members and veterans of the Armed Forces;

(d) To uphold the Constitution of the United States;

(e) To promote Justice, Peace and Good Will.

MCA Officers 1995-1996

President - Lorraine K. Potter
Vice President - David E. White
Secretary - James P. Lauer
Treasurer - Eric S. Renne

Executive Committee

Ernest B. Newsom, 96
JoAnn Knight, 96
Edward J. Kelley, 97
Michael L. McCoy, 97
Jay Boggs, 98
Kenneth Seifried, 98

Trustees

Clifford Weathers, 96
E.D. "Doc" Ellison III, 97
Marlin Seiders, 98

Past President

Herbert B. Cleveland

Executive Director

G. William Dando

Executive Director Emeritus

Karl B. Justus

National Headquarters

P.O. Box 42660, Washington, DC 20015-0660

Phone or Fax: In Washington 574-2423. Outside Washington 717-642-6792

E-Mail Address: CHAPLAINS @ charitiesusa.com.

Presidents of MCA

Charles H. Brent	1925-1929
John M. Thomas	1929-1931
William Hughes	1931-1932
Gustav Stearns	1932-1933
Howard E. Snyder	1933-1934
Arlington A. McCallum	1934-1938
Nils M. Ylvisaker	1938-1946
Robert M. White	1946-1949
Fred C. Reynolds	1949-1951
Daniel A. Poling	1951-1952
Henry Darlington	1952-1955
Stanton W. Salisbury	1955-1956
Maurice S. Sheehy	1956-1957
Edward L. R. Elson	1957-1959
Leslie Glenn	1959-1961
Patrick J. Ryan	1961-1966
Pardee Erdman	1966-1968
James Roy Smith	1968-1970
Philip L. Green	1970-1972
Richard W. Ricker	1972-1974
Leonard F. Stegman	1974-1976
Simeon Kobrinetz	1976-1978
Milton S. Ernstmeyer	1978-1980
William F. Emery	1980-1982
Simon H. Scott	1982-1984
Marlin D. Seiders	1984-1986
James E. Shaw	1986-1988
Frank H. Ebner	1988-1990
S. David Chambers	1990-1992
Herbert B. Cleveland	1992-1994
Lorraine K. Potter	1994-

Sites of National Conventions-Institutes

Washington	1931
New York	1932
Baltimore	1933
Cleveland	1934
Louisville	1935
St. Louis	1936
Chicago	1937
Washington	1938
Cincinnati	1939
New York	1940
Washington	1946
New York	1948
Chicago	1949
Washington	1950
San Francisco	1951
Fort Slocum	1952
Washington	1954
Fort Meyers	1956
Chicago	1957
New York	1958
Washington	1959
Annapolis	1960
West Point	1961
Colorado Springs	1962
Pasadena	1963
Chicago	1964
Boston	1965
Atlanta	1966
San Francisco	1967
Colorado Springs	1968
Seattle	1969
Chicago	1970
Washington	1971
Santa Monica	1972
Boston	1973
San Antonio	1974
New York	1975
Philadelphia	1976
Winter Park	1977
Colorado Springs	1978
Chicago	1979
Washington	1980
Atlanta	1981
Dallas	1982
Albuquerque	1983
Cape May	1984
Tacoma	1985
Nashville	1986
Newport	1987
Colorado Springs	1988
College Park	1989
Tampa	1990
San Antonio	1991
Hampton	1992
San Diego	1993
Carlisle	1994
Jacksonville	1995
Tacoma	1996

The Emerson Foundation

The Emerson Foundation was established by the Trustees of the Association to provide a means whereby members and friends could contribute to the Trust Fund. The Foundation was named for Chaplain William Emerson, the first chaplain in the military, being pastor of the fighting congregation at Concord, MA. When the alarm was sounded by Amos Melven that the British were afoot, Chaplain Emerson was the first to arrive. While the Continental Congress did not take action to establish the chaplaincy until July 29, 1775, Chaplain Emerson is honored as the first chaplain in the Revolution.

The Foundation works to support our special organization for chaplains and all that we do. Each year at our National Institute members of the Foundation are honored for their dedication to the Association and New members are inducted. Membership can only be granted by the trustees to those who have contributed, or been honored by a contribution of $1,000.00 or more to the Foundation. Each member is presented a numbered medallion and plaque and their names are placed upon a large plaque on display at each National Institute.

Emerson Foundation Members

1. Alva R. Appel
2. E. James Kingsley
3. Herbert B. Cleveland
4. James B. Martin
5. Edward A. Synan
6. Wilma J. Appel
7. J. Harold Ellens
8. Rita DeSanto Pollard
9. M. Douglas Blair
10. Howard A. Andrews
11. Frank H. Noll
12. Rev. & Mrs. William S. Koschny
13. Rudolf Devik
14. Ralph Smith
15. G. William Dando
16. Edward G. Wulfekuehler Jr.
17. William H. Sanford
18. Ernest B. Newsom
19. Cecil J. Knight
20. Mark R. Thompson
21. Jean W. Thompson
22. Harry Rhodes Miller
23. S. David Chambers
24. Robert H. Pepple
25. Edward B. Mulligan

Cutting the birthday cake, Navy Chaplain Corps 202nd Anniversary Celebration, November, 1978, at the Washington Navy Yard. From left: Lt. Michael D. Halley, CHC, USNR; Capt. James W. Conte, CHC, USN; Rear Admiral John J. O'Connor, CHC, USN (Chief of Chaplains); Rear Admiral Withers M Moore, CHC, USN (Deputy Chief of Chaplains) (Courtesy of Michael D. Halley)

Easter Sunrise Services on Christmas Island in April 1962. Chaplain Robert Maase conducting services. (Courtesy of Robert Maase)

Military Chaplains Special Stories

THE KOREAN BIBLE

by Arthur E. Lyons Jr.

A little more than half way through my second tour in Korea (1966-67) a Korean national had asked me to help him get a Korean text Bible. After several weeks he returned. I had not yet been able to get a Korean text Bible for him, so I loaded him into my Jeep with my American assistant and one of my KATUSA assistants, Park, as an interpreter.

We went to a nearby village where we located a bookstore. We found a Korean text Bible. Through Park I asked the price. The storekeeper gave a price and Park translated. Following the usual custom of bargaining over the price I made a counter offer through Park. The storekeeper became quite excited, jumping up and down gesturing and speaking very rapidly. I asked my assistant, "Park, what did he say?" Park looked at me and said, "Sir, he said, 'I will not bargain with the Word of God.'" Without another word I paid his asking price.

THE PERSIAN GULF

by David John Holland

I was privileged to be one of about two dozen or so Assemblies of God chaplains serving in the Persian Gulf. I was sent there to be a chaplain and at no time in theater, in the Kingdom of Saudi Arabia, was I asked to be anything less, like a morale officer, or to remove the cross from my collar. We were asked not to parade our being Christians but other than that there were no restrictions on my ministry as you will see. We were restricted in having our flag flying but military personnel are ingenious so these guys and gals had their flags flying in their offices, in their quarters and in the cabs of the vehicles which they drove all over Saudi Arabia. When the war was finally over I saw trucks and tanks and armored personnel carriers heading southward toward their points of debarkation with large American flags flying from their turrets, proudly waving in the open breezes of Saudi Arabia. They were proud to be Americans.

God is our provider and even in Saudi Arabia I found him to be a strong provider.

HE PROVED HIS PRESENCE. Easter Sunday, 1991, saw us meeting out in the open right on the Persian Gulf in the Port of Al Jubayl and God's presence overwhelmed us. Seventy men and women were present in this one of three Easter sunrise services on the Bay, and the Lord was present in power; four of these guys received Jesus as Savior that morning and six others rededicated their lives to him. In every worship service I held each weekend, and for several weeks I was doing 12 of them each Friday through Sunday, the Spirit of God was present in power. In one place, which I did not consider to be a Pentecostal or charismatic, this group of about 20 broke out in spontaneous applause as each one experienced the presence of God, and none of them could refrain from raising their hands in praise.

HE PROVIDED HIS PROTECTION. Shortly after I arrived in country, I was assigned to General Support Group Two, which was located about 15 to 20 miles south of the Kuwaiti border and about five miles from the town of Al Kafji. Once the bombing war began every hour of every day, we could hear the droning of United States and Allied aircraft as they made their way to Iraq and Kuwait on bombing missions—full of death for some; full of life and protection for others. We were not far from Al Khafji where the Iraqi made an incursion into what was an ill-defended town. Were the air wing guys and a few men on the ground not able to hold and defend that city, it would have fallen on us in

A liturgy service is conducted prior to a baptismal service for Marines in the Persian Gulf during the Gulf War, February 10, 1991. (Courtesy of Bradford Ableson)

Troops pray and receive communion during the Gulf War on March 17, 1991. (Courtesy of Bradford Ableson)

Chaplain Bradford E. Ableson, USN, Marine Aircraft Group-11, celebrates communion for Marines during Desert Storm, February 17, 1991. (Courtesy of Bradford Ableson)

Chaplain Bradford E. Ableson, USN, (foreground) and Chaplain Alan T. Baker, USN, (background) both of Marine Aircraft Group-11, distribute elements of Holy Communion during the Gulf War, March 17, 1991.

General Support Group Two to defend the route to the rest of Saudi Arabia. Ours was to have been only a hold action for it was guaranteed that we would have been overrun. And all we had to defend ourselves were clerks, cooks, truck drivers, mechanics, Seabees and chaplains. Not the best combat training, but we would have done our job if called upon. We were on the front lines under the umbrella of God's protection, for God's people were praying and we were the recipients of His blessing. None of the people in my area were killed by hostile fire.

HE PROVIDED HIS PORTION. Daily I made my way around to visit my troops. In my area there was an average of 1200 to 1300 personnel assigned over a 300 square mile area throughout the war. One out of every six U.S. military personnel in the zone made some kind of a decision for Christ. Easter Sunday afternoon, in the last service I would have in country, I held a service at the naval airport in Al Jubayl. One guy who attended had been away from the Lord, but that man fell in love with Jesus during that hour, rededicated his life to Jesus and told me that he made it his commitment to live for him when he returned to his family and home.

HE PROVIDED FOR HIS PEOPLE. It was estimated that between 10 to 20 percent of the 540,000 American personnel in Saudi Arabia were Christians. That meant that there were between 50 and 100 thousand Christians in that Islamic country. God planted His kids where they could be influential. Week after week I was able to encourage believers in every service. One young man who was instrumental in seeing that about 50 of his fellow Marines were in service each week, wrote a letter to me after the first week of services in which he said that he was so glad that I had heeded God's call and was there in Saudi Arabia.

There were seven of us from our church in Fallbrook, California who were ordered to Saudi Arabia, and I was able by the provision of God to see each one of them throughout the country even though I did not know at the beginning where they were. One by a xerox machine at the time that I entered a building. Another was the Marine who would check us in when we arrived in country. One young man was a Marine aboard a ship that just "happened" to pull into and dock at the port of Al Misha'ab where I spent the war. One young man was on a bus I was riding. Another we "happened" was in an open "tank" field.

HE PROVIDED HIS PASSPORT. He cares for us personally. The war was winding down. I wanted to get home to attend both of our daughters' graduations from college and high school respectively and to celebrate the 25th anniversary of our marriage, so I began praying. The retrograde tempo was on the increase, so I prayed, "God I would like to be out of this country by April 4." Not only was I out of Saudi Arabia by that day, but I was also home by that day. Praise God for his tender-loving care.

OPERATION "GITTMO"

by Earl V. Deblieux

It was quite a shock to receive a phone call early December 1991 from the Air Force Chief of Chaplains Office informing me that I was selected to be a Catholic Chaplain at Guantanamo Bay (Gitmo), Cuba to assist the Haitian boat people. Then another shock when I left so early (December 12) out of Eglin AFB, Florida by C-141 with my assistant, Staff Sergeant Al Centeno from Offutt AFB, Nebraska. But the greatest shock was to find about 7,000 Haitians in a tent city behind razor wire on the old McCalla Airfield here at Gitmo. In the sun, I find mostly young males, some families and children, all fleeing the killing army and growing poverty on the island of Haiti. They are seeking the safety, freedom and opportunity of a new land. Detained here by politics and legal decisions of higher authority. The job of the United States Military (about 1700 of us attached to the Joint Task Force (JTF) is to supply them with basic shelter, clothing, food, medical and spiritual care. The 13 chaplains assigned to JTF come from all branches of the service. The chaplains plunge into the camps with a ministry of loving, prayerful presence. We arrange for Catholic and Protestant worship services, conduct Bible studies, Choir and Worship Committee Meetings. We travel daily through row after row of tents, with lots of good mornings (bon jour), shaking hands, playing ball with children and passing out French and Creole Bibles. They spend their days gathering in groups talking, men play dominoes or cards, women wash clothes in white buckets. All line up three times a day for meals of MREs (Meals Ready to Eat) with rice and beans. Time drags on and on.

Some of the chaplains speak French which helps but most of us use American or Haitian interpreters to communicate. But it is the sign language of love that communicates far more than words. These are a gentle, open and prayerful people, all suffering a frustrating wait, wondering if they will be sent to the United States or back to Haiti or to another country. The United Nations (UN) the Immigration Naturalization Service (INS) and Community Relations Service (CRS) all work hard to process these people. As chaplains we encourage our Haitians to be patient, to be supportive of one another, to follow rules, especially hygiene, and above all to have faith and trust in God. We show our caring seven days a week by our constant presence in the camps. Often into the night you will hear the joyful voices and hand clapping of these Haitian people as they sing their songs of praise to God with their chaplains leading. Chaplains are here for a 90 day TDY in this great humanitarian effort. Please pray for the Haitian people, for the United States Military and the Chaplains serving at Guantanamo Bay, Cuba. For most chaplains, and I include myself, this is the most challenging and yet most rewarding service I have ever performed in the military. May God and others bring it quickly to a peaceful conclusion.

BROTHERLY SACRIFICE

by Chaplain Frank R. Griepp

"Unafraid they left a peaceful parish
For ministry in a bloody melee
Concerned about men who served their nation
Doing so they found themselves in harm's way.

Soldiers fulfilled their sacrificial vows
To the country to which they gave their oath.
Chaplains true to their ordination vows
Sacrificed their lives to preserve their oath.

One in fidelity, they faced danger
Enduring heat and cold they won victory
Brotherly sacrifice of life itself
Awards to them the conquerors trophy."

AN ACCIDENTAL ENCOUNTER

by Ronald Scott Bezanson, Chaplain (COL) USA (RET)

Chaplain coverage for troops in combat in an airmobile theater of operations demands a lot of flying time, much of it under very stressful conditions. Since chaplains have no dedicated air assets, if a chaplain is to reach his troops in the field, he must become a hitchhiker on helicopters of all sizes and shapes, on a wide variety of missions.

In the First Cavalry Division, deployed in III Corps, South Vietnam in 1969-70, I logged more than 500 hours in combat support and combat service support missions, flying with commanders in command and control helicopters, flying with logistical resupply "log" helicopters, and flying in light observation helicopters. I walked away from three crash landings during this period, one due to enemy fire, two the result of mechanical failure.

It was a sultry afternoon in February 1970, while serving as 2nd Brigade Chaplain, 1st Cavalry Division (Airmobile), that I was riding a log ship to provide chaplain coverage to a unit that was positioned along the edge of a Michelin rubber plantation, west of Song Be City. We were approaching a landing zone that had been cleared for us when suddenly power to the tail rotor was lost and the helicopter began to spin, tail around cockpit, and we plummeted toward the ground. We seemed headed directly into the rubber trees, and as my life flashed before me, I could picture a fatal encounter. Suddenly we dropped short of the rubber trees, into a small banana grove. The soft banana trees slowed our rotation and cushioned our impact, so that everyone on board walked away from that crash with only minor scratches.

I retrieved my combat chaplain kit, and with the others walked quickly away from the crash site. I announced services as usual about an hour later and nearly everyone attended the service.

Thirteen years later, I was standing in a Pentagon corridor talking with a visiting chaplain, when a tall young major walked by. He passed by once, and then turned and passed again, observing closely. Out of the corner of my eye I could see him stop and wait for us to finish our conversation. When I began to move on, he approached me and asked, "Aren't you the chaplain who walked away from a helicopter crash at the edge of a rubber plantation in Vietnam in February 1970? The bird had lost its tail rotor and went down in the trees, but you came out and conducted a service a little while later." I admitted that I remembered such an experience. He shook my hand and said, "I was a young sergeant, the pathfinder (air traffic controller) on the ground at that location. I wasn't in the habit of going to worship services, but when I saw you and the others walk away from that site, I went to that service. And chaplain, you know I haven't missed chapel on many Sundays since. I decided on the spot that there must be something to this faith thing after all. And I just want to say thank you."

Chaplain George Ambrose conducting field service in the Mekong Delta, Vietnam, 1968. (Courtesy of George Ambrose, Jr.)

NO GREATER LOVE

by Ronald Scott Bezanson, Chaplain (COL) USA (RET)

It was hot and steamy during early spring in the jungles of South Vietnam. The year was 1970. The area was known as the Parrot's Beak, an enemy infested jungle territory along the Cambodian border of III Corps. I provided chaplain ministry to the men of 1/12 Cavalry, 1st Cavalry Division. We were an airmobile division where ground vehicles were few, and resupply for units in the jungle was accomplished every fourth day by helicopter "log" ships, Hueys which were stripped of doors and all but fold-down seats in order to facilitate maximum cargo capacity: food, water, ammunition, mail, and replacements.

Since chaplains had no direct call on transportation assets, except on Christmas and Easter, hitchhiking a ride on the "log bird" was the standard means of reaching the troops. A platoon or company would clear a landing zone, radio that it was ready to receive "log" and the resupply began. Whenever possible the chaplain hitched a ride on the first bird in, and, unless he planned to spend the next three days in the jungle with that unit, caught one of the last backhauls out. Whatever day the chaplain arrived in a unit location was "Sunday" as far as the troops were concerned.

The chaplain would visit as widely as possible with the deployed troops in that location, taking care not to compromise the security or safety of the men. A place for services would be found and the word spread, and soon a majority representation of the unit would gather for a short worship service. Some were regulars, attending every service unless on patrol, others seemed to attend only when there had been recent enemy contact or when reports of enemy activity indicated that contact was imminent.

One of the regulars in B Company was John. John was a squad leader. John was also a devout Christian, a man who read his Bible and prayed daily. John was concerned for the men in his squad who did not come to worship services and who made no profession of faith. His prayers and his conversation reflected that concern.

One dark night, John and his squad were assigned night defensive responsibility. They were moving into position when an enemy grenade was tossed into their midst. John, with total disregard for his own safety, grabbed off his helmet, placed it over the grenade and fell on it. The impact of the explosion tore the helmet apart and John was gravely wounded. Medevac was on the scene within minutes and I encountered John in the forward aid station on Fire Support Base Buttons, the first stop in his journey to the Evacuation Hospital in Long Binh. For John the war was over. He was horribly wounded; his entire midsection was perforated with shrapnel; he was in pain; but he was conscious and his eyes lighted up when he looked up from his litter and saw my face. "Chappy," he said, "pray for me." We had a brief prayer there amid all the hustle and bustle, and then he was on his way. I saw him again a few days later in the Evacuation Hospital. The road to recovery would be long, the rehabilitation difficult, but his faith remained strong, and still he prayed for those he had left behind in the jungle.

I covered that unit for several more weeks, and John would have been proud to know that every member of his squad became regulars in worship. They were hungry for information about John, and determined to find that faith which had been so much a part of his life among them.

After he left Vietnam, John spent many months in hospitals

Baptismal Service in the Cua Viet River, five miles soth of the dimilitarized zone, RVN, July 28, 1968. Chaplain Elden H. Luffman performs the baptism. (Photo by Sgt. Al Stirling, courtesy of Elden Luffman)

"For such is the Kingdom of Heaven" Chaplain Elden Luffman poses with Vietnamese children in Hue during TET, March 1968 (Courtesy of Elden Luffman)

in Japan and in the United States, and several years had passed before I was next able to contact him. For his heroism and sacrifice he had been awarded the Congressional Medal of Honor, and finally I was able to tell him of the lasting impact his living witness had made upon his squad. Greater love has no man than this, that he was willing to risk his life for his friends.

THE CHAPLAIN

by Richard Y. Bershon, Chaplain USA

Somewhere over the Republic of Vietnam an army helicopter approaches a small landing zone that has been cleared out of the dense jungle. This is a logistical resupply helicopter usually referred to as a "log bird." Along with the supplies this one carries a chaplain. The pilot radios to the platoon leader to "pop smoke." A smoke grenade is tossed marking the landing zone and the helicopter descends.

The chaplain helps toss off the cartons of C rations, water cans, mail bag, and other supplies, grabs his combat chaplain's kit and gets out quickly. He knows the pilot doesn't want to remain on the Landing Zone (LZ) any longer than is absolutely necessary.

After the chopper takes off and the dust settles, the chaplain talks with the platoon leader who announces to his men that they will be having Protestant services in a few minutes. The platoon leader selects a location away from the LZ for the service and the chaplain makes preparation. Often two chaplains, Protestant and Catholic, will travel together. In that case the services are usually consecutively. However, they may be conducted simultaneously. This depends on the desire of the platoon leader and the tactical situation.

No attempt is made to conduct all services on Sunday in airmobile units. The men in the bush tend to lose track of days of the week. Any day that the chaplain can make it is Sunday, so far as they are concerned.

The men gather around for the service which is necessarily brief. Log day is busy and it isn't safe to have several men bunched up for a long period of time.

One or two hymns are sung, perhaps a responsive reading is used, prayer is offered, and reading from the Word of God along with a short message is ministered. After the service there is time for the chaplain to chat with the men and counsel with any that may have a problem.

The chaplain remembers the words of the Apostle Paul, "For I long to see you, that I may impart unto you some spiritual gift, to the end ye may be established. That is, that I may be comforted together with you by the mutual faith both of you and me" (Romans 1:11, 12). He hopes that in his brief time on the LZ that he has been a blessing to the men and helped to strengthen their faith in Christ and their spiritual lives.

He is sure that they have been a blessing and encouragement to him. These airmobile infantry soldiers ("Grunts" as they are called) have more to complain about than the other soldiers, but they complain the least. They many not have strong convictions about the war; but their country has called them to do a job, so they do it to the best of their ability. Everything they have is carried in their rucksacks. They each may get two or three cans of soda pop on log day. They always offer one to the chaplain. They have so little but they wish to share what they have. It may have been several days since they were on a fire base and perhaps weeks since they have seen a base camp; for they stay in the bush under the blistering tropical sun and through the drenching monsoon rains. However if the chopper seems to be a little slow in returning for their chaplain, they express concern.

When the bird comes back, the chaplain departs having been encouraged by the faith and concern of the men to whom he came to minister. In this way Christians in the military service and throughout the world are a blessing and a source of strength one to another.

Chaplain Krabbe conducts services aboard the USNS Geiger for units bound for Vietnam, 1966. (Courtesy of R. D. Daniell)

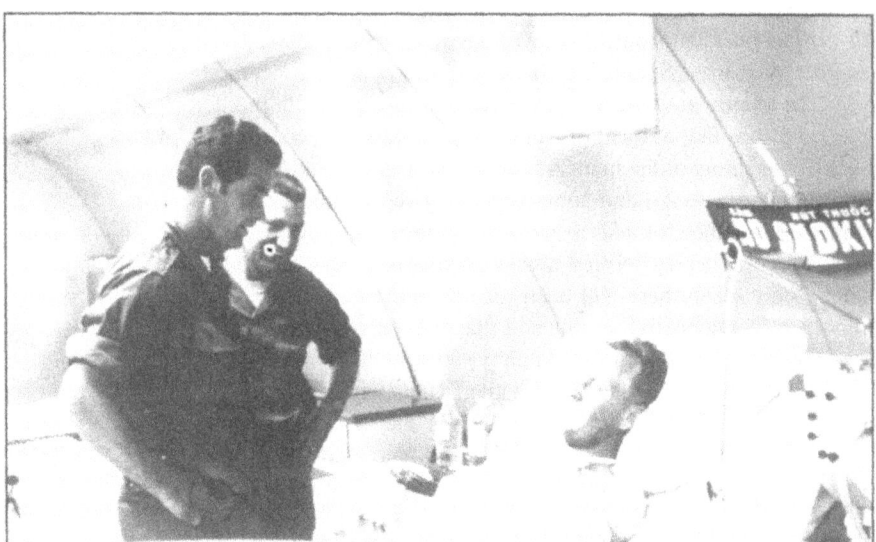
James Garner and Chaplain Daniell visit patients at the 24th Evac Hospital in 1967. (Courtesy of R. D. Daniell)

Daniell conducts character guidance session at Long Giao, RVN, for members of the 36th Sig. Bn. Detachment. (Courtesy of R. D. Daniell)

BURT FIRE SUPPORT BASE

Vietnam, January 1968

by Rev. Fr. Alister C. Anderson

The code name for one of the many fire support bases in Vietnam was Burt. It was a small clearing in a dense jungle area near the village of Katum, 68 miles northwest of Saigon and five miles south of the Cambodian borders. On my circuit around the artillery units attached to the 25th Infantry Division, of which I was the Division Artillery Chaplain, I visited Burt on January 26, 1968. At 0815 a mortar attack was launched on our position by the North Vietnamese. In less than 30 minutes three men were killed and 26 were wounded. As our artillery returned fire, I went to the perimeter to minister to the wounded and dead. Dust-off choppers arrived in 20 minutes and evacuated the seriously wounded to the 12th Evacuation Hospital in Cuchi. As I comforted the wounded and administered Last Rites to the dead, I was shocked to see that two of them I had baptized several days before in a rice paddy at another fire support base. Their faces were staring wide-eyed in astonishment that death had come so suddenly. I touched each eye and closed them upon the violence of this life. An overwhelming feeling of sorrow swept over me while I fought back tears of grief for those two new-found friends. Then I comforted myself with that inspiring fact that they had come to the Lord through Holy Baptism before He had called them through battle to His home.

I began thinking about all those other soldiers in our nation's history who perhaps not baptized in church or chapel were, nevertheless, considered to be so by their own blood which they shed sacrificially in death for a cause they believed to be righteous and just. I anointed their foreheads and recited the ancient Christian prayer: "The almighty and merciful Lord grant thee pardon and remission of all thy sin and the grace and comfort of the Holy Spirit. Depart, O Christian soul, out of this world; in the Name of God the Father Almighty who created thee; In the Name of Jesus Christ who redeemed thee; In the name of the Holy Ghost who sanctified thee. May thy rest be this day in peace, and thy dwelling place in the Paradise of God."

Then I recalled their baptism. I had led them out into a rice paddy, filled the steel pot of my helmet with water from that paddy and poured it over their heads and bodies which were stripped to the waist. I recited another ancient prayer as the water streamed over them: "I baptize you in the Name of the Father, and of the Son, and of the Holy Ghost. We sign you with the sign of the Cross that hereafter you will not be ashamed to confess the faith of Christ crucified, and manfully to fight under His banner, against sin, the world, and the devil; and to continue Christ's faithful soldier and servant unto your life's end. Amen." I believed I saw their faces reflecting hope and confidence that now they knew nothing could separate them from the love of God.

After the mortar fire, the expected ground attack did not occur and the senior commander present permitted me to hold a Communion Service for some of the soldiers. I invited as many who could crawl into a sand-bag bunker only about four feet in height and no more than 20 feet square. We knelt in semi-darkness with two flashlights held over my Prayer Book, Bible, Chalice and paten. As I recited the comfortable words from the Episcopal Service, "Come unto me all ye that travail and are heavy laden, and I will refresh you," I thought of all those Christians through the ages in Catacombs and other secret places, who had to worship this way so as not to be detected by those who hated their faith and sought to kill them. After the service I preached a short sermon that I repeated many times around our infantry division. I reminded them that we were fighting a just war. In spite of the news broadcasts which condemned the war; in spite of letters received from family and friends that their friends were demonstrating, burning draft cards and going to Canada and Sweden to avoid being called up, I said there was a good and honorable reason for us to be in all this mud, blood and sweat. We had come to this place to defend peaceful, freedom-loving people from a ruthless, invading enemy. We were waging a war with the right intention to protect the good and remove the evil. We can believe that the South Vietnamese fight for national survival was part of the free world's struggle against belligerent, atheistic Communism and therefore it was in the best interest of our own country for us to be fighting there. We were not fighting the Vietcong or the North Vietnamese in revenge but only for the protection of all freedom loving people.

When I finished my sermon we crawled out of the bunker into the bright sun and scorching heat and the soldiers went back to their posts. I packed up my mass kit, strapped it to my back and walked along the protected rim of our defensive perimeter. I spoke to the men at each point, reminding myself that as I slept the next night, it would be these men who would defend us against another attack. I thanked God for them and then recalled another mortar barrage that was followed by a ground attack that overran part of a fire support base at Sui-Tre. Our division lost many more men that day than we did at Burt today. I also thought about a seminary professor who had criticized my being involved in what he called "this immoral war." I reminded him in a letter, which I wrote when I returned to base camp, that I should go where Jesus goes and that he calls his chaplains to be with his people wherever they go. I also reminded him that this was a just war and he could find a theological explanation for it in the Summa Theological of St. Thomas Aquinas.

THE BIRTH OF A KOREAN SYNAGOGUE

by Chaplain, Seoul Military Post, Seoul, Korea

On March 2, 1954, the order to move was given. True, the shooting stopped several months before, but changes in troop locations were continuously taking place. Seoul Military Post was releasing its headquarters area to another Korean aid group as the city was returning more and more to civilian status and control.

To the barren area we came, the chaplain section in the vanguard being the first to move. Two days later all our supplies and equipment were placed in the two 75x20 foot quonset which needed repair and remodeling before they were to become the office space for the chaplains and the Seoul Military Post Chapels, one of which would be the first Jewish Chapel and Synagogue in the history of Korea. Beth Yehee Shalom, the House of Let There Be Peace was my task, a job that took nine weeks to perform.

All through the Korean Conflict Jewish Chaplains used the field, tents, and shared army chapels for services, but now there was to be a separate building dedicated for Jewish Worship. With my assistant, I set upon the work with great fervor. Construction material and supplies were at a premium. We had to travel far from our home to locate the lumber, nails, paint and varnish. There were days when I traveled as far as 35 miles to obtain a donated sheet of plywood or a gallon of much needed paint. Gradually the items began to accumulate and the laborers came to work.

These artisans, Koreans who had never seen or heard of a Jewish Synagogue and who could speak no English, were prepared to take direction from the Jewish Chaplain who could speak no Korean. For six days we worked; hammering, sawing and putting the mosaic pattern into form. By then the carpenters had to leave so that the construction shifted to night hours lasting till close to midnight. Perhaps it was for the mitzvah or the added compensation they received; the work progressed nicely. By Purim most of the partitions were in. The chaplain's office and the space for his assistant were completed. The wires for the electricity was installed and the lights put in. Even the bimah was made. Haman received his "due reward" at the hands of GIs who came to Purim services held in a shul in Korea.

More expeditions, letter, and calls brought the remainder of the needed materials so that the work of nightly construction could continue. A jig saw was discovered so that the Hebrew letters forming the Shema could be carved out of wood and placed upon the wall above the ark. Stateside gold paint was located to ornament these letters. The two coats of paint were completed and the fixtures designed by the chaplain and made by the assistant were installed. With the words of the Shema placed upon the wall, the shul was ready for Pesach, the holiday of freedom.

For Yomtov services the GIs came from near and as far as 57 miles to be in the House of Let There Be Peace; to pray for peace in this land and for his loved ones at home. But the shul was not yet complete, there was still need for new benches, the dedicatory plaque, the red carpet, and the walk in front of the building.

At the Passover Seder, General Maxwell D. Taylor, commanding general, 8th United States Army, was our guest. At that time he expressed the desire to participate in the dedication. Arrangements to complete the building were made; the dedication set for May 2. The Honorable Ellis O. Briggs, United States Ambassador to Korea was extended an invitation to attend and he accepted.

The missing items were built, bought and installed. Special generators were obtained to furnish the electricity for the tape

Marine Private First Class Leo J. LeMaitre, son of Mr. and Mrs Charles LeMaitre of Swanton, OH, talks with Chaplain John H. Craven during the 7th Marines campaign in reservior area, Korea. (Courtesy of John H. Craven)

recordings and motion pictures taken by the Army Signal Corps to record the historic event. At the appointed hour (1500/3:00 p.m.) Sunday, 29 Nissan 5714 with all the guests present, the dedicatory service began. All eight of the Jewish Chaplains stationed in Korea participated and I, as the host Jewish Chaplain who built and directed the construction of Beth Yehee Shalom, had the pleasure of presenting Colonel Kammerer, the post commander, Ambassador Briggs and General Taylor. On concluding the dedicatory address General Taylor dedicated the synagogue with the act of lighting the nerbtamid (eternal light).

Four thousand years of history was changed. Dedicated "In honor of the men who made possible the establishment of Beth Yohoo Shalom, the House of Let There Be Peace" a synagogue was now established in Korea. Many took part in forging the historic chain of history and as I prayed at the dedicatory service: to the men and officers of the 8th United States Army who made it possible that this house of the Lord be built, to the National Jewish Welfare Board back in the States, to those who participated in its construction, and to those who donated towards its erection, the everlasting thanks of an eternal people.

THE VILLAGE CHIEF

by Clyde Northrop

I heard the burst of automatic rifle fire and saw the two men fall to the sand about 500 yards down the beach from where I was standing in my jeep straining to get a better view and concerned about whether they were still alive. The two had gone down the beach toward the make-shift village against my advice and in direct violation of normal procedures. We had a humanitarian mission planned for the village that morning. An armed escort was arranged for every village visit. Sometimes we took lumber for village construction and other times we took food. Our visiting dentist even went a couple of mornings. Any assistance to the villagers brought out the whole population and there was swift competition to vie for the limited resources. We never visited without the Vietnamese "Village Chief" appointed by our authorities as a liaison. Our escort was a little late on that day and the Chief and his assistant did not want to wait. No amount of talk would dissuade them. Things seemed to be going better between the village people and our Army compound, so they started walking toward the fishing village which was just out of sight beyond the sand dunes on the beach. From where I stood I could see some of the boats at the village shoreline through the haze created by the bright sun bouncing off the beautiful white sand.

The chief and his assistant never even reached the village. It must have taken five minutes for our armed escort to arrive and reach them. The chief was dead and the assistant chief was wounded in the arm. Our medics put the body in a bag and placed the bag on a trailer behind the jeep. I was accompanied by the bandaged assistant chief, arm in sling, in carrying the dead official back to his family in Quang Tri City. Normally we went to Quang Tri in convoy. This was just after TET of 1968 and conditions had become a little more secure. There was no convoy this morning and we set out on the dirt road alone, my assistant riding "shotgun," the soon to be appointed new chief of the village in the back and with me driving. I had no idea how we would be received by the family of the chief. This was a mission that I approached with much dread and some fear. I was surprised when

Appreciation ceremony from the Orphanage for support by the Battalion. Chaplain Daniell receives the award with Col. Hendricks looking on Daniell served as interpreter between the orphanage priest who spoke French, and the battalion. Daniell also taught English to the priest and nuns during 1966-67. (Courtesy of R. D. Daniell)

we arrived and presented the chief's widow with the body of her husband, that we were well received. We were invited into the thatched roofed home with no glass in the opened windows. The deep sorrow did not keep the family from treating us as honored guests. This Southern Baptist Army Chaplain was presented with a glass of warm Vietnamese beer. I am not a beer drinker, and certainly not warm Vietnamese beer. I believed it too hard a communication task and inappropriate under the circumstances to try to explain that I would rather not accept that part of their hospitality. So I drank as much of the beer as I could get down, a small sip at a time. Through a very limited vocabulary and much gesturing with the hands, over the course of a half hour I conveyed my regret concerning the death of the beloved husband and father. I shall never forget the grace with which I was received and the manner in which his family ministered to this very young chaplain in his second year in the Army.

I have seen it multiplied throughout my ministry. It is difficult, if not impossible, to minister to others without receiving more ministry than you give.

AN OPEN LETTER

by Capt. Raymond G. McPherson, CHC, USNR

To: Maj. Everett A. McPherson, USMC/Pilot
Status: MIA March 18, 1966; still missing,
Panel #6E, Line #21
FM: Older brother, Captain, Chaplain Corps, USNR
The Moving Wall, Baton Rouge, LA, Sept. 27, 1989

Dear Brother,
The last time I wrote to you was in March of 1966 just before you were reported "presumed shot down." You were flying an EF10B with Bret Davis as your back seat radar man. Your mission was reconnaissance in nature; to locate missile sites and try to jam their signals.

I wondered for a long time afterwards whether or not you received my last letter. It wasn't until several years later, after that unforgettable day of learning you were down and when your status was changed to "Presumptive Findings of Death" that your personal effects were returned to the family. In your returned things I was much relieved to find you had received and apparently read my last letter, since it had been opened.

I was also relieved to know you had read that particular letter because I had felt led of the Lord to share with you one of the beloved Psalms of David. After searching the scriptures, I settled on Psalm 91 that speaks of God's protection and deliverance. You can imagine how confused I was, and for quite some time, when it seemed you did not have what I was expecting from God; namely His protection for you.

The purpose of this letter now, is to simply remember and, once again, put into perspective the experience we call "Nam" and the journey that has been mine in reference to you and all we have learned and shared together from this end of things.

First I want to say I think it would be important for you to know that I am now at peace on your behalf. I somehow feel that this is what you would want for me as well as for the family, to be at peace. But it has not always been so.

It has been a painful journey since that fateful day on March 18, 1966. I was taking a break between seminary classes when the phone rang in our trailer home. It was dad. Most unusual to get a call from dad; and especially during the day. He was very upset with a quiver in his voice when he said "Ray, he's down. Everett's down! Your brother's been shot down!"

I will never forget my own reaction of total disbelief and non-acceptance. For I had trusted you to God for his protection and I am also now aware that I had relied too much on the fact that you flew a jet. I thought you were invincible.

None-the-less, dad's message was all-to-soon to be confirmed by a telegraphed message from the Commandant of the Marine Corps followed by a letter from the Army Commander in Chief. Wanda and I took immediate leave of absence from the seminary and drove to mom and dad's in Norfolk to be with them and the rest of the family. We stopped along the way every hour or so to call home to see if there was any late word of your possible rescue.

When we got home, none of us knew what to do. We were afraid to cry for fear of conveying hopelessness to each other. So we mostly buried our heads in our pillows at night and sobbed our hearts out. Some of us swallowed our tears or choked them down. Dad was best at that. Mom couldn't help crying off and on. But she never gave up believing you were alive and would one day walk through the door of home again. She died on July 25, 1978, at the young age of 62. For 12 long years she never gave up. Now she knows the whole story, far better than we.

For awhile I was angry, not only with the enemy, but with God; and also with you. I was angry with the enemy for taking you away from us, with God for awhile, thinking He had forsaken us, and with you for breaking your promise.

Remember when we stood outside in front of the trailer there at Wake Forest? You didn't have permission to tell me you had orders for Vietnam, but we both knew it. It was our last meeting together and final farewell. We hugged each other a little awkwardly and I said, "Brother, you don't have to be a hero in this war. Just go and do your duty; get it over with and bring yourself home." You nodded your head in agreement as our hands held tightly to each other. I still remember how your huge hand enveloped mine even though I was "the big brother." Well, you broke your promise...so far. I'm still holding you to it, but you'll be happy to know I'm not angry anymore over what you had no control over.

Remember that time you told me a flyer's worst fear was burning? Well, for quite awhile after you were reported down, I kept having these terrible recurring nightmares of you in a burning plane in a nose dive. The dream was always the same. I always saw you, in this dream, sitting behind the controls of your plane helplessly engulfed in flames. One day, by God's loving providence, I attended a special seminar on dream therapy dealing with other people's problems. That night I had that terrible dream again. When I awoke the next morning, I decided to apply some of the techniques I had learned from the God-fearing therapist I had heard the day before. Step-by-step I walked myself through the principles and each detail of the dream, facing you in the worst part, the flames. Amazingly, I discovered what God wanted me to learn from that dream. I discovered that one of your great hopes was to one day take me for a ride. In order to tend to that unfinished hope and dream of yours, God gave me the means to put out the flames in the dream, climb aboard your plane in the imagination of my heart, and go for a ride. Your dream has been fulfilled, brother, and my nightmares are finished. God is good. He has shown me, and allowed me, to fly with you in my heart.

I am also at peace to know that God has been with you all these many years since that fateful day. And whether you are alive in the flesh or alive in the spirit, I know you are not dead. I am convinced you are with the Lord.

John Gillespie Magee Jr. wrote a poem entitled *High Flight*; it has been an inspiration from God that speaks the heart of the flyer and comfort to so many like myself. I am comforted by the poem in the knowledge that you have reached out "and touched the face of God." Even more importantly, I am eternally thankful in the knowledge that you have been touched by Him.

There are so many more things I would like to tell you. Time or space does not permit it now. One day it will. But these final words in closing.

I want you to know that your name lives on in our first and eldest son, David Everett. You would be proud of him, your first nephew. He's now 21, married to a beautiful lady from Louisiana, and wears the uniform well of the ROTC at LSU. You also have a niece, Jennifer, whose a grown woman now who recently completed basic training for the Army National Guard. Can you believe it? She fired expert on the rifle range! Your youngest nephew, Jonathan, will soon turn 14, and guess what? He wants to be a flyer. Well, I don't know about that. Well, I'll just have to trust each one of them to our heavenly Father like I did you.

Your name, by the way, has been memorialized. It's on a Vietnam Memorial called "The Wall" in Washington, DC with hundreds of other names of those killed in action and still missing. Its a massive and awesome sight to behold. The first time I saw your name up there, I found myself weeping all over again; just like a baby. You would have laughed. But that time it was somehow different. I can't quite explain it, it's too deep for words. Your name, alongside hundreds of your fallen comrades, who gave up their lives in obedience to the call of our nations to service. Please know, brother, you are not forgotten.

For too long I was unable to visit The Wall in Washington. There are still hundreds of families and citizens who cannot get there to see it. I am happy that today there is a replica of that same wall on a smaller scale. Its called The Moving Wall and is being taken to the people across the country of America. My prayer is that it will facilitate healing in the hearts of many; even as it has helped me to come face-to-face with my own grief.

Please know, brother, it was not in vain that you went to Nam. Countless numbers of us have been literally brought to our knees before our Maker, the God in Whom We Trust. We have learned much. And we continue to learn as we unravel the mysteries of the Vietnam story, and our part as a nation, in it.

Our wounds are healing. But there is still much unfinished business. I believe the final victory in overcoming our pain and hurt, will be in the obedience to God and his sovereign way of doing things. This is going to be the hardest thing of all for many of us, accepting God's way and...forgiving the enemy. I read about that recently in Matthew's Gospel, the fifth chapter, verses 43-48 (Matt.5:43-48). When I am able to do that, forgive the enemy, then I think my peace will be complete in your regard. Then, perhaps, God will hear my prayer for the release from the bondage we have too long felt about Vietnam, and the bondage of those who may still be held captive against their will. And one day, perhaps, those whom we have called our enemies, will come to know and love the same Lord, God, and Father of us all Who is our peace. Let the will of God be done.

Until I see you and embrace you again, my dear brother, and I most certainly will, I remain faithfully

Your older brother,
Raymond.

BLONDE IN THE MUD

by Talmadge F. McNabb

It was Springtime, 1985. The United States Army chaplain was sitting in his little tin covered chapel, near Ujonbu, Korea, 10 miles north of Seoul. He was preparing his worship service bulletin for the forthcoming Sunday morning.

Suddenly, unannounced, a jeep stopped outside the chapel; a young soldier sprang out, rushed into the chaplain's office, excitedly proclaiming, "Chaplain! I was in a convoy and couldn't stop. We just passed a little village next to us, and I saw a little blonde haired girl being pushed into the muddy paddyfield by some Korean children. Could you go see about her?"

A little blonde haired girl being pushed into a paddyfield. Ostracized! Chaplain McNabb knew this was what was called a GI baby. He must rush to help. The story and subsequent significant developments were told in a 1955 published book, *Bring My Sons From Afar*.

The saga was intertwined with the chaplain's rescue of the little GI baby, an Oregon farmer, his wife Bertha. This was to lead to developments whereby over 70,000 needy children would in later years be placed in good homes worldwide.

The chaplain was Talmadge Ford McNabb from a small village in Tennessee. As if by strong compulsion, he tossed aside his office work, jumped in his jeep, sped away to the village.

There he saw the little two year old blonde haired girl, now pushed into the miry paddyfield. As she would try to climb out, up the slick bank, the Korean children would step on her fingers, causing her to fall back down.

The Chaplain, after shooing away the other children, reached down for the little girl, pulled her into his arms, her clothes and hair matted with mud.

He took her to his chapel, cleaned off the mud. Some GIs found bright clothing, a little white dress, blue shoes, socks, even a ribbon for her hair, in some chapel packages previously sent to the chapel for distribution.

The little girl looked so beautiful it seemed every GI in the compound wanted to adopt her. Chaplain McNabb found the girl's mother who wanted him to take the little girl and try to find a good home for her, as she had been ostracized by the other village children because of her different physical features.

The Chaplain found a missionary in Seoul with whom he could temporarily leave the little girl. Meanwhile, he visited the head of the Korean Department of Child Welfare, who told him a letter had just arrived from a retired Oregon farmer, Harry Holt, who was interested in coming to Korea to adopt eight GI babies into his own family, even though the farmer had reared six children of his own.

The chaplain contacted Mr. Holt, soon received a letter from his wife stating Mr. Holt was on his way to Korea. The Oregon Farmer met Chaplain McNabb, was presented little Christine (the name of the rescued child) and Mr. Holt fell in love with her from the very beginning. Chaplain McNabb helped Mr. Holt find seven other GI babies; Mr. Holt took them back to Oregon, where widespread publicity was given in large national magazines and news publications.

Mr. Holt had told Chaplain McNabb that prior to the farmer's leaving for Korea, he was plowing his tractor on his farm. He perceived, almost as in a vision, a little blonde haired girl in Korea reaching her arms out to him. He stopped his tractor, rushed to his house, told his wife he must go to Korea now. No further delays. As if to confirm his feelings, Mrs. Holt handed him the letter she'd just received from the chaplain in Korea.

That was not the end of the story. Mr. Holt later set up the Holt International Children's Service, an adoption society. He also came back to Korea, built a huge orphanage north of Seoul. While working with his orphanage in Korea, he died of a heart attack and was buried on a hilltop overlooking the institution he loved so well.

Mrs. Holt continued Harry Holt's vision of placing children in good homes, not only in the USA, but worldwide. The Loretta Young national TV program made a dramatic television movie of the Holt story, portraying Chaplain McNabb, the little girl Christine and Mr. and Mrs. Holt.

Mrs. Holt is still living, well into her 90th year, very active, sometimes jogging three miles a day, still making international flights to place children in good adoptive homes. She was one year selected as American Mother of the Year and was called to the White House to personally meet the then President Lyndon Johnson.

A little blonde haired GI baby pushed into a muddy paddyfield. A GI passing in convoy seeing the pathetic sight, rushing to tell his chaplain. The chaplain hastening to rescue the little mud covered girl. A kind Oregon farmer hastening to Korea to adopt her. His inspiration leading him to adopt eight GI babies into his family; later setting up and adoption program whereby tens of thousands of needy children were placed in good homes. An inspiration! Obedience in trying to help others. The results almost unbelievable.

Chaplain McNabb has never considered his part in the dramatic saga as little more than any other chaplain would have done under similar circumstances. But he strongly believes when people are obedient to their inner urgings to help others, great happenings can result.

Sacrament of baptism on the USS Iwo Jima (LPH-2) with Chaplaim Schade. (Courtesy of Sigmund Schade)

Chaplain Captain Robert L. Maase conducts Easter Sunrise Service on Christmas Island in April 1962. (Courtesy of Robert L. Maase)

The Rev. Edwin L. Bishop conducting services at NTC Orland, 1975. (Courtesy of Red. Edwin L. Bishop)

CDR Thomas A. Schultz, CHC, USN (Ret.)

Field Service, Military Police Officers, Fort Hood, Texas. (Courtesy of C. W. Edwards, Jr.)

Baptismal service in a river in Vietnam (Courtesy of F. E. Bentley)

The Commander, the chaplain's clerk and Chaplain Virgil Daley in Germany on field manuevers. 1960s. (Courtesy of Virgil Welden Daley)

Chaplain "Connie" Walker, 173rd Airborne Brigade, hold a service for paratroopers in the field during an operation.

CDR Thomas A. Schultz, CHC, USN (Ret.)

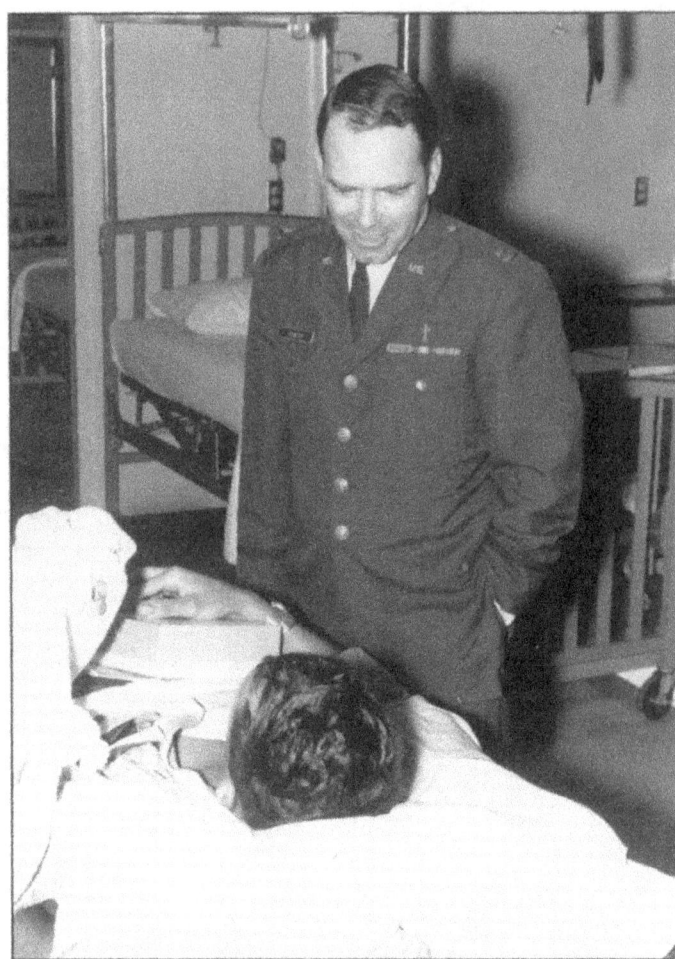

Sawyer visits a wounded soldier. (Courtesy of D. M. Sawyer)

Chaplain Griepp and his congregation on the fighting line, Yongpyoug, Korea, 1951. (Courtesy of F. R. Griepp)

Major Fisher and Major R. Mehring of the 7th Infantry help a Korean orphan who has been crippled since birth. 1964 (Courtesy of R. A. Mehring)

Even the chaplains learned how to jump. 188th AIR, 11th Airborne Division, Ft. Campbell, KY, March 1953.

Chaplain Craven returns the church bell from the Central Church of Chong-Chin, to the pastor the Rev. Lee from Seoul. The Chinese Communist took the bell from the destroyed church building and used it is a tower for an air raid alarm Korea. (Courtesy of John H. Craven)

The Chaplain rides along as the troops prepare for "All-American" field exercise at Ft. Bragg, November 1957. (Courtesy of Frank O. Varvin)

Chaplain John F. Wakefield and Pfc. Richard Williams are shown presenting a Christmas gift to a Korean boy at the Naichon school, 4th Signal Battalion. (U.S. Army photo by Pvt. Nelmes, courtesy of John F. Wakefield)

The hood of a jeep is sufficient space for Herbert Cleveland to conduct a service. (Courtesy of Herbert Cleveland)

Dedication of Armed Forces Flag Pole at Bethel Theological Seminary's new campus, St Paul, MN. (Courtesy of Chaplain Col. Bruce Herrstrom)

A Christmas Eve candlelight service with Chaplain M. H. Jay. December 1953. (Courtesy of M. H. Jay)

John F. Wakefield was assigned to the 4th Signal Battalion of the 10th Corps in Korea and had seven preaching stations scattered over the area. He used to stop and hunt on his way to visiting the troops in outlying areas. (Courtesy of John F. Wakefield)

Church services for A 1/1 in Hue between buildings for safety using the hood of a jeep for an altar. Chaplain Elden Luffman was the regimental chaplain for the 1st Marine Divison. February 1968. (Courtesy of Elden Luffman)

LTG Richard Stillwell and Col. Clayton Day, Chaplain, escort Dr. Billy Graham from his helicopter to XXIV Corps HQ prior to his Christmas Service for the troops of the Hue Phu Bai area. (U. S. Army photo by SSG James Harmon, courtesy of Clayton E. Day)

Dr. Billy Graham makes a dramatic point during his Christian service for the troops of the Hue Phu Bai area. From left: MG Melvin Zeis, CG 101st Airborne (Airmobile) Div, LTG Richard G. Stillwell, (G XXIV Corps, Phu Bai, RVN) Col. Clayton E. Day, Chaplain, XXIV Corps, Phu Bai and soloist for Dr. Graham, James McDonald. December 22, 1968. (Courtesy of Clayton E. Day.)

Ecumenical Memorial Services are conducted aboard the USS Iwo Jima (LPH-2). Jewish XO is at the rostrum, Catholic Chaplain is seated (wearing white) and Protestant Chaplain Sigmund Schade is wearing black robe. (Courtesy of Sigmund Schade)

Chaplain Capt. S. J. Payne of the 6220th Air Base Squadron, Vietnam, baptized T/Sgt. Osburn J. Middleton while S/Sgt. Robert T. Walker waits his turn. Both men are assigned to the Second Air Division, Tan Son Nhut. This was the first immersion baptism by an Air Force chaplain in the three-year history of the Southern Baptist mission.

Chaplain Maj John J. Castellani and Pope Paul VI at Kindley AFB, Bermuda, August 24, 1968. (Courtesy of John Castellani)

Services were also conducted in the trench lines around Khe Sanh Luffman used sand bags as an altar and kept his helmet and flak jacket close by since it was unsafe in the open because of constant shelling from the enemy (Courtesy of Elden Luffman)

The Rev. Dr. Billy Graham talks with personnel following services at Long Binh, 1967. (Courtesy of R. D. Daniell)

A taste of home. Daniell enjoys a real treat at Di-An, RVN, post for the 1st Infantry Division. (Courtesy of R. D. Daniell)

Reunited! Daniell is reunited with Chaplain Samuel Graves, who performed his wedding ceremony in La Rochelle, France ten years earlier. Graves did not know Daniell had become a chaplain, or that he had served as a role model for him. (Courtesy of R. D. Daniell)

Daniell checks location of units during field exercises in Germany, 1972 as he "circuit rides" to various locations to provide chaplain services. (Courtesy of R. D. Daniell)

Burial at sea, USS Coral Sea (CV-43) 1988, Cdr. Michael D. Halley, CHC, USN, presiding. (Courtesy of Michael D. Halley)

Chaplains Professional Development Training Course, Rota, Spain, 1982. From left: CDR David B. Fountain, CHC, USN (Naval Station, Rota); Capt. Charles L. Keyser, CHC, USN (Fleet Chaplain, CINCUSNAVEUR, London); and CDR Michael D. Halley, CHC, USN (USS Puget Sound (AD-38). (Courtesy of Michael D. Halley)

LCDR Michael D. Halley, CHC, USN, Ship's Chaplain, USS Puget Sound, (AD-38) and CDR John Wright, CHC, USN, Fleet Chaplain, U. S. Sixth Fleet, tour Jerusalem with Fr. Gregory of the Franciscans as tour guide, 1981.

Easter Dawn Service at Fleet Hospital 15 outside Al Jubail, Saudi Arabia, April 1991. Chaplain Hazel Thomas playing the organ, Chaplain Stan Dombrowski at right extreme and Chaplain Ted Bowers, center. (Courtesy of T. E. Bowers)

Chaplain Lt. Col. Jerry L. Martin giving benediction at Easter Sunrise Service at Walter Reed Army Medical Center, Easter 1986. (Courtesy of Jerry L. Martin)

More than 3000 troops of the Hue Phu Bai area join in singing Christmas carols at the Billy Graham Christmas service at Phu Bai, Dec. 22, 1968. (Courtesy of Clayton E. Day)

Military Chaplains Biographies

BRADFORD E. ABLESON, Lieutenant Commander, born Jan 2, 1959, Tulsa, OK Graduated from Yale Univ with M.Div. degree and ordained a Cumberland Presbyterian minister in 1985. Commissioned in the Navy Theological Student Program and completed Chaplains School in 1984 Served as a reservist until recalled to active duty in 1987 after two years of parish ministry.

Military assignments include: Recruit Training Cmd., San Diego, CA (USNR); USS *Lexington* (AVT-16), (USNR); Naval Weapons Station, Concord, CA; USS *Mars* (AFS-1); 3rd Marine Aircraft Wing, FMFPAC, El Toro, CA, Marine Aircraft Gp. 11 and Marine Air Control Gp. 38; and Commander Submarine Sqdn. 2, Groton, CT.

Aboard *Mars*, Chaplain Ableson deployed to the Persian Gulf in 1988 as part of Operation Earnest Will escorts of Kuwaiti reflagged tankers. With MAG-11 he again deployed to the Persian Gulf in support of Desert Shield/Storm. During combat operations to liberate Kuwait, he provided ministry in the field to FMF units. Following cessation of hostilities, he remained in the field as Air Combat Element (ACE) Chaplain, 3rd MAW SWA

Awards/Medals: Navy Commendation Medals, two Navy Achievement Medals and the appropriate campaign and expeditionary ribbons. Married to the former Julia Tevis Narz of Louisville, KY.

RAYMOND A. ACKER, Lieutenant Colonel, born Jan 4, 1932, Hartford, CT. First tour of duty was as enlisted man during Korean conflict. Overseas assignment was Thule AFB, Greenland, where he was assigned as radio operator with an AAA battalion.

Education Philadelphia Bible College (BS in Bible), Philadelphia Theological Seminary (M Div.) and Dallas Theological Seminary (Th M.). Also earned MS in 1973 from Long Island Univ.

Received commission in Chaplain Corps, 1963, returned to active duty in July 1965. Assignments took him from Fort Polk, LA to Okinawa; Vietnam; APG, MD; Fort Hamilton, NY; Germany: Fort Hood, TX and Fort Meade, MD, where he served as deputy post chaplain until retiring in 1983

Awards/Decorations: Bronze Star, Meritorious Service Medal and Army Comm Medal w/2 OLCs.

Currently serves on staff of Grace and Truth Evangelistic Assoc. and as director of the World Wide Bible Institutes. Upon retirement in 1983, served as director of Alumni, Philadelphia College of Bible (1984-90) assistant to the general director, Biblical Ministries Worldwide. Has been at Camp of the Nations since September 1990

Married Jean Rineer and has two sons, Thomas and Douglas, and six grandchildren. Both sons served in the Army and during his active years, the family served together except in Vietnam.

WALLACE ALCORN, Colonel, native of Milwaukee, was sworn into the USN on his 17th birthday and retired from the Military District of Washington on his 60th in 1990 in the rank of colonel after 43 years of continuous service, active and largely Reserve

A graduate of Wheaton, Grand Rapids Baptist, and Princeton, he holds a Ph.D from New York Univ. First a Navy QM/SM, CIC agent and MP officer, he served 29 years as an Army chaplain

Overseas tours included the Atlantic sea duty, Germany and Honduras. Assigned to four USAR training divisions, hospital, engineer, and logistic commands.

Received Meritorious Service, Army and Navy Commendation Medals.

Ordained within the General Assoc. of Regular Baptist Churches, he was pastor in four states and taught at Moody Bible Institute, Northwest Baptist Seminary, and Austin, MN Community College. Author of eight books, contributor to four and he has written over 300 periodical articles

JOHN KENNETH ALLYN, Lieutenant Colonel, born July 26, 1942, Coral Gables, FL. Joined the Army in August 1965 Received BA from Univ. of Miami and M Div. from Princeton Theological Seminary

Stationed at Fort Hood, TX, Fort Gordon and Fort Benning, GA, Fort Irwin, CA; Wertheim, Augsburg and Stuttgart, Germany. Served with 1st Cav., 2nd Armd. Div., VII Corps, 17th FA, Signal Corps School, 2nd Corps Supply Co.

Memorable Experiences Commander C TAB; Wertheim; chaplain for troops of 17th FA and families in Augsburg, Germany; special ministry to troops and families in Nellingen, Germany with 2nd COSCOM, and with troops in Saudi Arabia

Discharged Sept. 1, 1992, as lieutenant colonel.

Married, 1966, to Annabelle Minear and has two children. Presently sole pastor of Lake Shore Presbyterian Church, Jacksonville, FL

GEORGE AMBROSE JR., Lieutenant Colonel, born June 11, 1929, Lake Charles, LA. Graduate of Leland College, Baker, LA (BS degree, 1951); School of Religion, Virginia Union Univ., Richmond, VA (BD degree, 1954); Andover Newton Theological School (1977, D.Min., Newton Centre, MA).

Joined US Army, January 1957, and stationed at Chaplain School, Fort Slocum, NY, January to March 1957; HQ, Fort Belvoir, VA, HQ, Kaiserslautern Post (Germany, Vogelweh); US Army Chaplain School, Fort Hamilton, NY (Career Crs); HQ, Fort Dix, NY; 7th Inf. Div., Korea; HQ, US Army, Korea, Fort Hood, TX; 22nd Repl. Bn., Cam Ranh Bay, Vietnam, 1968; Army Air Def. Ctr, Fort Bliss, TX; HQ, 2nd US Army, Fort Meade, MD; US Army, Ryukyu Islands (Okinawa) 2nd Log. Cmd, 46th Cbt. Spt. Hosp., Med. Bn and Cutler Hosp, Fort Devens, MA.

Received Bronze Star, Meritorious Service Medal, Army Commendation, National Defense Service Medal, Armed Forces Expeditionary Medal, Vietnam Service Medal, Vietnam Cross of Gallantry with Palm, Vietnam Campaign Medal w/60 Device and Meritorious Unit Citation w/OLC. Retired January 1973 as lieutenant colonel

Memorable experience was participating in parade in NYC honoring all veterans who fought in the Vietnam War At the time he was serving as chaplain at Fort Dix, NJ (1973). During 1973, the end of Vietnam War, troops enjoyed a time of "Peace."

Was pastor of Quioccasin Baptist Church, Richmond, VA; Nazarene Baptist Church, Hanover County, VA; Protestant chaplain, East Orange General Hosp., NJ; assistant pastor, Calvary Baptist Church, East Orange, NJ. He is certified science teacher and currently employed at West Side HS, Newark, NJ.

Member of Optimist Club, East Orange, NJ; American Legion, Trenton, NJ; TROA, VFW, American Baptist Churches USA, National Baptist affiliated by attending annual conventions; and member of Phi Beta Sigma Fraternity

Married Novella Susan Finney of Powhatan, VA, Oct 18, 1952, and has one son George Spencer; granddaughter Nikia Tamara; and grandson Travis Ambrose.

E.H. JIM AMMERMAN, Colonel, born in Conway, MO, July 20, 1925. Served in the USN in WWII as a radioman in combat, then became a naval aviator. After ordination and graduation from Southwestern Baptist Theological Seminary, Fort Worth, TX, he served as an Army chaplain 23 years.

Had the duty and privilege of building the 8th Army Retreat Center in Seoul, Korea. As a paratrooper and Green Beret, he served in the 82nd Abn. Div., the 101st Abn. Div. (while Gen Westmoreland commanded), the 10th Special Forces Bad Tolz, Germany and Special Warfare Center.

Served in the 1st Cav. Div in the Far East and again as division chaplain, Fort Hood, TX, where he was also 1st Armd. Div. Chaplain. In Vietnam, 1967-68, he was senior chaplain for 18th Engr. Bde. Serving last overseas as V Corps Chaplain, his retirement assignment was at the Command and General Staff College, Fort Leavenworth, KS, as a colonel.

After military he founded the Full Gospel Chaplaincy serving as their endorser many years.

ALISTER ANDERSON, Colonel, graduated from the USN Academy and served aboard a destroyer in the Pacific in the last year of WWII. He graduated from Union Theological Seminary, NYC and was ordained a priest in the Episcopal Church in 1951.

Commissioned a Regular Army Chaplain and from 1956 until 1977, he served with the 4th Armd. Div at Fort Hood and in Germany, assistant post chaplain, Fort Jay, NY; Tripler Army Med Ctr., Hawaii, 25th Inf. Div., Vietnam, chaplain, Landstuhl Gen. Hosp and Support Cmd., Kaiserslautern and staff chaplain, Walter Reed

Army Medical Center from which he retired as a colonel. His awards include the Legion of Merit, Bronze Star, Meritorious Service and Army Commendation Medals

Ordained an Eastern Orthodox Christian priest in 1992 and serves an Orthodox Christian parish in Bethesda, MD. Married to Ann Stuart and has five children and six grandchildren.

ARVID LAWRENCE ANDERSON, Lieutenant Colonel, born April 12, 1914, Randolph, MA. Graduated Gordon College, Wenham, MA, TH.B. 1936; Gordon/Conwell Theological Seminary, South Hamilton, MA, M.Div., 1940; State College, Bridgewater, MA, M.Ed, 1967, Harvard Univ. Divinity School, Post-Graduate Studies (1955-1957).

Served with 519th MP Bn., 1952-54, during Korean War. From 1954-74 in the USAR with 94th Inf Div., 399th Evac. Hosp and 352nd Area Cmd., Civil Affairs.

LTC Anderson was discharged on April 30, 1954. He received the Commendation Medal

Civilian employment and positions held include: pastor of Baptist and Congregational churches, Lebanon, ME; Baptist churches, Blue Hill, ME, Baptist Church, Bath, ME; Wendell Ave. Congregational Church, Brookton, MA; executive director, Greater Brockton Council of Churches, chaplain and volunteer chaplain coordinator for the Greater Brockton Area Hospitals, pastor, Church of New Jerusalem, Elmwood, MA; contract chaplain, VA Medical Center, Brockton, MA (1985-94); Interim Ministry, Assonet, MA. He and his wife were resident caretakers and coordinators for the Avon, MA, Blanchard Museum House and its educational program from 1970-89

Married Ruth Williams Blair June 4, 1937, and has three children and five grandchildren.

JOSEPH RUSSELL ANDREWS, Colonel, born May 29, 1918, Landrum, SC. Graduated from Wofford College, Duke Divinity School and Teachers College, Columbia Univ. and ordained a Methodist minister

After serving three years in Virginia churches, he entered active duty as an Army Chaplain, June 6, 1944, and served continuously for almost 34 years (a record) until his retirement as colonel, post chaplain, Fort Lee, VA on Jan 31, 1978. Served overseas in three wars: Evac Hosp ETO, WWII, 3rd Inf Div., Korea, and IFF, Vietnam. Among his other assignments: director, resident instruction, Army Chaplain School; post chaplain, Fort Benning, GA; Chief, Plans and Operations, staff chaplain USAREUR; and staff chaplain, Military District of Washington.

Among his over 25 awards and decorations are the Bronze Star, Legion of Merit w/3 OLCs, Commendation Medal w/4 OLCs and four foreign decorations.

Upon retirement Chaplain Andrews held a position as Director of Operations for five years at the United Methodist Retreat Center, Lake Junaluska, NC Married Frances "Betsy" Babb and has three children and six grandchildren

ROGER M. ARENDSEE, Lieutenant Colonel, born in Rockford, IL on Feb 3, 1923. He flew as a radio operator and gunner on a B-24 bomber from Italy during WWII. Graduated from Wheaton College, IL and from Northern Baptist Theological Seminary in Chicago, IL

After entering the USAF as a chaplain in August 1953, he served at F E. Warren AFB, WY; Itazuke AB, Japan; Eglin AFB, FL, Izmir, Turkey; Luke AFB, AZ; Phan Rang AB, Republic of South Vietnam and Shaw AFB, SC, where he retired in August 1974.

Studied church history after retirement from USAF at the Graduate School at Wheaton College, IL Following a brief stint of teaching in San Antonio, TX, he served as pastor of an English language church in Brasilia, Brazil, for two years.

Returning to San Antonio, he served as president of the TIME for Christ, Inc. Executive Board for about eight years and as president of the Executive Committee of Mexico Ministries of TIME for Christ for over 10 years

Married to Darlin Bailey and has three children and eight grandchildren.

JOHN STERLING ARMFIELD, Commander, born Jan. 24, 1915, Fayetteville, NC. Received AB degree from Univ of North Carolina, 1936 and M.Div. from Virginia Theological Seminary, 1939.

Joined the USNR in January 1943. Active duty for training assignments included: USNAS, Jacksonville, FL; Aircraft Carriers, USS *Midway* and USS *Lake Champlain*, troop transport, USS *General Rose*; Research vessel, USS *Compass Island*; USMC Amphibious Forces, Little Creek, VA; USNH, St. Albans, NY; USN Submarine Base, New London, CT; and USN Disciplinary Barracks, Portsmouth, NH.

Military locations and stations included USNTS, Great Lakes, IL; USS *Luzon*; Naval Receiving Station, Norfolk, VA He retired in June 1969 as commander.

One of his best memories was Christmas Eve 1944, Apra Harbor, Guam There were dozens of crafts there too small to rate a chaplain, so his CO made available to him a motor launch and crew. He rounded up three musicians and far into Christmas Eve night pulled alongside one small craft after another playing the beloved carols and wishing each crew a Merry Christmas. In addition he left a printed liturgy for a brief Christmas service at each boat The "carol boat" was indeed a unique experience.

Married Oct. 3, 1942, to Margaret Anne Swain and has three children and five grandchildren. As Episcopal priest he has served as rector of parishes in North Carolina, Florida and New York. Retired from ministry, May 1981

PAUL EDWARD ARMSTRONG, Major, born Dec. 23, 1941, Anderson (Madison) IN Received M.Div., Evangelical Theological Seminary; Univ. of Virginia at Charlottesville, Western Piedmont College; Durham Tech Institute; numerous military schools including the Institute of Administration at Fort Ben Harrison, IN, Army Chaplains School at Fort Monmouth, NJ

Joined the US Army, Jan 11, 1960. Stationed in Germany twice, South Korea, Dominican Republic, Thailand, Alaska and all over the Lower Forty-Eight.

Served with 7th Army, Wuerzburg, Germany, 4th Inf. Div , Fort Lewis, WA; 8th Army Support Command, Seoul, Korea, US Army Spt , Thailand Khorat; US Army Strategic Communications Cmd , Fort Huachuca, AZ, TRADOC Troop Cmd., Fort Ben Harrison, IN; Trng Bde., Fort Dix, NJ.

Military Awards Joint Services Commendation Medal, Army Commendation Medal, National Defense Service, Vietnam Service, Armed Forces Expeditionary, Meritorious Unit Citation, Vietnam Campaign, Young Veteran of the Year 1980

Member of MCA, National Chaplains Assoc ; life member of VFW, Military Order of the Cootie, American Legion and DAV.

Married Betty Becker and has five children and two grandchildren.

DONALD EDWARD ARTHER, Colonel, born Jan 26, 1931, Denver, CO Received BA in Sociology, William Jewell College, Liberty, MO; M.Div. in Theology, Christian Theological Seminary, Indianapolis, IN, DMn., Eden Theological Seminary, St. Louis, MO and graduate work, Univ. of Chicago, Chicago, IL. Attended 10 weeks AF Chaplain Courses and Air Command and Staff College by seminar.

Commissioned in AF Chaplaincy and from 1963-77 was chaplain at Chanute AFB, IL; Ton San Nhut Chapel, Vietnam; USAF Academy Base Chapel and Prepatory School; RAF Alconbury, England; Mt. Home AFB, ID. (1977-81) member AF Chaplain Resource Board, Air Univ., Maxwell AFB, AL. (1981-82) installation staff chaplain, Hahn AB, Germany. (1982-84) chief, Personnel Division, USAFE Cmd. Chaplain's Office. (1984-88) installation staff chaplain, Mather AFB, CA (1988-90) asst. command and command chaplain, Scott AFB, IL.

Awards include Bronze Star, Meritorious Service Medal w/3 OLCs, RVN Service Medal, RVN Cross of Gallantry w/palm, National Defense Service Medal and Legion of Merit. Retired from AF Chaplaincy July 1, 1990. Currently part-time instructor in philosophy and theology and director of Lay Ministry Education for Eden Theological Seminary, St. Louis.

Married Shirley Von Derau and their foster son, John Neff, is ordained UCC clergyman.

LEE W. BACKMAN, Lieutenant Colonel, retired from active duty at Howard AB, Canal Zone after 24 years on active duty in the USAF He is a resident of California and now considers Sacramento his hometown Began his military career at Mountain Home AFB, ID as a 1st lieutenant in September 1954 after completing the basic USAF Chaplain Crs. at Lackland AFB, TX

Overseas assignments included Hahn AB, Germany; Shulin Kow AB, Taiwan; Bien Hoa AB, South Vietnam and Howard AB, Canal Zone. Other Air Force assignments were Greenville AFB, MS; Mather AFB, CA; Kirtland AFB, NM; Blytheville AFB, AR; Moody AFB, GA and McClellan AFB, CA.

Served with distinction as installation chaplain at each of his last four assignments. Among awards and decorations earned during his many years of professional excellence are the Bronze Star, Meritorious Service Medal w/cluster, AF Commendation Medal and numerous theater, campaign and service medals.

At the close of a long and dedicated military career as a USAF chaplain, he retired on Aug. 1, 1978.

JOHN B. BAHAN, Colonel, born in New Orleans, LA, April 14, 1913 Worked in the business world for 12

43

years before being drafted into the US Army April 17, 1942. After basic training, he attended OCS at Mississippi State College and was commissioned 2nd lieutenant, TC, Feb. 3, 1943. Assigned to New York Port of Embarkation, Desert Trng Ctr., Banning, CA, then assigned to the G4 section of HQ, X Corps, where he served in Leyte and Mindanao, Philippines, and in Japan after WWII ended.

Discharged as major in April 1946, he entered St Mary's College, St. Mary, KY. to study for the priesthood in September 1946. Completed theological studies at Notre Dame Seminary, New Orleans, and was ordained as a priest of the Archdiocese of New Orleans on May 30, 1953. Re-entered military service in 1954 as chaplain, 39th DIVARTY, LANG.

Called to active duty in 1961 in the Berlin crisis, he served at Fort Eustis, VA and Heidelberg, Germany Recalled to New Orleans in 1963, he returned to military service as chaplain of the 204th Trans. Gp., LANG and later of the 377th Support Bde, USAR Retired as colonel in April 1973 and holds the Bronze Star Medal, Army Meritorious Service Medal and various service awards.

He is currently pastor emeritus of St Henry's Church, New Orleans

CHARLES A. BAKER, Lieutenant Colonel, born Feb. 24, 1922, Spice Run, WV Upon graduation from high school in May 1941, he enlisted in the USAAC. Basic training was at Jefferson Barracks, MO and Aircraft Mechanics Tech School at Chanute Field, IL Arrived Dec. 7, 1941, at first duty station, Kessler AFB, MS.

During WWII Rev. Baker was involved in a variety of Air Crew Training Programs. Enlisted Pilots, Glider Pilot, Flexible Aerial Gunnery, Bombardier Navigator

Following WWII he attended Taylor Univ., Upland, IN; graduated from Drew Theological Seminary Madison, NJ and was ordained Elder in the North Indiana Conference of the Methodist Church.

Commissioned 1LT, USAF as chaplain and called to active duty in June 1956. For the next 26 years he served in the Chaplain Ministry to Air Force personnel and their families. Assignments included Westover AFB, MAS, Wimpole Park Hosp. and RAF Sculthorpe, England, Minot AFB; Osan AFB, Korea; Eglin AFB, FL, Shu Lin Ku AS, Taiwan, Duluth, MN, Lajes Field, Azores Islands; Sheppard AFB, TX

Awards include AF Commendation Medal w/2 OLCs, AF Outstanding Unit Awd., AF Organizational Excellence Awd, Good Conduct Medal, American Defense Service Medal, American Campaign Medal, WWII Victory Medal, National Defense Service Medal with Bronze Star, Humanitarian Service Medal w/Bronze Star, AF Longevity Service Awd. Ribbon w/6 OLCs and Meritorious Service Medal

Married to Bernice Schell of Adrian, MI, and has two children, Barbara Ann and David James, and two granddaughters. Retired July 1, 1982

RICHARD CARL BAKER, Lieutenant Colonel, born July 25, 1932, near Kittanning, PA. Education Kittanning HS, Univ. of Cincinnati; BA from Gettysburg College, PA; BD from Lutheran Theological Seminary, PA; four units clinical pastoral education at Institute of Religion and MD Anderson Hosp., Houston, TX; MA in behavioral science from Univ of Houston in Texas; ordained June 3, 1959; commissioned as chaplain USAR, Feb. 13, 1967

Military Assignments APG, MD, 1967-68; 7th DIVARTY, ROK, 1968-69; Fort Sill, OK, 1969-71; Military Assistance Cmd , RVN, 1971-72; Fort Polk, LA, 1972-75, released to USAR Control Group. 1975-79, 4005th US Army Augmentation Hosp., 1979-80; 491st Medical Clearing Co., Houston, TX, 1980-82; 114th Evac. Hosp., San Antonio, TX, 1982-86, 810th Station Hosp , North Little Rock, AR, 1986-90.

Called to active duty to do family support ministry at Fort Bragg, NC, in support of Operation Desert Shield/Desert Storm, 1991. Released to 810th Station Hosp . North Little Rock, AR, July 1991; released to Control Group, August 1991-July 1992. Retired from the US Army, July 25, 1992, with over 24 years of service (over nine of those years active duty)

Awards include the Army Service Ribbon, National Defense Service Medal with Bronze Service Star, Army Reserve Component Achievement Medal (3), Vietnam Service Medal, Vietnam Campaign Medal w/60 device, Vietnam Cross of Gallantry w/palm, Armed Forces Reserve Medal, Presidential Unit Citation, Armed Forces Expeditionary Medal, Overseas Service Ribbon (2), Vietnamese Staff Service Medal 1/c, Army Achievement Medal (3), Army Commendation Medal (3) and Bronze Star Medal.

Life member of the MCA Civilian employment included parish pastorates and civilian chaplaincies.

Married to Marjorie and has two sons (one deceased), one daughter and two grandchildren.

CHARLES STANLEY BALDWIN, Lieutenant Colonel, born Sept. 12, 1937, Knoxville, TN. Educated at St. Paul's HS and College, Concordia, MO; Concordia Sr College, Fort Wayne, IN, BA, 1959; Concordia Seminary, St. Louis, MO, M Div., 1963; Long Island Univ , Brooklyn, NY, MS, 1974; Southern Baptist Theological Seminary, Louisville, KY, D.Min., 1982

Joined US Army May 30, 1960. Military assignments (1967-90). 931st Engr Gp and 51st Engr Bn., Ft Campbell, KY, 1967-68; 554th Engr. Bn., Cu Chi, Vietnam; Walson Army Hosp., Fort Dix, NJ; 101st Abn. Div. Arty., Phu Bai, Vietnam, 91st and 11th Engr Bn. and US Army Engr. Ctr., Fort Belvoir, VA; Chaplain Advanced Crs., US Army Chaplain Ctr. and School, Fort Hamilton, NY, US Army Europe and 7th Army Spec. Troops Gp., Heidelberg, Germany, 10th Air Def Arty. Gp., Darmstadt, Germany; US Army Armor Ctr , Fort Knox, KY; US VII Corps HQ, Stuttgart, Germany; US Army Trng Ctr., Fort Jackson, SC, and US Army Garrison, Fort Sheridan, IL

Awards and decorations include the Bronze Star w/OLC, Meritorious Service Medal w/2 OLCs, Air Medal, Army Commendation Medal w/OLC, Meritorious Unit Commendation, National Defense Service Medal, Vietnam Service Medal w/7 campaign stars, Armed Forces Reserve Medal, Army Service Ribbon, Overseas Service Ribbon (2), RVN Campaign Medal, RVN Cross of Gallantry w/Palm Unit Medal, RVN Civic Action Unit Medal and Saint Martin of Tours Bronze Medal Life member of MCA and member of numerous professional organizations

Married Elva Marie Heidle, Dec 12, 1970, and has two daughters, Amy Melinda and Joy Angela. He is now pastor of Grace Lutheran Church, High Point, NC

ROBERT G. BALNICKY, ADF1, USN, Lieutenant Colonel, CAP, born April 18, 1922, Elizabeth, NJ. Education Pensacola Jr. College; Emory Univ , Columbia Theological Seminary, Decatur, GA; B. Ministry, M Ministry, International Seminary, Plymouth, FL. DD, 1980 and D Min , 1985

Served as flight engineer first class, USN, 1942-49. Recipient of four Chaplains Citations and the Meritorious Service, Grover Loening Aerospace, Paul E Garber and Gill Robb Wilson Awards. Memorable experience was serving as acting chaplain of Peleliu Island, Palau Group (1946) as second class petty officer.

Member of DAV (life), American Legion (SC state chaplain 1956-58, post cmdr. 1953-54), Navy League, MCA (life) and several civilian organizations.

Married Cdr Annette Virginia Hawkins on Dec 24, 1977. Children by previous marriage, Richard Ozzie and Barbara Gail, also has three grandchildren. He retired from Evangelical Presbyterian Church on April 18, 1992

BENSON COZBY BARRETT, Lieutenant (jg), born in Norcross, GA, Aug. 1, 1915 Graduated from Emory Univ in 1938 and Candler School of Theology in 1940 Ordained Methodist minister in 1941; commissioned lieutenant jg in Chaplains Corps of Naval Reserve in 1943 and stationed on USS *Lamar* until end of WWII; NAD, Hastings, NE until end of 1945

Civilian pastorate, 1946-51 Recalled to active duty in 1951. Duty stations included MCRD, San Diego; Naval Base, Kwajalein, 14th District Staff; USNH, Memphis, TN; 9th Marines, 3rd MARDIV; NMD/NWS. Yorktown, VA, USS *Valley Forge*; NAS, Alameda, CA: NSCS, Athens, GA. Retired in 1969 and returned to pastorate

Married to Lois Fay Douglas and has four children and six grandchildren.

WILLIAM P. BARRETT, Lieutenant Colonel, born March 23, 1920, Pikeville, KY. Education. BA, Univ. of the South, Sewanee, TN, 1940, M.Div., Univ. of the South, 1959, graduate work, George Washington Univ .

Washington, DC, 1962-63; graduate work, Texas Christian Univ., Fort Worth, TX, 1967-69; ordained deacon, Jan 11, 1943 and priest, Aug. 6, 1943, Church of the Good Shepherd, Lexington, KY

Served in Chaplain Corps, US Army, 1944-65 Overseas service: ETOUSA, 1944-45, MTOUSA, 1946-47; Korea and Japan, 1951-52; US Army Alaska, 1960-62, USAREUR, 1954-55.

Received the Bronze Star Medal and Army Commendation Ribbon w/2 OLCs. Retired Aug. 31, 1965, Fort Lee, VA with rank lieutenant colonel

Married Ida Belle Armstrong, Aug 6, 1949, at Post Chapel, Fort Riley, KS They have two children, William Barrett Jr. and Martha Hasni, and five grandchildren

Civilian churches in Kentucky, New York, North Carolina, Kansas and Texas. Civic and military clubs include post commander, American Legion, member, VFW, president, Lions Club; member, Kiwanis and Rotary; member of American Legion, VFW, AUSA, AFA and TROA.

Supply priest, Episcopal Diocese of Fort Worth, 1985 to present

STEPHEN R. BARTELT, Colonel (currently LTC-P), born Dec. 3, 1945, Milwaukee, WI. Received M Div., Concordia Seminary, 1971; MM, Emporia State, 1974, MPA, Univ. of Kansas, 1988

Joined the USAR Aug 29, 1968; served with STARC, KSARNG; 84th Div, Milwaukee and 86th USARCOM, Forest Park, IL. His memorable experience was being activated for Desert Storm, staff chaplain, 86th ARCOM in 1993.

Highest rank achieved was colonel, currently LTC-P. Married Peggy Sandelin on July 1, 1972, and has two children. Parish pastor, Kansas, IL; School Assoc of Greater Milwaukee, director of finance, Lutheran High.

DONALD E. BARTONE, Lieutenant Colonel, born May 13, 1923, Detroit, MI Attended Sacred Heart Seminary College, Detroit; Mt. St. Mary Theological Seminary, Norwood, OH; ordained Catholic priest in 1948.

Joined the USAF in November 1957 Stationed in Europe, Middle East, Far East and in the States Discharged in September 1980 with the rank lieutenant colonel

He was pastor of Archdiocese of Detroit and retired in July 1987.

WILLIAM E. BASKETT, Private First Class, USAAC, born July 11, 1921, Mountain View, OK Finished Gotebo HS in Oklahoma, 1938; Frank Wiggins Trade School (radio electronics), 1940, Bible Institute, 1943; LeTourneau College, BA in Bible, 1962; Seattle Pacific, BA in soc/anthropology, 1969; plus graduate study

Joined the USAAC in February 1994 Stationed at Amarillo AAB and Douglas AAB, AZ He was still in training when war ended and took COG discharge

Saved at age 13. Did "pioneer" missionary work in tribal area of Philippines. Began ministry with college students in Manila Also, served over 22 years with International Students, Inc ministering to internationals in the States Began ISI's Northwest outreach. Now with Mission Ministries, a mission begun and directed by retired military chaplains and "ministering wherever there are needs."

Married former Daisy Ruth Bates on March 1, 1942, and has three children and five grandchildren.

Civilian employment: machinist, tool and die maker, sales and customer relations manager

EDWARD C. BASTILLE, Captain, GM-13, born April 21, 1943, Gardner, MA. Received BS from Springfield College in 1966; M.Div in 1975, D.Min. in 1980

Joined the USAF in 1967. Served with 366th MMS, 341st PACAF, SAC, stationed in Texas, Colorado, Japan, Vietnam, Ohio and Mississippi.

Memorable experiences. learning to duck in Vietnam, receiving the MCA Distinguished Service Award in 1993; graduating from LVA in 1994; becoming a fellow in COC and NAVAC. Medically retired in 1978, still in Reserves.

Married to Louise; no children He is chief of chaplains PALO ALTO VAMC.

WILLIAM FREDERICK BATEMAN, Colonel, born in Memphis, TN, Sept 22. 1935 He attended public schools through high school, graduated from Union Univ., Jackson, TN with BA degree; subsequently pursued theological and graduate level education. He earned the following degrees, respectively: BD, Southern Seminary, Louisville, KY, MA in sociology, Long Island Univ, Brooklyn, NY; and the Ed D., Indiana Univ., Bloomington, IN.

Became a minister of the United Church of Christ in 1965 and served as a mission church pastor until beginning military service in 1970. Key assignments included. duty with airborne units, staff and faculty of the Army Chaplain School, training officer for all Reserve Component chaplains in First US Army, deputy post chaplain of Fort Bragg, staff chaplain of Combined Field Army (Korea/US) and he was the first person to hold the command and staff chaplain position of US Army Spec. Ops. Cmd.

Assignments carried him to six US installations and to Vietnam, Germany, Panama, Korea and Honduras. Awards include the Legion of Merit which was presented for duty with Rangers, Special Ops and Special Forces.

He retired with the rank of colonel in 1991 and became pastor of Emanuel UCC, Sanford, NC He and his wife Jo Frances (Fayettville VA Patient Education Coordinator) have three grown children. Member of MCA since becoming a staff specialist/chaplain candidate in 1961 Also served as national secretary for two years

The United Church of Christ appointed him their Associate Military Chaplains Endorsing Agent in 1994.

FRANK J. BAUER, Colonel, born Feb. 3, 1919, New York City. Attended Concordia Seminary, St. Louis, MO, BA, 1941 and M.Div. in 1943

Joined the USARNG on May 30, 1950. Served with 174th Regt., NYARNG, Buffalo, NY; 126th AAA BN, 26th DIVARTY, 26th Div HQ, State HQ, MAARNG, Boston, MA, US VA, Hospital Chaplain, Boston and West Roxbury, 1957-87

Discharged in July 1977 with the rank of colonel Married Jean Elizabeth Helman of Cleveland, OH, June 12, 1943, and has three children and six grandchildren. He retired Feb 3, 1984.

ROGER M. BAXTER JR., Lieutenant Colonel, born Sept. 17, 1927, Slagle, LA Educated at Horatio HS, Horatio, AR, Ouachita Baptist Univ., Arkadelphia, AR, BA in business, May 1950; New Orleans Baptist Theological Seminary, New Orleans, LA, BD, 1953 and upgraded to MD in 1975

Served during WWII in the USN, Pacific area, Unit AD #100, yeoman 3/c, December 1944 to August 1946, in the Korean War as USN chaplain, lieutenant jg, June 1953 to June 1957; in USS *Maury* (AGS-16) and the Marine Corps Recruit Depot, Parris Island, SC. Discharged June 30, 1957.

Pastor of Baptist Church in Bassett, TX, 1949-50; Chaplain, Corsicana State Childrens Home, TX, 1957-58; Director, Home Mission Board Mission Ctr., San Antonio, 1958-60; pastor, Bethany Baptist Church, Dayton, OH, 1960-64; chaplain, CAP from May 1959-present, serving as units in San Antonio and Dayton area. Served as Ohio Wing Chaplain from August 1981-1993, and as inspector, city of Dayton, OH, June 1965-February 1991 Retired

Married Ruth Marie Jordan, Metarie Baptist Church, Metairie, LA, Aug 19, 1950 They have two children, Roger III, Lt Col, USAF (wife Cheryl and children: Tami, Kori and Nathen) and Rebecca Marie, teacher (husband Rodney Lee Lucas and children: Stacey, Katie and Zachary).

DONALD G. BELANUS, Captain, a native of Prospect Park, NJ. He began his Chaplain Corps career through the Theological Student Program, graduating from the Chaplains School Basic Crs. in 1972 After serving civilian pastorates in New York and Michigan, he was recalled to active duty and detailed to the Naval Communication Area Master Station Western Pacific, Guam in 1979

Subsequent duty assignments included the 2nd Bn., 2nd Marines; 2nd Marine Regt., Naval Officer Post-Graduate Program at the School of Education, Catholic Univ of America; the staff of the Naval Chaplains School, Newport, RI; command chaplain, USS *Blue Ridge* and staff chaplain, US 7th Fleet; component chaplain for USN Forces Central Cmd. during Operations Desert Shield and Desert Storm; and command chaplain, Naval Weapons Station, Charleston.

Presently serving on the Chief of Chaplain's Staff as director, Manpower and Recruiting

Chaplain Belanus has been awarded the Meritorious Service Medal (2 awds), Navy Commendation Medal, National Defense Service Medal. SWA Service

45

Medal and Kuwait Liberation Medal. A minister of the Christian Reformed Church, he earned his BA degree from Calvin College, Grand Rapids, MI and the BD, M Div. and Th.M from Calvin Theological Seminary.

Married to the former Margaret Rose Muir of Imlay City, MI. They have two daughters, Mary Jean and Nicole Ruth.

FRED A. BENDER, Captain, born Oct. 14, 1927, Haynesville, LA. He holds BA, M.Div., MA and Ph.D. degrees. Served in the USAAC from 1946-49 and in the Army from 1956-64. Stationed at Fort Hood, Fort Sill, Germany and Korea.

Assigned to the 4th Armd. Div., I Corps Arty. His memorable experience was getting home alive. He was discharged in June 1964 as captain.

Professor, San Antonio College; pastor, Memorial Baptist Church, Pasaden, TX; professor, philosophy, Univ. of Maryland; Hardin Baylor, Belton, TX

FRANK E. BENTLEY, Colonel, born Jan 26, 1914, Taboa, IA. Attended Iowa State Teachers College, Southern Illinois Univ., Central Baptist Baptist Theological Seminary in Kansas and Burton College and Seminary of Colorado. Earned BS in education in 1947, BD, 1950, master of theology, 1952 and DD in 1957. He pastored churches in Illinois, Kansas, Missouri, California and Arizona.

Enlisted in the US Army Sept. 2, 1942; discharged Feb. 5, 1946, and called to extended duty as a chaplain in the US Army in 1957. After 20 years of active duty and 28 years of total service he retired from military service in August of 1973 as a colonel.

Military career took him to many interesting places, including Korea, Japan, Germany and many other European countries, Vietnam, Hawaii, Guam, Thailand and many of the states in the U.S.

Decorations include the Meritorious Service Medal, American Theater, Bronze Star w/2 overseas bars, RVN Campaign Medal w/60 device, Vietnam Service, Army Commendation, National Defense Service Medal w/ OLC, Armed Forces Reserve Medal, Meritorious Unit Citation, WWII Victory Medal and Good Conduct Medal.

In July of 1989, his wife of 47 years, Jeanette, passed away. He has two children, Gary and Carolyn, and two grandchildren. He married Velda Reynolds in December 1990. He is still doing supply and interim work.

JOHN WELLONS BERGER, Commander, born Aug. 6, 1920, Mt. Shasta, CA. Received AB, Stanford, M.Div., Pacific School of Religion. Joined the Army Dec. 9, 1944, and the USN Nov. 11, 1952.

Stationed at CONUS; 143rd Med Trng Bn.; MSTS Pac, NMTC Pt. Mugu; 3rd Marine Div.; MinPac; San Miguel, PI; DASA Lake Mead, NV; ServRon 3, NAS Lemoore; NSA Da Nang, NAS Moffett Field, USS *Prairie* (AD-15); COMSERVRON ONE. Retired June 30, 1982 as commander 05.

Memorable experiences: ship's chaplain for Korean POW returnees, POW/MIA ministry at NAS Lemoore; Ombusman Program, SF Bay area.

Married first, N. Carolyn Hitchock and second, Ione Ingraham Mosher. He has four children and five grandchildren. Civilian employment as United Methodist pastorates.

MURRAY J. BERGER, Colonel, born Oct. 18, 1937, Brooklyn, NY. Attended Univ. of Cincinnati, Hebrew Union College, Ohio, Troy State Univ., Alabama; Indiana State Univ., Indiana. Has BA in psychology, MAHL, theology; MS, counseling and guidance; Ph.D., counseling and psychological services.

Joined the Army May 21, 1963, and completed 12 courses while in the military. Served as chaplain with the following units: Post HQ, Fort Sill; 375th Gen. Spt. Gp.; 129th MASH; 38th DISCOM, 604th MP Bn.; Control Gp., 36th Abn. Bde.; 386th Engr. Cbt Bn., CPE Residency, BAMC, Fort Sam Houston; State HQ; HQ STARC, 94th Gen. Hosp.; Post HQ, Fort Belvoir, VA, and from December 1990 to present with 4003rd US Army Garrison.

Medals include the Meritorious Service Medal, Army Commendation Medal, Army Reserve Components Achievement Medal w/3 OLCs, National Defense Service Medal, Armed Forces Reserve Medal and Army Service Ribbon.

Has a private, full-time counseling practice specializing in marriage and family therapy. He is a consultant to the Dallas VA Hosp. CPE Program; is a contract chaplain for the US Federal Correctional Institutions in Fort Worth and Seagoville, TX. Serves as Rabbi for congregation Anshai Emet, Plano, TX (part-time).

Married to Roberta and has three children.

CHARLES J. BERMEL, Colonel, born Sept. 25, 1912, Brooklyn, NY. Attended Cathedral College and Immaculate Conception Seminary, Brooklyn Diocese. Ordained a priest Jan. 10, 1937, St James Cathedral, Brooklyn, NY. Assigned to St. Peter of Alcantara Parish, Port Washington, LI, NY.

Commissioned 1st lieutenant July 23, 1941, and entered active duty Sept. 10, 1941. Stationed at Aberdeen Ord. Trng. Ctr.; Canal Zone, Panama; Chaplain School, Harvard Univ., Camp Claiborne and in Europe. Returned to civilian life in December 1945 and assigned as curate at St. Paul Church, Brooklyn, NY.

Re-entered military service in November 1950 and served with 297th Engr Avn. Bn., Fort Totten/Fort Leonard Wood; 1952-53, Camp Kilmer, NJ, 1953-55, Fort Richardson, AK; 1955-57, Fort Hamilton, NY and Fort Slocum, NY; 1957-58, 7th Inf. Div. and 1st Cav Div., Korea, 1958-64, post chaplain, Fort Monmouth, NJ; 1964-66, USACOMZEUR chaplain, France, 1966-68, post chaplain, Fort Knox, KY.

Retired from federal service Nov. 1, 1968, as colonel. Received the Legion of Merit, Bronze Star, Army Commendation Medal w/OLC and ETO w/3 Campaign Stars.

After retirement from US Army, he was assigned to St. Pancras Parish, Glendale, NY, Feb 11, 1969. Retired from pastorate Sept. 25, 1982. Since retirement from pastorate, he is assisting in various parishes in Brooklyn. He is single.

RICHARD Y. BERSHON, Colonel, graduated from Brigham Young Univ. in 1953. Served in the USAF as a ground equipment maintenance officer from 1953-55. Following his graduation from Fuller Theological Seminary in 1960, he pastored Church of God congregations in Parshall and Ryder, ND.

Entered active duty as an Army chaplain in January 1962. His assignments included Fort Carson, CO, Korea, Fort Hood, TX; Germany and Vietnam. In 1974 he became chaplain at the VAMC in Biloxi, MS. In 1977 he was appointed chief of Chaplain Services at the VAMC in Tomah, WI.

Has MS degree from Long Island Univ. and Ph.D. from California Graduate School of Theology. His awards include the Army Commendation Medal, Meritorious Service Medal, Bronze Star Medal and the Church of God Distinguished Chaplain Award.

He is the author of *With the Cross of Jesus*, a history of the Church of God chaplaincy and ministry to the military.

Bershon retired from the US Army Reserve in 1987 with the rank of colonel and from the Department of Vietnam Affairs in 1990. Has been a member of MCA almost continually since 1962.

EUGENE WILLIAM BEUTEL, Colonel, born July 27, 1927, Sanborn, NY. Graduated from LaSalle HS in Niagara Falls, NY in 1943. Received a BA degree in 1949 from Capital Univ., Columbus, OH; BD degree from Trinity Lutheran Seminary, Columbus, OH, 1952; ordained by the American Lutheran Church July 27, 1952; and subsequently awarded two graduate degrees from Princeton Theological Seminary (Th.M. in 1970 and D.Min. in 1975).

Served two years with the US Army Engineers during his college years, including a year's service with the 1st AD on Okinawa. Commissioned a 2nd lieutenant in 1946, after completing OCS at Fort Belvoir, VA, and recalled in 1952 for three years of EAD as chaplain during the Korean War. He served with the 40th Inf. Div. in Korea, where the hostilities ceased on July 27, 1953.

Other EAD assignments included Fort Slocum, NY; Fort Lee, VA; Fort Meade, MD; and completed US Army Cmd. and Gen Staff College Crs. After 32 years of total USAR service, including 11 years as division chaplain, 78th Inf. Trng. Div., he transferred to the Retired Reserve Dec. 21, 1979, in the grade of colonel. MEDALS: Bronze Star, Legion of Merit and Meritorious Service Medal.

Pastorates with the American Lutheran Church included serving as pastor/developer in Baltimore, MD; 13 years of service as area service mission director in the Northeastern US, and five years of service as coordinator, Region 8, Evangelical Lutheran Church in America (out of Harrisburg, PA). Retired July 31, 1992, and continues to serve in a variety of consulting roles. Married to the former Dolores Hanson and has three sons and seven grandchildren.

ROBERT HANNA BEVERIDGE, Lieutenant Colonel, born July 11, 1932, Richmond, VA. Attended St. Lawrence Univ.; Emory Univ., AB, 1956; The Church Divinity School of the Pacific, M.Div., 1969; Whitworth

College. Served in the USAFR 1954; extended active duty from 1956-66, weapons director at radar sites in California and British Columbia, Pilot School, Class 60F, Bartow, FL and Greenville, MS; Beale AFB, CA (B52G copilot and aircraft commander). Reappointed as a category B Mobilization Augmentee Chaplain in 1972, with training attachments to Fairchild, McChord, Bolling, Andrews and Griffiss. Served with 31st and 744th H Bombardment Sqdns. and the 456th Strategic Aerospace Wing.

Memorable experiences include flying the Cuban crisis and preaching to the dependents at Fairchild July 4, 1973, while its crews were bombing Cambodia Retired in April 1988 as lieutenant colonel Awards: Meritorious Service Medal and Combat Readiness Medal w/OLC

Married Aug 29, 1959, to Alberta Anne Whittle and has four sons. Curate, Trinity Cathedral Church, Sacramento, CA, 1969-70, Rector, St. Mark's Episcopal Church, Moscow, ID, 1971-80, Rector, St Bartholomew's, Beaverton, OR, 1981; Associate, St George's, Arlington, VA, 1982-87; Rector, Trinity Episcopal Church, Fayetteville, NY 1988-94. Retired from the active ministry Jan. 1, 1995.

RONALD SCOTT BEZANSON, Colonel, born Oct. 28, 1936, Laconia, NH. Graduated with BA from Aurora College, Auroa, IL, M Div., Evangelical Theological Seminary, Naperville, IL, MBA, Univ of Texas, ordained a minister of the Advent Christian Church and commissioned a chaplain in the US Army in 1962

Became an MCA life member in 1969, served on active duty for 30 plus years, retiring in July 1992. Service includes: battalion and brigade chaplain with 1st Cav. Div. (Korea and Vietnam), division chaplain with 2nd Inf. Div. (Korea), Chaplain School Instructor, TASCOM and USARV admin chaplain, Army Materiel Cmd and Air Def Cmd. deputy staff chaplain, OCCH director of administration and management, Western Command and Tripler AMC staff chaplain.

Awards include two Legions of Merit, three Bronze Stars, three Meritorious Service Medals, 10 Air Medals, three Commendation Medals

Since retirement he has served as a hospital chaplain with Interfaith Ministries of Hawaii. Married to Mary Jo Arthur since June 28, 1958. They have four children and two grandchildren

ARVID E. BIDNE, Captain, born June 29, 1924, Kiester, MN. Received BA, Stolaf College, Northfield, MN and M Div., Luther Seminary, 1952. Joined the USN in 1943 and discharged in 1946 as QM3/c

Commissioned in 1956 and participated in Navy Chaplain programs Stationed in Leyte Gulf, Philippine Sea Frontier and served with Aviation Rescue, crash boat and NROTC appt Retired in 1982 as captain, USN.

Last parish was First Lutheran Church, Albert Lea, MN as senior pastor, 1963-75; last administrative position was as vice-president for development at Luther Seminary, St Paul, MN, 1975-88; member of Advancement Committee, Assoc. of Theological Schools, 1985-88

LOUIS H.G. BIER, Lieutenant Colonel, born Jan. 12, 1933, Chicago, IL Received BE from Chicago Teachers College in Illinois, Ed M, Boston State College, Boston, MA; M.Div, 1973; BT in 1959 and M.Div in 1973 from Concordia Seminary, Springfield, IL. Joined the USAF, AUX, CAP, serving as squadron and Massachusetts Wing Chaplain.

Ribbons: Meritorious Service, Commanders Citation, Excellence (2), Special Service, Levels I, II, III, Civil Defense, Attendance, Military Preparedness, Disaster Prevention (Silver OLC), Longevity (three Bronze OLCs). He was the 1994 Chaplain of the Year and received several civilian awards.

Served as pastor/chaplain/vicar in Boston, Jamaica Plain, West Roxbury, and Holyoke, MA; West Frankfort, IL and Philadelphia, PA. 1961-present, pastor of Trinity Church in Boston, 1966-present, chaplain, Boston VA Hosp ; 1961-present, part-time chaplain, German home for the elderly in Boston

Married Helen July 29, 1962, and has three children and one grandchild. He is a life member of MCA

DARRIS YATES BINGHAM, Lieutenant Colonel, born Nov. 24, 1922, Monroe, NC. Received BA, Wake Forest Univ ; M.Div., Th D., Ph.D., Southwestern Baptist Theology Seminary, Fort Worth, TX; MA, Reading, MA, guidance/counseling; MA, BBL/ESL, UTSA, San Antonio.

Joined the USAF Nov. 5, 1951. Stationed at Randolph AFB; Wakkanai AS, Japan, Chitose AB, Japan; Tinker AFB, OK; Ramstein AB, Germany; Malmstrom AFB, MT, USAFE, Wiesbaden; England AFB; Kelly AFB, TX and others

He had many memorable experiences but the most outstanding was participating in Operation Bootstrap to finish requirement for Doctor of Theology Also memorable was helping numerous officers and enlisted to find a Christian purpose for life and working with uprooted AD and ANG in temporary and permanent situations. Discharged Aug 1, 1975, as lieutenant colonel.

Married Ann Barnwell and has two sons and four grandsons Pastored in Texas, South Carolina and North Carolina Retired Aug 1, 1975, then South SAISD, Reading Specialist, Sp. Ed Counselor, initiated and director of Boston Center, Baptist School of Ministry.

DALLAS A. BIRD, Colonel, born March 26, 1919, Sheridan, WY. Received BA from Univ. of Nebraska and Th.M from Iliff School of Theology

Joined the USAF on June 18, 1950, stationed at Davis-Monthan AFB, AZ; Ben Guerir AB, French Morocco; Elsworth AFB, SD; High Wycombe AB, England; Lowry AFB, CO; Great Falls Defense Sector, MT; Naha AB, Okinawa, Williams AFB, AZ; Tan Son Nhut AB, Vietnam; Chanute AFB, IL and Mountain Home AFB, ID

Memorable experience was conducting an Easter Sunrise Service at 18,000 feet altitude aboard a MATS charter plane on their way to assignment in England. As senior school chaplain, he and the other school chaplains established the first pre-marital clinic in the USAF. Professionals used included a doctor, psychologist and a Red Cross financial advisor. The clinic had the full support of the Tech School commander and the student squadron commanders.

Retired Sept. 1, 1978, with the rank of colonel Military awards include the Legion of Merit w/OLC and the Bronze Star.

Married Betty (Fosbury) Bird on June 25, 1942 They have four children and nine grandchildren Was pastor of Friedens UCC, Goehner, NE. Retired Sept. 1, 1978

EDWIN L. BISHOP, Captain, born Feb 24, 1930, Seattle, WA Received BA from the Univ of Washington, completed theological studies at the General Theological Seminary, New York, NY, receiving STB in 1955. Graduate studies at the Presbyterian School of Christian Education, Richmond, VA, MA degree and the Virginia Commonwealth Univ. with M.Ed degree Ordained a priest in the Episcopal Church in February 1956.

Enlisted service from 1947-52, USN (NAS Sandpoint, Seattle; VP-892, NAS Alameda) Combat Aircrew. Deployed to Japan for Korean service, 1950-51 Commissioned in the Chaplain Corps, 1968.

Assignments included NTC, Great Lakes, IL, Naval Mobile Construction Bn ONE (deployment to Vietnam and Puerto Rico), NAS, Milton, FL. Naval Surface Weapons Ctr., Dahlgren, VA, Naval Station, Norfolk, VA, 2nd Marine Force Service Support Group, Camp Lejeune, NC, 1st Marine Amphib Bde., Kaneohe, HI, USS Lexington (AVT-16), NTC, Orlando, Naval Shipyard, Norfolk, VA; Naval Reserve Readiness Cmd Region SIX, Commander US Atlantic Fleet.

Awarded the Meritorious Service Medal, Navy Commendation Medal, Air Medal, Presidential Unit Citation, Navy Unit Citation, Navy Good Conduct Medal, Navy Occupation Medal and service ribbons for Korea, Vietnam and United Nations Retired in September 1990.

Married Joan Gail Avery and has three children and two grandchildren. Parish priest in Washington, Oregon and Nevada Currently serving as an Interim Pastoral Specialist with vacant congregations in Virginia, Maryland, North Carolina, Texas and Hawaii.

DON BJORK, Colonel, was given, on March 9, 1993, the Faithful Servant Award by the Social Action Commission of the National Assoc of Evangelicals He pastored churches in four states over 23 years and was a USARNG/USAR chaplain for 27 years in Minnesota, New Jersey, Illinois and Florida (retired 1988)

Promoted to colonel in 1980, he earned the Humanitarian Service Medal (for working among Cuban refugees) and the Meritorious Service Medal

From 1977-93, he served as an executive and editor with World Team Missions (five years), then director of Refugee Resettlement (35,000 resettled) and Associate Executive Director of World Relief (11 years) He was president/acting director of the Assoc of Evangelical Relief and Development Organizations (AERDO), board

47

member or consultant for 'umbrella' service agencies, and, at Capital Hill and UN conferences, a frequent spokesman for suffering people.

Graduate of the Moody Bible Institute and Univ. of Buffalo, he was ordained a Baptist minister in 1951 and commissioned an Army chaplain in May 1960 Active in retirement, he and his wife, Barbara, rejoice in their four sons, three daughters and seven grandchildren

JOHN C. BLACKFORD, born April 9, 1921, Minneapolis, MN, the son of Albert E. (WWI Army veteran who served in France) and M. Barbara Larson Blackford Graduated from Minneapolis South High School; Hamline Univ., St Paul, MN; and Asbury Seminary, Wilmore, KY; and was ordained June 10, 1945

Entered the USN and received training in Chaplain School at the College of William and Mary, Williamsburg, VA with the rank of LTJG, USNR Duty assignments included regimental chaplain, Recruit Training Base, Camp Peary, VA; Chaplain, Marine Retraining Cmd., Camp Peary; Chaplain, German POW unit, Camp Peary; NOB, Norfolk, VA, with two Atlantic cruises; Quantico Marine Barracks, Quantico, VA, with training for the invasion of Japan, and train commander for a company of recruits being transported from Camp Peary to Treasure Island, CA To his knowledge, he was the youngest chaplain in the USN at the time of enlistment. He was separated to inactive duty in July 1946.

Married to Tulida (nee Klein), and their ministry was in the United Methodist Churches in Minnesota and North Dakota. They have four children and 10 grandchildren. Retired, they live in Forest Lake, MN, where he is associate pastor in their local congregation. A member of the American Legion, the VFW and the MCA. He serves on the City Planning Commission and on the Board of Minnesota Goodwill/Easter Seal

ROBERT ERIC BLADE, born Oct 31, 1923, Philadelphia, PA Educated at Columbia Bible College, Columbia, SC, 1946-47; Temple Univ., Philadelphia, PA, BA in 1951 and MA in 1959. Princeton Seminary, Princeton, NJ, BD in 1954. Ordination, June 1, 1954, Presbytery of Philadelphia, PCUSA. Pastor of James Evans Mem. Pres Church, Philadelphia, PA, 1954-59; Hamptonburgh Pres. Church. Campbell Hall, NY, 1969-82

Military service in US Army Infantry, Signal Corps and Air Corps. Stationed in Hawaii, Christmas Island and the Marianas Isles from 1942-45

USNR duty, Chaplain Corps, Co. 4-1, Reserve Trng. Ctr., Philadelphia, PA; CG Recruit Trng. Base, Cape May, NJ; NAS Norfolk, VA. NAS. Willow Grove, PA, 1956-59 USN active duty, Chaplain School, Newport, RI, 1959, Marine Corps Base, Camp Lejeune, NC, 1960; Destroyer Sqdn. 8, Newport, RI and Mayport, FL, 1960-62 (deployment to North Atlantic, Mediterranean Sea and Caribbean Sea); Marine Corps Recruit Trng. Base, Parris Island, SC, 1962-64, Naval Station, Keflavik, Iceland, 1964-66 (service to Air Force, Marine Corps and Coast Guard). Mobile Construction Bn. 58. Davisville, RI, 1966-68 (two deployments to Vietnam), duty and patient status at Naval Hospitals in Newport, RI and Philadelphia, PA, 1968. Disability retirement, Dec. 30, 1968. His work in Vietnam was a very memorable experience.

RUSSELL L. BLAISDELL, Colonel, born Sept 4, 1910, Hayfield, MN. Received BA from Macalester College, 1934 and M Div from Presbyterian Theological Seminary, 1937

Joined USAAF, July 1938, with active duty, July 1940. Stationed at Fort Sheridan, IL with 61st Coast Arty. Antiaircraft and Reception Ctr. Stations from 1941-47 included Fort George Wright, WA, base chaplain, staff chaplain at Alaskan Wg. ATC, Edmonton, Alberta. Pacific Wg. ATC, Hickam Fld, HI, HQ 8th AF, Fort Worth, TX; HQ 5th AF, Korea, HQ Japan Air Def. Force, Nagoya, Japan, HQ Flying Trng. AF, Waco, TX, 17th AF, Wheelus AB, Libya. He was command chaplain at HQ Tactical Air Cmd, Langley AFB, VA and HQ Military Airlift Cmd., Scott AFB, IL

Memorable experience was the evacuation of 1,000 orphans from Seoul, Korea to Chejie Do Founded Seoul Orphanage (a movie was made of the event and also an AF chaplain training film)

Retired June 30, 1964, as colonel A widower, he has three children, 10 grandchildren and six great-grandchildren. Pastor of Eastern Iowa Sr. Social Services, 1937-40 and representative of State Dept. of Social Services, 1966-77

TRAVIS LEROY BLAISDELL, Lieutenant Colonel, born Dec. 12, 1927, Corpus Christi, TX Received BA, Howard Payne Univ., 1948, BD, Southwestern Seminary, 1950; MRE, Southwestern Seminary, 1951.

Joined the USAF July 18, 1953. Stationed at 10 CONUS bases and five overseas bases. Served with all major AF Commands except Alaskan. Holds record as youngest, activated AF Chaplain (age 25) He is a graduate of all three air university schools.

Served as chaplain at Indian Springs AFS during stateside atomic bomb tests and later as first security services chaplain in Black Sea area at Turkey, was battalion chaplain in Korea, 1952, Sandia Army Hosp. chaplain, 1955, sr. chaplain, Azores, 1964-65; last chaplain at Amarillo AFB, 1968; Sr. AF chaplain in Panama when Canal Zone changed hands, 1979.

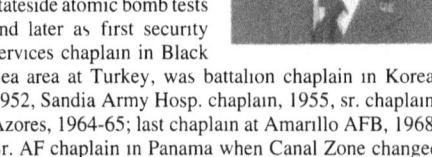

Married Carolyn Gates, June 23, 1962; they have three daughters and two grandchildren. He is minister-at-large, American Baptist Churches, USA

PHILIP B. BLISS, Lieutenant Colonel, born March 8, 1930, Somers, CT Graduated high school; college with BA, Seminary with M Div.

Joined the US Army in January 1962. Stationed at Fort Carson, CO; Korea, Fort Knox, KY; Vietnam Served with 5th Div and 2nd Div. Spt. Cmd, basic training, Fort Knox, KY, 13th Avn Bn., Vietnam

Memorable experiences included hospital assignment in Germany, CPE at Walter Reed AMC; assistant staff chaplain, Fort Hamilton, NY and with the 13th Avn. Bn. in Vietnam. Retired Feb. 28, 1982, as lieutenant colonel (0-5).

Married Margarette Bigg and has two children and two grandchildren. Interim pastor, substitute teacher at high school, retired March 1, 1982.

JOHN O. BLOM, Colonel, born Feb 9, 1929, Woodville, WI. Graduated from the Univ. of Idaho in 1953 and Luther Theological Seminary, St. Paul, MN in 1956. Received ordination in 1956 and was assigned to Fort Huachuca, AZ, after completing the basic course at the US Army Chaplain School, Fort Slocum, NY

Served in USAREUR, 1958-65, with a brief interlude at Fort Hood, TX in 1961. After completion of Advanced/Career Crs at Chaplain School, Fort Hamilton, 1966 Assigned to Fitzsimons Army Hosp., Denver, then to USAR Vietnam, 1967-68. Was division chaplain and deputy post chaplain, 24th Inf. Div. and 1st Inf Div., Fort Riley, KS, 1969-70.

Civilian schooling, 1970-71 (counseling), then to Fort Sam Houston, TX, 1971-73. Family Life Center Chaplain, Fort Ord, CA, 1973, with promotion was assigned to Staff, USAR Chaplain School, Fort Wadsworth, NY, 1974 Received Regular Army Commission and assigned to Fort Lewis, WA, 1976-79 Retired on June 1, 1979.

Married Carol Jean Erickson of Troy, ID, and has three children and one grandchild. Rural parish pastor, 1980-88; interim pastor

WILLIAM ARMISTEAD BOARDMAN, Colonel, born Feb. 16, 1922, Winston-Salem, NC Graduated Griffin, GA HS, 1939; Univ. of the South, Sewanee, TN, BA, 1943; Union Theological Seminary, NYC, M Div., 1945; Air War College, diploma, 1966; George Washington Univ., MS, 1966; Iliff Seminary, Denver, CO, D.Min., 1980.

Military Service: 54th Ftr. Gp, GAANG, commissioned captain Sept 9, 1946, 278th Reg. Cbt Team, TNNG Regimental Chaplain, 1947-51; 118th Tac Recon Wg. TNANG, called to AD, 1951 Stationed in Memphis, TN, 118th TRW, 1951-52; 63rd Recon Wing, Shaw AFB, SC, 1952, Misawa AB, Japan, 1953-55; Sampson AFB, NY, 1955-56, Lackland AFB, TX, 1956-58; Torrejon AB, Madrid, Spain, 1959-62

Promoted to major in 1960 Clinton-Sherman AFB, OK, 1962-65, base chaplain, Air War College, 1965-66. Promoted to LTC, 1965 Pacific Security Region, Honolulu, 1966-69, staff chaplain Promoted to full colonel, September 1968. Lowry AFB, CO, Center Chaplain, 1969-70; HQ. 7th AF, Vietnam, all of 1971, command chaplain; HQ Norad/ADC, Colorado Springs, 1972-75. Retired, with 29 years of service, in September 1975

Married Ann Lowrey Webster in April 1946 and has two children, Thomas and Rebecca. Instructor pilot (glider, 25+ years) and commercial pilot (SEL, 31+ years) After retirement he and wife Ann founded St Matthias Episcopal Church, Monument, CO, and served 10 years without pay He left the parish six acres and a cemetery.

THEODORE E. BOWERS, Commander, born in Ellwood City, PA Received his BA from Geneva College, Beaver Falls, PA; M.Div from Winebrenner Seminary, Findlay, OH; and he is an ordained minister of the United Church of Christ

Ordained in 1962 and received his commission in the USNR as a lieutenant jg in 1965. Served as pastor in churches in central Pennsylvania while also providing leadership to various boards and commissions of the Penn Central Conference of the UCC.

Military assignments consisted of tours at NRC Great Lakes, MCSD Barstow; MCB Camp Lejeune, MCRD Parris Island, NB Guantanamo Bay; NAS Whidbey Island; MCDEC Quantico; NAS Alameda; MCAGCTC Twenty-nine Palms; CGTC Cape May; NAS Bermuda; NAS Brunswick; NH Philadelphia; MCAS New River; MCAS El Torro; and MCTC Kaneohe Bay.

Among his supervisory responsibilities in the USN, he was XO, SURFLANT (REL) 104; CO, 4th MAF (REL) 304, battalion chaplain (CAX), director of Family Services; OCE Staff Chaplain (CAX 8-89), group chaplain, MCR MAG-49; and senior chaplain, Fleet Hosp. 20/15.

Recalled to active duty for the Persian Gulf War to be the senior chaplain of Fleet Hosp 15, Al Jubail, Saudi Arabia Received the Navy Commendation Medal for his outstanding ministry in the hospital and among the Kuwaites. Retired from the USNR in 1992.

Most memorable event was celebrating an ecumenical Easter dawn service with American and foreign civilians at an outside service at FL HOSP 15 in Saudi Arabia during the Persian Gulf War. It was the first "public" worship most of these civilians had ever attended since coming to work in Saudi Arabia.

Married to Lowanda (Price) Bowers and has four children and four grandchildren.

DAVID GAILLARD BOYCE, a graduate of Davidson College, Columbia Seminary and Princeton Seminary. As an Army chaplain, he served as a paratrooper with the 101st Abn. Div at Fort Campbell, KY and with the Army Spec. Forces at Fort Bragg, NC. In Vietnam he was a Green Beret Chaplain with the 5th Spec. Forces Gp.

A graduate of the Army Abn. School and Army Spec. Warfare School. His awards include the Air Medal, Bronze Star Medal, Armed Forces Expeditionary Medal and the Legion of Merit. He is a master parachutist. Army retirement took place at Fort Meade, MD.

Since military retirement, he has won international awards as a writer/producer of documentary and motivational video productions. Currently, continues his award-winning work in the field of film and video and makes his home in Alexandria, VA.

SEYMOUR BRICKMAN, Lieutenant Colonel, born June 30, 1932, Bronx, NY. Received BA, Yeshiva College; MA, professional diploma, Columbia Univ.; ordained rabbi at Theological Seminary.

Joined the USAF in December 1956. Stationed at Lackland AFB, TX; Chanute AFB, IL; Floyd Bennett Field, Brooklyn, NY; Dover AFB, DE; Langley Field, VA. Served with HQ 3345th TT Wg; 106th Cbt. Spt. Sqdn, 9018th Air Res, 436th ABG, HQ TAC, AF Academy, liaison officer.

Memorable experience was serving troops at Dover AFB while they were preparing to leave for mission in Persian Gulf during Desert Shield, Desert Storm. Also memorable was serving in the Command Chaplain's Office at Langley AFB.

Retired in December 1958 as lieutenant colonel. Married, with three children and four grandchildren. Consultant, Board of Jewish Education, New York, NY and director, Fund for Jewish Education. Retired in June 1990.

FRANCIS P. BROSIUS, Captain, born Nov 21, 1930, Nanty Glo, PA. Graduated Blacklick Twp HS; Indiana Univ. of Pennsylvania; master's, St. Francis, Loretto, PA; D.Min, Lancaster Theological Seminary.

Joined the USAF in June 1948; served with Air Sea Rescue and CAP, Johnstown, PA Memorable experience was USAF from 1948-52 during Korean War Flew with brother, Herb, on KC10 tanker from Westover to Azores. Served at Ramey AFB, Puerto Rico. Still active in CAP.

Married Shirley Bradley and has three children and four grandsons. Still serving as pastor and court judge in Pennsylvania.

BENEDICT JOSEPH FLAGET BROWN, Lieutenant, born Oct. 6, 1947, Louisville, KY. Educated at St. Columbia School and St. Thomas Preparatory Seminary, BA and M.Div. from St. Meinrad Seminary, IN; post graduate studies, Indiana Univ; ordained August 1973 and served as associate pastor in Elizabethtown and Louisville For six years he was director of seminary students and for 11 years he pastored St Thomas Parish and School in Bardstown, KY

Served three years at the Naval and Marine Corps Reserve Ctr., Louisville Had active duty at Diego Garcia in the Indian Ocean and at Arlington National Cemetery in Washington, DC for six weeks. Served the Haitian migrant community (who were predominantly HIV infected) in Guantanamo Bay, Cuba, which had two characteristics of military service in the 1990s, its mission was humanitarian and included all US military branches of services.

In 1993 he became a member of the MCA and began an active duty tour with the 1st Marine Div at Camp Pendleton, CA Priest for Archdiocese of Louisville, KY

MONTE BARTLE BROWN, Captain, born Jan. 29, 1912, Eugene, OR. Graduate of Univ of California; San Francisco Theological Seminary with BD

Joined US Army Sept. 1, 1950. Stationed at Camp Cooke, Lompoc, CA; Japan and Korea Served with 223rd Regt., Camp Sendai, Japan, 1951; Camp Whittington, 1951; 140th AAA Bn. Div., Camp Palmer, 1951; 960th FA BN, Camp Fuji McNair and Kumsong, Korea in 1952

Discharged May 27, 1952, as captain. Received Occupation Medal (Japan), Korean Service Medal, UN Service Ribbon, Commendation Ribbon with medal pendant.

Pastorates from 1947-1973: St James Presbyterian Church, San Gabrial, CA, St. Paul's Presbyterian Church, San Francisco; Presbyterian Church, San Leandro, CA, interim pastor; field representative, Board of National Missions, Presbyterian Church. Director of National Missions of the Synod of Oregon, Portland, OR, Counsellor of Stewardship, Synod of Colorado Took an early retirement in 1973

Interim pastorates in Prescott, AZ; Bethany Church, Glendale, pastor, Interdenominational Church of Seroe, CO; Aruba, Netherlands Antilles, 1976-78, interim pastor and pastor emeritus, Bethany Presbyterian Church, San Bruno, CA, 1979. Retired, Ojai, CA, 1983.

Married Dorothy E Sullivan on Sept. 19, 1938, Casper, WY. They have two children, David and Joseph, and four grandchildren. Trust officer, Bank of America, 1938 National Bank Examiner, 1942-44.

JOHN ACIE BURGESS, Lieutenant Colonel, born near Waterville, WA. Received his education from Phillips Univ. and at Seminary, Pacific School of Religion. He was ordained in the Christian Church, Disciples of Christ.

As civilian minister he served pastorates in Santa Fe, NM; Berkeley, CA; and Camp Springs, MD. In November 1940 he was commissioned chaplain, 1st lieutenant, US Army, serving stateside as base chaplain at Stockton, CA; La Junta, CO, Davis-Monthan AFB; Edwards AFB, Hurlburt AFB, Barksdale AFB; and senior chaplain at Wilford Hall AF Hosp.

He was circuit rider chaplain with AACS and weather units MATS in Canada and Alaska. Overseas he served with 79th Ftr. Gp, North Africa, Sicily, Italy, Corsica, Southern France, ending 12th AF HQ, Florence; Korea-8th Ftr. Wg.; Clarke AFB, Philippines and 10th TAC RECON, Alconbury, England. Took part with combat units in 11 major campaigns and two invasions in WWII Retired as a lieutenant colonel in July 1963.

He and his wife are the parents of four children.

CHARLES LEE BURGREEN, Colonel, born March 6, 1924, Davis, Tucker, WV. Received BA from Maryville College, Maryville, TN; BD from Univ. of South, Sewanee, TN.

Joined the US Army April 16, 1951. Stationed at Fort Benning, Germany, Fort Dix, Japan, Fort Hood, Slocum, Alaska, Vietnam, Fort Sheridan.

Memorable experience was as instructor at Chaplain School. Retired March 31, 1973, as colonel.

Married Helen Florence Lord, March 31, 1948, and has two children and four grandchildren. Bishop, Armed Forces, the Episcopal Church. Retired March 3, 1989.

WAYNE L. BURKEY, Colonel, born Aug. 23, 1921, near Murphysboro, IL. After three and a half years in the Navy V-12 and V-12 during WWII, he graduated from Southern Illinois Univ. in 1948 and from Asbury Seminary in Wilmore, KY in 1950 Ordained an elder in the United Methodist Church in 1950 and served churches in Ashley and Lebanon of the Southern Illinois Conference until being commissioned as a chaplain in the USAF in 1955.

Served assignments at Ent AFB, CO; Birkenfeld and Furstenfeldbruck, Germany; Larson AFB, WA; Don Muang AB, Thailand; March AFB, CA; Wheelus AB, Libya; and Dyess AFB, TX. He retired as a colonel from active duty on March 1, 1974, and pastored Tuscola United Methodist Church near Abilene, TX until his retirement in June 1989 after 43 years in the ministry.

Married to Marcella and has one son, two daughters and five grandchildren. They live in Abilene, TX.

WILLIAM G. BURNS, Colonel, born Jan 5, 1936, Iowa City, IA. Received BA from Univ. of Iowa, 1959; M.Div from Eden Theological Seminary, 1963; MS, Long Island Univ., 1973; D.Min, Eden Theological Seminary, 1992.

Joined USAR as chaplain in May 1966. Stations included Armor Trng. Cmd., Fort Knox, KY, 1966; 2nd Div. Arty , Korea, 1967-68; Msl Bn., Edgemont, PA, 1968-69, 6/31 Inf. Bn , 9th Inf. Div., RVN, 1969-70; HQ CMD, Fort Ord, CA, 1970-72, Adv. Crs., Fort Hamilton, NY, 1972-73; 8th Div., Mianz, Germany, 1973-74. Left active duty in May 1974.

Reserve Units served from 1974-91: 498th Engr. Bn.; 103rd COSCOM; 5th US Army, Ft Sam (IMA), 1991-94, Inactive Reserve Called to active duty Jan. 2, 1991, for Desert Shield/Storm until July 12. Retired as colonel, 1991, and from inactive Reserve, 1994.

Memorable experience was being saved from injury and possible death by a young Vietnamese boy. It was late in the evening when the command element came to the fence surrounding a small village. As the commander stopped to re-group, the boy came to the gate where they stood and explained that they were under a daisy chain. Had they opened the gate, the explosives would have been detonated.

Married Florence and has five children and six grandchildren Employed at VA Hosp. since May 1988.

WILLIAM E. CALBERT, Lieutenant Colonel, is a life member of the MCA and a former trustee. A native of California, he has served in three different military ranks and in three wars: enlisted and warrant officer in WWII; as a commissioned officer in Korea and Vietnam, with intervening service in the US and Germany

A graduate of San Francisco State College, American Baptist Seminary of the West; and Teachers College, Columbia Univ.; in addition to the Army Chaplain School where he later served four years on the staff and faculty.

One of his memorable experiences was that of participating in the very first Ecumenical Service ever in St. Patrick's Cathedral, NY, Oct. 16, 1966, when chaplains (Protestant, Catholic and Jewish), in the presence of Cardinal Francis Spellman, participated in a service sponsored by the Military Order of the World Wars.

One additional memorable military-related experience was that of serving as the representative of the MCA on the occasion of the groundbreaking ceremonies for the Vietnam Veterans Memorial, Washington, DC.

He is married to the former Madlyn Williams, retired school administrator, and has four daughters and one son

RICHARD CARR, Major General, is a native Californian who graduated from Whitworth College, Spokane, WA, 1949, with a BA in history, from Fuller Theological Seminary, Pasadena, CA, 1954, with a M.Div; and awarded the DD from Whitworth College, 1981. He flew as combat crew member in WWII and Korea; entered active duty as an AF chaplain in 1955 and retired in August 1982 as chief of Chaplains.

His career included base and command positions, being appointed deputy chief in 1976 and chief of Chaplains in 1978. Special interests centered in POW/MIA activities from 1965-73, race relations in military commands and bases, early drug programs in the AF, and pioneering AF Family programs, 1975-81, culminating in establishing the AF Family Matters Office, HQ, USAF and AF Family Support Centers throughout the AF.

Awarded the AF Distinguished Service Medal, Legion of Merit w/OLC, Meritorious Medal w/4 OLCs, AF Commendation Medal, plus WWII, Korean and Vietnam Service medals and ribbons.

An ordained minister of the United Church of Christ, he holds standing in the United Presbyterian Church (USA), currently serving as interim minister for pastoral care, National Presbyterian Church, Washington, DC.

Married to the former Jeanne Maurece Robertson and has three children and two grandsons. Since his AF retirement, he has conducted marriage and family workshops at military installations world-wide with his wife Jeanne, and has worked with humanitarian agencies in developing countries with relief and rehabilitation programs.

MARTHA A. CARSON, Lieutenant, born March 24, 1958, Parkersburg, WV. Received BA and a regular commission as a Marine lieutenant through Ohio State's NROTC Program, June 13, 1980 After Basic School at Quantico, VA, she attended the Disbursing Officers Crs. at Camp Lejeune, NC and served at various disbursing offices, including 2nd FSSG and MCAS(H) New River With 3rd FSSG on Okinawa, October 1983-April 1985 Was the assistant disbursing officer at MCAS Kaneohe Bay, HI. Released from active duty in June 1987.

She felt led to become a Navy chaplain and entered the Divinity School at Duke Univ. in August 1987. Was awarded an M.Div. degree May 13, 1990. While at Duke she was commissioned an ensign in the Navy's Chaplain Candidate Program.

After changing affiliation from the United Methodist Church to the Full Gospel Churches, she was ordained a Christian minister May 17, 1992.

Recalled to active duty in 1994. Presently serves with 2nd Marine Expeditionary Bde., Camp Lejeune.

JAMES PAUL CARTER, Captain, born April 30, 1940, Kirbyville, TX Holds AA, BS, Th.M and D.Min. degrees and is a licensed professional counselor Most of his ministry has been in the area of helping people work through times of crisis, disabilities and sickness.

Commissioned June 25, 1967, in USAR and entered active duty as a chaplain (CPT). Attended Basic Chaplain's Crs. at Fort Hamilton, NY, then went to Fort Polk, LA. Left for South Vietnam Nov. 18, 1968, and served in 1st Air Cav. Div. Wounded July 25, 1969 and returned to Fort Sam Houston, Brook Gen. Hosp., TX.

Separated for permanent disability retirement with a 100% disability rating on Oct. 14, 1970. Awards include the Purple Heart, Bronze Star w/V, Air Medal, Vietnam Service Medal, Vietnam Campaign Medal and National Defense Service Medal.

Married Nancy Kathryn Van Pelt and has two children, James Paul Jr. and Mark Stephen, and one grandson. Chaplain, Audie L. Murphy VA Hosp., San Antonio, TX (1973-1979); Chief, Chaplain Service, Olin E Teague Veterans' Center, Temple, TX, (1979-1995). Retired April 31, 1995. Enjoys camping, coin and stamp collecting and the computer

JOHN J. CASTELLANI, Colonel, born May 1, 1923, New Britain, CT. Attended St. Joseph's Parochial School, New Britain, CT; St. Thomas Seminary, Bloomfield, CT; St Bernard's Seminary, Rochester, NY (BA and M Div); graduate work (partial) Catholic Univ. of America, Washington, DC; Univ. of Oklahoma, Norman OK, 1972; Univ. of San Diego, San Diego, CA, 1978; North American College, Rome, Italy, 1980; various military courses on management, budgeting and personnel planning. Ordained to the priesthood May 6, 1948, and was assistant pastor, 1948-56, St. Peter's Church, Torrington, CT.

Entered the USAF Oct. 22, 1956. Stateside assignments at Lackland AFB, TX; Geiger Field, Spokane, WA, Patrick AFB, FL; Andrews AFB, Washington, DC, Wright Patterson AFB, OH, HQ Aerospace Def. Cmd., Ent AFB, CO; Norton AFB, CA, Scott AFB, IL; March AFB, CA. Overseas assignments at Wiesbaden, Germany; Kanto Mura, Tokyo, Japan; Korat, Thailand, Kindley AFB, Bermuda; and Ramstein AFB, Germany.

Retired from service July 1, 1980 Decorations include Legion of Merit, Meritorious Service Medal w/ 2 OLCs, AF Commendation w/4 OLCs, National Defense Medal, Armed Forces Expeditionary Medal, Vietnamese Service Medal w/Bronze Star and RVN Service Medal.

Member of MCA, DAV, AFA and TROA. Appointed pastor, St. Lucy's Church, Waterbury, CT, May 15, 1981; appointed Dean of Waterbury Catholic Clergy, June 1982-86, retired July 28, 1993.

ALSTON R. CHACE, Colonel, born Feb. 22, 1932,

Fall River, MA Graduated from Gardner HS, Gardner, MA in 1950; earned bachelor's degree from Tufts Univ., Medford, MA, 1954; seminary training at Episcopal Divinity School, Cambridge, MA, M.Div degree in 1957; second master's in counseling and guidance from Troy State Univ., Troy, AL, 1973. Graduate of Air Command and Staff College, the Academic Instructor Crs. and the Air War College, Maxwell AFB, AL.

Ordained a deacon in St. Paul's Episcopal Church, Gardner, MA; advanced to Sacred Order of Priests, All Saints Episcopal Church, Belmont, MA, Jan 4, 1958.

Entered the AF in July 1961. Stateside assignments included: Langley AFB, VA; HQ USAFA, CO, Bolling AFB, Washington, DC, Kirtland AFB, NM, HQ Mil Airlift Cmd., Scott AFB, IL, and HQ AF Systems Cmd., Andrews AFB, MD. Overseas assignments included RAF, Kirknewton, Scotland, RAF, Mildenhall, England, Phu Cat AB, RVN; U-Tapao AB, Thailand; Incirlik AB, Turkey; HQ USAF in Europe, Ramstein AB, West Germany.

Retired from the AF Aug. 1, 1991. Military decorations include the Legion of Merit w/2 OLCs, Bronze Star, Meritorious Service Medal w/2 OLCs, AF Commendation Medal w/OLC, AF Outstanding Unit Awd. Ribbon w/6 OLCs and V device, AF Organizational Excellence Awd., RVN Gallantry Cross w/palm, AF Overseas Ribbons (short and long).

Life member of MCA, served on Executive Committee and is past-president of the National Capital Area Chapter He is four-time recipient of the George Washington Honor Medal for his patriotic essays.

Married to the former Beverly Ann Morse, Brewster, MA. They are parents of three children Carey Anne, John Scott and James Stewart (deceased). In the Diocese of Western Massachusetts, he serves as Dean of the Episcopal Church in North Worcester, is on the Ecumenical and Diocesan Councils, and is Diocesan representative to the Armed Forces.

DAVID CHAMBERS, Lieutenant (jg), born Feb. 13, 1921, Newark, NJ Graduated from Grove City College and Princeton Theological Seminary where he joined the USN V12S Program Feb 7, 1944 Commissioned LTJG upon graduation and served in the Fleet Chaplains Office, Pearl Harbor, aboard the USS *Altair;* and at the Bikini Atoll for the first Navy A-bomb tests

From 1946-52 he was on the faculty of Lafayette College until recalled to the USN. Served at Camp Lejeune and with the 1st Mar Div. during the Korean War, followed by NTC, San Diego; Naval Base, Yokosuka, Japan; Navy Chapel, Washington, DC; USS *Antietam;* Chief of Chaplains Office. Retired in 1970 as chaplain of the Naval Postgraduate School, Monterey, CA

Retired in 1983 as Director of the Presbyterian Council for Chaplains. He is married to Betty Rehn and has four children and three grandchildren.

JAMES V. CHAMBERS, Lieutenant Colonel, born May 2, 1920, Brooks Station, GA, the son of James F and Nellie Mince Chambers Attended Mercer Univ., Macon, GA; Southern Seminary, Louisville, KY; Luther Rice Seminary, Jacksonville, FL; ordained a minister May 8, 1957, and served 35 years as pastor of the Baptist faith

Entered military service Feb 4, 1941; assigned to Co L 121st Inf. Regt., 8th Inf. Div., Fort Jackson, SC. Landed on Omaha Beach and fought through the hedge rows of France. Wounded in Dinard, France, Aug. 8, 1944, where he and his battalion were cut off and held for 10 days The Annals of the 121st; the infantry recorded this event as "The Lost Battalion."

Decorations include the Purple Heart, Bronze Star, Combat Infantry Badge, Campaign Ribbon w/4 stars and a number of other medals.

One of his most memorable experiences was running into a barn which caved in, leaving him buried alive under tons of wheat. He survived by putting his helmet over his face to trap in air.

Commissioned a chaplain in the CAP in 1957, with the rank of captain and is active in all their activities He is a licensed pilot with 2,000 plus hours. Present rank is lieutenant colonel. He is a life member of the MCA, MOPH, the Elberton Flying Club and Georgia Wing of the CAP.

Married to the former Anne Kelly and has two children, E. Timothy and Linda Dianne Chambers Kanazawa His name is one of those inscribed on "The Wall of Liberty" in Normandy, France.

GERALD R. CHANCELLOR, Brigadier General, born July 25, 1935, Cooper, TX. Graduated from Adamson HS, Dallas, in 1953. Earned BA from East Texas Baptist Univ., 1957; BD in 1961; M.Div. in 1968; D.Min., 1976, all at Southwestern Baptist Theological Seminary Completed Air Cmd. and Staff College and Academic Instructors School, both in 1978 and Air War College in 1987.

Received direct commission in 1962 and assigned to the 136th Ftr. Gp., TX ANG, Dallas. From April-August 1969, he served as chaplain area representative for the Office of the Chief of Chaplains. Became an individual mobilization augmentee in January 1970; served at Bergstrom AFB, TX; England AFB, LA; Carswell AFB, TX; Pope AFB, NC, and Langley AFB, VA. Became mobilization assistant to the command chaplain, July 1981, HQ TAC, Langley. February 1988 became mobilization assistant to the deputy chief of AF Chaplains in Washington, DC until retiring June 1, 1992.

Decorations include the Meritorious Service Medal, National Defense Service Medal, AF Longevity Service Award Ribbon w/4 OLCs, Armed Forces Reserve Medal w/HG Device and Distinguished Service Medal.

Served as chaplain to the Buckner Baptist Children's Home in Dallas and as pastor for the Buckner Home Baptist Church on the campus Member of the Dallas Baptist Pastors Conference, and since 1992 has been the pastor of First Baptist Church, Seagoville, TX. Life member in the NGA of Texas, MCA and ROA.

Married to the former Frances Kathleen Bateman of Baton Rouge, LA. They have five children: Gerald, Timothy, Richard, Jerrell and Angela.

RADOMIR CHKAUTOVICH, Lieutenant Commander, born Dec. 27, 1935, Serbia, Yugoslavia. As a priest in Communist Yugoslavia, with the dictator at that time, Josif Broz-Tito, he did not have any freedom to do the work God and his Holy Church appointed him to do. Left Yugoslavia, Aug. 8, 1963, and spent nine months in Greece (nobody knew his plan) and came to the US on April 20, 1964. Finally, his family came on Nov 17, 1968.

Joined the Navy SCC May 31, 1972. Served with "Saratoga," Tulsa, OK; "Joe Causino," St. Louis, MO; "NAS," Memphis, TN His memorable experience was becoming a US citizen on May 1, 1970. He wanted to give something to his new country in return for his freedom so he became a USN SCC officer. To wear the Navy uniform was for him a sacred privilege.

Married Vera Maksimovich of Medvedja kod Trstenika, Serbia, Yugoslavia and has three children and seven grandchildren He is parish priest at Holy Trinity Serbian Orthodox Church, St. Louis, MO.

AMOS E. CLEMMONS, Colonel, born Sept. 25, 1939, Great Falls, MT. Graduated from The Master's College, Newhall, CA with BA degree; M.Div from Northwest Baptist Seminary, Tacoma, WA, MA in marriage and family counseling from the Univ. of San Francisco. Organized and pastored Santa Clarita Valley Baptist Church before entering active duty in July 1966.

Served as Service Group Chaplain and the Range Chaplain at US Army Air Def. Ctr., Fort Bliss, TX; battalion chaplain for 2/2 Mech Inf. and 2/28th Inf. of the 1st Div. in RVN, post chaplain and deputy, 6th Region Air Def. Cmd. Chaplain, Fort Baker, CA

Reserve assignments included: 579th Cbt Engr. Bn., CAARNG, hospital chaplain, 352nd Evac. Hosp (MUST), 2nd Hosp. Ctr. and 6th US Army Chaplain's Office.

Retired from the USAR March 20, 1994. Awards include the Legion of Merit, Meritorious Service Award, Bronze Star (Service) w/OLC, Army Air Medal, Army Commendation Medal w/2 OLCs.

Married Ernestene (Janes) Dec. 17, 1960, and has two married daughters and three grandchildren Served Grace Baptist Church, Eureka, CA for 22 years and has since served as a pastoral counselor and interim pastor.

HERBERT B. CLEVELAND, Chaplain, born Feb. 20, 1931, on a "company farm" in the Red River Valley near Gardner, ND. The family of nine moved to Detroit Lakes, MN where he was raised on a farm until he enlisted in the US Army. He got a taste of infantry life in the 10th Mountain Div. at Fort Riley, KS, then to Fort Bragg, NC until being sent to USAEUR in Germany, finishing his first three years as a sergeant

Returned to Grand Forks where he married his longtime dream girl, Connie Borlang, on Sept. 9, 1955, at Univ. Lutheran Church where they would intern some years later. After the Univ. of North Dakota, they moved to Saint Paul where they attended Luther Seminary where he was commissioned as a butter bar in the Chaplain Corps of the US Army. Graduated Chaplain School at Fort Slocum and Fort Hamilton, NY.

Served various USAR assignments with the Engineers, Chem. Corps, 452nd Gen. Hosp , 84th Div. where some 28 years later he completed his service during Desert Shield and Storm in 1991. He served parishes in Minneapolis, MN; Lead and Sturgis, SD; and he and his wife had a religious talk show for 10 years.

His real love was with the VA In 1963 they moved to Fort Meade where he rose to chairman of the Pastoral Care Department. Fort Meade was a great time for family growth where he and wife, Connie, raised their four children: Laurie, Beth, Rob and Tim.

In 1983 he was selected as Deputy Chief of Chaplains in Washington, DC, selected in 1988 as Chief of Chaplains for the Dept. of Veterans Affairs. As Chief he brought women into the Chaplaincy, broke the Judeo Christian mold by bringing in the first Buddhist and Moslem Chaplains; organized the Black Chaplains Assoc.; established the National Chaplain Ctr. at Hampton, VA and the National Pastoral Care Institute at Palo Alto, CA. Other Chaplain activities included 21 CPE sites in the VA, the Northwest Ethics Trng. Ctr at Portland, OR.

Active in the MCA service as board member, vice-president and national president. The most exciting conversion and institute in his memory was held in Gettysburg, PA, when sessions were held on famous battlefields and sites with re-enactments including chaplains, soldiers and even President Lincoln.

He was active in establishing relations with foreign chaplains, including the Russian military. As his career closes, he serves the Evangelical Lutheran Church HQ in Chicago, the Specialized Pastoral Care Coordinator. This has been a time of excitement, satisfaction and privilege to be a chaplain and living Pre Deo Et Partice.

When he retired Secretary Derwinski placed the gold Exceptional Service Award around his neck. The Washington experience will never be forgotten

JAMES V. COLEMAN, Colonel, entered US Army active duty with the KYNG in January 1941. Graduated from Army Infantry OCS and served through the North African and Italian campaigns as a combat officer with the 34th Inf. Div., leaving active service in the grade of captain in the infantry in January 1946.

Graduated from Union Theological Seminary, New York; re-entered active service as a chaplain, US Army, in September 1950. He served in Korea with the 40th Inf. Div and seven years with 11th Abn. Div. in the US and Europe. Graduated from George Washington Univ. with a master's degree in public administration in 1960 Served successively as assistant 3rd US Army Chaplain, and as USA Element and International Staff Chaplain, SHAPE, in Paris.

Closed his active duty years serving as deputy, then as staff chaplain, USA Material Cmd., when promoted to colonel in 1969, 8th US Army and UN Cmd Staff Chaplain, Seoul, Korea, 1970-72, and staff chaplain,

52

USA Arty. Ctr. and Fort Sill, OK. Retired from the Army at Fort Sill, June 1, 1975.

Following Army retirement, Chaplain Coleman served as pastor of First Presbyterian Church (USA), Jasper, TX, 16 years, retiring June 1, 1992.

JOSEPH I. COLLINS, Captain, born March 28, 1914, Norwood, MA. Education Elementary, HS, Holy Cross College, St. John Seminary, Boston Chaplain School, first class at Fort Devens, Ayer, MA, September 1944.

Joined the US Army, Aug. 21, 1944. Stationed at Fort Devens, MA; Camp Butner, NC and ETO. Served with 89th Inf. Div , 16 Port at LeHavre, France, Port Chaplain.

Memorable Experiences: staging at Camp Myles Standish, MA; sailing from Boston, MA on SS *Uraguay* with 6,000 men of the 355th Regt. of 8th Div., landing at LeHavre after 13 days on the Atlantic, combat in Germany and seeing the German Concentration Camp in Ordruf, Germany, March 1945.

Discharged on Oct 26, 1946, with the rank of captain. He is pastor of St. Paul, Cambridge, MA and also at St Pius V, Lynn, MA

JAMES THEODORE COLSON, O-5, born Feb 13, 1922, Tampa, FL Received AB degree from Tulane Univ., LA; BD and M.Div from New Orleans Baptist Theological Seminary. Served in the FLNG, Btry. B, 265th Coast Arty., October 1939-November 1940; joined the USMC, November 1940-May 1947 (acting 1st sergeant); USAF from June 1953-until medically retired in May 1971 (rank O-5)

Stationed at Camp Foster, Jacksonville, FL, while in the NG; MC Base and Camp Elliott, San Diego, CA, South/SW Pacific, USN Station, Washington, DC; Cherry Point, NC; Quantico, VA and Tientsin, China with the USMC; and Biggs AFB, TX; Turner AFB, GA; Matagorda Bombing and Gunnery Range, TX; RAF Brize Norton AFB, England, Donaldson AFB, SC, Lincoln AFB, NE; Minot AFB, ND; RVN; MacDill AFB, FL with the USAF.

Served with (NG), 265th Coast Arty., (USMC) 2/3 Bns., 2nd Mar. Div., Shore Patrol HQ, Washington, DC; 1st Mar. Air Warning Gp., Cherry Point, NC, control tower, Quantico, VA, and 1st MAW, Tientsin, China; (USAF) 810/811 Air Divs , 4080th SRW, 4004th AB Sqdn , 3920th Cbt. Spt. Gp., 63rd Troop Carrier Wing, 818th Cbt. Spt. Gp., 810th Strategic Aerospace Div., 12th Tactical Fighter Wing and 836th Cbt. Spt. Gp.

Memorable experience was preaching "Remembrance Day" services at Tewkesbury Abbey, England in 1958; becoming a "mach-buster" chaplain in 1966 and developing and building the Cam Ranh Christian Love Center in RVN, 1966-67.

Married Ernestine Celeste Brady in 1945 and has three children and three grandchildren. Chaplain at DeSota Correctional Institution and Missionary Associate with SBC Foreign Mission Board.

KENNETH R. COLTON, Chaplain, born in 1944, Pontiac, MI Served as an enlisted member of the USAF from 1962-66. Graduate of Oakland Univ and Colgate Rochester Divinity School, NY Earned BA, MA and M.Div. Served United Methodist churches in Michigan before entering the chaplaincy in 1978.

Military assignments included Clark AB, Philippines; Bentwaters AB, England; Kelly AFB, TX; Kunsan AB, Korea; Andrews AFB, MD; the AF Chief of Chaplains Office, DC; the AF Chaplain School, Maxwell AFB, AL, Hellenikon AB, Greece; Kirtland AFB, NM; and McConnell AFB, KS.

Awarded more than 18 military decorations, including the Meritorious Service Medal w/2 OLCs, the Joint Service Commendation Medal and the AF Commendation Medal w/2 OLCs.

He considers his most enjoyable assignment was working in the Chief of Chaplains Office, and his most demanding was while assigned as a Senior Camp Chaplain to Cuban refugees at Guantanamo Bay, Cuba

Married to Laura and has two children, Sarah and Andrew. He is a life member of the MCA.

LYNN DALE COOPER, Commander, born Aug. 11, 1932, Aberdeen, WA. Attended Northwest Christian College, Eugene, OR, BTH, 1955, graduated seminary, Phillips Univ., M.Div., 1961 and D.Min., 1977; ordained First Christian Church, Hoquiam, WA, Oct. 30, 1954. Was assoc. pastor/pastor of First Christian Churches at Olympia, WA, Aline, OK, and Sumner, WA. Author of *The Chaplain's Relationship to and Responsibility for Non-Traditional Minority Religions in the USN* (D.Min. project).

(1966-86): CS, Newport, RI; COMDESRON 13, Long Beach, CA; COMDESDIV 132, Long Beach, CA; NAS Whidbey Island, Oak Harbor, WA; Marine Pre-Dep Tr., Camp Pendleton, CA; 1st MAW, Da Nang, RVN; 3rd MAW, MCAS El Toro, CA; TAD, Subic Bay NS, Philippines; NAVCOMMSTA H E. Holt, Exmouth, West Australia; Phillips Univ. (DUINS), Enid, OK; USS *Hunley*, MAG 26, 2nd MAW, MCAS New River, NC, USS *Camden*; Naval Hosp., Bremerton, WA; USS *Tarawa* (LHA-1) 1986-88.

Awards/Decorations: Combat Action Ribbon, Bronze Star w/Combat V, Navy Unit Citation, Meritorious Unit Citation, RVN Meritorious Unit Citation (Civil Actions Color w/palm, Navy Commendation Medal with Gold Star, seven campaign and service medals, Letter of Commendation from CINCLANT and Letter of Appreciation from CG, Joint Control Group of Exercise Solid Shield. Retired from USN, March 1, 1988. Served as Pastor of Central Christian Church, Prosser, WA from March 1988 to present. Life member of MCA.

Married D. Marlene Aydelott on June 2, 1956, and has three children. Kevin, Kathy and Karen, and six grandchildren.

RUFUS A. COOPER, Lieutenant Colonel, born Jan. 28, 1912, in Barnsville, GA, the eldest son of the Rev Gilliard and Elizabeth Cooper. His early years were spent in Pasadena, CA where he attended elementary school. Completed his secondary education in Los Angeles where he later attended the Bible Institute of Los Angeles. Graduated from San Jose State College with a BA in sociology and anthropology. During his 24 years of military service he attended numerous service institutes, including two levels of training at Chaplains School and the California Institute of Family Relations.

Military career began Oct 1, 1942, at which time he was commissioned as chaplain of the 7th Inf. Regt. of the California State Guard. This was the first black regiment in the state of California When this regiment was deactivated, he was commissioned, Oct 31, 1943, as chaplain in the US Army. Served in various installations Stateside and overseas during WWII, the Korean War and in the peacetime Army.

Assignments included Transport Chaplain, combat and occupation duty in Germany and Japan, and with the 2nd Inf. Div. in Korea. Retired as post chaplain at Fort Ord, CA with the rank LTC. Holds 12 decorations which include the Bronze Star, Army Commendation Medal w/ 2 OLCs and the Gliderman Badge.

Pastored (as civilian) congregation in California under the auspices of the African Methodist Episcopal Zion Church. Served churches in Los Angeles, Monrovia, Modesto, San Diego, Oakland and San Mateo. Always interested in improving the quality of life for all persons, he served on the boards of many community agencies and received many awards recognizing his services to the community. One of these awards was the Family of Man Award presented by the Conference of Religion, Race and Social Concern of San Matio County, an interfaith council.

Life member of the MCA, TROA, VFW and National Assoc. for the Advancement of Colored People. At the present time he resides with his wife, Helen Williams Cooper, at AF Village West, a retirement community for retired military officers in Riverside, CA.

Married Helen Cooper and has one daughter, five grandchildren and three great-grandchildren.

RAYMOND H. COSGROVE, Lieutenant Colonel, CAP, born April 14, 1935, Los Angeles, CA. Received master of ministry, Bethany Bible Seminary, AL. Joined the USAF March 25, 1954.

Stationed in Japan, 1956-58; England, 1965-68; Thailand, 1970-71. Served with 45th TAC Recon Sqdn., 307th BW, 79th TFS, 33rd TFW. Retired from USAF Jan. 1, 1977, as E-6. Received two National Defense Service Medals, two AFOUA, two Good Conduct Medals, two AFGCM, four AFLSA, SAEMR, two AFCMs, VSM, RVCM and RVGC Medals.

Married Constance and has three children and two grandchildren. Worked for civil service, USAF, until he retired Feb. 2, 1990.

JOHN HAROLD CRAVEN, Captain, born April 12, 1915, Cape Girardeau, MO. Enlisted in USMC Oct. 24, 1933, and was granted special order discharge in 1935 (member of USMCR, 1935-39) while attending SW Baptist College, Bolivar, MO and William Jewell College, Liberty, MO, receiving BA in 1939. Ordained in 1937 and served as pastor of Baptist Churches in Calhoun and Leeton, MO, while a student at the Central Baptist Seminary, Kansas City, KS, receiving Th M in 1942. Attended Navy Chaplains School in Norfolk, VA and appointed acting chaplain in the USN.

Assignments: NTS, Sampson, NY; served with

1st, 2nd and 4th Mar. Divs. Served in USS *Okaloosa*, USS *Cambria*, USS *Mt Olympus* and USS *Coral Sea*.

Fought in Marshall Islands, Saipan, Tinian, Iwo Jima, Inchon, Seoul, Chosin Reservoir and Central Front in Korea with 7th Mar. Regt.

Awarded the Legion of Merit w/Combat V, Bronze Star w/Gold Star and Combat V, Ribbon w/3 stars for the Presidential Unit Citation and Navy Unit Commendation Ribbon, American Campaign, Asiatic-Pacific Campaign Medal w/4 stars, WWII Victory Medal, Navy Occupation Service Medal (Europe Clasp), Korean Service w/3 stars, UN Service Medal, National Defense Medal and Navy Commendation Medal.

Married July 1940 to Betty May Smith and has two daughters, Carol May and Margaret, and two grandsons. Retired Aug. 1, 1973; left August 15 for missionary work in Okinawa. Served as Director of Ministries for Norfolk Baptist Assoc., 1975-89, since then serving as the Chaplain-in-Residence at Vinson Hall. His wife passed away in March 1990, and he married Mrs. Verna Hyde in February 1992.

HAYWOOD K. CROSS, Lieutenant Colonel, born Aug. 9, 1909, Robbins, TN. Received BA from Lincoln Memorial Univ., 1934 and MA from CRDS, Rochester, NY. Ordained in Baptist Church, 1937, and was missionary to Crow Indians in Montana.

Active duty Dec. 7, 1941, Harbor Defenses of Puget Sound. Chaplain at Presidio of San Francisco, then Amphibious Trng School in Hawaii. Served with 111th Inf. Cbt. Team in the Marshall and Palau Islands. Other stations: Fort Lewis, WA; staff chaplain, Rome Arno Cmd., Italy; 6th Army Presidio of San Francisco, CA, 1st Cav Div., Sugamo Prison, Korea; Cmd. and Gen. Staff College; Chaplain School, Fort Slocum, NY; HQ USAREUR, Heidelburg, Germany.

Memorable experience was duty with the 6th Army Escort Det for the return to the US of those killed in the Pacific Theater.

Married and has two children and two grandchildren. Has held two pastorates after retiring: 1st Christian Church, Alameda, CA and 1st Christian Church, Oceanside, CA.

DAVID CLIFFORD CRUMMEY, Lieutenant Commander, born May 19, 1913, San Jose, CA, the son of John D. and Vivan Crummey. Attended the Univ of the Pacific, Stockton, CA; received his divinity degree at Boston Univ and then a master's in theology at Union Theological Seminary. The Univ of the Pacific awarded him a DD in 1958. He earned the Ph.D. from the Univ. of Chicago in 1961.

Served Methodist churches in Gerber and Mill Valley, CA before going into the service. After the war he was appointed to churches in Palo Alto, Stockton and Berkeley. For six years he was Methodist superintendent in San Francisco and then executive director of the Northern California Ecumenical Council for five years

In February 1943, Crummey was ordered to the Navy Chaplains School in Norfolk (school moved to the College of William and Mary before his class graduated) After a year at the NAS, St. Simons Island, GA, he was assigned to the USS *Estes* under construction in Brooklyn. The *Estes* carried RADM W H P Blandy who was in charge of bombing at Iwo Jima and Okinawa previous to landings. After a trip back to Alameda for repairs the ship started back to the Pacific War Zone just as the war ended. The new flag officer, RADM R.O Davis was ordered to the Philippines to help load troops to support Gen MacArthur in Japan. The ship was then sent to Shanghai, China, where he left it.

Memorable experience was celebrating the 50th anniversary of the *Estes'* commissioning in Newport, RI in 1994. Chaplain Crummey used the original commissioning prayer there.

Member of the MCA for most of 50 years. Married Ethel Elizabeth of Providence, RI in 1937. They have four children and 10 grandchildren. He lives with his wife in retirement in San Francisco.

THOMAS F. CURRIER, Colonel, born May 16, 1926, Mason City, IA. Graduated from Loras College, Dubuque, IA in 1946, St Louis Theological (Kenrick) Seminary in 1950. Ordained Roman Catholic priest, Dubuque Archdiocese, May 27, 1950. Commissioned chaplain in IANG, March 20, 1956, in 224th Engr Bn. (SCARWAF).

Reserve assignments from 1957-66: 103rd Inf. Div., 394th Engr. Bn. and 84th Div. (Trng.). Active duty assignments from 1966-72 were with 5th Inf Div. and 1st Inf. Div. in Vietnam (1967-68); Deputy Post Chaplain, Fort Irwin; Cbt. Developments Cmd, Fort Ord. Korea to I Corps Group, 7th Inf. Div and division chaplain of 2nd Inf Div. 103rd COSCOM USAR 1972-86. His memorable experience was TET Offensive 1968.

Promoted to colonel in 1976 and retired May 15, 1986. Awarded the Army Commendation Medal w/2 OLCs, Bronze Star w/OLC, Air Medal, Meritorious Service Medal, Legion of Merit, Vietnam Campaign Ribbon w/4 stars

Civilian assignments included pastorates, hospital chaplaincy and education.

VIRGIL WELDEN DALEY, Colonel, born May 29, 1923, Ellington, NY. Attended Anderson College; Theological Seminary, Anderson, IN, BTH, and various military schools. Joined the US Army on Oct 5, 1952.

Military Stations and Units. 41st FA GP and 653rd Obs. Bn, Fort Sill, OK; 11th Abn Div, Fort Campbell, KY (twice); 29th Inf and 8040th Rycom Ord. Svc., Okinawa; 82nd Abn. Div. Arty and 3rd USA Msl Cmd., Fort Bragg, NC; 42nd Arty., Frankfort, Germany, HQ USA Spt Cmd, Vietnam; HQ USAG and USA Northern Warfare Trng. Ctr, AK; USA Munitions Cmd., Picatinny Arsenal, NJ; Fort Buckner, Ryukyus Islands. He was discharged May 31, 1973, with the rank of colonel

Married Alice Van Hoose and has two sons and two grandsons. He has pastored churches in Louisiana, Maryland and Pennsylvania. Retired in March 1988

ROBERT DOUGLAS DANIELL, Lieutenant Colonel, a native of Birmingham, AL. He enlisted in the USAF, 1953-57, met and married his wife, Suzanne Fombellida, in La Rochelle, France (her hometown). Upon discharge he began his education for the ministry and was ordained in 1961 and commissioned chaplain, USAR in 1963. He served several pastorates before entering active duty in 1966.

Education includes a BA, Samford; M Div., NOBTS; MS, LIU; MA, Pepperdine; D.Min., Vanderbilt; American Institute of Family Relations; and training in Holistic Health and Addictions, with certification as an addictions counselor and clinical supervisor.

Served with the 36th Sig. Bn. in Vietnam; Army Avn Ctr., Fort Rucker; 4th and 1st Armd. Divs. in Germany; 101st Air Assault Div., Fort Campbell; and Walter Reed AMC.

Awards include the Legion of Merit, Bronze Star and Meritorious Service Medal w/OLC. Since retirement in 1982 from Walter Reed, he has served as a chaplain at the Soldier's and Airmen's Home, Washington, DC; program director of the Tri-Services Addictions Facility, Naval Hosp., Bethesda, MD; hospital chaplain and director of the Addictions Program at Charter Hosp., Savannah, GA

Resides in Savannah with his wife; they have two children and two grandchildren

FRANKLIN D. DANIELS, Lieutenant Colonel, born Dec. 3, 1933, Tarboro, NC Graduated from High Point College, 1959; Wesley Theological Seminary, 1963 and ordained a United Methodist minister. Received BA, M.Div, MA in Sociology and MA in marriage, family and child counseling.

Drafted into the US Army in 1956 and served with the 82nd Abn. Div. for two years. Volunteered for the Army Chaplaincy in 1967 and served with the 47th Engr. Bn.; 14th Inf Bn , 25th Inf Div. in Vietnam; 173rd Abn Bde., the 101st Abn Div.; 1st Inf. Div. (Fwd.) Germany, Director of Family Life Ctrs. in Stuttgart, Germany, Fort Bragg, NC and Seoul, Korea.

Awarded the Legion of Merit, Bronze Star w/V Device, Meritorious Service and Army Commendation Medals. Discharged in October 1991 with the rank lieutenant colonel.

Served as chaplain to the Methodist Home for Children, Raleigh, NC, 1963-67, and at civilian parishes in Hartwood and Springfield, VA and Grays Creek, Fayetteville, NC. Married since June 8, 1957, to Marjorie Alene Payne. They have one son and one granddaughter.

BERNARD L. DANNER, Colonel, born March 19, 1918, Rhinelander, WI. Attended Concordia College, Milwaukee; Concordia Seminary, St. Louis, MO; post graduate, Univ. of Nebraska.

Joined the service Aug 13, 1943, and served in both the Army and USAF. Stationed at Burtonwood, England; Tempelhof AB, Berlin; Samson AFB, NY; Keesler AFB, MS; Chin Hae and Pusan, Korea; Manhattan Beach AFS, NY; Ankara, Turkey He served with 55th Field Hosp., the 75th Air Depot Wing and others.

Memorable Experiences: re-uniting an American staff sergeant with his German fiancee in Berlin after seven years of separation; Istanbul, Turkey, private audience with Athenagoras, Patriarch of Orthodox Church.

Discharged from active duty, Feb. 28, 1958, and retired from the USAF March 19, 1978, with rank of colonel. Married Caroline Geres, Manhattan Beach AFS, NY, April 27, 1957. They have one son. He was a roving

pastor in Europe from 1958-1967; Lutheran Hosp. chaplain at VA hospitals in Chicago area 1967-. Retired Oct. 31, 1985.

CLAYTON E. DAY, Colonel, born Aug. 3, 1920, Grapeland, TX, and grew up in Palestine, TX Attended East Texas Baptist College and Baylor Univ., BS degree; Southwestern Baptist Theological Seminary, Th.B degree; Univ. of Wisconsin, graduate study in public relations, Basic and Career Courses, US Army Chaplain School; US Army Mgmt. School, Fort Belvoir, VA; US Army Cmd. and Gen. Staff College, Fort Leavenworth, KS, MS degree. Ordained to preach by First Baptist Church of Palestine and served pastorates in several Baptist churches before entering the Army Chaplaincy in 1949

Stationed on various US Army posts in Europe, Korea, Vietnam and the States. He has been staff chaplain, US Army 2nd Armd. Div.; XO, Office Chief of Chaplains, Washington, DC; post chaplain and chaplain in charge of Arlington National Cemetery, Fort Myer, VA; Corps Chaplain, XXIV Corps, Vietnam; and post chaplain, Fort Jackson, SC.

Honors include the Legion of Merit w/OLC, Army Commendation Medal w/OLC, Bronze Star, Army of Occupation Medal (Germany), Distinguished Unit Citation, Korean Presidential Unit Citation and Vietnamese Armed Forces Honor Medal. He received the honorary DD degree from Dallas Baptist Univ. in 1989.

Subsequent to military retirement, Dec 31, 1970, he was for nine years director of Institutional Resources at Southwestern Baptist Theological Seminary, Fort Worth, TX and for seven years vice-president for Administrative Affairs at Dallas Baptist Univ.

Active in civic organizations, served as Governor of the North Texas Dist. and currently is director of Evangelism and assistant to the executive director/treasurer for Baptist Convention of New York.

Married for over 48 years to Junita Virginia Dowdy until her untimely death. He has two grown sons and three grandchildren He recently wed Maxine Patrick Crouch.

EARL V. DEBLIEUX, Lieutenant Colonel, born Dec 22, 1931, Pittsfield, MA. Graduated from St Joseph's HS, 1951; Fordham Univ., Bronx, NY, 1956 with BA in history and philosophy; Our Lady of Angels Seminary, Niagara Falls, NY, 1960, with master's in Sacred Theology. Ordained a Catholic priest June 28, 1960. After two assignments at civilian parishes in the diocese of Springfield, MA, he was commissioned as a captain in the Air Force Chaplaincy in September 1964

Assignments include: Altus AFB, OK; Elmendorf AFB, AK, Ellsworth AFB, SD, Loring AFB, ME; Da Nang AB, RVN, Keesler AFB, MS; Wiesbaden AB, Germany; Reese AFB, TX; Lakenheath RAF, England; Langley AFB, VA, Incirlik AB, Turkey, Patrick AFB,

FL; Yokota AB, Japan, Keesler AFB, MS; and now at Fort Meade, MD. He spent 90 days at Guantanamo Bay, Cuba with Haitian humanitarian relief from December 1991-March 1992. Was the installation staff chaplain at Incirlik AB and Patrick AFB and the senior catholic chaplain at his other assignments.

Completed Air Cmd and Staff College in 1977 and Air War College in 1979. Awards include the Bronze Star, Meritorious Service w/7 OLCs, Air Force Commendation w/3 OLCs, Joint Service Achievement, Air Force Outstanding Unit Award w/valor device, National Defense Service, Vietnam Service w/4 devices, Foreign Decoration, Vietnam Medal of Honor, RVN Cross of Gallantry w/device, RVN Campaign Medal and several ribbons.

He is interested in travel, photography and music. Published a book of poetry, *Of Life and Love*, in 1970.

His parents have passed away, he has two older sisters, Marlee Manns and Rosemary Ditello, a younger brother, Donald; all are married with children.

JUANZEN KANADA DeGREY, Captain, born May 6, 1944, Idabel, OK. Received his M.Div, degree from seminary in Atlanta, GA. Joined the military service in September 1966 and served in the US Army and National Guard. Stationed at Fort Ord, Fort Lewis, Fort Lee and Korea. Served with the 87th Army, 2nd Army, 11th MN BN (NG). High light of his career was when chosen to be acting state chaplain in August 1990 for two weeks training at Fort Stewart, GA.

Retired Aug. 1, 1992, as captain. Married Dericka and has three children Employed 23 years as the Senior Recreation Center Director for city of Atlanta.

BERNARD M. DELOS, Colonel, born Sept. 16, 1918, Amsterdam, NY Educated at Siena College, Albany, NY; St. Joseph Seminary, Yonkers, NY; Catholic Univ., Washington, DC, STL degree

Served in the USAF from March 22, 1949, until retirement Sept. 1, 1975, as colonel. Stationed at Lowry AFB, CO; Kadena/Naha, Okinawa; Sampson AFB, NY; Randolph AFB, TX; Dhahran AB, Saudi Arabia; Turner AFB, GA; Hahn AB, Germany; Mitchel AFB, NY;

Westover AFB, MA; Wheelus AB, Libya; Walker AFB, NM, Gunter AFB, AL; HQ PACAF, Hickam AFB, HI, McGuire AFB, NJ

Awards: United Nations Medal, AF Longevity Service Ribbon, Korean Service Medal, National Defense Service Medal, Army of Occupation Medal, American Defense Service Medal, Presidential Unit Citation, AF Commendation Medal and Legion of Merit.

Life member of MCA, TROA and K of C, member of Rotary International, American Legion, VFW, Catholic War Veterans, AMVETS and Siena College and Catholic Univ. Alumni Assoc. After retirement he had pastoral assignments in Arlington, VA; volunteer chaplain for VA Medical Facility, District of Columbia; volunteer service in Fort Lauderdale, FL

WILLIAM G. DEVANNY, Colonel, born in Buffalo, NY on June 24, 1925. Upon graduation from high school, he served with the 17th Abn. in Europe during WWII and earned a field commission during the Battle of the Bulge

During his career as Army Chaplain, he served with the 504th AIR, 82nd Abn Div., Fort Bragg, NC; HQ, 24th Inf. Div. FECOM; 19th Inf , FECOM; 325th AIR, Fort Bragg, NC; HQ 10th Inf. Div., USAREUR, HQ, 87th Inf. Div USAREUR; 7th US Army NCO Academy, USAREUR; 101st Abn Div., Fort Campbell, KY; TUSLOG, Det 27, Ankara, Turkey; instructor, USACHS, Fort Hamilton, NY; Cbt Dev. Cmd., Fort Lee, VA, HQ MACV; director, Plans, Policy and Programs, Office Chief of Chaplains, Washington, DC; CONARC.

Awards: Bronze Star, ARCOM w/OLC, Purple Heart, Good Conduct, Combat Infantry Badge, Master Parachutist Badge, Vietnam Campaign Medal and Legion of Merit.

After discharge he entered Brown Univ. and earned his degree in 1949, attended Princeton Theological Seminary, graduating in 1951. Ordained into the ministry by the Presbytery of Elizabeth, NJ.

Chaplain Devanny was a graduate of the US Army War College, Class of 1966; he died while on active duty at Fort Monroe, VA on July 3, 1973.

MONROE DREW JR., Commander, born in Oakland, CA, in 1916; graduated from Univ of California at Berkeley; received M Div. from San Francisco Theological Seminary. Has done graduate work at Rutgers Univ and Princeton Theological Seminary. He is a signer of the MCA Congressional Charter, was editor of the *Military Chaplain* for many years and a member of the MCA Executive Committee.

As special projects officer on the staff of the Navy Chief of Chaplain, 1946-50, he edited the first *Navy Chaplain Newsletter*, produced the first recorded sacred music kit for chaplains, the first Navy Chaplain Corps poster series, and conceived and put into production the *For Which We Stand* Navy motion picture series. He also produced and narrated the films, *Navy Chapels in the Pacific*, *Of Monuments and Men* and wrote the script for *Thine is the Power in the Navy Goes to Church* film series In addition, he wrote the words and music for Padres of the Sea, a song for the *Navy Chaplain Corps*

During WWII he was the first chaplain assigned to Coast Guard HQ in Washington, DC and in the Pacific Fleet was the only chaplain to serve a single destroyer, the *Heywood L. Edwards*. As the last chaplain of the heavy cruiser *Chester*, he earned a commendation for organizing outstanding entertainment programs for Army as well as Navy units participating in the Occupation of Northern Japan

In 1959 he founded the AEREON Corp. of Princeton, NJ to develop more suitable aircraft for the world's developing countries. The company built and tested two proof-of-concept vehicles, one of which was successfully flown at the National Flight Experimental Center in Pomona, NJ

In 1972, he became national chaplain of the ROA and for the next 20 years served the ROA's Department of New Jersey as senior chaplain. They made him a "Minuteman" and in 1993 he was awarded an unusual distinguished service plaque. His word arrangement for Taps, *The Call Has Come*, was recorded and distributed nation-wide by the ROA and has been used in many ROA Memorial Day observances

Two of his 29 years of military service were spent in the AF, 1951-53, as chaplain of the 111th (L) BG, PA ANG, based at Philadelphia International Airport.

After retiring from the USN in 1976, he established the New Jersey Employee Advisory Service, a counseling program for all New Jersey state employees, retiring in 1991 as director of Employee Services for the state of New Jersey.

Married in 1939 to Dorothy Edna Langlois and they reside in San Antonio, TX. They have three children and eight grandchildren.

CLARENCE EDWARD DRUMHELLER, born June 2, 1922, Clifton Forge, VA, son of Zack and Bertha Drumheller. Graduated from Randolph Macon College, Ashland, VA in 1945 with a BA degree. Then in 1955 he graduated from Boston Univ School of Theology with M.Div. degree; ordained elder in the United Methodist Church and entered the AF as chaplain.

His most unforgettable experiences were in Korea as site chaplain of the 6314th Spt. Wg. (Osan, AB) for 13 months, 1961-62. He enjoyed the travel, fellowship with isolated groups of airmen in the remotest corners of Korea, and the friendships of many Korean people. While there he adopted a two year old Korean boy who returned with him to the States and became his third child (joining two daughters)

Stationed at Ardmore AFB, OK; Glasgow AFB, MT; Suffolk County AFB, L.I , NY; base chaplain at RAF Croughton, England and chaplain at RAF Upper Heyford, England. Returned to the States and was assigned to Hurlburt Field, FL. While there in 1969, he preached his sermon, *Honor To Whom Honor is Due*, in the base chapel and received the coveted first prize award given annually by the Freedoms Foundation at Valley Forge, PA for the best sermon of the year.

Next assignment was to Minot AFB, ND from which he retired in February 1975. Church activities included serving as assistant pastor at Trinity Methodist Church, Richmond, VA, 1941; pastor at Hi-Line Methodist Parish, MT, 1951-53; First Methodist, Clinton, MA, 1953-55, Bridger-Belfry UM Churches, 1958-59, Salem United Methodist Church, Virginia Beach, VA, 1984 Founded and ministered to Sunnyside Community Church, Virginia Beach, VA, 1985-88.

In civilian life he taught English in the Chesapeake Public schools for 10 years, 1976-87. Life member of TROA, American Legion, member of MCA and several professional organizations.

Due to the progression of Parkinson's disease and heart problems, he now ministers through his everyday life and freelance writing. Publishers include *The Upper Room, Purpose Magazine* and *Science of Mind*. Married to Geneva and has six children and 12 grandchildren.

JOSEPH A. DUNNE, born in New York City, NY Sept. 14, 1916. Ordained a priest May 30, 1942, and assigned to St Peter's Church, Poughkeepsie, NY. Commissioned a chaplain at West Point, July 21, 1944, and then served the 90th Inf. Regt. He joined the 250th FA Gp. participating in the Rhineland Campaign in Germany, 513th Prcht. Regt., 17th Abn. Div.; 506th Prcht. Regt., 101st Abn. Div. and 508th Prcht. Regt., 82nd Abn. Div which remained in Frankfurt as honor guard for Gen. Eisenhower until November 1946

Rejoining the 82nd Abn. in Fort Bragg, NC, he was given a RA Commission serving the 325th Abn. Regt. and was sent to Japan in 1948, HQ Kobe Base, and to Korea, July 12, 1950, HQ Pusan Log. Cmd., 21st Inf Regt., 24th Inf. Div. near the Yalu River Transferred to 187th Abn Inf Regt to make an airborne assault at Munsani on March 23, 1951 He was promoted to major and five days later, wounded by a land mine.

Hospitalized for a year at Phoenixville, PA, he returned to Fort Bragg as asst. Corps Chaplain, XVIII Abn. Corps, May 5, 1952, and retired for physical disability Aug 31, 1953. Awards include the Silver Star, Bronze Star, Purple Heart, Army Commendation Medal and Senior Parachutist Badge w/Arrow Head.

Back in New York he was assigned to St. John's parish, White Plains and appointed vice-chancellor of the Military Ordinariate and given the rank of monsignor. He became chaplain of the New York City Police Dept. on Sept. 8, 1958, with the rank of inspector; designed and directed the Counseling Service, recovering 2,000 police officers from alcoholism. He earned a MPA at John Jay College of Criminal Justice, founded the National Council of Compulsive Gambling and retired Dec. 30, 1981, after a small stroke

In Florida, he continues rehabilitating police officers Has suffered a more serious stroke limiting his function, but not his spirit He is single.

GEORGE H. DUPUIS, born Jan. 29, 1924, Hartford, CT. Completed elementary, high school, college, seminary and continuing education in Rome, Italy. Served 37 years in CAP as squadron chaplain, deputy wing chaplain, wing chaplain and summer encampment chaplain. He is a life time member of MCA.

Among his awards are the National Award, Catholic Youth Organization for God and Youth; CAP awards: Meritorious Service and Longevity Certificate.

Chaplain, 1982-94, Vermont State Fire Fighters Assoc.; Pastoral Care SV Medical Ctr , 1992-94; charter member and board of directors, 251 Club of Vermont; Weeks School chaplain for 10 years, state training for juvenile delinquents; diocesan moderator for Vermont Council of Catholic Women, 1976-94; diocesan spiritual director for Vermont World Apostolate of Fatima, 1977-94; diocesan moderator for Vermont and upper state of New Hampshire for St. John Therapist Councils; diocesan counselor; Dean of Bennington, Addison and Franklin Counties; Member of Presbyterian Council and executive committee, Vermont Council of World Affairs; and pastor of Saint Margaret Mary Church, 1982-present.

HENRY L. DURAND, Lieutenant Colonel, born June 17, 1916, St Benoit du Lac, Quebec, Canada. Educated at Rosary High, Holyoke, MA; LaSalette High, Enfield, NH; LaSalette College, BA; LaSalette Novitiate, Bloomfield, CT; LaSalette Seminary, Altamont, NY, Ph.B; St. Joseph Seminary, Trois Rivieres, Quebec, Canada; LaSalette Seminary, Attleboro, MA, Th.B. Ordained May 30, 1942.

Entered military in August 1944. Attended Basic Crs., Chaplain School, Fort Devens, MA; Career Crs., Chaplain School, Fort Slocum, NY and CGSC, Fort Leavenworth, KS. Other stations include: Camp Van Dorn, MA; Camp Swift, TX; Germany; France; London, England; Austria; Fort Dix, NJ, Fort Bragg, NC; Camp Stoneman, CA; Japan; Korea; Fort Campbell, KY; Fort Monroe, VA.

Retired June 1, 1968. Awards include the EAME Campaign Medal w/3 stars, WWII Victory Medal, Medal of Occupation (Germany), Bronze Medal of the French Reconnaissance, Parachute Badge, Korean Service Medal w/3 stars, Army Commendation Medal w/2 OLC, Bronze Star w/OLC, American Campaign Medal, National Defense Service Medal w/OLC, UN Service Medal and Legion of Merit

His memorable experience was serving I Corps in Korea and being chosen to be the Catholic chaplain aboard the ship which was taking back to the States the first group of our POWs returned to us by the North Korean

ROBERT M. DURKEE, Brigadier General, born in Belmont, MA, Nov. 8, 1926. Enlisted in the USN in 1944 and served as a gunner on an ammunition ship in the Pacific Theater where he participated in the invasion of Okinawa and the liberation of the Philippines. After the war, he made several trips to Japan and there witnessed the freeing of the POWs at Wakayama. He was among the first Americans to enter Hiroshima.

Graduated from Tufts College in 1950 and worked  for two summers directing a refugee camp for children in France Commissioned a 1st Lt in the USAF and later stationed in Texas, England and France.

Was rector of Grace Episcopal Church in Medford, MA for 25 years while also serving as division chaplain to the 26th (Yankee) Inf Div. as well as state military chaplain for the Commonwealth of Massachusetts Currently chaplain to the MOWW, the Lawrence Lightguard Armory, 1st Corps of Cadets in Boston and to the Ancient and Honorable Artillery Co. of Massachusetts, the oldest military organization in the country (charted in 1638). Also active in the New England Chapter of Military Chaplains

Father Durkee is married to Diane and they have two married children, Joseph and Sandra Rigazio III and Scott and Ellen Durkee, and two grandchildren.

Decorations and Awards Meritorious Service w/ OLC, Navy Medal, American Campaign, Asiatic-Pacific Campaign w/BBS, WWII Victory, Army of Occupation, Humanitarian Service Award, AF Service Ribbon, Armed Forces Reserve Medal with HG, ARCOM w/3 OLCs, Army Service Ribbon, Philippine Liberation Ribbon w/BBS, Philippine Independence Ribbon, Massachusetts Service Medal with Gold and Silver Star and Massachusetts Emergency Service Ribbon w/BS.

GERALD HENRY DZIEDZIC, Captain, born Aug. 11, 1947, Bristol, CT. Attended St. John Seminary, Brighton, MA, 1974, M.Div.

Joined the USAR, Jan. 6, 1968; served with 819th Sta. Hosp , 405th CSH, W. Hartford, CT. His memorable experiences are all the hours preparing soldiers from Massachusetts and Connecticut units going over to the Persian Gulf War. It was hectic and a time of confusion, excitement and worry.

Parish Catholic priest at St. Lawrence O. Toole, Hartford, CT, St Stanislaus, Bristol, CT; and is now priest director, Academy of Our Lady of Mercy HS, Milford, Ct.

FRANK HENRY EBNER, Colonel, born June 14, 1922, Elk River, MN, the son of Eric and Bernadette Ebner Attended St John's Univ., Collegeville, MN and St. Paul Seminary, St. Paul, MN. Ordained a priest May 31, 1947.

Was assistant pastor of St. Boniface Church Melrose, MN, 1947-51, when he began six years of active duty with the USAF. Stationed at Fort Slocum Chaplain's School, Lockborne AFB, OH, Johnson AFB, Japan with sub bases at Shiroi and Nugata and a dozen radar sites in the mountains; Manhattan Beach AFS processing to and from Europe, Africa, South America and the Arctic.

One of his most memorable experiences was when American fighter planes from Johnson AFB accompanied bombers from Yokota AFB on raids in Korea. He also had the privilege of offering Mass on top of Mount Fuji in Japan when he climbed with the choir and met many service people as they went overseas and returned Stateside.

Retired with the rank of colonel in 1982 after 30+ years in the USAFR. Awards include the National Defense, Korean Service, UN, Armed Forces Reserve, AF Longevity, Meritorious Service (USAF), (First Bronze Clasp, CAP), AF Outstanding Reserve Chaplain, 1973; Golden Crusader Awd., Venezuelan Mission, Special Service Awd. for the K of C, Clara Barton Centennial Honor Awd , Long Timers Awd ROA, Red Cross, CAP, Boy Scout, American Legion Americanism Awd and WCCO Radio Good Neighbor Awd.

Has BA degree plus four years of seminary, attended numerous military schools, three levels of AF Chaplain Schools, Instructor School, Squadron Officer School, Command and Staff College, War College, extension Institute Courses, Seminars, workshops, career development institutes, and many church related retreats, conferences and institutes.

Pastorates include St Francis Xavier Church, Sartell, MN; St Mary of Mt. Carmel Church, Long Prairie, MN; and St Andrew Church, Elk River, MN. He retired July 7, 1993.

Activities include membership in MOWW, American Legion, VFW, MCA, Northland Chapter (CAP), Chief of Chaplains (CAP), ROA, K of C, National Retired Teachers Assoc., Todd and Stearns County Historical Societies and St John's Univ. Associate and Catholic War Veterans.

LEONARD S. EDMONDS, Colonel, born in McLouth, KS, March 4, 1914. Graduated Park College 1935; Louisville Presbyterian Seminary, 1938; ordained and became supervisor for Council for Clinical training of Theological Students and Protestant Chaplain for District of Columbia prison system.

Commissioned in US Army Oct. 12, 1943. Subsequent assignments as chaplain included Laughlin and Randolph Fields, TX during WWII, 811th Engr. Avn Bn in Korea during Korean Conflict, and MACV HQ, Saigon during Vietnam War Other career assignments included Chanute, Sewart, Bolling, Andersen and Charleston AFBs; and ADS, MAC, TAC and AU HQ. Awards included Legion of Merit and Bronze Star

After retirement on May 31, 1973, he did graduate study, then worked for U and state of Arizona in vocational rehabilitation. Since second retirement in May 1980, has been a volunteer in church and community ministries, Tucson, AZ. Married to Virginia Saum and has two children and four grandchildren.

CHARLES W. EDWARDS JR., Lieutenant Colonel, born Dec. 2, 1943, Wharton, TX. Attended Southwestern Christian College, Terrell, TX, associate's degree in 1965; Jarvis Christian College, Hawkins, TX, bachelor's in 1970; Christian Theological Seminary in Indiana, master's in 1973; Austin Presbyterian Theological Seminary in Texas, doctorate's in 1989.

Military Schools: basic cbt trng , Fort Jackson, SC; AIT, Fort Dix, NJ, Armor Trng School, Fort Knox, KY; Chaplains Asst. School, Fort Hamilton, NY; Race Relations Discussion Leaders Crs., Fort Knox, Chaplain Officer Basic  Crs., Fort Wadsworth, NY; Fifth US Army Chaplain School/Conference; Annual Trng. Chaplain School/Conference, Fort Hood, TX; Hosp. Ministry and Pastoral Care Crs, Fort Sam Houston, TX.

Chaplain Officer Adv. Crs , Fort Monmouth, NJ; 49th Armd. Div. Chaplain School/Conference, Camp Mabry, TX; Chaplain Reserve Components General Staff Course, Fort Monmouth

Stationed in Camp Hovey, Korea; Camp Atterbury, IN, Fort Lewis, WA; San Antonio, TX; Austin, TX; Camp Mabry, TX; with present assignment as hospital chaplain with 217th Evac. Hosp., San Antonio, TX

Awards Army Commendation, Army Achievement, Good Conduct, Army Reserve Components Achievement, National Defense Service, Armed Forces Expeditionary, Armed Forces Reserve Medal, Army Service Medal, Overseas Service Medal and Texas Faithful Service Medal.

Member of DAV, MCA, Military Order of the Cootie, NGA of Texas and the USA, American Legion and VFW (national chaplain 1993-94) Civilian pastorates from 1968-92 in Texas, Illinois and Indiana. Since 1992 employed at William Jennings Bryan Dorn Veterans' Hosp., Columbia, SC, as staff chaplain.

HUBBARD SCUDDER EDWARDS, Captain, born in New Haven, CT, Aug. 9, 1928. Graduated from Rutgers Univ in 1951. He was called to active duty and served as a line officer with Service Force Atlantic Fleet and Commander Cruiser Destroyer Force Atlantic Fleet, with duty aboard USS *Chukawan* (AO-100), USS *Tidewater* (AD-31).

Released from active duty to attend Theological Seminary at Princeton and Bloomfield. He accepted a commission as chaplain USNR. Ordained in 1956 a Presbyterian minister at the Brick Presbyterian Church, NYC In April 1962 he was recalled to active duty and served as chaplain to the President with further orders to Destroyer Div. 102, aboard the USS *Joseph P. Kennedy* (DD-850). He continued to serve with Desron 10 until transferred to the USNH, Philadelphia, PA.

Released from active duty in 1968 but continued to serve as chaplain at Willow Grove, NAS, while serving as pastor at Grace Presbyterian Church, Jenkintown, PA. Remained at the Air Stations while serving as pastor at the First Presbyterian Church, Ridgewood, NJ.

Achieved the rank of captain while on the staff of the Naval Air Reserve Commander. Following his call to the South Salem Presbyterian Church, NY, he served as chaplain, Naval Submarine Base, New London, CT, Readiness Command Chaplain Region Two; Commanding Officer Naval Reserve Chaplain's Company, Fort Schuyler, NY, and chaplain, at Bethesda Naval Hosp.

Retired from the USN in July 1987 and retired from the Presbyterian Church, Marietta, GA.

Married Patricia Van Dyke and has four children: Amy Lynn Hilliard, Timothy, Mark, Alexander and four grandchildren: Chelsea, Jacob, Zachery and Kayla

JAMES R. EICHELBERGER, Lieutenant (jg), born May 27, 1954, Niagara Falls, NY. Attended Westminster Theological Seminary, Philadelphia, PA (D.Min.); Faith Theological Seminary, Elkins Park, PA (M Div.); Shelton College, Cape Canaveral, FL (BA).

Joined the service July 25, 1983, and served in the USNR Served with 4th MAF (Rel) 304 NAS Willow Grove, Willow Grove, PA; SURFLANTREL 104, Naval and Marine Corps Reserve Center, Wilmington, DE

Returned to Western New York in 1989 to pursue a career as minister, Evangelical Methodist Church; ministry as Christian counselor Christian Counseling Services of Greater Buffalo; consultant, program developer and planner, Niagara County Dept. of Mental Health, Alcohol and Drug Abuse

JAY HAROLD ELLENS, Colonel, born July 16, 1932, McBain, MI. Received BA in 1953; Th.B in 1956; M.Div. in 1982; Th M in 1965; Ph.D in 1970, Ph D in 1994. Joined the US Army on June 10, 1955. Served with the 1st Div., 8th Div., 8th Army, LAMC, C&GS, USAWC and NDU in the European Theater, Korea, Vietnam and Beirut Retired after 37 years with the rank of colonel in 1992.

Married Mary Joe Lewis Ellens on Sept. 7, 1954 They have six children and six grandchildren. Professor of Philosophy and Psychology and pastor. Retired July 16, 1992

JOHN A. ELLIOTT, Lieutenant, born Dec. 12, 1923, Hammett, ID. Received BA degree and BD degree from San Francisco Seminary Joined the USN in August 1951 and served in the Chaplain Corps. Discharged in August 1958 with the rank of lieutenant.

He and wife Elaine have two children and five grandchildren. Employed with Social Security Adm ; retired November 1972.

HAROLD T. ELMORE, Colonel, USAR, RET, is a life member of the MCA, joining in 1955. He was born at Seebert, WV on July 26, 1930; graduated from Hillsboro HS in 1948; Morris Harvey College in 1952; and Vanderbilt Univ in 1955. Served as campus pastor, local church pastor, and district superintendent in the WV Annual Conference of the United Methodist Church from 1955-93

As a 2nd lieutenant he attended the first Chaplain Basic Crs. for seminarians in the summer of 1954 at Fort Slocum. Commissioned a chaplain, 1st lieutenant, in 1955 and completed, in residence, both the Chaplain Career Crs. at Fort Hamilton in 1968 and C&GSC at Fort Leavenworth in 1972.

Served on active duty from 1959-62 at Fort Bragg; Thule, Greenland and Fort Benning. His reserve assignments were with the 83rd Inf. Div., 100th Div (trng.), 38th Ord. Gp., MOBDES 1st US Army, Fort Meade and IMA, Military Dist. of Washington, Fort McNair Retired in July 1990 with 34 years of service.

In the UMC he served as a member of the Division of Chaplains and Related Ministries, 1972-76, the 1984 and 1988 Northeastern Jurisdictional Conferences and Board of Trustees of WV Wesleyan College, 1979-94.

Awards and decorations include the Meritorious Service Medal, Army Commendation Medal, Alumni Key from Morris Harvey and a honorary degree from WV Wesleyan in 1982.

Married Sylvia Conklyn of Martinsburg, WV on Dec. 27, 1956; they have four children: Thomas, Wesley, Heather and Jonathan, and six grandchildren. His uncle, Maj Samuel Azo F. Wagner, served as chaplain during WWII, 1942-46, at Carlisle Barracks and Fort Lee. He was a Methodist pastor for over 50 years.

MILTON SIEBERT ERNSTMEYER, Captain, born Sept 16, 1916, Hayland, NE. Graduated from Concordia Seminary, St. Louis and ordained at St. Luke's Lutheran Church, St Louis, before being commissioned as a Navy chaplain for active duty in 1943.

With graduate degrees from Nebraska and Harvard Universities, he later received the DD degree from Concordia Seminary

During WWII he was assigned to the attack transport USS *Grimes* (APA-172) in WESTPAC. After serving several Marine Corps units and bases, he also became division chaplain for the 3rd Marines in Okinawa.

Other ship board assignments were on the USS *Philippine Sea* (CV-47), staff chaplain of landing ship Flotilla Two, the USS *Princeton* (CVS-7), as well as with the flagships of the 6th Fleet, the USS *Des Moines* (CA-137) and the USS *Springfield* (CGL-7).

Stateside assignments included those as staff chaplain for the Chief of Naval Air Trng., the District Chaplain for the 5th, 13th and the Naval Dist., Washington, DC.

Awards include the American Defense Service Medal, Asiatic-Pacific Campaign Medal, WWII Victory Medal, Navy Occupation Service Medal w/Asia Clasp and w/European Clasp, China Service Medal, National Defense Medal, Navy Commendation Medal and Letter of Commendation

Requested Navy retirement in 1972 to accept the call as executive director of Armed Forces Commission, LCMS as well as the LCMS staff member of DSMP, LCUSA Elected president of the MCA of the USA (1978). Retired in 1983 as executive secretary, Ministry to the Armed Forces, LCMS, and was honored with the Silver St. Martin of Tours Medal. He has written devotions for *Portals of Prayer* as well as articles and books, such as *They Shall Not March Alone*, a compilation of experiences of LCMS military chaplains since the Civil War.

Since retirement he and his wife Muriel reside in Myrtle Beach, SC. They have three married daughters and six grandchildren.

DOUGLAS A. ETTER, Captain, born Oct. 22, 1960, Butler, PA. Received BA from Grove City College in 1982 and M.Div from Princeton Theological Seminary Joined the USARNG on Aug. 23, 1985; served with 50th Armd. Div Arty., 3/126 Inf. 38th Div ; 1/107 FA 28th Div., stationed in Trenton, NJ; Grand Rapids, MI; Pittsburgh, PA.

His memorable experience was organizing and administering a support group for families of all military branches during Desert Shield/Storm.

He has two children, Bruce and Erin, and is pastor of Leesburg Presbyterian Church.

LESTER G. FELKER, Colonel, born Feb 27, 1931, at Oshkosh, WI Attended Northwestern College in Minneapolis and Trinity Seminary in Chicago; was ordained Sept 15, 1956, and pastored churches in Polk and Clarks, NE and Flint, MI. Served seven years in the USNR as an airplane mechanic and eight years in the USAR as a staff specialist, then chaplain. He entered the USAF on active duty in October 1963

Assignments included Keesler AFB, MS, Kadena AB, Okinawa; Grand Forks AFB, ND; Shemya AFB, AK; Lackland AFB, TX; Ramstein AB, Germany; Air Reserve Personnel Ctr , Lowry AFB, CO, and Wright-Patterson AFB, OH Retired with the rank of colonel in February 1984.

Currently serving as executive pastor at Faith Presbyterian Church in Aurora, CO. He and his wife Gloria have five sons, three grandsons and three granddaughters.

HARRY FISTER FENSTERMACHER, Lieutenant Commander, born March 21, 1913, Hamburg, PA. Graduate of Ursinus College, Collegeville, PA and Lancaster Theological Seminary, PA of the United Church of Christ

Served as a chaplain in the USN from Dec. 8, 1943-Jan. 1, 1964 Stationed at NTC, Camp Peary, VA, NAS, Whiting Field, FL, NAS, Oceana, Virginia Beach, VA, 2nd Mar Div and Naval Hosp., Camp Lejeune, NC; NTC, Bainbridge, MD; Naval Hosp., Key West, FL.

Made landing with 1st Mar. Div. at Okinawa, April 1, 1945, was with them through the taking of the Island, the end of the Pacific War and the occupation of North China which followed while stationed in Tientsien. Division received Presidential Unit Citation.

Served in the USS *Mississippi* (EAG-128), 1948-50; the Korean War, 1952-53 with 1st MAW and received Bronze Star for meritorious service; NAS, Atsugi, Japan, 1956-58, USS *General J C. Breckinridge*, 1960-62, MSTS, Pacific Retired as LCDR, USN, Jan. 1, 1964.

Married Harriett and has two step-daughters, four step-grandchildren and three step-great-grandchildren. He is interim pastor, UCC Churches in and near St. Petersburg, FL and associate pastor, First Congregational UCC, 1968-80, St. Petersburg Retired Dec. 1, 1980

LAWRENCE R. FENTON, Lieutenant Colonel, born Oct. 30, 1936, in Santa Barbara, CA Graduated Santa Barbara HS, 1955, Pasadena/Point Loma Nazarene College, San Diego, CA, with BA; Nazarene Theological Seminary, Kansas City, KS, with M.Div in 1968; and one year CPE education at Yale New Haven Medical Center, CT, 1982-83

Enlisted with the USAF and served four years active duty as air traffic controller. Then entered the US Army chaplaincy July 4, 1975 From 1972-92 he was stationed at Fort Riley, KS; Korea; Fort Carson; Fort Ord, MEDDAC, Camp King, Oberursel, West Germany, 4 TRANSCOM Chaplain; Fort Hood, TX; and Yuma Proving Ground Post Chaplain, 1992-94.

Awarded the Legion of Merit, Meritorious Service w/3 OLCs, Army Commendation w/3 OLCs and Good Conduct Medals, the Army Service Ribbon, AF Longevity Ribbon and Overseas Ribbon w/#3.

He and Janet Tedman were married Dec. 12, 1963, and have four children: L. Richard Jr., Jon D., Amber J. and LeAnn K.; daughter-in-law Delna, and grandson Thane. Since 1994 he has been pastoring the Los Banos Church of the Nazarene in California.

THOMAS M. FIALKOWSKI, Lieutenant Colonel, Born Jan. 25, 1940, in Erie, PA Received BA from St. Bonaventure Univ.. Joined the USAR on July 19, 1978; stationed with 99th ARCOM, Oakdale, PA; and served with 339th Gen. Hosp., 475th QM GP

His memorable experience was working with the Haitian and Cuban migrants at Guantanamo, Cuba. Discharged with the rank lieutenant colonel. He is pastor of Our Lady of Mt. Carmel Catholic parish.

CHARLES E. FIX, Colonel, born Sept. 20, 1924, in Cincinnati, OH. Drafted March 17, 1943, and served with the 8th Armd. Div. at Fort Polk, LA Departed Nov 6, 1944, for Southampton, England and the ETO. Following V-E Day he served with the Army of Occupation in France and Czechoslovakia Returned to the US and was discharged Feb. 6, 1946 as tech sergeant.

He will always remember the thrill of V-E Day as an enlisted man and the horror at seeing concentration camps in Germany.

Attended Lakeland College and United Theological Seminary, graduating in 1953. Ordained in the Evangelical and Reformed Church which eventually became the United Church of Christ He served in parishes in Andrews, IN and Louisville, KY.

Recalled to active duty June 20, 1960, at Fort Belvoir, VA. Additional Stateside assignments were Fts. McNair, Knox, Benning and Gillem (Atlanta Army Depot) Overseas tours were 809th Engr. Bn. in Thailand, 18th Engr. Bde. in Vietnam and Msl Spt. Cmd in Italy Retired Feb 1, 1977, as colonel. Married Irma M. Scheve in 1947 and has two children and one grandchild.

MARTIN M.P. FLEMING, Colonel, born Feb 22, 1927, in St. Paul, MN. Attended Nazareth Hall Preparatory Seminary, 1940-45; St. Paul Seminary, BA, church history and classical languages, 1948; ordained June 7, 1952, St. Paul Cathedral. Pastoral associate at Basilica of St. Mary, Minneapolis and St. Mary's Shakopee and chaplain, Minnesota State Reformatory for Women.

Joined the Army Reserves, Oct 9, 1959; commissioned 1st lieutenant USAR Chaplain Corps with active duty from June 6, 1967-March 1, 1992. Duty as brigade chaplain, deputy post chaplain and community chaplain at Fort Carson, CO; Fts Wainwright and Richardson in Alaska; 9th Inf. Div., Tan An RVN; Cambodia, Kaiserslautern, Stuttgart and Hanau in West Germany; Fts. Benning, McPherson and Gordon in Georgia; and Fort Belvoir, VA. Retired March 1, 1992, as colonel.

Presently co-pastor of St. Mary's Convalescent Home and senior resident of Bethany Village, a cluster of homes near the Cathedral of St Paul, which encourages Catholic communal living and he is coordinator, Bethany Manor and Coach House.

EMMETT OWEN FLOYD, Rear Admiral, born March 21, 1928, in Griffin, GA. Received BA from Mercer Univ. in 1948; M.Div. from Southern Theological Seminary, Louisville, KY, 1951, and S.T.D., San Francisco Theological Seminary, San Anselmo, CA in 1973.

Commissioned LTJG, CHC, USNR on May 12, 1952, USMC recruit TD, Parris Island, SC, September

1952-March 1953; 7th Mar Regt., 1st Mar. Div. (Korea), April 1953-April 1954; 2nd Mar. Div., Camp Lejeune, NC, April 1954-July 1954. Recalled to active duty in March 1962; MAG 26, New River, NC, March 1962-December 1963; USS *Okinawa* (LPH-3), January 1964-July 1965; RAD, July 1965 Memorable experiences: service with Marines in combat, being first chaplain assigned to a MAG, and serving as director of Naval Reserve Chaplains, 1981-84.

Retired from USNR Dec 1, 1984 Decorations include the Legion of Merit, Commendation Medal w/ Combat V, Navy Unit Commendation, National Defense w/star, Armed Forces Expeditionary, Korean Service w/ 2 Battle Stars, Armed Forces Reserve w/2 Hour Glasses, United Nations, and Korean Presidential Unit Citation.

Served parishes in Georgia, Florida and North Carolina; conference minister (CEO), Southeast Conference, United Church of Christ; president, United Church Board for World Ministries and selected as "Atlanta's Outstanding Young Man of the Year in 1959."

LOWEL D. FOSTER, Colonel, born Oct. 28, 1932, in Elmore County, AL. Graduated HS, 1949; received BA from Trevecca Nazarene College, Nashville, TN, 1953; attended Nazarene Theological Seminary in Kansas City, MO and obtained M Div. in 1956. Ordained clergyman of the Church of the Nazarene and pastored for 10 years in Georgia.

Entered the Air Force as captain on May 7, 1966, and first assignment after Chaplain School was Shaw AFB, SC, 1966-68. Completed Squadron Officer School Resident Crs. and from 1968-92 served at Osan AFB, South Korea; March AFB, CA; Wheeler AFB, Hawaii; Air Cmd. and Staff College Resident Crs.; Andrews AFB, MD, AF Inspection and Safety Ctr., Norton AFB, CA, deputy command chaplain with US Forces at Yongsan Army Installation, Seoul, South Korea; chief of personnel and inspections in the command chaplain's office, TAC, Langley AFB, VA; installation staff chaplain, Kirtland AFB, NM; and last position of command chaplain, AF Military Personnel Ctr., Randolph AFB, TX. Retired in September 1992.

Married to the former Inez Miller of Winchester, VA and they have a daughter Pamela and a son Brent

JAMES L. FOX, Lieutenant Colonel, born March 4, 1930, in Hale Center, TX. Received BA, BD and M.R.E. degrees. Joined the USAF in November 1958; stationed at Maxwell AFB; Goose Bay AB; Yokota AB, Japan; Radar Sites, Michigan; Bolling AFB, DC; Osan AB, Korea and Lackland AFB, TX. Served with Air Univ.; ADC; SAC; PACAF; Mil. Dict. of DC; ATC.

His memorable experience was meeting the air evac flights from Vietnam while he was at Yokota AB, Japan. Discharged in November 1978 with the rank lieutenant colonel.

As a civilian he was pastor at West Glendale Baptist Church, Glendale, AZ and First Baptist Church, Sun City, AZ and last position as pastor at South Reno Baptist Church, Reno, NV. Retired in October 1992.

He and wife Betty have two children and two grandchildren

PAUL J. FREEMESSER, Lieutenant Colonel, born Nov. 9, 1933, in Rochester, NY. Graduate of Theology School, he joined the US Army on Dec. 17, 1964, and served with the 98th Div (TNG-ENGR), USARSO, Garrison, Fort Sam Houston

Military stations include Fort Dix, West Point, Fort Leonard Wood, Walter Reed Hosp., Fort Devens, Fort Drum, Seneca Depot, Indiantown Gap, Fort Davis, Fort Sherman, Fort Clayton, Gorgas Hosp., Howard and Allbrook AFBs and Rodman Naval Base.

He was in the 98th Div. (Rochester, NY) from 1964-87; Panama from 1987-90; Fort Sam Houston, June 1990-December 1991. IRR to retirement Nov 9, 1993. Memorable experiences include being the second Catholic priest assigned to West Point in 1971; assisting in Panama and invasion; anointing Navy lieutenant at Gorgas Hosp (DOA); saying mass for PW camps (5,000-8,000) and providing mass for captured PDF officers at Clayton Detention Center for four weeks. Spent his whole career as a troop chaplain and garrison pastor

SHARON MAY FREETO, Lieutenant Colonel, born June 7, 1948, in Laconia, NH Received AB from Syracuse Univ.; Th.M from Boston Univ., and MA from Ball State Univ..

Joined the USAF on April 16, 1976 Stationed at Mississippi, Germany, Korea and Texas. Her memorable experience was remote duty in Korea and being the first United Methodist clergywoman to serve as AF chaplain.

Still on active duty, she is married to William R. Irwin and has two step-children

EUGENE W. FRIESEN, Colonel, born 1929 in Madrid, NE. Graduated with BA from Owosso Bible College and Taylor Univ.; Ph D from Michigan State Univ., and D.Min. from the Jesuit School of Theology at Berkeley.

Commissioned a chaplain in 1953 and assigned to Infantry Division at Fort Jackson, SC; Munich, Germany; Fort Ord, CA; and he was with the 82nd Abn. Inf Div at Fort Bragg, NC from 1956-58

Active duty for five years and reservist for 30 years Initially with an artillery unit, he served 19 years as a psychology instructor at the US Army Chaplain School and six years with the Health Command, finishing his final tour of duty at Triper Hosp. in 1988.

In addition to being a licensed psychologist, he is an ordained minister in the United Methodist Church and is the founding pastor of the Fountain of Life UMC. He and wife Leta have three children and three grandchildren.

IVAN RICHARD FULLER, Capatain, born Feb. 7, 1936, in Lafayette, IN Received BA from Butler Univ and M.Div from Christian Theological Seminary Joined the USN on June 29, 1965; student at Chaplain School in 1966 and again for advance course 1978-79

Military stations from 1966-92: Destroyer Sqdn. 16, Mayport, FL; Clarksville Base, TN; USS *Sanctuary* (AH-17) Vietnam, MCRD, Parris Island, SC; 3rd Mar. Div., Okinawa; Naval Training Center, Great Lakes, IL; 2nd FSSG, Camp Lejeune, NC; USS *Nimitz* (CVN-68); assistant force chaplain, Surface Forces Atlantic; Marine Corps Air Station, Cherry Point, NC; and in USS *Theodore Roosevelt* (CVN-71). Still on active duty with the rank of captain, he has been at the National Naval Medical Center, Bethesda, MD, since 1992.

Medals: Legion of Merit, two Meritorious Service Medals, three Navy Commendation Medals.

Civilian employment included pastor of Alaska Christian Church and Olive Christian Church, Morgan County, IN (1957-59); associate minister of First Christian Church, Marion, IN (1959-61); pastor of Champion Christian Church, Warren, OH (1961-66). Married to Valre Jean (Belden) Fuller and has five children and five grandchildren.

WILLIAM H. GARRETT, Sergeant, USAF, born Feb. 24, 1947, in Akron, OH, and raised in Luxembourg, Europe. Served in the USAF from March 23, 1971-Dec. 15, 1977, was assigned to 432nd CSG, 1606 SPS Keflavik (PACAF); and served in Southeast Asia as a K-9 security policeman and at NORAD Cheyenne Mtn. as well as in Iceland and New Mexico.

Obtained an AA in criminal justice at College of the Redwoods and a BA in theology at another college He is a licensed pastoral counselor/temperament therapist by the NCCA and will be pursuing an M Div. or master's degree in the future.

Commissioned a 1st lieutenant with the CAP in 1993, he serves as CAP chaplain. He is also a chaplain at San Jose International Airport in San Jose, CA Some of his awards are the Vietnam Cross of Gallantry w/palm Unit Citation, Expert Markmanship Ribbon, AF Good Conduct Medal, National Defense, Vietnam Campaign Ribbon and Vietnam Service Award.

Married Janet and they currently reside in Mountain View, CA He works full-time for the 129th Rescue and Recovery Group, Security Police at Moffett Field

GORDON E. GARTHE, born June 8, 1931, in Traverse City, MI. Graduate of Candler School of Theology, he earned BS from Western Michigan Univ., M.Div. from Emory Univ., MA from Univ. of Oklahoma, D.Min. from San Francisco School of Theology.

A naval aviator during the Korean War, he returned to serve as United Methodist (Florida Conference) Navy

Chaplain during Vietnam and remaining on active duty until his retirement as commander in 1983 Duty stations were the 3rd MAW, El Toro; 1st MAW, Da Nang; NAS, Corpus Christi, Naval Station Guam; Naval District, Washington; Fleet Religious Support Activity, Charleston, Naval Station Norfolk.

Garthe was chaplain to the Corps and Director of Religious Activities at The Citadel from 1983-90 Personal decorations include the Navy Commendation w/ Combat V and the Meritorious Service Medal.

Married to the former Jeane Lawrence of Norfolk, VA. They have five children and reside in Sedona, AZ, where they serve the Episcopal Church

ALVIN J. GILLIAM, Lieutenant Colonel, born May 13, 1921, at Westmoreland, TN. Graduated from Kentucky Wesleyan College in 1943 and the Candler School of Theology, Emory Univ., GA, in 1946. Ordained a United Methodist minister in 1945, and served as a civilian pastor in Tennessee and Kentucky from 1946-53 and later from 1976-83.

Commissioned as a chaplain in the USAF in 1953 and served until 1976. Assignments included tours of duty in Oklahoma, Texas, Morocco, Hawaii, New Hampshire, Alaska, Mississippi, Thailand and California. Upon retirement in 1976 in the rank of lieutenant colonel, he received the AF Commendation Medal for Meritorious Service. Dr. Gilliam was also awarded the honorary degree of Doctor of Divinity from Kentucky Wesleyan College in 1978.

Married to Mary Catherine Hacker in 1944 and they have two daughters and three grandsons Since retirement in 1983, they have resided at Henderson, KY.

CHARLES H. GLAIZE, Lieutenant Colonel, born Feb 2, 1916, Strasburg, VA. Graduated Strasburg HS, 1935; AB from Emory and Henry College, Emory, VA, 1940; BD from Candler School of Theology, Emory Univ., Atlanta, GA, 1942; Chaplain School, Harvard Univ. in May 1943, and ordained elder, United Methodist Church, Virginia Conference, Richmond, VA, February 1943

Called to active duty in the US Army in May 1943; assigned to 16th Armd. Div., Camp Chaffee, 25th Inf. Div., 967th AAA Gun Bn in the South Pacific, 1944-46; and discharged in June 1946. Teacher and Dean of Men, Ferrum Jr College, 1946-48; recalled in September 1948 to 3rd Armd. Div., Fort Knox

Transferred to AF as regular AF chaplain in August 1949. Stationed at Lackland AFB, (1951) Sampson AFB; (1952) wing chaplain, Laredo AFB; (1953) 6146th AF Advisory Gp ; (1954) reassigned to Lackland AFB; (1955) wing chaplain, Dover AFB; (1958) wing chaplain, Wheeler AFB; (1961) wing chaplain, Mather AFB; (1964) wing chaplain, Homestead AFB; (1967) senior installation chaplain, RAF Bebtwaters, England.

Participated in the 25th anniversary of D-day in Normandy, June 1969. In 1970 was senior Protestant chaplain, Eglin AFB, FL. Retired as lieutenant colonel on Sept 1, 1973, with over 28 years of active duty.

Married Nancy Robertson on June 16, 1948. They have four children: Beth Butler, Charles Jr., John and Edward, and 10 grandchildren. Since retirement he has preached in three nearby Presbyterian churches.

BERNARD CHARLES GOERTZ, Colonel, born July 4, 1928, in Red Rock, TX. On Sept 15, 1941 (at the tender age of 13) he entered St. John's Seminary in San Antonio, TX and was ordained a priest for the Diocese of Austin on May 31, 1952.

While serving as associate pastor of St. Mary's Church in Temple, he was commissioned a chaplain (1LT) in the TXNG on Dec. 1, 1954. After seven years of reserve service and while serving as pastor of St. Mary's Church in Lampasas, he was mobilized into federal service with the 49th Armd. Div. at Fort Polk, LA, on Oct. 15, 1961, when the Berlin Wall went up. Remained on active duty for 23 years, retiring from Fort Sam Houston, TX on June 30, 1984, with the rank of colonel.

While on active duty Chaplain Goertz served overseas for six years in Germany with the 4th Armd. Div. at Zirndorf and Bamberg, with the 8th Inf. Div. in Bad Kreuznach, and with the 130th Gen. Hosp. in Nurnberg. Spent one year in Vietnam with the 54th Arty Gp. at Xuan Loc, five months in Honduras with the 41st Cbt. Spt. Hosp. at Palmerola AFB near Comayagua.

Stateside assignments were to Fort Polk, LA; William Beaumont Army Medical Center in El Paso, TX; the Chaplain School at Fort Hamilton, NY; Dugway Proving Ground, UT; Walter Reed Army Medical Center in Washington, DC; and Fort Sam Houston, TX.

In retirement Chaplain Goertz serves as a permanent "floating replacement" throughout the Diocese of Austin, filling in for priests while they are on sabbatical, vacation, sick leave, etc. He lives with two dogs and a cat in his own home on 10 acres of land near Bastrop, just a few miles from his childhood home.

RALPH A. GOFF, Lieutenant Colonel, born May 4, 1927, in Oklahoma and served in Germany with the 309th Regt., 78th Inf. Div. in 1945. Following graduation from Oklahoma Baptist Univ. and Southwestern Baptist Seminary, he was ordered to active duty as a chaplain at Fort Sill, OK.

During his army career his assignments included the 14th Armd Cav. Regt., 82nd Abn. Div., 503rd Abn. Battle Gp., 101st Abn. Div. and 7th Corps. Staff assignments included post chaplain, Fort McClellan, AL; assistant corps chaplain, 7th Corps and Kaiserslautern (Germany) Support Group Staff Chaplain.

Retired a lieutenant colonel in 1973 and served Baptist churches in Arkansas and Arizona. He lives in Rogers, AR and has five children (son Matthew is an Army Chaplain with the 82nd Abn. Div.) and 11 grandchildren.

GEORGE WALTER GOODLEY, Lieutenant Colonel, born June 11, 1912, in Bethel Twp., Delaware County, PA. Graduated Chester, PA, High School in 1929; Penn State Univ., 1933, AB, Temple Univ., STB, 1939 and STM, 1954. Joined the USAAC on April 17, 1942, stationed at Randolph Field, TX; and served with Air Trng. Cmd and overseas duty with the Air Trans. Cmd. in North Africa, Middle East and the Persian Gulf. Also had temporary duty in Saudi Arabia.

Memorable Experiences. becoming post chaplain at Randolph Field after only four months in the service, visits to Holy Land on military missions; and his 11 months of duty in Egypt. Discharged March 1, 1946, as lieutenant colonel and retired from USAR June 11, 1972

Command and General Staff School for several summers, taught C & AS courses and chaplain courses. Served eight years on original State Human Relations Commission of Delaware by appointment of the governor, 1962-70. Was pastor of the UMC from 1937-77.

Married Margaret Elizabeth Brown and has two children and two grandchildren.

DAVID E. GRAETZ, 2nd Lieutenant, USAR and Captain, KYNG), born Jan. 1, 1957, at Montgomery, AL, the son of Robert and W. Jean (Ellis) Graetz Attended Circleville Bible College, Circleville, OH and Ashland Theological Seminary, Ashland, OH Ordained in the Brethren Church on Nov. 15, 1987.

Served as senior pastor at Highland Brethren Church in Marianna, PA from 1986-1990. Completed a residency year in CPE at Riverside Methodist Hosp in Columbus, OH, and was employed as a staff chaplain at the Louisville VA Medical Center in Louisville, KY in 1992 where he currently serves. Chaplain Graetz enlisted in the USN in 1975 as an aviation structural mechanic in hydraulics. He served his four year enlistment with Patron Sqdn 24 (VP-24). Stationed in Jacksonville, FL (NAS JAX) and went on three deployments, two to Sigonella, Sicily and one to Keflavik, Iceland Served his last two and a half years as a 2nd mechanic on the P3C aircraft flight crew After being honorably discharged, he spent five years in the USNR and achieved the rank of PO1/c

In 1984 Chaplain Graetz was commissioned 2nd lieutenant in the USAR as a chaplain candidate He joined the ARNG in 1985 and was commissioned a chaplain in 1989. He served in Ohio, Pennsylvania and Kentucky National Guards and currently holds the rank of captain.

Awards include the Army Commendation Medal, Army Achievement Medal, Navy Good Conduct Medal, Army Component Achievement Medal w/OLC, Navy Reserves Meritorious Service Medal, National Defense Service Medal, Armed Forces Reserve Medal, Army Service Ribbon, Kentucky Service Ribbon w/2 OLCs, Navy Meritorious Unit Commendation, Navy Battle Efficiency "E" Ribbon and the Navy Aircrew Insignia.

Member of the National Association of Brethren Church Elders, life member of the MCA, member of National Assoc. of Veterans Affairs Chaplains, the KYNGA and USNGA.

Married to Gale Unger and has two daughters, Sarah and Rachel.

RICHARD PONTER GRAVES, Captain, born Dec. 25, 1952, in Pine Bluff, AR. Graduated Pine Bluff HS in 1971; Univ. of Arkansas in Monticello with BA in history in 1983; and Concordia Seminary, St. Louis, MO with M.Div. in 1989. Ordained into the ministry of LCMS July 23, 1989, Trinity Lutheran Church, Pine Bluff, AR.

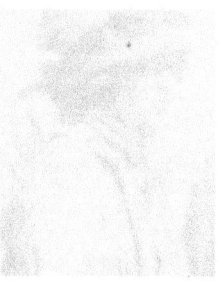 

Joined the US Army on May 9, 1985; stationed at Fort Hood, TX, and served with IRR, 1985-89; 1/127th FA, 35th ID, KSARNG, Ottawa, KS, 1989-93; 1/8 Cav., 2nd Bde, 1CD Fort Hood, TX, 1993-present. Memorable experience was his introduction to prison ministry at Fort Leavenworth, KS, in 1986 and to hospital ministry BAMC, Fort Sam Houston in 1989.

Civilian Employment: musician (1971-82); department manager, Wal-Mart (1982-84), field worker, Chapel of the Cross Lutheran Church, St. Louis, MO (1984-89); vicar, Our Savior's Lutheran Church, Sheboygan, WI (1987-88); pastor, Trinity Lutheran Church, Burlington, KS (1989-93).

Married Renita Gayle Norton on July 23, 1978, and has three children: William Richard, Shaun Matthew, and Laura Michelle Gunter Graves.

PHILIP LAMBETH GREEN, Colonel, born Sept 15, 1914, at Leicester, Buncombe County, NC. Educated at Guilford College, NC, 1936; Phillips Univ College of Bible, 1951, Ed for ordination

Joined the USAAC and USAF, June 19, 1943. Assignments from 1943-63: Harvard Univ., MA; Grand Central Air Term, Glendale, CA; Ontario AAF, CA, Avon Park AAF, FL, Page Field, Fort Myers, FL, MacDill Field, FL; Rhein-Main AB, Frankfurt, Germany; Hoersching AB, Linz, Austria; Bad Kissingen AB, Germany, Wiesbaden AB, Germany, Vance AFB, OK, Spence Field, Moultrie, GA; Parks AFB, CA; Joint US Military Gp., Madrid, Spain; Whiteman AFB, KnobNoster/Sedalia, MO, USAFA, Colorado Springs, CO and Kincheloe AFB, MI. Retired July 31, 1963, as colonel.

Memorable Experiences Berlin Airlift, 1948-49; National President, MCA, 1970-72; Host Committee

Chair of MCA Conventions 1968, 1978, 1988; Founder "Operation Southern Hospitality" for MDAP pilots training in USA, Spence Field, Moultrie, GA; music director, 1st USAF Spiritual Life Conf., Ridgecrest, NC.

Married to Lois Dawson Ritter from 1936-88 and to Helen Thompson McMillan since 1989. He has three children, eight grandchildren and five great-grandchildren.

DELBERT W. GREMMELS, Colonel, born Feb. 19, 1930, in St. Louis, MO Received BA, BD, M.Div. (Concordia Seminary, St. Louis) and MA (Monterey Institute Foreign Studies, Monterey, CA, Army War College). Joined the US Army on Jan. 3, 1959

Served as chaplain at Fort Hood, TX; 46th FA GP, Germany; 194th Armd Bde., Fort Ord, CA; MACV Advisory Team #33, Ban Me Thout, Vietnam; 1st Log Cmd, Long Binh, Vietnam, Army Chaplain School, Fort Hamilton, NY, Chief of Chaplains Office, Washington, DC, Defense Language Institute, Monterey, CA; director, Religious Resource Ctr., Munich, Germany, and post chaplain and command chaplain, US Army Msl Cmd., Redstone Arsenal, AL Memorable experience: serving troops at 31 different locations in Vietnam; as instructor of religions and cultures at US Army Language School, Presidio of Monterey, CA, and instructor at Army Chaplains School. Left the service Aug. 1, 1985, as colonel.

Pastor of Holy Trinity Lutheran Church, Gulfport, MS, retired Dec. 31, 1994. Married Lela and has three children and four grandchildren.

FRANK R. GRIEPP, Colonel, born Aug. 6, 1913, in Wisconsin. Earned his BA degree in history at the Univ. of California; theological training at North Central Bible College in Minneapolis; commissioned in the Chaplain Corps in July 1944 Graduated from the Chaplains School at Fort Devens, MA, Advanced Crs. at Fort Slocum, NY; and from the Command and General Staff College at Fort Leavenworth, KS. Stateside tours of duty include Camp Shelby, MS, Fort Lee, VA; Fort Meade, MD; Hospital Chaplain at Fort Belvoir, VA; Arlington Hall, VA; Fort Ord, CA; and as post chaplain at the Presidio of Monterey, CA.

Overseas tours of duty were in the Pacific Ocean area at the end of WWII and through 1947, as regimental chaplain of the 10th Inf. in Germany, 1953-56 Prior to that as chaplain for the 7th Cav. Regt. in the first year of the Korean War. Most memorable of his entire military ministry was that privileged duty with one combat unit moving up and down the whole Korean Peninsula. Frequent meetings with the surviving veterans of that unit, including present ministry to them, form the highlights of his retirement years.

Awarded the Bronze Star with "V" for Valor for heroism in ground combat near Yongpyong, Korea. He pastored churches in Minnesota for several years and retired with a total of 29 years of active and reserve duty.

Married Muriel over 58 years ago and has three children and six grandchildren.

HERMAN E. GROSSMAN, Lieutenant Colonel, born Nov 7, 1922, in Boston, MA. Graduated from Harvard with the Class of 44; enrolled in the Jewish Theological Seminary in Manhattan, graduated the Hebrew Teachers College with bachelor of religious education.

Joined the US Army in August 1947; stationed at Fort Jackson, SC Joined USAF in 1947, stationed at Keesler AFB, MS, and discharged from active duty in August 1949. Retired from USAFR on Oct 30, 1993

Memorable experience was being Jewish chaplain at the dedication of "4 Chaplain Stamp" in St. Louis (February 1948). Present was a mother whose son drowned with the sinking of the *Dorchester* Also memorable was conducting the High Holyday services at Fort Jackson in August 1947.

Married Rosalind Gewirtz on June 17, 1947, and they have three sons Theodore, Joel and Daniel, and 11 grandchildren. Staff Chaplain, VA Medical Center, Northport, NY; acting chief of chaplains at the VA for 10 months prior to retirement in October 1993. Lives in Kfar Saba, Israel.

FANNALOU GUGGISBERG, Major, Chaplain Fannalou Guggisberg joined the MCA in the early 80s, as a chaplain candidate/seminarian She was born May 12, 1947, at Fort Sheridan, IL; graduated from William H. Burges HS, El Paso, TX, in 1965 and from the Univ. of Texas at El Paso in 1969, with a bachelor of arts, cum laude. She received her master of arts degree in 1971.

Entered the USAF in December 1974 through the delayed enlistment program and attended Officer Training School at Medina Annex, Lackland AFB, TX She was commissioned a 2nd lieutenant in March 1975, attended the administrative management and Executive Officer Course at Keesler AFB, MS, and served two years as chief of administration of the 4754th Radar Evaluation Sqdn. (ADCOM), Hill AFB, UT. Promoted to 1st lieutenant and moved to a special assignment as an instructor of English at the USAFA in 1977.

At the academy she received a regular commission and was promoted to captain and assistant professor of English. In 1980 she responded to God's call to become a chaplain and soon became a chaplain candidate, 2nd lieutenant, seminarian. She was ordained in April 1983, and received her master of divinity degree from Southwestern Baptist Theological Seminary in May 1983 She then served as a chaplain, 1st lieutenant, in the USAFR and entered active duty as a chaplain, captain, at Scott AFB, IL, in 1985. In June 1990 she moved to Howard AFB, Republic of Panama and in May 1992 returned to the States.

Her military awards and decorations include the Meritorious Service Medal, Air Force Commendation Medal w/2 OLCs, AF Outstanding Unit Award w/3 OLCs, National Defense Service Medal and the Armed Forces Reserve Medal.

Chaplain Guggisberg has written several Air Force songs and hymns: *The Red, White and Air Force Blue*, additional verses to *Eternal Father, Strong to Save, Tri-Service Benediction*, and *God the All-Powerful* (tune, Russian Hymn).

Chaplain Guggisberg currently serves at Wilford Hall Medical Center, Lackland AFB, TX.

MYRWOOD K. GUY, Colonel, born June 12, 1929, in Holland, MI. Received AA, BA, MA, M.Div and D Min. He joined the USAF on Oct. 12, 1955 and was stationed at Lackland AFB, TX; Altus AFB, OK; Elmendorf AFB, AK, Nigerian AF in Kaduna, Nigeria; Hamilton AFB, CA; McClellan AFB, CA, and Travis AFB, CA.

Memorable experience was flying in KC-9F's into Adak on the Aleutians in Alaska and being 4th AF HQ, staff chaplain, Liaison officer for AFA Academy. Discharged Oct. 11, 1985.

Married Coral A Guy, since Dec. 19, 1951, and they have six children and eight grandchildren. Coach, school teacher, pastor, he plans to retire in 1999.

MICHAEL DAVID HALLEY, Commander, born in Barboursville, WV on March 11, 1943 He graduated from public schools in Saint Albans, WV, received his BA from Marshall Univ., Huntington, WV, in 1965 and his M.Div. from Southern Baptist Theological Seminary, Louisville, KY in 1970.

From March 1970-June 1973, he served as pastor of First Baptist Church, Ravenswood, WV, October 1971 was sworn into the naval Reserve as a chaplain endorsed by the American Baptist Churches, USA; and served on inactive duty through June 1973 with a Reserve SeaBee Bn. in South Charleston, WV.

His duty stations on active duty include Naval Chaplains School, Newport, RI; USS *Jouett* (DLG/CG-29), San Diego, CA; 2nd Mar Div., FMF, Camp Lejeune, NC; administrative officer, Office of the Chief of Chaplains, Washington, DC, postgraduate study, Eastern Baptist Theological Seminary, Philadelphia, PA; USS *Puget Sound* (AD-38), flagship of the US 6th Fleet, Gaeta, Italy, pastor, David Adams Memorial Chapel, Naval Station, Norfolk, VA, command chaplain, USS *Coral Sea* (CV-43) Norfolk, VA; Armed Forces Staff College, Norfolk, VA; plankowner, USS *George Washington* (CVN-73), Newport News, VA; History Project Officer, Chaplain Resource Board, Norfolk, VA.

Military awards include the Meritorious Service Medal, Navy Commendation Medal, Meritorious Unit Commendation, Navy "E" Ribbon, Navy Expeditionary

Medal, National Defense Service Medal (2 awds.), Sea Service Deployment Ribbon (7 awds.) and Expert Pistol Shot Medal.

In 1987 the American Baptist Churches named Chaplain Halley the Outstanding Military Chaplain at the biennial convention in Pittsburgh, PA. He retired from active duty on July 1, 1993.

He is a member of the USS *Coral Sea* (CVA-43) Assoc., American Vets, the National Assoc. of Life Underwriters and the National Assoc of Professional Financial Planners. While serving as the Chaplain Corps History Project Officer, he compiled and wrote Volume X of the *Chaplain Corps History Series*, biographies of chaplains on active duty 1982-91

In 1993 he joined Metropolitan Life Ins. Co. as an account representative and registered securities representative and is now an area marketing representative for the American Mutual Funds Group in Norfolk, VA.

Since 1964 Chaplain Halley has been the proud husband of Carmen Blair Halley, an accomplished piano teacher and chapel organist. They reside in Virginia Beach, VA and are the parents of two adult sons, David and Jeffrey

RICHARD ELLIS HALVORSEN, Lieutenant Colonel, born on Dec. 12, 1935, in Chicago, IL Educated at Elmhurst (IL) College in 1961; Lutheran School of Theology in Chicago, 1964; Ball State Univ., receiving MA degree in 1974 He joined the US Army on July 31, 1967, and completed his clinical pastoral education at Fort Benning from 1979-80 He previously served four years in the USN and was discharged in December 1956.

Military stations included Fort Bliss, TX; Vietnam, Fort Polk, LA; Germany; New Cumberland Army Depot, PA, Fort Benning, GA, and Presidio of San Francisco He served with the 11th Armd. Cav Regt in Vietnam and the 8th Inf. Div in Germany. Retired July 31, 1983 as lieutenant colonel

His memorable experience was serving with Col. George Patton in Vietnam

In counseling (with Lutheran Social Services, Racine, WI) and hospital ministry since 1983, he is now chief of VA Medical Center, Fresno, CA.

Married Barbara Ann Bouton and they have three children and one grandchild

RICHARD HASKELL HARGETT, Lieutenant Colonel, born March 8, 1944, in Lexington, KY. He graduated from Asbury College in 1966 with BA degree, Asbury Theological Seminary with a M.Div degree; and completed one-third of the work for his doctor of ministries degree at the Virginia Theological Seminary. He has also completed three units of CPE (one at Jacksonville Methodist Hosp. and two at Georgetown Univ. Med. Ctr. in Washington, DC.

Joined the US Army Feb. 3, 1970 and attended Chaplain Officer Basic Crs., Airborne Jump School, Chaplain Advance Crs., and Chaplain Command and General Staff College.

Military assignments were at Fort Sill, OK; Florida; Fort Belvoir, VA; and Mannheim, Germany. From 1989-93, he was chaplain of 100th Div USAR in Kentucky and is currently serving as full time chaplain at the Cincinnati/Fort Thomas VA Medical Center

Discharged from active duty Jan. 21, 1988, with rank lieutenant colonel. He is still serving in the USAR His highest award is the ARCOM (1st OLC) Member of MCA, ROA, Kentucky Ministerial Assoc and American Baptist Churches, USA.

He has served from youth director to senior pastor in churches in Kentucky, Virginia and Florida. An evangelist, he has preached in eight states and several foreign countries: Spain, Israel, Germany, France, England, Italy, Belgium, Switzerland and Austria.

Married to Dorothy and they have four children and one grandchild.

DONALD J. HARLIN, Major General, born Aug. 14, 1935, in New York City and graduated from Flushing (NY) HS, 1953. Earned BS in theology from Nyack College, 1958; M.Div. from Gordon-Conwell Theological Seminary, 1961; DD from Nyack College, 1991, and completed Air Command and Staff College, 1975

Entered the USAF in November 1965 and assigned as Protestant chaplain with the 862nd Cbt. Spt. Gp , Minot AFB, ND; 12th Cbt. Spt. Gp., Cam Ranh Bay AB, South Vietnam, 1094th Spt. Sqdn., Manzano Base, NM; 4900th AB Gp., Kirtland AFB, NM; 6135th AB Gp., Naha AB, Japan; 824th Cbt. Spt. Gp., Kadena AB, Japan

Attached to the 1143rd AB Sqdn. with duty at Arlington National Cemetery, VA. He was instructor with the AF Chaplain School, Air Univ., Maxwell AFB, AL; transferred to Osan AB, South Korea as installation staff chaplain with the 51st Cbt. Spt Gp Returned to the States in July 1981 and served successively as chief, Budget and Logistics Div ; chief, Personnel Div.; and command chaplain at the Air Trng. Cmd., Randolph AFB, TX.

Since December 1991 he has served as chief of chaplains, HQ USAF, Washington, DC. His military awards include the Distinguished Service Medal, Legion of Merit w/2 OLCs, Bronze Star Medal, Meritorious Service Medal w/3 OLCs and AF Commendation Medal w/2 OLCs. He received the award of Outstanding Military Chaplain of the American Baptist Churches, USA in 1977 Promoted to major general on July 1, 1992

Married to the former Carol A. McCandless and has two sons, Matthew and Timothy.

ERHARD HERMAN HARMS, Colonel, born Jan 22, 1916, in Batavia, IL. Attended schools in Davenport, IA, including Brown's Business College. Took his theological training at Concordia College, Milwaukee and Concordia Seminary, St. Louis, graduating in 1941. Assigned to religious survey work in Texas and was ordained and installed as pastor of Immanuel Lutheran Church, Iowa Falls, IA, on Dec. 7, 1941

Joined the US Army June 15, 1945, and reported for active duty to the Brooklyn AB. Military assignments include the Army Ground Forces Replacement Depot #1, Camp Pickett, VA; US Constabulary in Germany, Fort Bragg, NC; South Korea; Presidio of San Francisco; Fort Benning, GA; XIV USAC, Minneapolis, MN; and 2nd Log. Cmd., Okinawa.

Military Schools. Army Chaplain School, US Constabulary School, Army Installation Management School and the Basic Abn Crs at the Infantry School.

Decorations include the WWII Victory, Army of Occupation, National Defense Service w/OLC, Korean Service, UN Service and Meritorious Service Medals, ROK Presidential Unit Citation, Parachutist and Glider Badges; plus several Certificates of Achievement.

After retirement he served as pastor of Trinity Lutheran Church, Coal Valley, IL, from 1971-74; member of Rock Island Arsenal Retirement Sub-council for seven years and served as emergency medical tech. with the Coal Valley Ambulance Service from 1977-83.

Chaplain Harms was married to Sylvia Klunder on Feb. 8, 1942, they have three children and three grandchildren.

VERNON P. HARMS, Colonel, born Nov. 5, 1926, in Meade, KS He joined CAP in April 1953, Hutchinson, KS, where he established a new inter-denominational church shortly after graduating magna cum laude from Grace College and being ordained by The Fellowship of Evangelical Bible Churches.

Due to numerous throat surgeries, he left the ministry and entered aircraft sales and did test flying for Lear Jet Corp Regained his speaking capability eight years later and returned to founding new churches.

He is a qualified mission pilot, check pilot and command pilot with CAP; holds a certified flight instructor rating in aircraft and instruments; and has completed Levels I through V of the Senior Member Training Program with numerous ribbons and commendations.

Served as Pacific Region Chaplain; squadron chaplain in Kansas, Nebraska and Oregon; Wing Chaplain in Nebraska and Washington; and appointed Chief of Chaplains of CAP in August 1991.

Married to the former Judy Hamilton and resides in both Sunriver, OR and Tucscon, AZ They have two sons in the Midwest and one in Bangkok, Thailand.

JAMES VERNON HARVESTER, Colonel, born Aug. 9, 1921, in Meridian, MS. Graduated Hillsborough High School, Tampa; BA from Florida Southern College; M.Div. from Emory Univ.; MA in public administration, George Washington Univ.

Joined the service on Sept. 10, 1940 and served in the Field Artillery, Signal Corps and Chaplain Corps. Some of his stations were Camp Blanding, FL; Camp Bowie, TX; Fort Monmouth, NJ; Fort Jackson, SC, Fort Benning, GA; Camp Casey, CO; Fort Monroe, VA, Fort Hamilton, NY; Washington, DC, and overseas in Korea and Germany.

Memorable experiences were serving with the troops, establishing a management program for chaplains in CONUS, and as secretary of US Army Chaplain School.

Retired Aug 1, 1970, as colonel. He and Helen Grace were married on July 3, 1944. They have six children, 18 grandchildren and 10 great-grandchildren. Pastor of Thonotosassa United Methodist Church in Florida from 1979-1992.

HARRY R. HATAWAY, 1st Lieutenant, born May 28, 1924, in Parsons, KS. Enlisted in the US Army in June 1943 and was sent to Camp Roberts, CA; Camp Adair, OR; then to ETO with the 70th Inf. from 1944-46. He stayed in Reserves and entered Phillips Univ and completed seminary in 1952 with BA and BD degrees Commissioned 1st lieutenant Chaplain in April 1952

Served with the 37th Inf , Fort Polk, 180th Inf., 45th Div., frontline in Korea (where he started "Pray for Peace"); 1st and 4th Armd. Divs , Fort Hood, TX; 25th Inf. Div in Hawaii; 4th Army at Fort Polk; 1st Div. at Fort Riley, KS and on frontline in Vietnam.

Retired when deputy post chaplain in August 1969. Awards include the Legion of Merit, Bronze Star, Good Conduct Medal, American Campaign, EAME w/2 stars, WWII Victory Medal, Army of Occupation, National Defense Service Medal with OLC, Korean Service w/3 stars, Armed Forces Expeditionary (Berlin), Vietnam Service w/3 stars, Armed Forces Reserve with device, UN Service Medal (Korea), RVN Campaign Ribbon, Distinguished Unit Citation, ROK Presidential Unit Citation and Vietnam Cross of Gallantry

Married to Cleo M. Miller and has four children, four grandchildren and one great-grandson He was a Disciples of Christ Minister in Crowley and Hammond, LA until retiring in September 1987.

BURTON G. HATCH, Colonel, served as an AF pilot in WWII. He also was awarded a secondary aeronautical rating as aircraft observer (flight engineer). Graduated from Biola Univ., attended Talbot Theological Seminary and graduated from Columbia Univ in New York City.

Entered the Army Chaplaincy in 1954 and served in the 11th Abn. Div., 7th Spec. Forces, as a member of the Staff and Faculty of the US Army Chaplain School, senior chaplain of Task Force Oregon (later Americal Division) in Vietnam and senior chaplain at Fort Rucker, AL, from which he retired as a full colonel

Awards include AF Pilot Wings, Aircraft Observer Wings and US Army Senior Parachutist Wings.

Chaplain Hatch is an ordained pastor in the Grace Brethren Church, and was commissioned a Regular Army Chaplain Awards include Legion of Merit w/ OLC. He is married to Marie Rudkin and has four children and six grandchildren.

LAWRENCE E. HAWORTH, Lieutenant Colonel, born Feb. 14, 1937, in San Fernando, CA Received M Div. from Bethel Theological Seminary, St. Paul, MN and MS from Long Island Univ., CPE

Joined the US Army in June 1966; attended Army Chaplain Basic and Advanced Courses at Fort Hamilton, NY, Clinical Pastoral Education, Letterman AMC, San Francisco; Staff and Faculty, Army Chaplain School, Fort Wadsworth, Staten Island, NY.

Stationed at Fort Ord, CA; Vietnam; Germany; Red River Army Depot, Texarkana, TX; Deputy Staff Chaplain, Army Materiel Cmd., Alexandria, VA and as post chaplain, Fort Huachuca, AZ, 1990 until retiring in September 1992

Married to Deanna, there are no children

JOSEPH G. HEARD, educated at Univ. of Pennsylvania, Harvard Univ. and doctorate from the Univ. of Miami. A former practicing attorney in Florida and member of Florida and American Bar Associations.

USN officer in WWII with the Amphibious Forces in the South Pacific and was a Protestant Naval Chaplain during the Korean War. Had numerous church missionary assignments in 45 countries, including North and South America, Europe, the Middle East, Far East and Asia.

Director of worldwide youth activities for his church's international headquarters, addressing students at over 700 colleges and universities, is the founder and current member of board of trustees of nationwide scholarship fund for college and university students; is Christian Science teacher and practitioner with healing practice for many years, and he is the author of numerous works, religious dramas, over 100 published articles, poems, lectures and various professional publications. He is a member of Dramatists Guild of New York

Married with one son and grandson He makes his home in south Florida.

ELMER WILLIAM HEINDL, Lieutenant Colonel, born June 14, 1910, on Flag Day. Ordained a Roman Catholic priest on June 6, 1936, Diocese of Rochester, NY and assistant pastor at Dansville, Coldwater, Auburn and Rochester Churches.

Released for Army Chaplaincy in March 1942; assigned to 268th Coast Arty., Fiji, July 1942 and was attached to the 37th Inf. Div in January 1943. Combat service with the 148th Inf. Regt. in Guadalcanal, April 1943; New Georgia, July 1943; Bougainville, November 1943; teamed with infantry medics, 148th Inf. as liberators of Luzon, Manila, Baguio and Cagayan Valley peace on Aug. 15, 1945.

Returned from overseas and re-enlisted in January 1946 He served at hospitals, POW camps, First Army and Aberdeen Proving Grounds. Joined the 98th Trng Div. of Upper New York as Reserve Chaplain in November 1948 and served as Division Chaplain (LTC) from 1958 until mandatory retirement to inactive reserves in July 1970

Awards include the Bronze Star w/V, Distinguished Service Cross, Silver Star, Presidential Citations of US and Philippines, Philippines Liberation Medal and the Legion of Merit Medal

Concurrent with the chaplain service were ministry appointments throughout the Rochester Diocese. St Mary's, Rochester, 1948, Holy Trinity, Webster, 1952; pastor at St. Bernard's Scipio Center, 1958; St Theodore's, 1960, St. Patrick's, Cato, 1961; St. Joseph's, Weedsport, 1972; and mandatory diocesan retirement in 1980

Ministering actively at St. Charles Borromeo Church, Rochester and continued chaplain ministry as National Chaplain of the 37th Div Veterans Assoc. in 1988, was Monroe County Chaplain VFW in 1980 and was honored as the Monroe County Veteran of the Year in 1994 for service with all veterans organizations He continues active priestly and chaplain services on request in 1995.

LOUIS DUANE HENDRICKS, Colonel, born July 24, 1932, in Copan, OK Holds a BA degree from Oklahoma Baptist Univ., M.Div from Southwestern Baptist Theological Seminary, Fort Worth, TX; graduated from the US Army Command and General Staff College, received four quarters of Clinical Pastoral Education at Fitzsimons Army Medical Ctr , Denver, CO and earned his Ed.M. at Sul Ross State Univ., Alpine, TX

Chaplain Hendricks served in the US Army from July 1, 1961-Aug 1, 1981. Accompanied troops of the 1st Inf Div. into Berlin after the infamous wall was built; was sent in 1965 to Vietnam, and served at William Beaumont Army Medical Ctr., El Paso, TX; Irwin Army Hosp., Fort Riley, KS and was Army Community Chaplain in Giessen, Germany.

Awards include the Legion of Merit, Bronze Star Medal, Meritorious Service Medal, Army Commendation Medal w/2 OLCs, Armed Forces Expeditionary Medal (Berlin), Army Occupation Medal (Germany), Vietnam Cross of Gallantry with palm (unit), Vietnam Campaign Medal and Vietnam Service Medal w/2 Bronze Stars. Retired from active duty as a reserve officer with the rank of lieutenant colonel.

Married to Mary Netherton and has three children and eight grandchildren Retired, he continues to help the chaplains at the Temple VA, is active in an Airstream trailer club and provides recreational ministry in campgrounds and other settings

SHELDON E. HERMANSON, Colonel, born April 5, 1930, in St Cloud, MN He graduated from Princeton HS, Princeton, MN, Luther College, Decorah, IA; and Luther Theological Seminary, St. Paul, MN. Ordained into the ministry of the Evangelical Lutheran Church on May 20, 1956, and entered into active duty as a Lutheran Chaplain in the USAF on June 21, 1956

Assignments included Chaplain School at Lackland AFB, TX; Ellington AFB, TX; Craig AFB, AL, Stead AFB, NV, Wheelus AB, Libya, Duke Theological Seminary in Durham, NC (receiving his Th M); Wilford Hall Medical Center, TX, Shemya AB, AK; Luke AFB, AZ; Reserve Personnel Ctr , CO, Torrejon AB, Spain, Lackland AFB, TX; and as command chaplain, Electronic Security Cmd , San Antonio, TX.

During his 30 years he attended all levels of training at the USAF Chaplain School, Squadron Officers School, four quarters of clinical pastoral education at Duke Medical Center, Durham, NC and numerous chaplain sponsored courses, seminars and educational programs. In 1972 his chaplain team at Stead AFB was chosen to receive the Edward R. Chess "Air Force Chaplain Team" Award. Other awards include the Meritorious Service Medal w/2 OLCs and the Legion of Merit w/OLC. He was promoted to colonel in 1973 and retired in 1986. Married to Renee J. Aust, author and editor. They reside in San Antonio, TX and have five sons and eight grandchildren.

BRUCE HERRSTROM (BREWSTER),

Colonel, enlisted in the USN in 1943. Served as sonar operator during WWII and was instructor until discharged in 1951. Graduated from Bethel College, St. Paul, MN; Bethel Theological Seminary; Fuller Theological Seminary; and Univ. of Minnesota.

Ordained as a Baptist minister in 1954 and commissioned as chaplain, 1st lieutenant, USAFR in 1956. His assignments include the ANG units in Illinois, Minnesota and California. AF Reserve assignments were at Forbes AFB, KS; Edwards AFB, CA; McChord AFB, WA and Chanute AFB, IL where he retired as a colonel.

Additional duty assignments as admissions liaison officer for the AF Academy, Colorado Springs, CO from 1981 to present. He was a CAP chaplain for 20 years. Civilian ministry includes five pastorates, regional minister and administrative staff of Bethel Seminary West in San Diego. Married to Shirley Brown of Spirit Lake, IA. He is a life member of MCA.

ROBERT D. HERSHBERGER,

Lieutenant Colonel, born May 30, 1942, in Cumberland, MD. Received BA from Marion College, IN and M.Div. from Asbury Seminary, Wilmore, KY.

Joined the USAR on July 16, 1976, and served with the 97th ARCOM, Maryland; 77th ARCOM, New York; 2122nd USA Garrison; 320th Evac. Hosp.; 74th Field Hosp.; 815th Station Hosp. and 343rd Cbt. Spt. Hosp.

All of his career with the US Army Reserve units was memorable. Key experiences have centered upon many field exercises with service and training in the field hospital environment.

Married Patricia and they have three sons. Chief of Chaplains, VAMC Castle Point, NY; presently active commissioned service with the USAR.

ROBERT R. HILDEBRANDT,

Colonel, born Oct. 20, 1934, in Chicago, IL. Graduated from Marion HS, Marion, WI; attended Univ. of Wisconsin for one year, then joined the ROTC. Graduated from Wartburg College, Waverly, IA with BA; Wartburg Seminary, Dubuque, IA with a M.Div.; Tulane Univ. with MSW in 1969 and DSW in 1978.

Served two churches in Waterloo, IA, then in 1967 received a call from an infantry battalion and asked if he would be their chaplain. Received a commission in May 1967 to serve in the IANG. The decision to move to New Orleans and Graduate School at Tulane was made a few months later.

After summer camp at Camp Ripley, MN, transferred to LAANG and was assigned to the 204th Trans. Gp., later served with the now 159th MASH; back to the 204th and with HQ STARC serving as state chaplain.

He is pastor of St. Mark Evangelical Lutheran

Church in Metairie. Recently left teaching at Our Lady of Holy Cross College after 11 years directing their counseling program. Holds the Board Certified Social Work (BCSW) and Louisiana Professional Counselor (LPC) state licenses and has a private counseling practice. He is also a state licensed realtor and serves on several boards.

Married to Beverly and has two sons, three stepsons and four grandsons.

LLOYD S. HINDMAN,

Commander, born in Cross Creek, PA on April 3, 1914. Graduated from Washington & Jefferson College in 1935 and from Princeton Theological Seminary in 1938. Ordained to the Gospel Ministry of the Presbyterian Church in May 1938.

Served in civilian pastorates in Maryland, West Virginia, Iowa, Texas and Colorado. As a missionary of the Presbyterian Church he served in Korea and Thailand on special assignment.

Commissioned March 26, 1940, lieutenant (jg) in the Chaplain Corps, USNR. Reported for active duty at the naval operating base in Norfolk, VA; served at NAS, Jacksonville, FL; USS *Denver* (CL-58); was faculty member at Navy Chaplains School, Williamsburg, VA; USMC Barracks, Quantico, VA; Wing Chaplain, 1st Mar. Aircraft Wing; assistant fleet chaplain, COMSERPAC; and Armed Forces Staff College, Norfolk, VA.

Commissioned a chaplain, USN in 1943, resigned from the Regular Navy in March 1946 and was commissioned a chaplain with the rank of commander in the USNR. Honorably retired in April 1974. He received the Navy Unit Commendation. Married to Billie McReynolds and has six children, 10 grandchildren and three great-grandchildren.

LaFOREST E. HODGKINS,

Lieutenant Colonel, born April 23, 1905, in Lisbon Falls, ME. Received BS in SS, STB and Stm. Commissioned Oct. 28, 1943, in the US Army and was stationed at Fort Eustis and in various European WWII areas with the 35th Inf. Div.

Memorable experiences: driving between single lines of men moving battle areas and knowing some would not be coming back; and being at the site where the Germans drove political men into a barn, then fired incendiary bullets into gasoline areas, killing 1,175 men.

Discharged in January 1945 and served with the 76th Inf. Div. in the Reserves until retirement in May 1965. Awards include five Battle Stars and the Bronze Medal. Married 61 years, has been a widower since June 6, 1993, and has one son and two grandsons. Taught school one year and was pastor in five Congregational Churches.

WAYNE W. HOFFMANN,

Brigadier General, born Aug. 17, 1937, in Hollis, NY. Received BA from Wheaton College; BD from Columbia Theological Seminary; MA from Univ. of Mississippi and Ed.D from Indiana Univ. Completed the Officer Basic, Advanced and Installation Chaplain Courses; Command and General Staff College; Senior Reserve Component Officers Crs. and Corresponding Studies at the Army War College.

Joined the US Army in June 1959 and was stationed at Fort Chaffee, AR; Camp Kaiser, Korea; and Oakland Army Base. He served with the 85th Evac. Hosp., 1st Bde., 7th Div., 63rd ARCOM, DACH.

His memorable experiences were serving in the office of the Chief of Chaplains during Operation Desert Shield/Storm; serving in Forces Cmd. as IMA; and serving three different infantry brigades in the ARNG.

Awards include the Meritorious Service Medal w/ 2 OLCs, Army Commendation Medal, Army Achievement Medal, National Defense Service Medal, Bronze Star, Armed Forces Reserve Medal (2nd awd.), Army Reserve Components Achievement Medal w/4 OLCs, Army Service Ribbon and Overseas Service Ribbon.

Married Nancy Evelyn Mangum and has two children. President of Independent Colleges of northern California.

THEOL S. HOILAND,

Colonel, received BA from Pacific Lutheran Univ. and M.Div. from Luther Theological Seminary. Enlisted in the US Army from 1944-46; commissioned service in Oregon ARNG, 1957-60 and Washington ARNG, 1960-79. Stationed in Hawaii, Okinawa, 1944-46; Office Chief of Chaplains, Dept. of the Army, Washington, DC, 1973-76. He retired in 1979.

Served Lutheran parishes in Washington, Oregon and Alaska, 1952-73 and 1980-87. Lutheran Council Field Service pastor for Europe and Near East (Frankfurt, West Germany), 1976-80.

DAVID JOHN HOLLAND,

Lieutenant Commander, born Aug. 18, 1940, in Los Angeles, CA. Received BA from Bethel College, MN; MA from Fuller Theological Seminary, CA; M.Div. from American Baptist Theological Seminary, CA and MA from Webster

Univ., MO. Joined the USN on Nov 10, 1958, and Aug 15, 1969 Stationed at NTC, San Diego, CA; Naval Air Tech Trng. Ctr., Norman, OK, NAS Lake Hurst, NJ; Washington, DC, Philippines, USS *Ticonderoga*, Los Angeles, CA; Newport, RI; Norfolk, VA; Barstow, CA; Camp Pendleton, CA, USS *Truxtun*; Bremerton, WA and Saudi Arabia. Memorable Experiences seeing Christian missions work around the world; serving in Saudi Arabia in Operation Desert Shield/Storm and providing back-up support for Operation Restore Hope.

Discharged March 31, 1994. Awards include the Navy Commendation Medal (3 awds), Navy Unit Commendation w/Bronze Star, Meritorious Unit Commendation w/Bronze Star, Battle Efficiency E w/3 devices, Navy Good Conduct Medal, Navy Expeditionary Medal, National Defense Service Medal w/2 stars, SWA Service Medal w/2 stars, Armed Forces Reserve Medal, Kuwait Liberation Medal and several ribbons. Married Gloria Jean Thompson and has two children, Carisa and Caran.

HAROLD B. HOWARD, Colonel, born March 9, 1910, in Farmington, KY. Received BA, BD and M.Div. degrees. Joined the service on July 13, 1943, and served in the Army and Air Force. Participated in the ETO, FEAF, TUSLOG and SAC with the 321st Fighter Gp and the 48th TAC Recon Wing

Retired April 1, 1970, as colonel. Married and has one child and one grandchild. Civilian position: Presbyterian churches in Franklin, KY and Lebanon, TN.

DAVID M. HUMPHREYS, Captain, born Oct. 29, 1917, in Kingston, PA. Received AA from Keystone Jr. College; BA from Maryville College, BD from McCormick Theological Seminary, Boston Univ. Divinity School.

Joined the USN in 1944 and was stationed in Guam, China, Japan, Hawaii, Florida, California, (OCS) Newport and Norfolk Served with the 1st and 3rd Mar Divs., NAS ATSUG, COMNAV for Japan, Barbers Point Force Chaplain and FMF Atlantic.

Memorable experiences having Sir Winston Churchill come aboard the USS *Randolph*; Holy Helo Hops from carriers to destroyers for Divine Worship Services; accompanying admiral from Cruiser USS *Manchester* on protocol visits to all of the Greek Islands.

Discharged Sept. 1, 1974, as captain. Married Wilmine (Billie) and has three children and five grandchildren. Civilian employment: Eastern Virginia Assoc Minister UCC interim pastorates Presbyterian Church USA Retired Oct. 30, 1994.

WILLIAM WALPOLE HUNTLEY, Colonel, born Sept. 25, 1917, in Morris, MN. Educated at Northwestern Bible School, 1939-42, Univ. of Minnesota, 1942-45 with BA; Bethel Seminary, 1945-46, BD, ordained in the South Elmdale Congregational Church, Sept. 25, 1946; and attended US Army Chaplain School Career Crs Served in the Wisconsin NG, 128th Inf. Regt., 32nd Inf. Div. from January 1949-February 1957. Active duty with US Army Feb. 17, 1957, serving at Walter Reed Army Med.Ctr ; Guam, Mariana Islands; Fort Riley, KS, Menwith Hill Station, Yorkshire, England, Fort Huachua, AZ; US Army Electronic Proving Ground, Fort Hamilton, NY; Korea, Germany; and Fort Dix, NJ Retired from the Army on Dec. 21, 1976, to Elk River, MN.

Married Joyce Davenport and has two children, Mary Kay Sauter and Maj. David Huntley, USA (RET), and four grandchildren Carrie and Mikkii Sauter and Jason and Kimberly Huntley.

VERNON P. JAEGER, Colonel, born on April 17, 1906, in St. Paul, MN His family moved to California in 1909 He attended the California Institute of Technology, the Univ. of Redlands, CA and the Northern Baptist Theological Seminary in Chicago. Ordained in 1931 and was commissioned as a chaplain in the Regular Army in 1932

Stationed in Panama at the time the US entered WWII. He was then assigned as the division chaplain of the 91st Inf Div., which position he retained all through the entire active service with that division. With this division he served in North Africa and Italy. Upon deactivation of the 91st Div. he was assigned as the XXIV Corps chaplain in Korea. Later he served at Fort Gordon, GA and at the HQ, US Army, Japan Retired in 1963 at Fort Knox, KY.

Since retirement from the Army, he has served as associate executive minister of the American Baptist churches of Oregon and as associate pastor, Mountain Park Church in Lake Oswego, OR. Currently he serves as the building manager of the Interchurch Office Center in Portland, OR.

HAROLD L. JARVIS, Lieutenant Colonel, born Aug. 3, 1930, in Waterloo, NY, the son of Lewis E. and Jennie (Hannah) Jarvis. Graduated from Waterloo High School and the Practical Bible Training School, Binghamton, NY. Further education completed included the American Institute of Banking, Orange County, CA

Ordained by the Waterloo Baptist Church and pastored churches in Prattsburg, NY, Huntingburg, IN, Garden Grove, CA; Sonoma, CA; Redwood Valley, CA, and Rohnert Park, CA He served the latter part of his ministry with the Fellowship of Baptists for Home Missions and then the board of Western Baptist Home Mission.

Jarvis made application with the CAP in 1964 and served with each level of command as a chaplain. He is the recipient of the California Chaplain Awd. and the National Chaplain of the Year Awd. He is credited with bringing the California Chaplain Program to first place in 1977 and maintaining that high position in ratings longer than any other wing.

He served as a squadron chaplain in Santa Rosa, CA; group chaplain in Petaluma, CA; wing chaplain in Oakland, CA; and special advisor to the National Chaplain Committee for recruiting and retention. He is serving as an advisor on chaplain affairs for the Pacific Region, CAP.

MEARLE H. JAY, Lieutenant Colonel, born in Everett, PA, on March 29, 1924, and grew up in New Castle, PA During WWII he was in the US Army from 1943-45 and spent six months in the ETO with the 20th Armd Div.

Attended Waynesburg College, PA for a BA and Boston Univ. School of Theology, STB. Ordained into the Western Pennsylvania Conference of the United Methodist Church in June 1952. In September of 1952, he entered the USN Chaplaincy, being aboard the USS *Bennington* (CVA-20) at the time of the disastrous explosion on May 26, 1954. Served in the USNR until 1959.

Transferred to the AF in 1960 and went on active duty in August 1960. Served at Amarillo AFB, TX; Pine Tree Line, Canada, Ellington AFB, TX; Anderson AFB, Guam; Keesler AFB, MS; Dover AFB, DE, Incirlik AFB, Turkey; Vandenberg AFB, CA; and at Wright Patterson AFB, OH . He retired on Aug. 30, 1980.

Pastored Rocky Point Chapel, Springfield, OH for almost six years. Married to Phyllis Ringer on July 29, 1944, and they have three children: Paula, Gary and Lanny He and Phyllis moved to Corry, PA in 1986 to be closer to family They are active in the local UM Church. In 1992 they served for two years on the Steering Committee to build a new 600 seat church complex.

FRANCIS E. JEFFERY, Lieutenant Colonel, born in Minneapolis, MN in 1923 He is a 1949 graduate of St. Olaf College; 1952 of Luther Seminary, St. Paul, MN; and 1995 of Faith Lutheran Seminary, Tacoma, WA. WWII service was with the US Infantry in France. Commissioned in the USAF he retired in 1975 as a lieutenant colonel.

Awards: Purple Heart, Bronze Star, Combat Infantry Badge Meritorious Service Medal, AF Commendation Medal, AF Outstanding Unit Award, RVN Campaign and others. He served in Greenland, France, Spain, Japan, Vietnam and in the States.

Married to Lillian Ruth Hathaway; their son Paul died in 1963 and daughter Naomi married Maj. Otto A. Petersen, USAF (RET). There are three grandchildren. Retirement enables his involvement in military organizations He is the National Chaplain for the MOPH. He is active as a Christian therapist and writer.

ARTHUR F. JENSEN, Lieutenant Colonel, born Oct. 8, 1938, in Baltimore, MD. Received BS from Virginia Commonwealth Univ ; M.Div. and Th.M from Union Theological Seminary in Virginia; MA in philosophy, the Catholic Univ. of America, and graduated from the US Army Command and General Staff College.

Enlisted Reserve, 1959-65, Reserve commission chaplain, January 1974, entered active duty as US Army Reserve chaplain, September 1976; and Regular Army commission, September 1984

Assignments: Fort Jackson, SC, 1976-79; Augsburg, West Germany, 1979-83; US Army Sergeant Major Academy, Fort Bliss, TX, 1984-86; Fort Myer, VA, 1986-90; US Army Transportation School, Fort Eustis, VA, 1990-94.

Current assignment as installation chaplain, Fort Monroe, VA, April 1994-present. Teaching military leadership and ethics, mentoring senior NCO and young officer students is a memorable experience.

Married to Marguerite Ray Seay since 1961 and they have sons, Andrew and Thomas, and one grandson

CHARLES W. JEWITT, Lieutenant Colonel, born on March 1, 1916, in Philadelphia, PA. Received AB, THB, Graduate (12 hours). Joined the US Army on Sept. 4, 1942 Stationed in the States, South Pacific, Germany, Korea and Hawaii. Retired at Fort Hamilton, NY in August 1969 with 27 years of credited service. Memorable Experiences: retreat at Bertchsgarden, Germany and two tours in Korea as division and deputy corps chaplain.

Has pastored several churches as an interim since retirement; act as director of admissions at Bible College; and is chaplain to TROA of Palm Beach County.

Married to Esther over 55 years and has three children, nine grandchildren and one great-grandchild.

GRAY GOULD JOHNSON, Colonel, born on Oct. 27, 1922, in East Stroudsburg, PA. Graduated from Johnson C. Smith Univ and Seminary in Charlotte, NC. Was pastor of Second Presbyterian Church in Brunswick, GA before entering the US Army as a chaplain in October 1948 at Fort George G. Meade, MD Stateside assignments were in Maryland, New York City, Connecticut, Massachusetts and Georgia. He had two tours in Korea and two tours in Germany. While serving with the 24th Inf. Regt. during the Korean War, he was awarded the Silver Star w/OLC for gallantry in action. He retired with the rank of colonel.

Lives with his wife Helen in Hershey, PA, and they have two children, Gray Jr. and Bonnie Johnson Glass, and three grandchildren.

HAROLD S. JOHNSON, Lieutenant Colonel, born Feb. 11, 1928, in Newport, KY Has BS, BD, MA, and honorary DD degrees. Graduated from the Great Lakes Region Chaplain Staff College, Grissom AFB, IN, Southeast Region Chaplain Staff College, Maxwell AFB, AL; Southeast Region Staff College, McGee Tyson ANG, Knoxville, TN; completed the CAP Senior Officers Crs. and several others.

Served in the military with the USAAF in the Pacific Theater of Operations. Served with the 3rd Armd. Div. and the Army Field Forces for a total of six years. Awarded the Good Conduct Medal, American Campaign Medal, Asiatic-Pacific Campaign Medal, WWII Victory Medal, National Defense Medal and the Philippine Independence Ribbon Discharged March 3, 1952, as corporal.

In civilian life he served as pastor, teacher, administrator and missionary with the Seventh Day Adventist Church for 37 and a half years. Has been a CAP member since May 1989 and served as chaplain for the London Composite Sqdn., London, KY; Highlands County Composite Sqdn., Sebring, FL and Gp. 3 Chaplain, MacDill AFB, Tampa, FL. He received numerous civilian and CAP awards. Married Harriet Dinsmore and has two children. Retired on Dec. 30, 1990.

ROY B. JOHNSTON, Colonel, born near Fort Scott, KS and grew up on a farm. Enrolled at Phillips Univ., Enid, OK and received BA degree in 1949 Was ordained in the First Christian Church, Disciples of Christ, Fort Scott, KS and attended the Graduate Seminary in Enid and graduated in 1952. Pastored churches in both Kansas and Oklahoma.

Commissioned a 1st Lieutenant in the Chaplain Branch of the USAF and called to active duty July 1, 1952. Served over 28 years of duty, retiring from HQ SAC in 1980. Served Stateside military parishes at Vance AFB, Enid, OK; Edwards AFB, CA; Bossier Base, Shreveport, LA; Wilford Hall Medical Ctr, San Antonio, TX; HQ TAC, Langley AFB, Hampton, VA; HQ SAC, Offutt AFB, Omaha, NE.

Overseas assignments included Korea, RAF Sculthorpe, England; Chateauroux, France; Bitburg AB, Germany; and Kadena AFB, Okinawa, Japan. Military decorations include the Legion of Merit, Meritorious Service Medal w/2 OLCs, AF Longevity Service Awd. w/6 OLCs, National Defense Service Medal, Bronze Star, AF Presidential Unit Citation, AF Outstanding Unit Awd., Korean Service Medal, Korean Presidential Unit Citation and United Nations Service Medal.

Since retiring from the USAF in 1980, he has served and continues to serve as pastor of the Anderson Grove Presbyterian Church He is life member of MCA, ROA and TROA and presently serves as state chaplain for the Dept. of Nebraska, ROA

Married 46 years to the former Virginia Huston of Fort Scott, KS. She holds a religious education and music degree from Phillips Univ., Enid, OK They are the parents of three sons and have three grandchildren

HENRY F. JONAS, Colonel, born Feb. 3, 1923, Chehalis, WA. Was attending the Univ. of Idaho when Pearl Harbor took place and entered the US Army on March 15, 1943, completing the basic infantry and engineer training with the 10th Mtn. Div. On Jan. 9, 1945, he completed Engineer Officer Candidate School and was assigned to an engineer construction battalion serving in the Philippines, Okinawa and Japan. Released from active duty in July 1946.

Graduated in 1949 from Albertson College of Idaho and Princeton Theological Seminary in 1952. Returned to active duty in August 1952 in the Chaplains Corps with the US Army and served at Fort Carson, CO and with the 3rd Inf. Div. in Korea, March 1953-July 1954. Placed on active Reserve status in July 1954 and served as minister of Christian Education, First Presbyterian Church, Twin Falls, ID until June 1956. From July 1956-June 1958, he studied at Teacher's College, Columbia Univ., New York City and received a master's and professional diploma in vocational counseling. For two years, he was employed as the advisor to the Student Christian Assoc. at San Jose State Univ, California

Moved to active duty with the US Army in October 1960 and was assigned as chaplain to the 1st Experimental Regt at Fort Ord, CA. Was in Vietnam with the II Corps Advisory Gp. from February 1963-July 1965. Attended the US Army Chaplain Career Crs. at Fort Hamilton, NY (August 1965-June 1966); at Fort Sill, OK, July 1966-June 1968, and served as AIT Ctr. Chaplain. After one year of CPE at St. Elizabeth Hosp., National Institute of Mental Health, Washington, DC, he worked as hospital chaplain in Wurzburg, Germany from August 1969-August 1970, then as deputy staff chaplain and staff chaplain, US Army Medical Cmd., Europe, in Heidelberg, Germany from August 1970-June 1972. Then assigned as deputy staff chaplain, US Army Surgeon Generals Office, Washington, DC, June 1972-June 1973. From June 1973-March 1975 his final assignment on active duty was with the Health Services Cmd. and Brook Army Med. Ctr, Fort Sam Houston, TX. He retired as colonel (06) on March 31, 1975.

Awarded the Silver Star, Bronze Star w/OLC, Air Medal w/OLC, Meritorious Service, Army Commendation Medal, Good Conduct Medal and service medals for WWII, Korea and Vietnam with Battle Stars for each.

After retirement he secured a license as a marriage, family and child counselor from California. Became a prison chaplain at the California Correctional Institution, Tehachapi, CA for eight years; then was a minister for five and a half years in the Community Presbyterian Church, Lee Vining, CA. Retired for the third time in October 1992. He is married to Joan Boice and has four children: Fred, Wayne, Jennisse and Winchell, and seven grandchildren

OTTO K. JONAS, Lieutenant Colonel, born in South Beloit, IL on April 14, 1910. Graduated from Beloit College, Beloit, WI in 1932 and Andover Newton Theological School, Newton Centre, MA, in 1936

Reported for active duty in the Army at Fort Sheridan, IL in July 1942. Served there as post chaplain before being appointed senior chaplain of the 228th Gen. Hosp., the first all male hospital to be sent overseas in WWII. The 228th served in St. Quentin, France, before relieving the Third Gen. Hosp at Aix en Provence, France. Final duty overseas was as chaplain of the American Univ. in Biarritz, France.

Served in the MANG with the 772nd Antiaircraft Bn. and transferred to the Reserves in 1961, serving as Boston's post chaplain. In 1962, he moved to Seattle, WA, serving numerous Reserve units and retired in April 1970 as a lieutenant colonel.

He served churches in Sharon, Lynnfield and Walpole, MA, before moving to the state of Washington to serve the Fauntleroy United Church of Christ and the Eagle Harbor Congregational Church on Bainbridge Island. After retiring in 1975, he served as interim pastor in New Hampshire and Washington state.

Married Ruth C. Morgan on June 15, 1933. They have three children, four grandchildren and one great-grandchild.

A. JASE JONES, Colonel, born in Corrigan, TX, Sept 2, 1913. Education includes the BA, Th.M and Th.D. degrees. A graduate of the US Army Chaplain School and the Command and General Staff College (Assoc. Course). Ordained in 1940, he served as pastor of Baptist churches and as a US Army chaplain. He was a field representative for the Home Mission Board, SBC, for 22 years. Served as adjunct professor at New Orleans Baptist Theological Seminary and Golden Gate Baptists Theological Seminary

Entered the US Army in 1943 and was regimental chaplain for the 398th Engr. (GS) Regt. throughout WWII. The regiment was in the ETO for two years, with special assignments in England, Wales and Cherbourg and Verdun, France. It served as infantry in Luxembourg, driving enemy forces back across the Moselle River and holding a long stretch of the river against counterattacks. During the post-war years, Jones was Chaplain Branch Director of the Fort Worth (TX) USAR School and in Kansas City, MO, the chaplain of the 5052nd Log. Cmd., staff chaplain of the 325th Gen. Hosp and the 139th Med. Gp He retired in 1973 after 30 years service with the rank of colonel He and his wife, Vivian, have two children and four grandchildren.

EDWIN S. JONES, Captain, born May 22, 1919, Philadelphia, PA. Received BA in 1941 from Pennsylvania State Univ.; M.Div. in 1949 from Drew Theological Seminary; and was ordained by West Ohio Annual Conference (Methodist) 1951 and served Briggsdale Methodist Church, Briggsdale, OH, 1949-51

Served in the USMCR from June 1941- March 1948 with 1st Avn. Engr Bn. in New Caledonia, Guadalcanal, New Zealand, Tinian and Okinawa. Discharged as captain Served in USN from October 1951-April 1973 in Korea; Cherry Point; NYC, Bainbridge, USS *Amphion*; Naval Prison, Amphib Base, Norfolk; San Diego, NAS Pensacola, USS *Grand Canyon*, Newport; and New London. Retired as captain.

Memorable experience was around-the-world cruise with the USS *Bexar* in 1960. Awards include the Navy Commendation Medal, Presidential Unit Citation w/2 stars, Navy Unit Citation, American Defense, American Theater, Asiatic-Pacific Theater w/2 stars, Victory, National Defense, Korea w/2 stars and United Nations Service Medal.

Married Jane Oglevee in 1945. They have two children, Robert and Barbara Jane, and one grandchild, Robert Maitland Jones. Minister of visitation, First United Methodist, Winter Park, FL from 1978-present.

ENOCH ROSCOE LUKENS JONES JR., Lieutenant Commander, born Sept. 8, 1905, in Williamsport, PA. Received AB from Univ. of California; SF Theological Seminary, San Anselmo, CA, STB Episcopal Theological School, Cambridge, MA, Graduate, social work, Univ. of Illinois.

Joined the USN in 1937, naval activities, Treasure Island, South Pacific, USS *Tuscaloosa* and many other ships Memorable experience was being first chaplain for Treasure Island and sitting across from him at Officer's Mess were Ens John Kennedy and Ens. Richard Nixon (little did he dream they would be future presidents).

Retired Oct. 1, 1965, as lieutenant commander Chaplain US Federal Prison, Terminal Island, South Louisiana; Louisiana Alcoholism Research, Louisiana Skid Row; now volunteer auxiliary chaplain special needs of US Armed Forces Personnel, San Francisco North Bay and volunteer assistant pastor for community-at-large, Los Angeles, CA

MARK ANDREW JUMPER, Lt Commander, born May 1, 1954, Austin, TX. Received BA, Oral Roberts Univ.; M.Div, Columbia Theological Seminary, Decatur, GA; ordained June 1982 by the Presbyterian Church and transferred to the Evangelical Presbyterian Church in 1993.

Joined the USN on Jan. 28, 1982, basic course, summer 1982 and advanced course, 1993-94. Reserve duty with 4th Mar. Amph. Force (Religious), New Orleans, 1982-85 Active duty from 1985-94 with 3rd Mar Div., Okinawa and Korea; Naval Hosp., Bethesda, MD; Navy Family Service Ctr , Guam; NAS Agana Guam, USS *Leyte Gulf*, Mayport, FL; Chaplain Advanced Crs., Newport, RI; and from 1994 to present at NAS, Dallas, TX.

Medals: Navy Commendation, Navy Achievement, National Defense, SWA Campaign w/3 stars, Armed Forces Reserve, Kuwait Liberation, Expert Rifle and Expert Pistol, Ribbons. Navy Battle "E" (3), Navy Marine Corps, Sea Service Deployment w/2 stars, Overseas and CG Special Operations; Joint Meritorious Unit and Meritorious Unit Citations; and Navy Unit Commendation

Married Ginger Lou Jones in 1991. They have two children, Christina Joy and Andrew Albert.

CHARLES CHRISTIAN KARY, Lieutenant Commander, born Dec. 25, 1918, in Milwaukee, WI. Received BS, BD, MA (Chr. Ed) MA (Ed.) Th M and D.Min. Ordained to the gospel ministry on July 2, 1950; pastored churches in Chicago; and commissioned as naval reserve chaplain on April 1, 1955

Served as chaplain with the USMC in Japan; with the USN ship in the Pacific, and with the Marines at Camp Pendleton, CA. Released from active duty in 1958 and served as pastor of the SW Baptist Church in Bridgeview, IL

Recalled to active duty as Navy chaplain and served in the Middle East, at the naval station and brig in Norfolk, Vietnam, Great Lakes, IL and in the USS *Orion* on the East Coast until his release on June 30, 1969.

Served as interim pastor, then pastor of the Rogers Park Baptist Church in Chicago; appointed VA Chaplain Aug 19, 1973 and attended VA Chaplain School at Jefferson Bks., MO; assigned as Protestant chaplain at the VA Hosp , Iron Mtn., MI, Sept. 29, 1973 Retired from the USNR on July 1, 1975.

Served as chaplain at the VA Medical Ctr , Iron Mtn., MI from Sept. 29, 1973, until retirement on Dec 27, 1981. Served as interim pastor in the Ministers-At-Large Program from 1982-92. Presently serving as retiree representative of the American Baptist Churches of USA.

Married to Ruth Naomi Myers since Aug. 26, 1944 and has four children and eight grandchildren.

REUBEN M. KATZ, Lieutenant Colonel, born Feb. 22, 1919, New York City. Received BA from Brooklyn College, 1941, Rabbi, Jewish Theological Seminary of America, 1944; DD in 1969 and named Rabbi Emeritus in 1989.

Joined CAP in 1951, stationed in northeast region and served with the National Chaplain's Committee, CAP. Memorable experience was leading cadet exchange to Israel in 1969.

Received Unit Citation for Northeast Region CAP and Citation from National HQ, CAP. He was national president, American Jewish League, 1984-94; national president, Bnai Zion, 1994.

Married Reba and has three children and six grandchildren. 1943-44, Zion Temple, Philadelphia, PA; 1944-45, Temple Israel, Wilkes Barre, PA; 1945-49 Bethel Congregation, Akron, OH and 1949-89 Cong Bnai Israel, Freeport, NY.

EDWARD J. KELLEY, Captain (0-6), born March 24, 1940 in Boston, MA. Graduated from Boston public schools, attended St. John's Seminary College and graduated in 1962 with a BA degree. Advanced seminary studies at St John's Seminary, Brighton, MA, received M Div and ordained a Roman Catholic priest May 26, 1966, and assigned in urban ministries to St. Christopher's parish in the Columbia Point Sect of Boston and subsequently to St. Mary's in Charleston, MA.

Entered the USN Chaplain's School at NETC, Newport, RI; assigned to the USMC Logistics Base, CA, 1972-74; Naval Station Roosevelt Roads, Puerto Rico, 1974-76 and augmented into regular Navy.

Duty Stations: USS *Guam*; Marine Corps Recruit Depot, Parris Island, SC; USS *Eisenhower*; NAS, Cecil Field, FL; NAS, Norfolk, VA; Marine Corps Air Ground Cbt. Ctr., 29 Palms, CA; Commander, Naval Air Forces, Pacific Fleet; Naval Sea Systems Cmd., Washington, DC; Naval Air Systems Cmd ; Naval Facilities Engineering Systems Cmd.; Strategic Systems Programs; Space and Naval Warfare Systems Cmd., Naval Supply Systems Cmd.; Military Sealift Cmd and Navy Special Warfare Cmd Retired February 1995.

Received Meritorious Service Medal (2 awds.), Naval Commendation Medal (2 awds.), Navy Unit Commendation, Meritorious Unit Commendation (2 awds.), Navy Battle E (2 awds) and various other service medals He serves as a member of the Executive Board of the MCA.

THOMAS W. KELLEY, born Dec. 24, 1923, Philadelphia, PA. Received AB, MA and STL degrees. Joined the USN on Sept. 8, 1957.

Stationed at San Diego; Japan; Pensacola; 29 Palms; St Albans, NY; Okinawa; Vietnam, and Parris Island, SC. Served with the 1st and 3rd Mar. Divs.; Phib Ron 3 and 5; NAAS Saufley Field, Pensacola, FL; NAVHOSP, NY, NAVHOSP ship, Vietnam, USS *Sanctuary* Discharged on Jan. 1, 1986, with the rank of captain, USN.

DAVID B. KENNEDY, Colonel, born on May 17, 1945, in Minneapolis, MN. Graduated from the Univ of Texas in 1967; Dallas Theological Seminary in 1971 with Th.M; further graduate study at St. Louis Univ.; ordained minister of the gospel in 1971 and served civilian churches in Texas, Oklahoma and Fairview Heights, IL. Served as a professor of Old Testament at Grand Rapids Baptist Seminary in Michigan from 1980 to the present.

He was commissioned as USAR chaplain in 1972 and served Army Reserve units, 95th Trng. Div. (Tulsa), 329th Supply and Spt. Bn. and 25th Cbt. Spt. Hosp., St. Louis and 300th MP Cmd. at enemy POW, Inkster, MI, 1980-92. From 1992 to the present, he serves as a reserve chaplain in the Office of the Chief of Chaplains, Pentagon. Promoted to the rank of colonel in 1992. He has been awarded the Meritorious Service and Army Commendation Medals.

He is married to Coila Nell Moss and has three children.

EARL C. KETTLER, Colonel, born, Sept. 7, 1921, at Deerfield, KS. Attended St John's Academy and College, Winfield, KS, 1936-42; Concordia Seminary, St. Louis, MO, 1942-47; ordained a Lutheran minister on July 13, 1947, and developed Lutheran missions in SW New Mexico.

Volunteered for Army Chaplaincy and entered service at Fort Sam Houston, July 18, 1951. Served in the Korean War with the 13th Engr. Cbt Bn, 7th Inf. Div.; 40th AAA Bde., Tokyo and Yokohama, Japan, Fitzsimons Army Hosp., 1954-57; Trois Fontaines, France, 1957-60; 1st BG of the 3rd Inf. at Fort Myer, VA and Arlington National Cemetery, 1960-63; Vietnam 1964; XIth US Army Corps and US Army Admin. Ctr., St Louis, MO, 1965-68; Office of Chaplains, 1968-71.

Memorable experiences crawling up hill called Jane Russell under Chinese fire; serving as circuit rider in Vietnam, the beauty and peacefulness of Arlington National Cemetery

Married Doris Hentschel of Denver, CO; they have three daughters and eight grandchildren. Retired from the service in 1971 and became a parish pastor in western Maryland and Silver Spring, MD. Retired in 1984 to Cincinnati, OH and recently completed a book on his ministry in Vietnam called *Chaplain's Letters: Ministry by Huey*

ERNEST CHARLES KLEIN, Lieutenant Colonel, born June 8, 1924, Vinemont, AL. Attended Cullman, AL public school and received his high school education at St Bernard High School which was a part of the nearby Benedictine Monastery.

Drafted July 1944 and served with the 95th Inf. Div. in Europe As an enlisted man, he earned the Combat Infantry Badge and the Army Commendation Medal.

Stationed at Camp Blanding, FL; Camp Shelby, MS and Fort Totten, NY Attended colleges: St Bernard Junior, AL; Bob Jones, TN; AB degree from Franklin and Marshall, Lancaster, PA; M.Div. degree from Eden Theological Seminary, St. Louis, MO; MS (Ed) St. Francis, Fort Wayne, IN. Ordained June 8, 1952 in the Evangelical and Reformed Church.

USAR, 12th Spec. Forces Gp. Retired from USAR as lieutenant colonel in 1977. Received the Master Parachutist Badge. Served churches in Pennsylvania, Illinois, Indiana and Michigan Retired January 1990 as VA Chaplain, Allen Park, MI. Doing research on the origin of Memorial Day to be placed in Memorial Day Museum, Waterloo, NY

Married June 14, 1952 to Dorothy Tripp and has four children.

JOSEPH M. KMIECIK, Lieutenant Colonel, whose parents were married in Poland in 1883, a native of Walker County, TX. Ordained a priest of the Congregation of Holy Cross in 1934. After early assignments in South Bend, IN and in Poland, he returned to the States after the war broke out.

He preferred the Navy, but was asked in 1942 to join the Army as chaplain. From Fort Lewis, WA he went to Alaska, landing in the battle at Attu and later in Adak. After the war, he was released from active duty as a major. In 1948 he chose the Air Force and was recalled in 1951 for the Korean War.

After duty in Korea he  served at Wolters AFB, TX, Ashya Base, Japan; Lackland AFB, TX; Brize Norton RAFB, England; Randolph AFB, TX and Tyndall AFB, FL. Retired as lieutenant colonel in 1968.

Parish assignments in Texas continued until 1983, when a car crossed the median on a Texas road and hit Father Joe's car head-on After walking away from the car, Father Joe was eventually diagnosed as having a broken neck Traction, long months of rehabilitation and an enduring spirit got him back on his feet. He now lives in retirement at Holy Cross House, Notre Dame, IN

ERNEST J. KNOCHE JR., Colonel, born Dec. 15, 1943, at Brooklyn, NY. Received BS from West Point, MS from Boston Univ., and M.Div. from Concordia Theological Seminary

Joined the USMA on June 9, 1965. Active duty, Branch ADA, 1965-74; C Btry. (Herc) 4th Bn., 4th Arty., Kingston, WA; D Btry., 52nd Arty., RVN Institute Military Asst, Fort Bragg, resigned RA commission in 1974.

Commissioned in Reserves in 1974; Reserve Br. CH, 1978 to present; 36th ABN Bde. Trng, Houston, TX; SOCOM, Fort Bragg, NC; 464th CM Bde, Johnstown, PA; 99th ARCOM Pittsburgh, PA.

Awards include the Bronze Star w/OLC, Meritorious Service Medal, Air Medal, Army Commendation Medal w/2 OLCs, National Defense Service Medal w/ star, RVN Campaign, RVN Cross of Gallantry and Meritorious Unit Citation

He and wife Donna have three children and one grandchild. Associate pastor of St. Matthew Lutheran Church, Houston, TX, 1978-82 and Christ Lutheran Church, Pittsburgh, PA, 1982-present.

RAYMOND C. KOOP, Captain, born Dec. 1, 1948, Pontiac, MI, the third son of five children to Deacon Lewis Carl Christian Koop and Deaconess Viva May Eldred. Graduated from Pontiac Northern HS in 1966 and went to Moody Bible Institute, Chicago, IL where he graduated in 1970. Entered the US Army and served as a chaplain assistant during the Vietnam era, 1970-73, serving two years overseas with TASCOM, SUPDIST Nordbayern, William O. Darby Kaserne, Fuerth, Germany, as a specialist 5/c.

Earned his BA in 1975; MA in 1977 in Christian education from Biola Univ, LaMirada, CA, M.Div. in 1982 and Th.M in 1984 in systematic theology from Talbot Theological Seminary, LaMirada. Member of the Kappa Tau Epsilon Honor Society In 1989 he received his Ph.D in Biblical studies, New Testament emphasis, from Golden Gate (southern) Baptist Theological Seminary, Mill Valley, CA, where he also served for a year as a graduate fellow. Doctoral dissertation was "God as Father in the Synoptic Gospels and Pauline Literature: A Comparison and Differentiation."

Christened Dec. 26, 1948, Remus Methodist Church, Remus, MI. Accepted March 20, 1955, Jesus Christ as his Savior and Lord at Perry Park Baptist Church, Pontiac, MI and was baptized there by immersion at the age of 12 Fully licensed on Oct. 1, 1977 and ordained Aug. 31, 1980, by the Missionary Church, Inc., Fort Wayne, IN.

Served as minister of Christian Education at Ventura Missionary Church, Ventura, CA, 1977-80 and as the Missionary Church Western Dist. Christian Education Director, 1980-82 Ministered as interim pastor at Ojai Valley Community Church, Ojai, CA, 1982-83. On Nov. 12, 1987, Chap. Koop received his endorsement by the National Assoc. of Evangelicals Commission on Chaplains and entered active duty, Nov. 30, 1988, as chaplain for the 299th Engr. Bn. (Cbt), 214th FA Bde., III Corps Arty., Fort Sill, OK. Served six months with them in SW Asia during Desert Shield/Storm, and Provide Comfort as part of the 197th Inf. Bde. (Mechanized), 14th Inf. Div. Presently serves as chaplain for the 123rd Spt. Bn. (Main), DISC, 1st Armd. Div., Anderson Barracks, Germany, ministering as the community chaplain and providing chaplain coverage to the 501st MI Bn. and the 5th Bn., 3rd AD Arty. Regt.

On July 11, 1975, Chaplain Koop married Shirley Jean Rudd, daughter of Clarence A. Rudd Jr. and Verbena Smit of Oxnard, CA. She is CHAMPUS marriage and family counselor and a licensed clinical member of the American Assoc. of Marriage and Family Therapists. They have one child, Stephanie Joy, born in 1985.

Member of the National Assoc. of Evangelicals and founding member of the Centurions; the Missionary Church Historical Society; the Assoc. of the US Army, and life member of the MCA. Has held membership with the American Academy of Religion, the Society of Biblical Literature, and the Evangelical Theological Society; has been recognized by several *Who's Who*.

Awards include the Saint Barbara Medal, Sharpshooter Rifle Badge, Kuwait Liberation Medal, Army Service Ribbon, NCOPDR, Overseas Ribbon, SWA Service Medal w/3 Bronze Stars, National Defense Service Medal w/Bronze Star, Good Conduct Medal, Army Achievement Medal and the Army Commendation Medal with OLC.

JOHN V. KOWALSKI, Lieutenant Colonel, born March 15, 1917, Albion, NY. Received BA from St. Mary's College, Orchard Lake, MI; MA from Niagara Univ., Our Lady of Angels Seminary, Niagara Falls, NY and ordained a Catholic priest on June 7, 1941, Buffalo, NY.

Army service extended over a period of approximately 23 years and included two terms in the Panama Canal Zone as well as assignments at Fort Jackson; Fort Niagara; Fort Knox; Fort Dix, Schofield Barracks, HI; Germany; Korea, and Vietnam (where he was stationed during the 1968 Tet Offensive)

Retired from Army service in 1970. Prior to Army service he served various parishes and hospitals in the diocese of Buffalo, NY In 1975 he became pastor of Holy Name of Mary Church in East Pembroke, NY where he served until 1990 when he retired due to ill health.

WALTER L. KOWITZ, EM Sergeant, born July 26, 1929, in St. Paul, MN. Received AA from Inver Hills Community College; BA from Metropolitan St. Univ. and MA from International Bible College and Seminary; ordained as minister at age 54.

Joined the USMC, May 1946-50 and USAF, July 1950-September 1951. Stationed at MCB San Diego; 5th Field Depot, Guam, FMF WESPAC North China; served with H&S Co., 1st Mar. Regt., 1st Mar. Div. Memorable experience was the transfer of Chinese Nationals from North China to Formosa in 1949
(USMC), opening new basic training camp at Sampson AFB, NY during the Korean War in 1950 (USAF). Discharged September 1951 from the USAF as EM sergeant. Married Arlene A Aldrin and has three children, seven grandchildren and three great-grandchildren. Employed as supt., Honeywell Inc.; chaplain, St Paul Union Gospel Mission. Still working full time as mission chaplain.

ROBERT O. KRIEGER JR., Lieutenant Colonel, one of very few VA Chaplains who was a VA chaplain before he became a military chaplain. Born July 30, 1944, in Oak Park, IL. Attended Trinity College, Southern Illinois Univ., Trinity Evangelical Divinity School, Garrett-Evangelical Seminary, has BA, M.Div. and currently in a doctoral program at Trinity Evangelical Divinity School.

Began his VA career in September 1973 at the North Chicago VA Med. Ctr Joined the USAR in 1976 and attended the Basic Chaplain Officer Crs, in New York Transferred to VAMC Palo Alto, CA and became Chief, Chaplain Service at the VA Med Ctr, Livermore, CA, where he has been for the past 12 years

In the USAR, he served in the 85th Div. Trng, Chicago, IL as battalion chaplain from 1976-80; became an Individual Mobilization Augmentee Chaplain in 1982 and served in WESTCOM, HI as a reservist during the summers until 1987. Served with the 91st Div. Trng located in Sausalito, CA as brigade chaplain with the 6253D US Army Hosp., Santa Rosa, CA. Chaplain Krieger was ordained in the Evangelical Free Church of America

He and his wife Beverly have two daughters, Pamela and Natalie Beverly is a certified alcohol and drug addictions counselor in the state of California. They reside in Fremont, CA.

WILFRED L. KRIEGER, Colonel, born Sept. 5, 1921, in St Louis, MO. Received master's in education and master of divinity

Military Stations/Locations installation chaplain at March AFB and Randolph AFB; assistant command chaplain at Air Trng. Cmd. (1971-74); command chaplain of Air Log Cmd. (1979-80) at Wright-Patterson AFB, Dayton, OH.

Served overseas in England, Philippines, Germany and Panama. Memorable experience was designing and presently editing the *Ecumenical Daily Appointment Planner* for clergypersons of all major faith denominations. Retired in September 1981 as colonel

RALPH E. KRUEGER, Captain, born Dec. 24, 1916, Madison, WI. Graduated from Concordia College, Milwaukee and Concordia Seminary in St. Louis, MO

Joined the Army on Nov 6, 1943. Stationed at Fort Leonard Wood, Camp Breckinridge, Camp Shelby and the ETO. Served with the 75th Inf. Div., 114th Evac. Hosp., 90th Inf and 70th Constabulary

Discharged Oct 1, 1946, as captain. Awards include the Bronze Star for heroic service in crossing the Main River in Germany Memorable experience was conducting services in Flossenburg Concentration Camp after peace was signed

Widowed in 1971 and has three sons and five grandchildren. He served parishes in Buffalo, NY and Glenshaw, PA and chief chaplain at Pittsburgh, VA Medical Center, 22 years. Retired in November 1981.

VERNON F. KULLOWATZ, Colonel, born Oct. 2, 1919, Portland, OR. Graduated from Northwest Christian College, BT in 1942 and DD in 1968; Christian Theological Seminary, M Th, 1949, Graduate Air Cmd. and Staff College, 1949; graduate studies in residence, King's College, Univ. of Aberdeen, Scotland; Graduate Marriage and Family Counseling Crs., Hogg Foundation, Univ. of Texas.

Ordained in the Christian Church in 1940 and entered active duty as Army Chaplain Sept. 19, 1943. After Chaplain School, Harvard Univ., he was assigned to the 80th Inf Div. and served through WWII with them. Returned to civilian status March 1, 1946, from the position of asst. division chaplain and transferred his Army commission to the USAF

Recalled March 1951 and served continuous active duty until retirement, July 31, 1974 AF assignments were many and varied, including among others: HQ USAF/CAP Cmd. Chaplain, Military Airlift Cmd. asst. command chaplain; staff chaplain, HQ 7th AF, Vietnam, command chaplain, AF Systems Cmd., and command, chaplain, Alaskan Cmd., a tri-service position.

Awards: Silver Star, Legion of Merit w/OLC, AF Meritorious Service w/OLC, Bronze Star w/OLC and V Device, AF Commendation w/OLC and Purple Heart

Celebrated 53 years of marriage with his wife Bernice (Bea) on Sept. 13, 1994; they have three children

ABRAM GRIER KURTZ, born April 25, 1909. Attended Carlisle High, 1928; Dickinson College, 1932; Princeton Theological Seminary in 1935 Was assistant pastor of Westminster Church, Scranton, PA, 1935-40; Kingston Presbyterian Church, 1940-43.

Entered the naval service in July of 1943 and attended the Naval Chaplain's Trng. School at William and Mary College. Navy assignments were NAS, Olethe, KS and MAG 24, in the Solomon Islands and the Philippine Islands.

Returned to the States in September of 1945 and was released from active duty in October of that year. Became pastor of the First Presbyterian Church, Merchantville, NJ in 1946 and joined the Chaplain Reserve Co. 4-1, Philadelphia NB. Became staff chaplain in 1951 of the 2nd Depot Supply Bn., USMCR, remaining in that position until 1958, then at Camden, NJ until 1966.

Selected for captain and was CO of the Chaplain Co. 4-1 for about a year before retiring in 1969 He is a life member of the MCA, TROA, the Presbytery of Carlisle, The National Rifle Assoc and two hunting and fishing clubs

Married Jane Elizabeth in 1935 and has one daughter, two granddaughters and four great-grandchildren. In 1973 he was widowed and later married Ellen Scheifly Johnson of Kingston, PA They moved in 1985 to Green Ridge Village, a Presbyterian Retirement Center in Newville, PA.

JOSEPH HEYDON LAMPE, born March 19, 1911, in Syen Chun, Korea Attended college, Wooster, OH; McCormick Theological Seminary, Chicago, IL.

Joined the USN, July 3, 1943. Military locations and stations: Naval Station, Key West, FL; USS *Bougainville* (CVE-100); Naval Hosp., Pensacola, FL; USS *President Adams* (APA-19); USS *H.W Butner* (AP-119), Naval Training Station, Great Lakes, IL, MAG-12, 1st Marine Air Wing, Pacific (Korea); NTS, Great Lakes, IL (second tour); MAG-31 (Rein) Opa Locka, FL; USS *Greenwich Bay* (sea plane tender); Naval Training Station, Pensacola, FL; 1st Marine Bde, FMFPac, Kaneohe, HI; Naval Home, Philadelphia

Additional service: 1970-72, director, Servicemen's Center, Bangkok, Thailand; 1972-76, Protestant chaplain, Servicemen's Center, Fenwick Pier, Hong Kong.

Memorable experience was the typhoon off Okinawa, June 1945. The ship (CVE-100) did not capsize, but they rolled to port 38 degrees and to starboard 42 degrees. They lost 18 planes during the storm and jettisoned three more to clear the decks for others to take off

During the time they were in Korea with MAG-12, he was responsible for an orphanage. They had started out with a large tent, but with the onset of winter (1952) they needed an enclosed building, so built one with funds from the chapel services They housed approximately 150 orphans and made sure they were warm and fed. With the cooperation of the men they received several tons of clothing from friends and relatives. They provided for orphans and needy people through the church in town

One of the most memorable occasions was Christmas that year, when they had approximately 300 orphans from the Protestant chapel, the Catholic chapel, as well as from three other groups being supported by other groups of men at the base It was a rousing success and many a "Daddy for the Day" made it a real Christmas.

Retired from service July 1, 1966, as commander, CHC, USNR. He was pastor in North Dakota, Illinois and Pennsylvania and retired from the church March 19, 1976.

Married Mary Catheryn Niestadt, Aug. 16, 1938, in Wilmette, IL. They have four children, seven grandchildren and three great-grandchildren.

STEVEN OLAF LANGEHOUGH, 1st Lieutenant, born in Osage, IA, in 1955. He graduated from St. Olaf College in 1977 and United Theological Seminary of the Twin Cities in 1983. Ordained by the United Church of Christ in 1983, he served a church in South Dakota until 1986.

He was commissioned a 2nd lieutenant, Chaplain Candidate (USAFR), in 1982, and a 1st lieutenant, chaplain, in 1983. From 1982-86, he served at Travis AFB, CA; Lowry AFB, CO and Offutt AFB, NE.

He entered active duty in 1986. During the next six years he was assigned to Carswell AFB, TX (staff and hospital chaplain), Kunsan AB ROK, Rhein-Main AB Germany, and Izmir AS TU (Senior Protestant chaplain) He deployed to the Gulf during Desert Shield and to England during Desert Storm.

Since 1992 he has served a church in Hawaii and transferred to the Hawaii ARNG in 1994.

WILBUR MILTON LAUDENSLAGER, Captain, born in Allentown, PA, June 28, 1913. Graduated from Muhlenberg College 1939 and Lutheran Theological Seminary, Philadelphia, PA, 1942. He was ordained a Lutheran minister in 1942 and served two parishes: St. John, Overbrook, Philadelphia 1942-1943 and St. Luke, West Collingswood, NJ 1946-1952. He was the first resident chaplain in Lankenau Hosp, Wynnewood, PA 1954-1978

On Oct. 5, 1943, he was commissioned a lieutenant (jg), USNR Following Chaplain School at William and Mary College he was ordered to Naval Hosp., Great Lakes, IL January 1944. Ordered to the USS *Anne Arundel* (AP-76) March 1945; RAD in March 1946, and recalled June 1952. Following Chaplain School, Newport, RI, he was ordered to Naval Hosp., Key West, FL, where he reopened the Chaplain's Billet in August 1952. RAD July 15, 1954. Retired June 28, 1973, with the rank of captain, USNR

Remained on inactive reserve with Chaplain Company 4-1, Philadelphia and served as its commanding officer for three years. He is a charter member of the Liberty Bell Chapter, Philadelphia of the MCA, USA 1970-present.

On July 7, 1942, he married Myrna E Bishop. They have five children, nine grandchildren and one great-grandchild.

JAMES ALBERT LEATH JR., born Sept. 8, 1931, in Asheville, NC Attended Wake Forest University and Southeastern Theological Seminary (Baptist).

Joined the ARNG Aug. 23, 1957. Military locations and stations: Greensboro, Charlotte and Raleigh, NC. Served with 30th Arty. Bde, 105th Engr. Bde, North Carolina State HQ. Memorable experience was working with the families and men of various units. Retired June 1985 as colonel (06).

Married to Audrey Slate and they have three children and one grandchild. Held positions in churches in Highpoint, Durham, Burlington and Charlotte, NC. He retired June 1985.

HUGH F. LECKY JR., Captain, born in Newark, OH, Nov. 3, 1931. Graduated from Baldwin Wallace College, Berea, OH, Wittenberg University and was ordained a Lutheran minister 1956. He served parishes in Ohio and pastor to Lutheran students at Miami University before going on active duty. During naval services he received Th.M and Ph.D from Duke University.

Enlisted in USNR in 1949 and served as a hospital corpsman through Korea until commissioned as chaplain in 1956. He served NTC Great Lakes, DESDIV 192, MCRD Parris Island, 1st MAW, Shufly-Danang, USN SEC GRU Germany, USS *Constellation*, USS *Long Beach*, MCAS New River, AF College, CRB director, and 2nd FSSG

Retired October 1985 as a captain. He holds many military and civilian awards including three Legion of Merit and a Purple Heart received as the first chaplain wounded in Vietnam (1965).

Married Janet Lee Storms in 1952 and they have four children and 11 grandchildren. They reside in Durham, NC where he still serves as interim pastor.

ALBERT F. LEDEBUHR, Colonel, born June 9, 1924, in Milwaukee, WI. Graduated from Concordia Seminary in 1948, was a member of the Lutheran Church Missouri Synod and entered the US Army, Fort Dix, NJ, 1951.

Military stations and locations (1952-67) Erlangen Germany, 1st Army; Fort Riley, three months; Fort Slocum, wrote character guidance, made films, Korea, built chapel; Fort Belvoir, deputy post chaplain; Fort Leavenworth, student; Fort Lee, VA, CDC, wrote info for Combat Dev. Com.; Staff College, Class of 1940.

From 1967-79. Vietnam, during TET worked with Vietnamese Ch. (Buddhist, Catholic); War College Class of 1970; Fort Benning, post chaplain, established teaching position at Infantry School; USAEUR chaplain; TRADOC chaplain, Fort Monroe where he retired July 1979 as colonel.

Subsequently he worked for the Bethel Bible Series in Madison, WI Finally, he restored Harmony Church which was pastored by Reinhold Niebuhr's father, 100+ years ago. In 1979 he joined the ELCA and left Missouri Synod Held position at Bethel Bible Institute (Director of Development). Retired in 1987.

Married Jean Kerghtley in 1949. They had four children and six grandchildren. He passed away Nov 16, 1993.

ESTES L. LEWIS, Lieutenant Colonel, born April 25, 1908, near Athens, TX. Attended Baylor University, Waco, TX and SW Baptist Seminary. Joined the AF June 4, 1941. At stateside assignments he encouraged the personnel to attend churches of their own faith. This was a help to the local churches. They served in various services and helped to finance the local budgets

His overseas assignments were different. He was assigned to the AF Reinforcement station. Most of the AF personnel coming into the European Theatre came through their station and he was a part of the orientation team. The men were only there for a few days and on Sundays the theatre was full with nearly 500 men He also had second service at another unit and sometimes a third. Conducted the Hebrew services, he would read the Hebrew and one of the officers conducted the introduction He preached from the Old Testament Scripture and also did this in Korea and Greenland. He would almost have a second service at another part of the base and sometimes at a base in a separate location. Their chapel attendance was normally about 3 to 500 each Sunday.

When he returned from Europe, he was assigned to McClellan AFB, Sacramento, CA and was there three years He was given the responsibility of coordinating the chaplains supplies for Western US and the Far East He next served at Chatham AFB, Savannah, GA Chaplains were given the task of serving as casualty assistance officers (assisting the families of those who had died). One young man that Lewis had refused to perform his wedding, because he had told Lewis in a counseling session that he had not received a divorce from the former wife, was killed in an accident and the first wife received the death benefits.

At Chatham AFB he visited the mother of an officer who had been killed in the Berlin Airlift He had known the officer and his family at Sacramento, however, his mother did not know that he was married and had two children. He wrote these things up and the regulations were changed to remove this duty from the chaplains. Next there was a regulation that, if the chaplain was on leave and a civilian minister supplied for the religious services, then the chaplain would personally pay the minister. He wrote to the Adjutant General that this deprived the chaplains of authorized leave. No other civilian or military were required to pay someone else to perform their duties when they were on leave. This regulation was also changed.

From Chatham AFB, GA he was assigned to the 3rd Bomb Wing, Iwakuni, Japan for a few weeks before they moved to Kunsan, Korea. When overseas he always had a large attendance. From the HQ in Tokyo blueprints were sent for chapels in Korea that would hold 70 people. The engineer on their base built a chapel for 300 When personnel from Tokyo came for dedication, they said they knew that Rev Lewis was lying on his reports, for no one had that many people in chapel. In addition to the Sunday a.m. service at the chapel, he conducted a service at the port in Kunsan, at 8 a.m. In the afternoon he conducted a service for the Koreans who worked on the base with an interpreter A service at the Marine base across from their main base, then back to the confinement facility for a service, and counseling Then the evening service at the chapel. At the briefing each afternoon, he had a prayer for the men and their missions. Some of the crews told him of their thinking of these prayers on the missions.

In 1952 he returned from Korea to Chanute AFB, Rantoul, IL This training base for new personnel was a real blessing, as it gave him opportunity to serve men and women as they were in school From Chanute AFB, he went to the base at Greenville, MS, a basic training field. From Greenville, he went to Sondrostrom AFB, Greenland. This base is isolated and considered a hardship assignment.

When he returned from Greenland, he was terminated from service. As he had nearly 17 years of service, he enlisted and became a statistical analyst He not only prepared the programs for the charts, but reviewed them after they were prepared for presentation to Congress and higher commands.

Retired from the AF in 1961 and chose to pastor smaller churches as he had enough income to support himself and family. In 1961, he was recognized at the Texas A&M University Town and Country Pastors Conference as the Outstanding Minister of the Year by the *Farm and Ranch Magazine.*

Married Ruth Martin May, May 10, 1936, she died Dec. 14, 1990 They have two children, four grandchildren and two great-great grandchildren

ROBERT C. LEWIS, Lieutenant Colonel, born Sept. 24, 1926, in Greensboro, NC, the only child of Chester and Ella Lewis. After attending North Carolina State College, he graduated from MIT in 1951, and shortly thereafter was commissioned in the Navy Reserve.

In 1959, he became an AF chaplain serving three years at Chanute AFB, IL. In 1962, he was called to his church headquarters, The First Church of Christ, Scientist, in Boston, MA, to assist in ministering to chaplains and military personnel of his denomination worldwide. Served on MCAs Executive Committee and was president of the New England Chapter. He and his wife Loetta retired to Sun City Center, FL, where they are active in the local branch of their church.

KENNETH MARTIN LINDNER, Lieutenant Commander, born in Edinburgh, Scotland (May 1, 1906) and in Scotland's capital city received his undergraduate education His parents, brother, and he emigrated to America. The family initially settled in the Chicago area. Lindner was active in Chicago's North Shore Congregational Church and later received their ordination.

Called to South Bend, IN, Lindner served the People's Church as assistant. Naturalized an American citizen and knowing personally the church's Pearl Harbor casualties, the seed was sown to volunteer as chaplain. His call to duty was to the Chaplain School, Harvard University (March-April, 1944) Later, as a Reservist, he was a student at Carlisle Barracks for the Field Grade Chaplain Course.

From Harvard he was ordered to Camp Van Dorn, MS (Medical Units). Next assignment was to North Camp Hood, TX, with HQ 23rd Tank Destroyer (TD) Gp. as Protestant chaplain. That unit was scheduled for Europe. Chaplain Lindner was with the advance party

In Europe the mission of HQ 23d TD Gp was changed to HQ Rear Security, HQ 1st Army. Chaplain Lindner was placed on Detached Service with Chaplain Section, HQ 1st Army. Duties were implementing the desires of the Commanding General (VOCG) and to work with Cbt. Engrs., specially with battalions whose Group HQ were 1110th and 1128th.

Hostilities ended, his status of Detached Service ceased and with HQ 23rd TD Gp , he arrived at Fort Bragg, NC Upon the arrival of HQ 1st Army at Fort Bragg, Chaplain Lindner was ordered from Special Troops to Chaplain Section, HQ, 1st Army. There he served until HQ 1st Army was relocated at Governor's Island, NY. Accepted discharge and transfer to active Ready Reserve. In Fayetteville, NC, he organized the Eutaw Community Church

In 1952 Chaplain Lindner was recalled to active duty at Fort Bragg for special duties with 503 MP Bn., the Post Stockades, and Chaplain Section, Post HQ Receiving orders to the Far East, he was assigned to Camp Drake Personnel Center, Tokyo. Exigencies at Yokohoma Chapel Center eventuated in Lindner's assignment there.

Upon his completion of maximum Far East service, he was ordered to Army Chemical Center, MD, as post chaplain. Requested by his denomination for temporary service to the First Congregational Church, Washington, DC, he obtained voluntary release from active duty His ministry completed at that church, the Veterans Administration Chaplaincy placed him in Huntington, WV, as hospital chaplain. Continued as hospital chaplain in Huntington for five years. Responding to Marshall Univ , he became a member of their faculty, teaching in the English Department.

Upon reaching mandatory retirement, he was transferred to the Retired Reserve He is a lifetime member in six veterans organizations, including the MCA

CHESTER R. LINDSEY, Colonel, born on May 25, 1915, in Tuscumbia, MO Graduate of Moody Bible Institute in Chicago, he received his BA degree from William Jewell College, Liberty, MO. Received his bachelor of divinity degree and his master's degree in religious education from Central Baptist Seminary, Kansas City, KS Ordained at Hickory Hill Baptist Church, Eugene, MO, on Feb. 22, 1942 On May 8, 1945, he began active military duty with the US Army.

During his 30 years in the Army, he has served with the 40th Inf. Div. in the Philippines and Korea and the 7th Inf. Div. in Korea as unit chaplain, the 11th and 101st Abn Divs., Fort Campbell, KY, as assistant division chaplain; the 25th Inf Div , Hawaii, as assistant post and division chaplain; the US Army Chaplain School, Fort Slocum, NY, as instructor and later chairman of the Military Subject Committee, Munich Post as deputy post chaplain; the Office of the Staff Chaplain, US Army Europe as Chief, Plans and Operations; 1st Cav. Div., Vietnam as division chaplain; CONRAC as deputy staff chaplain; and US Army Pacific as command chaplain.

On Feb. 1, 1971, he was assigned as deputy commandant and director of instruction of the US Army Chaplain School. He was appointed commandant on July 30, 1971. As commandant of the Chaplain School, he supervised training for all chaplains and chaplain's assistants in the US Army.

Military decorations and awards include: Legion of Merit w/2nd OLC, Bronze Star, Air Medal, Parachutist Badge, Presidential Unit Citation, Asiatic-Pacific Campaign Medal, WWII Victory Medal, Army of Occupation Medal, National Defense Medal w/OLC, Korea Service Medal, Vietnam Service Medal w/3 Campaign Stars, Armed Forces Reserve Medal, Philippine Liberation Ribbon, UN Medal, RVN Campaign Medal and Vietnamese Cross of Gallantry with palms. In May 1967 he received the award of Military Chaplain of the Year at the American Baptist Convention, in November 1967 he was awarded the Citation of Distinguished Achievement by William Jewell College; and in 1968 he was named Alumnus of the Year by the Moody Bible Institute

Married to the former Cecile E. Hess of Grundy Center, IA They have three children: Gordon is a graduate of Yale Divinity School and assistant pastor in Long Island, NY; Linda of Minneapolis, MN; and Karla Lindsey Davies of Fort Lauderdale, FL

Chaplain Lindsey retired from the US Army on March 31, 1975. On July 1, 1975, assumed duties as assistant dean, Bethel Theological Seminary, St Paul, MN He passed away April 27, 1980.

JOHN A. LINDVALL, Colonel, born June 29, 1920, at Muskegon, MI. He graduated from Central Bible College, Springfield, MO, Southern California College and attended the Universities of Basel, MD and New York.

Was ordained in the Assemblies of God in August 1942 in Framingham, MA. Married Mae Nelson of Clearfield, PA in 1947 and they have four children and five grandchildren

Commissioned in the US Army in 1944, served with 36th Inf. Div. (TX) in WWII; 40th Div (CA) in Korea; six years with the 82nd Abn Div (including service in the Dominican Republic); was the first senior chaplain in Vietnam (MACV); and served with the 10th Div., Bamberg, Germany; was Rhineland District chaplain in Bad Kreuznach, Germany, command chaplain for the Munitions Command, Edgewood Arsenal, MD and Defense Atomic Support Chaplain, Sandia Base, NM. He retired June 30, 1971.

Civilian ministry included pastoring in Augusta, IL, organizing churches in Waterbury and Stamford, CT. After retirement, he became vice-president of Southern California College, Costa Mesa, CA. He also served Plymouth Congregational, Newport Beach, Hollywood Congregational and Anaheim Congregational churches.

He founded Mission Ministries, Inc., has served as VP of Worldscope Ministries, Asian Outreach, Major Market Stations and served on boards of a number of other missions and corporations.

LEWIS C. LONG III was born March 4, 1941 in Deland, FL. He attended Howey Academy, Howey-in-the-Hills, FL, John B. Stetson University (B.S.), The Lancaster Theological Seminary, Deland, FL (M.Div.) He joined the USAF on November 18, 1963 and was discharged in 1967, USAFR from 1972-1976 and the UDAF from 1976 to the present. Military locations and stations: Lackland AFB, TX. Amarillo AFB, TX, Itazuke AB Japan, Randolph AFB, TX, Osan AB, Korea, Patrick AFB, FL and remote sites above the Arctic Circle while stationed at Elmendorf AFB, AK, Wright-Patterson AFB, OH, Lindsey AS, Germany, Keesler AFB, MS, Contingency Hospital in Little Rizzington, England during Operation Desert Storm. In 1992 he retired from the United States Air Force at Keesler AFB on April 30.

His civilian employment included being the Senior Pastor at Pilgrim Community Church in Orange City, FL. He is married to Caryn and they have two sons: Lewis C. Long IV (Clark) and Chase Bond Long. He was ordained as a minister in 1974.

PERCIVAL LOVSETH, Lieutenant Colonel, born in South Dakota and graduated from Augustana College in Sioux Falls and in 1949 from Luther Theological Seminary in St Paul, MN. Served in WWII, both in enlisted and officer status, and was commissioned a chaplain, US Army in March 1951. Retired as a lieutenant colonel in 1968.

His military assignments included X Corps Arty. during the Korean War, 8th, 9th and 31st Inf. Div., 40th Arty. Gp (Redstone), 505th Signal Gp., post chaplain, Fort Totten, New York, and Corps Chaplain, VI US Army Corps. He was awarded the Legion of Merit, Bronze Star and Army Commendation Medal.

More recently, he has served as a field service pastor for the Lutheran Council in Texas, California and the Philippines and as executive director of the Volunteers of America in Sacramento. He is married to Anne Zima and has two sons and four grandsons.

KURT A. LUEDTKE, Colonel, is a life member of the MCA and the National Guard Association of the United States.

After commissioning in the US Army, he served for almost 25 years in infantry, artillery, armor, medical, aviation, special forces, and chaplain assignments, retiring from active reserve status in 1991. Although he had a rather unusual and diverse career, Col. Luedtke recounts his years of service as battalion chaplain with 1/246 FA, Virginia Army National Guard, as the most special.

Holds a baccalaureate, masters, doctoral and post doctoral degrees in professional psychology, and is licensed as a clinical psychologist and marriage and family therapist in multiple states. Currently serving as clinical director of Waynesboro Family Clinic in Goldsboro, NC, he has been board certified in professional psychotherapy, medical psychotherapy, behavioral medicine, and pain management, intensively practicing Christian psychology within a community mental health context.

Happily married (for 25 years) to Peggy Powers and they have two children, Peggy Leigh and Erik Von Luedtke.

ELDEN H. LUFFMAN, born on Aug. 23, 1925, in Ocala, FL, the eldest son of Mr. and Mrs. Leland Luffman

Graduated from Ocala High School at the peak of WWII and enlisted in the USN on Aug. 10, 1943, where he served for three years, attaining the rating of petty officer first class.

After graduating from Stetson University, Southeastern Baptist Theological Seminary, and serving as pastor of two churches, he re-entered the Navy as a chaplain and served in a variety of ministries until his retirement on Nov. 1, 1979 He served a total of 34 years of active and reserve military service and retired as lieutenant commander.

He had the distinction of serving as squadron chaplain from the world's first guided missile squadron DESRON 18. He was chaplain for the 1st Marine Regt. when it received the Presidential Unit Citation for its action in the Battle of Hue during the 1968 TET offensive in Vietnam. He was honored to be at the White House when President Nixon presented this award.

Other awards include: the Navy Commendation Medal w/Combat V (two awards), Combat Action Ribbon, Meritorious Unit Commendation (two awards).

Married to Joyce Cheek on Nov. 27, 1947 They have three children and nine grandchildren.

LOUIS LULJAK, son of Paul and Pauline Luljak, born May 5, 1935. Baptized May 26, 1935, in Roman Catholic faith and ordained priest, May 27, 1961.

Direct commission to Army Chaplain Corps, Jan 17, 1967. Units served 452nd Gen. Hosp (USAR), 5th Inf. Div. (Mech.), 2nd Inf. Div., (Korea), Fort Wolters PHC, 101st Inf. Div. Airborne (AirMobile) Vietnam, 1st Inf. Div. at Fort Riley, 452d Gen. Hosp. (USAR).

Civilian schooling: Saint Joseph Parochial Grade School, Saint Francis Minor Seminary (BA), Saint Francis Major Seminary (BT); School of Pastoral Ministry (M Div.), Long Island University (MS).

Military schooling: Chaplain Basic Course (Fort Hamilton, NY), Chaplain Advanced (Fort Wadsworth, NY); Command and General Staff College.

Military awards: National Defense Service Medal, Army Commendation Medal w/1st OLC, Vietnam Service Medal w/3 Bronze Service Stars, RVN Campaign Medal w/60 Device, Civic Actions Medal (1st Class), Armed Forces Expeditionary Medal, Bronze Star Medal and Staff Service Medal. Promoted to full colonel, Nov. 15, 1984. Retired July 12, 1990.

Civilian assignments. Saint Anthony (Kenosha, WI), Saint James (Muckwonago), Saint Roman (Milwaukee), Church of the Divine Word (Cedarburg) and Saint Stanislaus/Holy Trinity (Racine).

WALLACE L. LUNDEEN, Colonel, born Feb. 1, 1928, in Fargo, ND. Received MA and M Div.degrees. Joined the Navy and Army 1947.

Military locations and stations, stateside plus Pacific and Mediterranean sea duty. Served with aircraft carriers, fighter squadrons, hospitals.

Memorable experience was the long continuous duty tour in battle zone-Korea and being listed in *Who's Who*. Discharged colonel, Feb. 1, 1988.

Married Barbara Pascal Serex. They have five children and four grandchildren. Held position as church pastor, hospital chaplain Retired February 1993.

ARTHUR E. LYONS JR., born on Sept. 13, 1927, Rock Island, IL, the son of Art and Elizabeth nee Teuscher Lyons. Attended Concordia High School, Junior College, Milwaukee, WI; Concordia Theological Seminary, St Louis, MO and was ordained June 19, 1955

Served in the US Army in 1951-1952 serving 12 months in Korea. Returned to active duty as a chaplain in 1963. His chaplain assignments included Fort Hood, TX; Fort Leonard Wood, MO; Fort Riley, KS, Korea and Vietnam. He was retired for disability June 29, 1974, as major.

His awards and decorations include the Good Conduct Medal, Bronze Star Medal, Army Commendation Medal w/4 OLCs, Bronze St. Martin of Tours Award (of the Lutheran Church-Missouri Synod).

One of his most memorable experiences was serving as acting battalion chaplain for a period of six months in Korea in 1952 as a private first class

Parishes served included Christ Lutheran Church, Fort Worth, TX; Zion Lutheran Church, Alamo, TX; St. Peter, Pearsall, TX; and Grace, Devine, TX (a dual parish), and Grace, Rockdale, TX He retired Dec. 31, 1987.

Married to the former Alleen Kuretsch; they have five children and seven grandchildren.

ROBERT L MAASE, born Jan. 18, 1923 in Gresham, NE. He received a Th. B. from Judson College; B.A. from Roosevelt University, and M. Div. from Northern Baptist Theological Seminary.

He was in the USCG from Oct 6, 1942 - Nov. 16, 1945 as a PhM1/c. He joined the USAF on Nov 11, 1952. His various duties and assignments included: 1952-1970 and 1955-1958: Chaplain, USAF, Director of Christian Education of largest Air Force Sunday School in Bitburg Germany. 1958-1960 Minister to 1,200 WAF in the Air Force in basic training, tech. school and Permanent Party, Lackland Air Force Base, TX. 1960-1962: Chaplain of Wilford Hall Hospital - largest in the Air Force. 1962: Only Protestant Air Force Chaplain assigned to Joint Task Force 8 Pacific Atomic test (Christmas Islands Atomic Tests – all branches of the military) 1963-1966: First Junior Grade Wing Chaplain of largest AF fighter base in England (Lakenheath). 1966-1969: Wing Chaplain and Assistant Command Chaplain Bolling AFB, Washington, D.C area, Pentagon Protestant Pulpit: Arlington National Cemetery. Wing Chaplain largest AFB in Udorn, Thailand, SEA. Organized orphanage and adoption agency in Udorn, Thailand for Amerasian children (150)

He was discharged from the service on June 1, 1970.

Civilian employment includes the following: 1970-1982 – Northern Baptist Seminary, Chicago, IL. Area Representative, Director of Church Relations, Alumni, Placement, Student Services, etc 1982-1988 – Associate Administrator and Director of Development at Atherton Baptist Homes, Alhambra, CA.

Denominational involvements and Air Force assignments: Director of Protestant Women of Chapel for United Kingdom, England, President S W Washington, D.C. Ministers Council, Chairman of Pentagon Protestant Pulpit Committee, President of American Baptist Public Relations Association, National ABC/USA

Collaborated with Dr. A. W. Balckwood in writing an introduction on *Memorials* for his book on *Funerals* to be used for returning deceased Korean veterans.

Medals: Commendation Medal, Meritorious Service, Chaplain of the Year for Headquarters Command, Washington, D.C.,

He married to Elda Apel on March 6, 1943, she died May 7, 1990 She was a retired professor of Education and English. They had three children: David (Ph.D.), Philip (B.A.), and Karen (B.A and B.S.) and three grandchildren Eric Maase, Kimberly Ann, and Carrie Lee Marie. Robert Maase enjoys travel, photography, reading and volunteering. He is a member of Rotary International, Mental Health Association, Public Relations Association, National Assoc. of Homes for the Aging, California Homes and Hospitals Association, and Ministers Council American Baptist Con., USA. His special honor was receiving the Alumnus of the Year Award in 1989 by his Alma Mater Northern Baptist Theological Seminary.

HARRY TER MAAT, Captain, born July 28, 1953, in Vesper, WI. Received a M.Div. Joined the US Army and joined the Reserve Oct. 8, 1983, and active duty Oct 17, 1988

Military locations and stations: Schofield Barracks, HI (four years), Fort Riley, KS (two years). Served with DIVARTY-25th Inf. Div. (L)/ 2-34 Armor-1st Inf. Div (Mech)

Memorable experience was being selected for Fort Riley Unit Ministry Team of Year - FY 94. Discharged as captain Oct 16, 1994, and continued serving in the Reserves

Married to Marilyn Ter Maat. Held a position in travel and is now fully retired.

JAMES R. MACARTHUR, Lieutenant Colonel, born New Britain, CT, March 17, 1917. Educated in the local schools, BA American International College, Springfield, MA, M Div Hartford Theological Seminary, Hartford, CT. Ordained, South Congregational Church, New Britain, CT. Post graduate work, United Seminary of the Twin Cities, St. Paul, MN. Pastor of the Congregational Churches, Lakota and Crary, ND.

Appointed first lieutenant AUS, Feb. 9, 1943, March 4, 1943. Attended Chaplain School, Cambridge, MA. Group chaplain, 78 Air Svc. Gp , 13th Abn. Gp. to ETO, England May 1943, had usual chaplain duties in various locations in England, served units of 82nd Abn. when at their base for missions, including D-day, 82nd Svc. Gp., Air Strip B, 54 in France.

Back to the USA from Belgium and became part of chaplain pool eventually to Detachment of Separatees, Santa Ana, CA, where separated. Continued in Massachusetts NG, Connecticut Reserve, became lieutenant colonel and North Dakota NG until March 17, 1973, max allowable age.

DEBORAH MARIYA, Lieutenant, a native of Luverne, MN, she graduated from the Luverne Consolidated High School in 1971, with honors. Received her BA Cum laude, from Augustana College, Sioux Falls, SD in 1977. Following mission work with Wycliffe Bible translators in Brazil and Mexico, she attended Theological School, graduating from Garrett Evangelical Theological Seminary, Evanston, IL in 1984.

Rev. Mariya was ordained by the Iowa Annual Conference of the United Methodist Church in 1982 She served as the pastor of the Hope Parish, the Danbury Oto Yoke Parish and Wesley UMC, Muscatine from 1982-90.

Commissioned in the Naval Reserve in 1988, she entered the call to active duty ministry in 1990 and assigned as the command chaplain of USS *Cape Cod* (AD-43) homeported in San Diego. Deployed to the Persian Gulf during Desert Storm and again in 1993. Deployed to the Philippines during operation Fiery Vigil, 1991 Currently assigned to The National Naval Med. Ctr. in Bethesda, MD and to the hospital ship, USNS *Comfort* (T-AH-20)

She will never forget leaving a small rural parish in Iowa and reporting aboard USS *Cape Cod* with a crew of 1,500 members, and shortly thereafter, finding herself deploying for war in the Middle East.

She is married to Sam Tangredi, a commander in the USN.

ARTHUR C. MARSTON, Colonel, born in Nov. 22, 1915, in Austin (Chicago), IL. Attended Iowa State Univ., Westminster Seminary, Army Chaplain School. Joined the US Army, Dec 28, 1944.

Military locations and stations: WWII, Italy, Iowa ARNG, served with 432nd AAA Bn , 87th Mountain Inf., 2nd Inf. Div., 168th Inf , 34th Inf. Div

Memorable experiences: assistant division chaplain, 2nd Inf. Div.; division chaplain, 34th Inf Div.; regimental chaplain, 87th Mtn Div., (10th Mtn. Div); 133rd Inf. Regt ; and 168th Inf Regt. (34th Inf. Div.) Achieved the rank of colonel Discharged Nov. 22, 1975

Married Lota Mae Adamson (deceased), then Dorothy G. Keeling He has eight children and one grandchild He held position as American Baptist minister in Iowa. Retired in 1975 to Florida

CHRISTIAN HESS MARTIN JR., Colonel, born May 29, 1928, and grew up on a farm near Lancaster, PA. He was his Manheim Township High School 1946 class president, valedictorian and varsity athlete lettering in five sports. After Army Medical Corps service as a staff sergeant, he studied at his hometown Franklin and Marshall College. Transferring, he later graduated from Harvard with a concentration in clinical psychology, and leadership as president of the Harvard Christian Fellowship

Seeking jet pilot training, he entered the AF Aviation Cadet program, later was commissioned and received his Silver Wings at Bryan AFB, TX, in 1955 where he served as cadet wing commander. Follow-on assignments were at Hickam and Dover AFBs, the Pacific and Atlantic Divisions of MATS, flying worldwide routes and special missions as aircraft commander, instructor, flight examiner, and an assistant operations officer.

In further preparing for the chaplaincy, he served congregations in Alaska, Trenton, NJ and West Chester, PA. Continued AF Reserve flight duties while studying at Princeton Theological Seminary, from which he graduated and was ordained a Presbyterian minister in 1961. Initial chaplain taskings were at Niagara Falls AFB 1965, Takhli RTAFB and SEA in 1967, and at Oxnard AFB, CA, 1969 Base chaplain (installation staff chaplain, ISC) responsibilities followed at Tempelhof/Berlin 1973, Kirkland AFB, Albuquerque 1980, and at Incirlik AB Turkey, 1984.

MAJCOM HQ assignments - in support, training, and supervision of especially AFRES and ANG chaplain programs nationwide - included "tours of duty" at ADC 1970, MAC 1977, and ESC 1982 as command chaplain. For all this, studies at Air University's Staff and Command College, Maxwell AFB, AL were especially valuable Also, various crew survival and rescue courses and parachute training at Lakehurst NAS with Navy Seals proved advantageous in interservice ministries and exercises worldwide

Retired as TFWC Center Chaplain at Nellis AFB, Las Vegas in 1986, at that time the AF's largest operation with over 16,000 airmen assigned, the only base with three wings, plus important (and some secret) auxiliary fields and sites, "home" of the AF Thunderbirds Aerial Demonstration Team also, with whom he occasionally traveled, as a chaplain.

Chaplain Martin is a Daedalian, the Association of Military pilots; a member (H.R.) of Donegal Presbytery, PA; has served PCUSA congregations in South Texas; and currently (1995) is a Protestant chaplain at AF Village II near San Antonio. Through the years he has been active in professional, aviation, service, educational, military, community, church, and chaplaincy-related institutions, with special interest in POW/MIA concerns and families

He met Geraldine, his wife and "copilot" of 40 years, in Honolulu where she was working for Pan American Airways. A native of Yakima, WA, Geri is now an editor in Civil Service at MPC, Randolph AFB,

TX. She has been a teammate in ministry too, in very significant ways. Their daughter Karen is a manager for a global computer-software firm. Her "assignments" have been at financial centers worldwide; she had earlier worked in D.C as a US Senator's staff member.

Son Frederick is a lieutenant colonel pilot and C-141 squadron operations officer at Altus AFB, OK who, with his AF Academy classmate and pilot-wife Barbara, are parents of three daughters.

Son Scott, with business-woman-wife Linda, is a corporate lawyer in Chicago after four years as an AF intelligence officer and graduate degrees in both religion and law from the Univ. of Chicago. This paragraph, to illustrate that in numerous ways. "it's been an Air Force 'family experience,'" and . . . peripatetic life."

For and through all the myriad dimensions of an Armed Forces chaplaincy career, Chaplain Martin's was ever a ministry of "outreach" and "presence," one stressing leadership and involvement of the laity, and closest coordination with chapel office and management personnel. A ministry, also, ever-animated by the fervent, deathbed appeal of his first base chaplain at Niagara Falls, Fr. Edmund Fleming, a gallant veteran of CBI jungle warfare in WWII as a padre with Merrill's Marauders.

Father Fleming's abiding hope and prayer - and his "credo" is included in this bio-sketch out of great respect for him, and profound appreciation for the collegial ministry which is the chaplaincy at its best (i.e. for four chaplains of the USS *Dorchester*) - was that all chaplains should 1) "get out among the troops," our people and their families too. We should 2) reassure them that God loves us all, and is with us. 3) Assure them that they count, that everyone's effort and teamwork is essential to the mission. 4) Be a "benediction" to them, as and wherenever one can - realizing that not everyone will be open or responsive to that. But, 5) "never giving up on anyone, for neither does our Lord, who is merciful and gracious," and in death as in life ever-poised to welcome us "home." "Requiescat in pace," Chaplain Fleming. Shalom. Salaam. Aloha. "Shaloha" to all.

HENRY LAWRENCE MARTIN, born Oct 25, 1925, in Clinton, TN. Received his training at Carson-Newman College, Jefferson City, TN; New Orleans Baptist Theological Seminary, New Orleans, LA; Southern Baptist Theological Seminary, Louisville, KY; McCormick Theological Seminary, Chicago, IL (D Min.); and George Washington Univ., Washington, DC. As a Southern Baptist clergyman, he served as pastor of First Baptist Church, Vanceburg, KY; Auburn Baptist Church, Auburn, KY; First Baptist Church, Dickson, TN; and Greenwich Baptist Church, Greenwich, CT.

Martin served as a hospital corpsman in the Navy during WWII, prior to his entering college. Entered the Navy as a chaplain Jan. 2, 1967, and served until retirement Nov. 1, 1987, in the grade of commander. Principal duty stations included Chaplains School, Military Sealift Cmd., Pacific; Naval Hosp., San Diego (under instruction), Naval Hosp., Oakland, CA; Naval Advisory Gp., Military Assistance Cmd., Vietnam; NAS, Memphis, TN; USS *Coronado* (LPD-11) Fleet Religious Support Activity, USS *Shenandoah* (AD-26), Norfolk, VA; Naval Station, Norfolk, VA: Naval Operations, Washington, DC; and NTC, Orlando, FL.

During his five year tour in Washington, he served as head, Chaplain Corps History Branch, during which time he established the Chaplain Corps History Resource Center, Oral History Program, and Writers Program. He edited *Chaplains With U.S. Naval Units in Vietnam 1954-1975: Selected Experiences at Sea and Ashore;* and *History of the Chaplains Corps, U.S. Navy 1972-1981.* (He was also responsible for numerous monographs articles, and extended oral history interviews).

Awards and decorations include the China Service Medal, Asiatic-Pacific Campaign Medal w/2 stars, American Campaign Service Medal, WWII Victory Medal, Philippine Liberation Medal w/2 stars, Republic of Philippines Presidential Unit Citation, Navy Occupation Service Medal w/Asia Clasp, National Defense Service Medal, Vietnam Service Medal w/Silver Star and two Bronze Stars, RVN Campaign Medal, Meritorious Unit Commendation w/star, Navy Unit Commendation w/ star, Presidential Unit Citation, RVN Meritorious Unit Commendation (Civil Actions Medal, First Class Color with Palm), Navy Commendation Medal, Sea Service Deployment Ribbon and Meritorious Service Medal.

Married to the former Carolyn Taylor. They have two children, Timothy (a Presbyterian clergyman) and Lisa (a marketing communications manager). Timothy and his wife Julie have two sons.

Since retirement, Chaplain Martin has spent his time preaching, teaching and writing. Currently serves on the adjunct faculties of Columbia College (Orlando Extension) and New Orleans Baptist Theological Seminary (Orlando Extension).

JAMES B. MARTIN, Commander, in almost 50 years of ministry, Jim Martin has been called chaplain most of those years. Born in Chicago June 2, 1921, to Mary Ruth Smith and James H. Martin, he studied in Texas with the Oblates and in St. Louis at Kenrick Seminary. Ordained in Peoria, IL December 1946, he remained at the cathedral until joining the Navy Chaplain Corps in 1951.

After USMC duty at Parris Island with Puerto Rican troops, he joined MAG-11 in North Carolina and went to Japan and Korea with them. NAS Key West was his last active duty. In 1956 he became a chaplain at the Univ. of Illinois and there earned an MA with honors. He then reestablished one parish and founded another, both close to the university.

Following his silver jubilee he resigned the second parish and studied Spanish in Mexico. To prepare for hospital ministry he interned in Washington, DC at the federal hospital for the mentally ill. He then served on staff, earning the title of supervisor, mental health chaplains, US Catholic Conference.

Having remained active in the Naval Reserve, he was promoted to captain in 1974. After serving as a chaplain in the Veterans hospital, Battle Creek, MI, where he developed a multi-disciplinary treatment for substance abusers, he was moved back to Washington as deputy director of Veterans Chaplain Services, and, in January 1982 became director.

During that period he headed a team of chaplains who developed "The Philosophy of Hospital Chaplaincy." The USCC, Cardinal Cooke, and Archbishop Joseph T Ryan, the Military Ordinary, incorporated the work into the official endorsement of Catholic hospital chaplains.

He has been active in the MCA, an early member of its Emerson Foundation, a national trustee and a local representative for both Virginia and Navy, as well as one of the search committee which nominated William Dando for executive director. He belongs to the American Legion and to CORPUS, the National Association for a Married Priesthood, serving on their national board and coordinating their first national conference in 1988 at American Univ. in Washington, DC.

Married to Margaret Woolley in 1984, they have six adult married children and, so far, two granddaughters "born on his watch." With family from Milan, Italy to San Diego, CA, they have travelled widely. To celebrate their 10th anniversary they bought a new home and moved to San Diego. There he expects to continue as a volunteer hospice chaplain, a work begun with the Montgomery County, MD Hospice Society.

JERRY L. MARTIN, Lieutenant Colonel, born Sept. 27, 1938, in Mt. Vernon, IL. Received a BA in education, MA in sociology; M.Div. Joined the US Army May 2, 1966 (active duty).

Military locations and stations: Fort Leonard Wood, RVN, Fort Ord; Thailand; Europe. Served with Fort Bragg; West Point; Walter Reed Army Medical Center. Memorable experiences: Served with 4th Inf. Div.; 82nd Abn Div., March 1971 ADA

Received Purple Heart, Legion of Merit, Meritorious Service Medal, Bronze Star, Army Commendation Medal. Discharged May 31, 1986.

Married Adell E Martin. They have three children and two grandchildren. Held position as pastor at Kensington Baptist Church. Retired May 31, 1986

ROBERT GLENN MASSENGALE, Commander, born June 14, 1915, in Stewart, AL. Received AB 1935, Birmingham-Southern College; BD 1939; PhD 1950, Yale Univ. Joined with the US Naval Reserve Nov 10, 1943.

Military locations and stations: NTS (chaplains), Williamsburg, VA, Jan. 15-March 13, 1944; Naval Air Facility, Columbus, OH, March 18, 1944-Feb. 1, 1945, Navy Yard, Puget Sound, Washington (temporary duty in connection with fitting out of USS *Siboney*, CVE-112), Feb. 14, 1945-April 18, 1945, commissioning detail, USS *Siboney* (CVE-112), Tacoma, WA, April 19, 1945-May 14, 1945; USS *Siboney* (CVE-112), May 14, 1945-Feb 12, 1946.

US Naval Reserve (active): February 18, 1946-June 30, 1969, Fleet Reserve, June 30, 1969-June 4, 1975. Retired June 4, 1975. Memorable experience was his extended duty as chaplain, USS *New Jersey* (BB-62) on midshipmen cruise to Europe, June 1-Aug. 2, 1956. Achieved the rank commander. Discharged from active duty, Feb. 12, 1946. From Naval Reserve, June 30, 1969

Professor of Religion and Philosophy and chaplain, Univ. of South Carolina, June 1946-September 1948; director, Wesley Foundation at Yale Univ, September 1948-May 1949, professor of Religious Education, Scarritt College, June 1949-May 1951, professor of Religion and Philosophy, Huntingdon College, June 1951-May 1980. Retired May 1980

Married Lessie Elizabeth Clements and has one

daughter, two granddaughters, and one great-granddaughter.

RAYMOND MATTHESON, Colonel, born July 3, 1915 in Lawrence, MA. Attended four years college, four years Boston Univ., Seminary M.Div. degree. Joined the Army and USAF in April 31, 1944.

Military locations and stations: HQ USAF, two tours, Alaska; Arabia; Europe Served with 15th AF, 17th AF, 4th Armd Div., HQ Air Defense Cmd

Memorable experience was a call from the White House for a copy of the prayer he had given at Tomb of the Unknown Soldier with Vice-President Hubert Humphrey Nov. 11. 1965. Discharged as colonel Aug. 31, 1974.

Held positions at First Methodist Church, Danuers, MA. Retired Aug. 31, 1974, Legion of Merit Award Widowed Nov. 22, 1991. He has three children and five grandchildren.

JAMES A. MCCALMANT, Lieutenant Commander, born Nov. 23, 1929, in Grainfield, KS Received BA St. Olaf, BD Luther Seminary; MA Roosevelt Univ, Chicago. Joined the USN March 1948-March 1952. Enlisted July 1961-May 1978, CHC.

Awarded the RVN Meritorious Unit Citation, Civil Actions Medal, 1st Class of Color with Palm, Vietnam Campaign Medal, Vietnam Service Medal, National Defense Service Medal (2), Good Conduct Medal, Korean Service Medal with Bronze Star, UN Medal, China Service Medal, Navy Occupation Service Medal, (Asia Clasp). Discharged USN as lieutenant commander, June 30, 1978.

Married Arlene L. McCalmant. They have two children and two grandchildren. Held positions as pastor - Belgrade, MN, pastor/chaplain, Montevideo, MN. Retired Dec 1, 1994.

DAVID MICHAEL MCCLARY, Lieutenant Colonel, born Aug. 29, 1943, in Oak Hill, WV. Received BA, MPA, M.Div., candidate D.Min., AC&SC, BCHOC, ACHOC, Tng Mgr Joined the USA, NG, USAR, CAP June 6, 1982

Military locations and stations: Fort Jackson, Fort Eustis, Fort Gordon, Fort Lewis, Fort Bliss, Fort Leonard Wood. Served with 95th Div., 117th Trans Co., 8th Bde (USATC), 6th ADA, ROTC

Awarded the National Defense Service Medal, Army Commendation Medal, Army Achievement Medal, US Reserve Components Medal, Reserve Components Achievement Medal, Army Achievement Medal, Basic Ribbon, NCO Ribbon 2nd Device, Colorado Commendation Ribbon, Artillery Olympic Survey Master Badge, State Emergency Ribbon, NCO Ribbon, 1st Device, Recruiter Badge, Recruiter Ribbon, Good Conduct Medal and several medals from CAP, American Red Cross, Hunter Safety instructors, band, choir and university

Memorable experience Desert Storm; Haitian Rescue Operation; Vietnam; Apollo 13, 14, commissioned at 39 1/2 years. Discharged in USA in 1968; USARNG-1978; USAR Sept 1, 1993; CAP 1991, staff sergeant-NG; captain-USAR, lieutenant colonel-CAP. Retired as lieutenant colonel, April 30, 1991.

Married Madalyn (Lynn) Carol McClary. Married and has one son, two stepchildren Held positions at Walt Disney World, All Star Resort and front desk.

LEMUEL D. MCELYEA, Colonel, until his retirement in August 1980, was the center chaplain, Sheppard Technical Training Center, Sheppard AFB, TX. He was responsible for budgeting, planning, organizing, implementing and evaluating a total religious program for all distinctive faith groups on base.

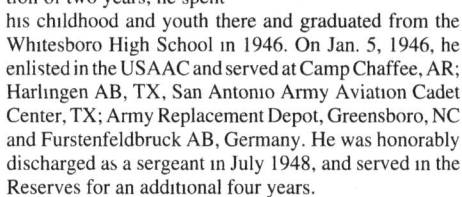

Born at Whitesboro, LeFlore County, OK, Oct 22, 1927. With the exception of two years, he spent his childhood and youth there and graduated from the Whitesboro High School in 1946. On Jan. 5, 1946, he enlisted in the USAAC and served at Camp Chaffee, AR; Harlingen AB, TX, San Antonio Army Aviation Cadet Center, TX; Army Replacement Depot, Greensboro, NC and Furstenfeldbruck AB, Germany. He was honorably discharged as a sergeant in July 1948, and served in the Reserves for an additional four years.

A graduate of Southwestern Assemblies of God College where he completed a BS degree in 1951 His seminary work was done at the Graduate Seminary, Phillips Univ., Enid, OK, where he received three degrees; bachelor of divinity in 1955 (later changed to M.Div.), master of religious education in 1961, and the doctor of ministry in 1988 Completed additional graduate rank courses at the Univ. of Puget Sound, Tacoma, WA, and Central State Univ., Edmond, OK. Attended the Armed Forces Staff College (Class 1950), Norfolk, VA, graduating in 1972. Completed the Air War College (Seminary/Correspondence Div.) in July 1974.

Chaplain McElyea was ordained for the ministry by the Oklahoma District Council of the Assemblies of God in 1951 Commissioned as a chaplain in September 1955 and ordered to extended active duty on Feb. 19, 1956. His chaplain assignments included tours at Travis AFB, CA; McChord AFB, WA; Clark AB, the Philippines; Lackland AFB, TX; Wheelus AB, Libya; Tinker AFB, OK; Armed Forces Staff College, Norfolk, VA; HQ US Military Assistance Cmd., Vietnam, Andrews AFB, MD, and Sheppard AFB, TX.

Presently serves as national secretary of the Assemblies of God Chaplaincy Department. He is administratively responsible for military, Veterans Affairs, industrial and institutional chaplains. He is secretary for the Assemblies of God Commission on Chaplains, Springfield, MO and maintains offices and a competent staff in support of these professional and administrative responsibilities

Served as president of the MCA, Texoma Chapter (North Texas-Southern, OK), 1977-78; also served from 1978-80 as vice president of the Wichita Falls, TX Ministers Fellowship

Chaplain McElyea's military decorations and awards include two Legion of Merit, Bronze Star Medal, Meritorious Service Medal, Joint Service Commendation Medal, a foreign decoration in 1973 from the RVN and the Civil Action Medal 1/c. Promoted to the grade of colonel on Feb. 1, 1973, and continued serving in that grade until his retirement from active duty in August 1980.

Chaplain McElyea resides with his wife, the former Naomi Rebecca Arnold, in Springfield, MO. They have four children: Theresa, Deborah, Bruce and Donald (now deceased).

CHARLES E. MCMILLAN, Lieutenant Colonel, born July 30, 1933, in Wellsburg, WV. Holds an AB from Washington and Jefferson College; M.Div from Princeton Theological Seminary; MS in education from the Univ. of Southern California, and MA from Columbia Univ. Ordained as a minister in the (now) Presbyterian Church (USA) in 1958 and served as pastor of the Pisgah Presbyterian Church of Corsica, PA, 1958-63.

Entered active duty as an Army chaplain in January 1963 and retired in February 1983 Military assignments included: Army Security Agency, Fort Devens; MA, 809th Engr. Bn., Thailand; 3rd Armd. Cav Regt, Baumholder, FRG; command chaplain, Advanced Wpns. Spt. Cmd , Pirmasens, FRG; MACV Advisory Team 2, Quang Ngai, RVN; Staff and Faculty, US Army Chaplain Center and School, Fort Hamilton and Fort Wadsworth, NY; Combat Developments Cmd., Fort Benjamin Harrison, IN; Army Mobilization and Readiness Region I, Fort Devens, MA.

Awarded the Bronze Star and other appropriate medals. He is a graduate of the Army Command and General Staff College

Associate director and director of the Presbyterian Council for Chaplains and Military Personnel, 1984-present. Currently resides in Vienna, VA, with his wife Mary Anne Crabtree McMillan and they are the parents of three children and grandparents of three.

A current life member of the MCA and intermittently active since 1963, having held national office as treasurer, and member of the Executive Committee.

TALMADGE FORD MCNABB, Lieutenant Colonel, served five years enlisted, sergeant; 20 years chaplain, US Army. Graduated Birmingham Southern College; Univ. Alabama; Southwestern College, Waxahachie, TX. He did graduate work at the Univ. of Texas, El Paso. Ordained 1950, Assemblies of God, pastored Warrior, Tuscaloosa, AL. Commissioned chaplain USA July 1, 1953.

In Korea rescued GI baby girl from paddyfield; contacted Oregon farmer Harry Holt who came to Korea and adopted her and seven more Saga made into national TV show, Loretta Young program, portraying McNabb, Holt, orphan girl. Out of inspiration of this first girl adopted, Holt set up adoption program whereby, since then, over 70,000 children have been placed.

At Fort Knox he developed unique Sunday informal services for basic trainees, with music, sing-alongs, films, becoming among largest and most popular services in US Army, 300-900 per night McNabb, since retirement, completed 18 years expediter in federal service, total 43 years federal service, counting military.

Active in Worldwide Christian Ministry, Inc., organization McNabb incorporated under NJ laws, doing benevolent work through Ecuador, India, Russia, Germany, France, Holland, Belgium

Married Pirrko Marjotta McNabb, a US Army nurse They have five children and eight grandchildren. Retired May 31, 1972

EDWARD J. MCNICHOLAS, Colonel, born Nov. 1, 1923, in Brooklyn, NY. Received a BA degree from St. John's Univ in New York. Served in the USAAF 1943-1946 and 1961-1978.

Entered the AF as a Catholic chaplain in October 1961 and served at McChord AFB, WA; Don Muang AB, Thailand; Bergstrom AFB, TX; Howard AFB, Panama; Ent AFB, CO, Bitburg AFB, Germany, Malmstrom AFB, MT; Wheeler AFB, HI. Also stationed in Camp Blanding, FL; Camp Robinson, AR; Camp Rucker, AL; St. Nazaire, France, Marseille, France,

Bischofshofen, Austria. Served with the Army in WWII in the 66th Inf Div. and with the 42nd Inf. Div.

Drafted into the Army in April 1943 and served as an enlisted soldier. Discharged in April 1946. Retired Nov. 1, 1978, after 20 years of duty as colonel Spent three years in the Army and 17 years in the AF. Served as Catholic priest, Parish priest. Retired July 1, 1994.

R.G. MCPHERSON, Captain, ordained to the Gospel ministry in February 1966 His theological training was accomplished at Southeastern Baptist Seminary, Wake Forest, NC, towards the M.Div. in 1968.

During a seven year period of active duty with the USN Chaplain Corps, 1968-75, he served two and a half years on Okinawa during the final stages of the Vietnam conflict, providing pastoral care and counseling to US Marines returning home from combat He is himself a former Parris Island trained enlisted Marine, (1955-58). Following his Okinawa assignment, he was attached to the 3rd Bn., 6th Marines at Camp Lejeune, NC, as battalion chaplain. Participated in special training exercises: NATO in Turkey, jungle training in Panama, Mediterranean and Caribbean deployment exercises.

From 1973-75, he served at the National Naval Medical Center, Bethesda, MD, where he became involved in a special research project entitled "Predictions of Results of Open Heart Surgery," using acceptance scale to help determine need and measurable outcome of persons going into open heart surgery At the conclusion of that tour he was commended by Rear Admiral R.G. Williams Jr for outstanding performance.

Active with the Naval Reserve Ready Command Forces since entering the civilian sector in 1975, he was promoted to the rank of captain in September 1988. Served for two years as commanding officer for a unit of chaplains in New Orleans. For six years he was the Special Cases counseling officer for a mobilization team at the reserve center in New Orleans. He was supervisory staff chaplain for Naval Reserve Readiness Cmd., Region 10, Naval Support Activity, New Orleans, LA 1990-92.

Elected to retire as a selected reservist on Oct. 1, 1992, after 28 years successful service. In 1975 he came to the GSL Hansen's Disease Center at Carville to serve as Protestant hospital chaplain. This is the only center of its kind in the continental US for the institutional care of leprosy patients. He provides pastoral care and counseling, patient visitation, and conducts regular divine services at Union Chapel. His wife, Wanda, is his volunteer musician, as well as son, Jonathan.

McPherson's: affiliates are Fellow, College of Chaplains; past president and secretary, Louisiana Chaplain's Assoc., Inc.; member of the MCA, Naval Reserve Assoc., and Baton Rouge Ministerial Assoc.

Married to the former Wanda Bass of Jacksonville, NC, May 1956 They have three grown children David Everett, Alexandria, LA. eldest son; Jennifer Sing, Gonzales, LA, only daughter; Jonathan Scott, youngest son still at home; grandchild, Dylan Sing (of Jennifer and Shannon Sing).

The eldest of eight children. He has one brother still listed as MIA in North Vietnam since March of 1966. He was on a reconnaissance mission as pilot of a USMC EF10B when he and his radar operator presumably took a SAM hit

In an agreement between the Federal Bureau of Prisons and the USPHS Hospital, he assisted in putting in place the religious program for the Federal Medical Center for Federal inmates. The program was highly successful until the withdrawal of the Federal Bureau of Prisons from Carville when the FBOP and USPHS failed to renew their agreement. The chaplain continues to provide pastoral ministry for Hansen's disease patients at Carville until his planned retirement from the center sometime 1996.

LESLIE MCRAE, Major, born Nov. 12, 1922, in Snowtown, Australia. Received BS, Lycoming College, Williamsport, PA and MST, Wesley Theological Seminary Joined the US Army-USAF, 1956. Military locations and stations: Portland International AFB, OR, Radar Sites, British Columbia; Sewart AFB, TN, Ramey AFB, Puerto Rico, Lowry AFB, Denver, CO; Loring AFB, ME.

Memorable experience. while stationed at his first duty station, Portland International AB, Portland, OR, in 1958, a citizen of Portland, voiced his concern over the negativism concerning AF jet fighters taking off, flying over, and landing patterns over the city As results, he was called upon by the base commander to come up with something to help the image of USAF in the community At the time he was the deputy base chaplain of the 337th Fighter Gp. Out of this came, "The Prayer for Pilots," which was printed on cards and circulated through the Portland Council of Churches and the congregations. It was carried in the local newspapers, and received with much enthusiasm throughout the city, and thus cemented relations between the community and the AFB.

A Prayer for Pilots: *O Lord, our God, Bless the great host of men dedicated to guarding our freedom in the air. Assure them of thy presence and protection as they wing through the skies and give them peace. Amen*

Discharged from the Army Nov. 12, 1945, and from the USAF, June 30, 1972. Married to Mary M. (Peggy) McRae They have three children and four grandchildren and two great-grandchildren. Held position at Central Pennsylvania Conference, United Methodist Church, retiring June 1985

RALPH A. MEHRING, Lieutenant Colonel, native of St. Louis, MO, graduated from Concordia Seminary, St. Louis, in 1952 Ordained on Sept. 14, 1952, and served Lutheran Churches in St. Charles, MO (2 1/2 years) Monett and Neosho, MO (5 1/2 years) Casey, IL, (three years) and Sparta, IL (four years). In July 1960 Mehring came on active duty as an Army chaplain.

Graduated from St. Paul's College, Concordia, MO and Concordia Seminary, St. Louis, MO. Also took extra educational courses at Concordia Teachers College, River Forest, IL. During his vicarage he taught in a Lutheran one-room school at Westcliffe, CO His degrees: BA, Bachelor of Divinity and Master of Divinity.

Awarded Legion of Merit, Meritorious Service Medal, Army Commendation Medal w/2 OLCs, National Defense Medal, Vietnam Service Medal, Vietnam Campaign Medal, ROK Presidential Unit Citation, Vietnam Unit Citation, Army Service Ribbon, Overseas Service Ribbon.

Mehring's 22 years of active duty brought him to Fort Gordon, GA (three years), Fort Sill, OK (two years); Fort Hamilton, NY (one year), Fort Hood, TX (one year); Fort Ord, CA (two years); St. Louis, MO (two years); Rock Island Arsenal, IL (three years).

His overseas tours were served: 13 months in Korea, 12 months in Vietnam, and six years in West Germany (Vilseck, Nuernberg and Kaiserslautern) with family. His last tour was as post chaplain of large Kaiserslautern community. He retired from active duty from the Army in October 1982 as lieutenant colonel. The Lutheran Church, Missouri Synod, awarded him in 1980 the St. Martin of Tours Bronze Medal.

On Nov 6, 1954, he married Ella Eckert. This union was blessed with two children, Michael of Edwardsville, IL and Mary of Scott AFB. They now have three grandchildren

WM. J. MENSTER, Commander, born in Cascade, IA. He received a BA from Loras College, Dubuque, IA Graduate St. Marys Seminary, Ohio 1938. Joined the USNR Dec. 19, 1942.

Military locations and stations 25 years in Naval Reserve, five years active. Served 20 months in South Pacific, WWII. Memorable experience Chaplain on the Fourth Byrd Antarctic Expedition, 1946-47 Conducted the first religious service in the Arctic, Jan. 26, 1947 Discharged June 27, 1947, as commander Retired from the Naval Reserve in 1967 and from parish work in 1972 He authored *Strong Men South,* (account of expedition)

RICHARD D. MEYER, Lieutenant Colonel, born in Chicago, IL, Feb. 2, 1914, raised in suburb, Maywood. Played clarinet in band of 202nd Coast Arty., antiaircraft National Guard seven and a half years to October 1938 Enlisted as Flying Cadet Dec 31, 1940, for pilot training, trained as aircraft observer (aerial navigator) by Pan American Airlines in the Univ. of Miami, FL. Commissioned as a second lieutenant, Dec. 7, 1941.

Assigned to Puerto Rico for defense of shipping lanes of the Caribbean, then in defense of the Panama

Canal, flying out of Guatemala City March 1943 returned to USA to serve as navigation instructor at Gowen Field, Boise, ID. At Geiger Field, WA, had special training to work with CNTs (Celestial Navigation Trainers) at Wendover Field, UT and Smoky Hill Army AFB, Salina, KS Completed Command and General Staff School at Fort Leavenworth, KS. Separated from active duty Dec. 18, 1945

Studied law at Univ of Illinois, became Assistant Dean of Men five years, switched to Educational Administration. First Reader in First Church of Christ, Scientist, Champaign, IL. Served as Christian Science minster for armed service personnel at Chanute AFB one year. Appointed chaplain, USAF. Attended Chaplain School at Fort Slocum, NY; then assigned Lackland AFB, TX 1953-55.

Served with WAFs, Reception Center, Basic Training Center, Confinement Facility and Retraining Center, transferred to Parks AFB, CA; Basic Training Center 1956-57, transferred to Elmendorf AFB, AK, serving as chaplain-at-large for all C.S personnel and dependents in Alaska. Also in charge of Protestant Sunday School during rapid expansion.

Assigned to Otis AFB, Cape Cod, MA April 1960-July 1964, among other things, ministered to personnel on Texas Towers near Cape Cod Transferred to Amarillo AFB, TX, 1964. Served in USAF Retraining Center and in charge of marriage seminars for Tech. School Airmen held bi-monthly with Protestant Airmen Retreats, 185 airmen each Sept 1, 1967, retired as lieutenant colonel, USAF, 35 years total military service (NG, US Army, USAF, Reserve).

Earned BS from Univ. of Illinois, 1947 and MS from Univ of Illinois in education admin, 1954 Moved to Joliet, IL for 10 years, served as volunteer CS practitioner in large mental institutions and as volunteer chaplain in city, county and state prisons, very active with college organizations and churches in greater Chicago area, then in Seattle area when they moved there in December 1977.

Married Lois Mae Taylor, still going strong. They have four children, eight grandchildren and three great-grandchildren Married 52 years thus far. Christian Science practitioner for 47 years, included in world-wide listing of practitioners for 35 years.

DONALD MIKITTA JR., Lieutenant Colonel, born March 10, 1950 in Fairview Park, OH. Received a BA Bible Lexington, KY, Baptist College (1976), Deland High School (1969). Joined the USAF September 1969 and CAP Nov 1, 1979. Military locations and stations: USAF Lowery AFB, Kadena AFB; Ubon AFB, Elgin, Minnesota Served with USAF, Munitions Maintenance SQ, CAP Redwing, MN and Minnesota Wing.

During his tenure in the enlisted ranks of the AF, Christ became his Lord and Savior, as a result he became a CAP chaplain in Minnesota. Discharged as sergeant in USAF Aug. 10, 1973 and still active as lieutenant colonel in CAP. Married to Nancy MacKeigan, 1973. They have two children. He held position as supervisor maintenance at Red Wing Technical College.

HARRY RHODES MILLER, Captain, born in Pittsburgh, PA to Harry and Georgia Miller June 25, 1930. Graduating Phi Beta Kappa from Boston Univ, he attended Western Seminary, now Pittsburgh Seminary, and ordained as an evangelist in the Presbyterian Church USA May 22, 1955.

In July 1955 he began 30 years of active duty ministry to the sea services His assignments included: MSTS, Pacific; MCB Camp Pendelton; 1st Marine Bde., HI; Naval Hosp., Philadelphia, USS *Shangri-La;* Oakland Hosp.; Naval Station, Norfolk; USS *LY Spear;* Naval Station, Quonset Point; Coast Guard Academy; Iceland Defense Force, Sub Base, Bangor; Shipyard, Mare Island.

Was the first Navy chaplain assigned to Vietnam. In Iceland he was pastor of the English speaking church in Reyjavik. From October 1983 until his retirement, July 1, 1985, he was the Gray Shepherd of the USN

Among his awards are the Legion of Merit, Defense Meritorious Service Medal, Joint Service Commendation Medal and the Coast Guard Commendation Medal. He is a life member of MCA, served on the board, was president of the Golden Gate Chapter and vice president of Liberty Bell. He is married to Doris Paasch and has three children and eight grandchildren.

LEWIE H. MILLER JR., Lieutenant Colonel, born Nov. 19, 1919, in Blackville, SC. Received the M.Div., Southern Baptist Theological Seminary, Louisville, KY Joined the AAF, Dec 27, 1941; AF, 1948, USAF, April 1951 as chaplain.

Military locations and stations: McDill AAF; Blythe (CA) AAB; March AAB; Great Falls AAB (Montana); Fort Dix AAB; Drew AAB (FL), Las Vegas AAB, Station 156 (England), William AFB, Vienna, Austria; Bitburg, Germany, Lackland AFB, TX; Donaldson AFB, SC; Evreux AB, France, Travis AFB, CA; Tan Sohn Nhut AB, Saigon, Vietnam, Hamilton AFB, CA.

He was a tailgunner on a B-17 for 11 missions, March-June 1945 flying from England Discharged Jan. 31, 1971, as lieutenant colonel

Married to Jackie McKenny Miller of Richmond, VA. He has two step-grandchildren. He has not yet retired President/founder/CEO, Computer Bibles International, Inc., Greenville, SC

RONALD A. MILLIAN, Colonel, born in Washington, DC in 1931. Received his AB from Dickinson College in 1953, a M Div. from Boston Univ. in 1956 and a D.Min. from San Francisco Theological Seminary in 1982. Ordained a Methodist elder on June 10, 1956.

His civilian pastorates include four years as founding pastor of Twinbrook, now Francis Asbury United Methodist Church in Rockville, MD. He was on active duty from 1956-59 and from 1963 -90, serving at 10 bases. He was the base chaplain at Thule AB, Greenland; the NATO chaplain at Oslo, Norway; the AF Iceland Chaplain, and the base chaplain at Williams AFB, AZ and Homestead AFB, FL.

Other assignments include: chief, Chaplain Inspection Branch; AF IG, Deputy Command Chaplain, Military Airlift Cmd.; and from 1986-90, command chaplain, Air Reserve Personnel Center at Denver. Retired on June 1, 1990, after more than 30 years of active duty Married to the former Constance Peterson of Washington, DC; they have two sons and four grandchildren.

BYRON LEITH MILTON, born April 8, 1915, in Aspen, VA Received BA Hampden-Sydney College Farmville, VA; BD Union Seminary, Richmond, VA. Joined the Navy in June 1945 and was a chaplain until discharged in June 1947. He achieved the rank of Lieu-

tenant (jg). FromJune 1945 - June 1946 he was a Student at the Navy Chaplain School, William and mary College. Next he was a chaplain at the naval Training Station, Treasure Island, San Francisco, then Naval Air Station, Santa Rosa, Ca, Navy Shipyard, Stockton, CA From June 1946- June 1947 he was a chaplain aboard the USS *Prairie* in San Diego Bay.

He was married on June 18, 1943 to Jane Jameson and they have one son and four daughters. They also has 12 grandchildren. He has been employed as a Presbyterian pastor and retired onJune 30, 1982. He lives in Kennesaw, GA.

ALBERT W. MITCHELL, Lieutenant Colonel, born Sept. 10, 1917, in Rochester, NY. Ordained in 1940 in the Christian Church (Disciples of Christ) Commissioned in the Army Chaplain Corps 1943.

Served with 134th Gen. Hosp. in Australian and Dutch New Guinea, then with 842nd Aviation Engr Bn in Leyte. Later served at Camp Breckinridge, KY (post chaplain) and Camp Campbell, KY (hospital chaplain). Active duty ended in July 1946.

USAR commission December 1946 Served with 384th MP Bn. Honorably discharged (medical) Aug. 8, 1951. Recommissioned Aug 13, 1956. Served 81st Inf. Div. USAR (Atlanta, GA), then 18 years with 4th Bde, 70th Div. (TRNG) in Indiana. Retired in 1977, 29 years total service Civilian service includes ministry to nine Christian churches, high school teaching, serving on faculty of Atlanta Christian College in Georgia, associate chaplain at a psychiatric sanitarium, and as a corrections counselor in Indiana Boys School

WILLIAM FRANKLIN MITCHELL, Colonel, born Aug. 27, 1916, near Edgemoor, SC. Graduated Erskine College 1938, Erskine Seminary 1942. Ordained April 14, 1942, in the Associate Reformed Presbyterian Church. Commissioned chaplain (first lieutenant) in the US Army Dec. 8, 1943.

Chaplain 304th Inf. Regt., 76th Inf. Div. and went overseas with the 346th Ord. Bn. Separated from the service March 12, 1946, to the ORC March 13 as a captain. He continued his chaplaincy with the Army Reserve and the Arkansas NG for more than 30 years During this time he had several pastorates in the Associate Reformed Presbyterian denomination and the Presbyterian Church US.

For more than 13 years he was executive secretary and Stated Clerk of South Carolina Presbytery, PCUS, until his retirement in 1978. He was promoted to colonel March 31, 1970, graduated Command and General Staff College, Oct 25, 1974, and retired from the Army on his 60th birthday, Aug. 27, 1976.

ROSARIO L.U. MONTCALM, Colonel, born on Feb 16, 1912, at Worcester, MA, and in 1932 received

his BA degree from the Univ. of Montreal, Canada. Ordained to the priesthood in 1936 after completing four years of theological instruction at St. Mary's Seminary, Baltimore, MD. Commissioned a first lieutenant on Aug. 6, 1943, and called to active duty on Aug 18, 1943.

Completing the five week indoctrination course at the Chaplain's School, Harvard Univ., Cambridge, MA, he was temporarily assigned to HQ 2nd AF, CO, before moving to Mountain Home AAF, ID. He remained there for 23 months as assistant base chaplain of the 213th Base Unit, the 426th Base Unit, and the 238th Base Unit. On Aug 31, 1945, he joined the 376th Air Svc. Gp. and moved with it to Biggs AAF, TX, McCook AAF, NE, and Fort Worth AAF, TX.

Discharged from the Detachments of Patients, Beaumont Gen. Hosp., TX, and, after convalescing at the Coral Gables Regional Hosp., FL, he was assigned to the Fort George Wright Regional Hosp., WA, for five months as hospital chaplain before transfer to Japan on Dec. 17, 1946 There, for the next two years, he served at Tachikawa AB as chaplain of the 317th Troop Carrier Wing. On Dec. 3, 1948, he moved with this organization to Celle RAF Station when it was committed to the support of the Berlin Airlift as part of the 1st Airlift TF.

Next followed a 20 month tour at Bolling AFB, Washington, DC, with the 1100th AB Wing In April 1951 transferred to Mitchell AFB, NY, where for three years, he was a member of HQ Continental Air Cmd., HQ 1st AF, and HQ 465th Troop Carrier Wing. As the wing staff chaplain of this last organization, he accompanied it when it deployed to France in March 1954 and served with it at Toul-Rosieres AB and Evreaux-Fauville AB until March 1957. After a 12 month tour at Westover AFB, MA, with HQ 8th AF, reported to HQ SAC, Offutt AFB, NE, for a 26 month assignment as assistant command chaplain. From June 22, 1960-June 12, 1963, he again served overseas as the staff chaplain, HQ 7th Air Div., High Wycome Air Station, England. On July 12, 1963, he was transferred to the USAF Academy and, in his terminal assignment, has performed exceptionally outstanding service as command chaplain and cadet Catholic chaplain.

During his distinguished military career, he has been awarded the AF Commendation Medal with two OLCs, American Campaign Medal, WWII Victory Medal, Army of Occupation Medal, Japan, Army of Occupation Medal, Germany w/Berlin Airlift Device, Medal for Humane Action, National Defense Service Medal, AF Longevity Service Award Ribbon w/4 Bronze OLCs.

Commissioned a 1st lieutenant on Aug. 6, 1943, and called to active duty on Aug 18, 1943. He was promoted to captain on June 22, 1944; to major on April 6, 1949; lieutenant colonel on Feb. 16, 1958, and colonel on March 25, 1963.

JOHN NELSON MONTGOMERY, Lieutenant Commander, born Dec. 4, 1916, in Grove City, PA. Received AB from Grove City College, PA; M.Div., Princeton Theology Seminary. Joined the USNR May 1943 Military locations and stations NTS, Newport, 28th CB, NCTC Davisville, RI Served with FASRON 6 NASJAX, AD-18 Sierra, MDLAB Panama City, FL. Memorable experiences include 25 years USNR. Retired from the USNR June 1, 1968, as lieutenant commander.

Married Virginia Gautier. June 16, 1942. They have two children. Held a position at Presbyterian Churches, Florida, Ohio and Aruba. Retired Dec. 4, 1976

SAMUEL FLEMING MORGAN was born October 20, 1945 in Hobbs, New Mexico. He received an AA in sociology at Pasadena City College, a BA in religion from Azusa Pacific University, an MA in religion from Azusa Pacific University, an MA in theology from Fuller Theological Seminary and has a pending Ph D in clinical pastoral care from Tidewater.

He joined the U.S. Navy in June 1963. His Navy career has been and is still full and varied. He has been stationed in California, Japan, Vietnam, Washington, Rhode Island, Memphis, TN, and Portsmouth His career has taken him from equipment operator, storekeeper, dental technician, student, recruiter, yeoman, awards judge, command chaplain district chaplain, staff chaplain senior resident to Director of Pastoral Care.

His memorable experiences include assisting Mrs. Coretta King establishing Dr. King's holiday in Hawaii, building the chapel at Coast Guard Base, Honolulu and assisting in Alex Haley's funeral service in Memphis, TN

Awards: Navy Commendation Medal, Coast Guard Commendation Medal, Coast Guard Achievement Medal, Coast Guard Unit Commendation, Coast Guard Meritorious Service Medal, National Defense Service Medal, Armed Forces Expeditionary Medal with/FMF, Combat Operational Vietnam Service Medal (three campaigns), Navy Sea Service Deployment Ribbon, Armed Forces Reserve Medal, Republic of Vietnam Meritorious Unit Citation (Gallantry Cross of Color), Republic of Vietnam Campaign Medal, Navy Marksman Ribbon (rifle), Navy Marksman Ribbon (pistol), and the NAACP-Roy Wilkins Meritorious Service Award nominee.

He married J. Marie Powell and they have six children and four grandchildren He is presently on active duty.

HENRY EARL MORRIS JR., Lieutenant Commander, son of Henry Earl and Eva Heatley Morris. Born Jan. 14, 1921, in Pueblo, CA. Received BA in Botany, 1944 in Univ. of Denver.

Joined the US Army, 1942-46; Camp Crowder Signal Corps Camp, 1942-43; Univ. of Pennsylvania, Chinese Studies 1943-44; Chief Clerk China Theatre Replacement Service, 1945-46. Discharged as technical sergeant, Jan. 10, 1946, with Bronze Star Medal.

Assistant Placement advisor, Lowry AFB 1946; Iliff School Theology, Masters of Theology, 1949, Colorado Annual Conference, Methodist Church, 1947-49; California-Nevada Annual Conference, United Methodist Church, 1949-present. Served 14 churches, retiring July 1, 1986.

Served USNR, 1955-73, lieutenant commander, Chaplains Corps. Chaplain, USNRTC Fresno 1955-58, Reno, NV, 1958-60; Fresno, 1960-67; Burlingame, 1967-69, Sacramento, 1969-73.

Member of MCA 1956-present (life member 1971), president Golden Gate Chapter 1965-69, area vice president, 1969-73; member TROA (life member); member The Naval Reserve Assoc., (life member); plank owner, USN Memorial; member Auburn (CA) Faith Community Hosp. Guild.

RONALD ARTHUR MOSLEY, Captain, born on Sept. 13, 1919, at Oak Lake, Manitoba, Canada, son of Canadian Army Chaplain T. Arthur and Ethel Hilda Mosley. Attended DePauw Univ., IN and received degrees from Boston Univ. (AB, STB, M.Div., STM) Ordained elder on July 18, 1943, in the Methodist Church.

Commissioned a chaplain (first lieutenant) in the Army of the US on Sept. 23, 1943, he served with the 106th Inf. Div and was wounded in Belgium on Dec. 30, 1944, in the Battle of the Bulge After hospitalization, he served with the 188th US Gen Hosp. in England and the Hosp. Annex, Percy Jones Hosp. Center, Fort Custer, MI. His terminal leave ended on March 10, 1946

Served Methodist and United Church of Christ Churches in Massachusetts, New Hampshire and Maine Receiving 100 percent service-connected disability compensation in 1970, he retired to his boyhood home in Nova Scotia Since 1975, he has written a weekly column, *"Consider This,"* for the Lighthouse Publishing Ltd., Bridgewater, Nova Scotia.

Military decorations include Purple Heart and two campaign stars Served as Massachusetts State Chaplain of AMVETS from 1950-53, president of the New England Chapter of MCA (of which he is a life member). Also holds life membership in the 106th Inf, Div. Assoc., the American Legion, the Royal Canadian Legion which also awarded him the Meritorious Service Medal, the Canadian Veterans Against Nuclear Arms, Veterans for Peace and is a co-founder of the International Veterans for Peace Liaison Committee.

Other awards include the 1985 American Legion Canadian Friendship Award, 1992 YMCA Canada Peace Medal, and in 1992 the Canadian government conferred on him the 125th Anniversary Commemorative Medal.

Married to the former Eloise Chapin; the Mosleys have three children and 10 grandchildren.

DONALD KARL MUCHOW, RADM, born Oct 20, 1937, in Framingham, MA. Awarded BA 1959, Concordia Sr. College, Fort Wayne, IN. Received M.Div., 1962, Concordia Theological Lutheran Seminary, St Louis, MO.

Joined the USN, Nov 4, 1964. Reserve duty, 1964-67, with USS *Observation Island,* Cape Canavarel, FL; Marine Corps Air Station, Cherry Point, NC; Marine Corps Base, Jacksonville, NC and Naval Reserve Center, Richmond, VA.

Active duty, from 1967-DESRON 22; Philadelphia Naval Hosp ; USS *Iwo Jima* (LPH-2); PHIBRON 10 and FOUR; Naval Station, Norfolk, VA, Basic Course Officer, Naval Chaplains School, Newport, RI, Ninth Marines, Okinawa; Rapid Deployment Task Force/US Central Cmd., Tampa, FL; Director, Plans, Policy, Programming and Fiscal Management Division (OP); director, Naval Chaplains School, Newport, RI; present duty, Deputy Chief of Chaplains (N097B) since August 1991.

Married Monie Eberhard 1960, Cordova, MD, graduate nurse from Johns Hopkins Univ. They have two children, Steve and Jeff They also have two grandchildren.

Has pastored St Matthew Lutheran Church, Balto, MD and Trinity Lutheran Church, Richmond, VA.

MERRILL GREG MULLER, Captain, born Oct. 25, 1952, in Margaretteville, NY. Received BA, Western Illinois Univ. M.Div. Brite Divinity School, TCU Joined the USAF/IANG Sept. 12, 1992.

Military locations and stations: Sioux City AB. Served with 185th Ftr. Gp. Memorable experience In his two years the best was his incentive ride in a F16.

Married to Deborah Anne Muller. They have three children. He is a United Methodist appointed minister. Presently still active in service.

EDWARD B. MULLIGAN, Colonel, a life member of MCA, having joined early in his AF career He held the office of national treasurer, working with Karl B. Justus, esteemed National Director Emeritus, in 1969-70. Attended St John's Seminary, Brighton, MA Received AB, Phil.B, and Th.B degrees. Ordained August, 1944, Boston, MA by Richard Cardinal Cushing. Served in civilian ministry: St. Mary of the Nativity, Scituate, MA; Our Lady of Lourdes, Boston.

Entered the USAF, Jan. 30, 1948. USAF overseas assignments: Germany, Saudia Arabia, Morocco, Philippine Islands and Alaska. USAF stateside assignments: Malmstrom AFB, MT; Scott AFB, IL; Patrick AFB, FL; Carlisle Barracks, PA, Davis-Monthan AFB, AZ; McGuire AFB, NJ; Langley AFB, VA; Wright-Patterson AFB, OH; Randolph AFB, TX, Bolling AFB, Washington, DC (Chief of AF Chaplains Office-Personnel Services).

Attended Squadron Officer's School, Air War College Seminar Program and AF Personnel Training, Maxwell AFB. Retired after 23 years, August 1971. Memorable experiences. Saudi Arabia, Morocco, US Army Ski School, Fort Greeley, AK.

He has held many positions since retiring active duty. Is counselor in private practice Vatican dispensation, 1973 Married to Helen F. Aylward.

RICHARD F. MUNSELL, Captain, was recently chosen for Air Command and Staff College, Maxwell AFB, AL. Ordained to the Roman Catholic priesthood, June 21, 1979, (Eastern Montana)

Entered active duty 1985. Served with the AF at Offutt AFB, Shemya AFB, Cannon AFB, RAF Upper Heyford and Dyess AFB. Served as senior chaplain Doha AB, Qatar (Operation Desert Shield/Storm). Also deployed in support of UPHOLD DEMOCRACY and SOUTHERN WATCH.

Education includes a BA from St. Thomas Seminary (Kenmore, WA) 1995, a M.Div from St John's Univ. (Collegeville, MN) 1979; and through the AF Institute of Technology a MA from the Graduate Theological Union (Berkeley, CA) 1995.

His military decorations include the Bronze Star, AF Commendation, AF Achievement, National Defense Service, Southwest Asian Service and Kuwaiti Liberation.

HENRY C. MURDOCH, Lieutenant Colonel, born Aug 14, 1908, in Grapeland, TX. Received BA degree,

Baylor Univ. 1936 and Seminary. Joined USAF October 1941.

Military locations and stations: San Luis Obispo, CA, Alaska, Aleutian Islands; Fresno, CA; Thermal, CA, San Antonio, TX, Lakeland, FL and Davis Monthan Field at the end of WWII. When recalled in 1950, he was at Brooklyn, NY Navy base; Mineral Wells, TX, France AFB in Tacoma, WA; Hamilton AFB, CA, Taiwan and L G. Hanscom Field, Bedford, MA

Memorable experiences aside from the real war, meeting famous people. Gen. MacArthur for one; getting to know the good people from all over the US and in foreign countries.

Discharged June 30, 1965, as lieutenant colonel. Married Margaret Sherman, June 18, 1934. They had two children and two grandchildren Held the position as teacher in Texas and New Mexico. He was also pastor Retired July 1965 due to poor health and he passed away July 7, 1994.

JIMMY LAIRD MYERS, Lieutenant, born March 11, 1953, in Winston-Salem, NC to Tildren R. and Mattie Lois Laird Myers. Received a BA cum laude in history from Wake Forest Univ. in 1975, and an M Div. magna cum laude from Emory Univ. in 1978 Ordained an elder in the United Methodist Church on June 8, 1979, and he served as pastor of Greer's Chapel and Mt Carmel United Methodist Churches of Lexington, NC from June 1978-September 1985.

Commissioned a lieutenant jg in the USNR Sept 19, 1985, and graduated with class B86001 at the Naval Chaplains School in Newport, RI in November 1985. Reported for active duty with the 2nd Marine Div., and was initially assigned to HQ Bn. as assistant battalion chaplain in December 1985, but in January 1986, he was assigned to 1st Bn., 10th Marine Regt. as battalion chaplain

Participated with this unit in NATO exercises 200 miles north of the Arctic Circle in Norway during February and March 1986 when it endured extreme cold weather conditions reaching a wind chill factor of -68 degrees F Promoted to lieutenant on Nov. 1, 1986, and received the Fleet Marine Force Ribbon for his service with the USMC in December 1986 In June 1987 Chaplain Myers was assigned to 5th Bn., 10th Marine Regt as battalion chaplain.

Chaplain Myers left active duty and entered the USNRR in October 1988, and reported for duty to Camp Lejeune Naval Hosp. Detachment 207 in Greensboro, NC in January 1989 He was given additional duty as unit chaplain with Communications Company, HQ and Service Bn , 4th Force Service Support Gp., 4th Marine Div., USMCR. While serving with this unit, he received the National Defense Medal and a Unit Commendation Ribbon for stateside service during the Persian Gulf War

Transferred to Personnel Mobilization Team 1007 of the USNRR based at Charleston Naval Station on Oct 1, 1992; promoted to lieutenant commander on Aug. 1, 1993, completed the Advanced Reserve Chaplain's Course at the Naval Chaplains School in Newport, RI in July 1994.

In May 1991 he received a Juris Doctor degree from the School of Law of the Univ. of North Carolina at Chapel Hill and practiced law with Garry W. Frank of Lexington, NC from September 1991-October 1992 when he opened his own law offices in Advance and Lexington, NC During this time, he held a special appointment beyond the local church as a legal mediator in the Western NC Conference of the United Methodist Church He also served on the Ethics Committee of the Lexington Memorial Hosp.. In November 1994 he was elected District Court Judge in the 22nd Judicial District of North Carolina. He took office in December 1994.

Chaplain Myers lives in Advance, NC and maintains a teaching and preaching ministry in addition to his duties as a judge and Naval Reserve Chaplain.

JAMES D. NELSON (SJ), Major, born Nov 14, 1927, in LaCombe, Alberta, Canada. He received an AB, STB and MA. Joined the Air Guard (Washington) on June 5, 1967.

Military locations and stations: Spokane International Airport, Hayward Airport (CA). Served with 142nd AD Wing, 141 CSS, 129th Troop Carrier Gp Discharged as major, Jan. 3, 1987.

He has held positions as high school teacher, hospital chaplain and computer technician. Retired June 16, 1991.

ERNEST BURCHIE NEWSOM, Commander, born Oct. 17, 1937, in Memphis, TN. Served with the USN Chaplain Corps.

Military locations and stations Great Lakes USN Base, Great Lakes, IL, Glenview NAS, Glenview, IL; Knoxville Naval and Marine Reserve Center, Knoxville, TN; Cherry Point Marine Corps Air Station, Cherry Point, NC; National Naval Medical Center, Bethesda, MD; 2nd MEB Camp Lejeune, NC, Nashville Naval Reserve Center, Nashville, TN

Memorable experience: while serving as commanding officer for Marine Expeditionary Forces (REL) 109, the Persian War broke out and the reserve unit was called to active duty to support that operation. All members of the unit were quickly and effectively merged into the active duty units and assigned to various units throughout the states. They took over functions left vacant by the active duty chaplains who had by this time been mobilized to the Gulf. The members of the reserve unit received great praise and admiration from their superiors for maintaining the religious programs at present levels and even enhancing them in many instances. The unit was even commended by the chief of naval operations for its contributions to the war's effort. Much of the success of the unit was attributed to Newsom. As a result of his efforts, he received the Distinguished Service Award for the Navy in 1993 in San Diego, CA This award is given to the outstanding chaplain who has given service and leadership to the Nation by the MCA

He is still a member of the Naval Reserve Chaplaincy and holds the rank of commander. Awarded the 10 Year Reserve Medal, Armed Forces Medal, Sharp Shooters Badge, Marine Expeditionary Medal, Good Conduct Medal and Overseas Badge.

Employed as Chief of Chaplain Service, Alvin C York VA Medical Center, Murfreesboro, TN. Also chairman of the Human Resource Committee at the Medical Center and serves on eight other boards and agencies. Married to Nolia (Sweatt) formerly of Mt. Juliet, TN. They have two children, Jacqueline Polk and Kelvin and two grandchildren, Michael and Brittany Polk.

CARL ANDREW NISSEN JR., Lieutenant Colonel, born June 26, 1930, in Manhattan, KS. Son of the Rev. Carl A. Nissen, and Bernice Lydia (Varney) Nissen. He attended Denison University, Ohio State University (BA, 1960). Studied at Graduate School of Theology, Oberlin; Berkeley Baptist Divinity School, United Theological Seminary, Dayton

Employed in contracting, as procurement analyst, Defense Electronics Supply Center, Dayton, OH, 1963-90 (retired) Bi-vocational: ordained, Ohio Baptist Convention, July 1985. Pastored Sinking Creek Baptist Church, Springfield, OH, 1985-90.

Enlisted in USNR (1947-50); RA (1950-53), USAR (1953-56); ARNG (1956-57), (1958-59), (1960-61), ANG (1961-75); Retired Reserve (1975-90); chief master sergeant, USAFR, Ret. enl. Ohio Military Reserve, 1976, commissioned, 1976, brigade chaplain, (1974-90), lieutenant colonel (1991).

CAP (1982-). Graduated Great Lakes Region Chaplain Staff College, Grissom AFB, IN (1987), assisted Moral Leadership program with cadets as "visiting clergy," Group VII, Ohio Wing (1986-90), Group III, Florida Wing (1990-94), squadron commander (1994-)

While on active duty during the Korean "place action" service with the 15th Inf. (received Combat Infantry Badge), and 557th Signal Radio Relay Company - "Boise" Relay in I ROK Corps area on the east coast of Korea.

Awarded George Washington Honor Medal, Freedom's Foundation, Valley Forge (1972), Minuteman Medal, Sons of the American Revolution (1991). Listed in *Who's Who in Finance and Industry*; *Who's Who in the Midwest*' *Who's Who in Religion*, and *Who's Who in America*.

Has been active in National Assoc. of Retired Federal Employes (ch. pres., 1991-93), Reserve Officer's Assoc (ch. pres., 1993-95); American Legion, Sons of the American Revolution (ch. and state pres., vice-pres. general (1986-87), chaplain general (1989-90); chaplain, Florida Society (1991-92, 1994-95), Society of Mayflower Descendants (Ohio: Colony lieutenant governor (1981-84) and Florida: elder (1993-96) Active in free masonry, has presided over four related bodies; remains active and with an inquisitive mind he researches the history and meaning of freemasonry.

CLYDE NORTHROP, Colonel, graduated from Chapman College, Samford University and New Orleans Baptist Theological Seminary Pastored churches in Alabama and Louisiana and was a high school band director for six years. Entered the chaplaincy in 1967 and served six years overseas in RVN, Korea and Europe. He was a unit chaplain at Forts Benning, Lewis, Rucker, and Stewart

Served as theater Army chaplain USARCENT, staff chaplain, Letterman General Hosp., post chaplain at Presidio of San Francisco, and Fort Polk from which he retired as colonel in 1994 with over 38 years of active and reserve Army service.

Married to Patricia Ann McGuinn and has three children and three grandchildren. He retired in Andalusia, AL where he serves as supply pastor and computer consultant

JOE O'DONNELL, CSC, graduated from Univ of Notre Dame in 1955, including two years in NROTC. Entered the Congregation of Holy Cross in 1953 and was ordained a priest in 1960 after theological studies at Holy Cross College, Washington, DC He joined the Naval

Reserve as a chaplain in 1965, and went on active duty to Vietnam in 1968 aboard Amphibious Sqdn NINE

Subsequent tours included naval hospitals (Bethesda, Portsmouth, Okinawa, San Diego); graduate study at Univ. of Texas Medical Center, Houston; Keflavik, Iceland; Pacific Fleet, Pearl Harbor; Surface Force Pacific, San Diego; Chaplains School, Newport, two separate tours as executive assistant to the Chief of Chaplains, Washington, DC, from which he retired as 0-6 in 1994

Awards include Legion of Merit (2), Meritorious Service Medal (3), Navy Commendation Medal "V" (2), other unit and individual citations In 1995, he returned to Notre Dame to serve as religious superior/administrator of Holy Cross House, a medical facility for religious of the Congregation of Holy Cross.

FREDERICK HENRY OGILVIE, Colonel, born March 18, 1922, at Melissa, TX, the son of Fred C. and Lily Mae Ogilvie. Attended Baylor Univ., Waco, TX, BA; Southwestern Baptist Theological Seminary, Fort Worth, TX, Th.M. degree and ordained on Sept 7, 1941

He began his military service as reserve officer and attended the Company Grade Course at the Chaplain's School located at Carlisle Barracks, PA. Called to active duty on July 7, 1950, and served in assignments which included Fort Bliss, TX; Korea, Camp Roberts, CA, Alaska; Fort Ord, CA; Germany; Fort Irwin, CA; Vietnam, Fort Jackson, SC; Fort Campbell, KY. Ogilvie retired as colonel with 22 years of service.

Activities include: life membership, MCA; pres., Upper Cumberland Ch., TROA. 1992-93, member, Assoc of the US Army, founding pastor, Fairfield Glade Baptist Church and now is pastor emeritus on the staff of Drug and Alcohol Rehabilitation Center; chaplain, Fairfield Lions Club; president, Kiwanis Club 1978; member Mental Health Assoc., Master Mason, Scottish Rite Shrine Mason; volunteer Christian Service Corp. (SBC) 1984 to present; fire chief of Fairfield Glade Volunteer Fire Dept., Who's Who in American Christian Leadership 1989; Two Thousand Notable Americans (Third Edition); Community Leaders of America (Twelfth Edition); Personalities of the South, Hall of Fame American Biographical Institute, Raleigh, NC.

Among his many awards and honors are National Defense, Korean Service, United Nations, Meritorious Service w/2 OLCs, Army Commendation w/2 OLCs, Bronze Star w/2 OLCs and Legion of Merit.

Post graduate studies include Univ. of South Carolina, San Jose State, Austin Peay State Univ , Vanderbilt Univ., Pepperdine Univ., American Institute of Family Relations.

GEORGE A. O'GORMAN, Colonel, born April 15, 1910, in Jersey City, NJ. Attended Seton Hall Univ. and Immaculate Conception Seminary. Joined the US Army January 1941.

Military locations and stations: Fort Dupont, DE; Los Angeles; Hawaii, Pacific area. Served with 122nd NG, NJ; 96th Inf. Div His memorable experiences include invasions, Bronze Spearhead, Leyte.

After the war he served as division chaplain of 50th Armd. Div., New Jersey NG and retired as colonel. Served as head chaplain for New Jersey NG and AF. Retired April 15, 1970, from the Army.

EILEEN L. O'HICKEY, Commander (05), born and reared in New England, she graduated from the University of New Hampshire, magna cum laude, with a BA in social work, 1974, and from Andover Newton Theological School with an M Div , 1978. She was ordained in the United Church of Christ in June, 1978, and was commissioned lieutenant (jg) in the Navy Chaplain Corps in September of that year.

Upon completion of the basic course at the Naval Chaplain School in Newport, RI, she served at Naval Training Center, Orlando, FL, from 1978-80. Following a tour at the Chaplains Religious Enrichment Development Operation (CREDO) in Norfolk, VA, she was assigned to the Pastoral Counseling Residency at Portsmouth, VA. Next assignment was at the NAS, Norfolk, VA, 1983-85. She had a tour overseas on Diego Garcia, British Indian Ocean Territory, followed by a tour with the Marines at Marine Corps Base, Camp Pendelton, CA, 1986-88.

In 1988 she attended the Advanced Course at the Naval Chaplain School, followed by a tour as the command chaplain at the Naval Submarine School, Groton, CT, where she was the first woman in the regular Navy in the Chaplain corps promoted to the rank of commander. She is currently serving as the command chaplain aboard USS *Emory S. Land* (AS-39).

Authorized to wear the Navy Commendation Medal (three awards), the National Defense Medal, and the Overseas Service Ribbon.

She is married to Captain Giles Norrington, USN (Ret), a former Vietnam Prisoner of War. In their blended family they have four children and five grandchildren.

JAMES T. OLDHAM, Colonel (06), born May 25, 1947, in Staten Island, NY. Received BA Wagner College, 1968; MS, Univ of Southern Mississippi, 1970, and M.Div. Eastern Baptist Theological Seminary, 1975 Attended Squadron Officer School, Air Command and Staff College, Air War College. Joined the USAF June 1968.

Military locations and stations: AFROTC,

80

NYU, 1966-68, administrative officer and squadron commander, Keesler AFB, MS and Galena AFB, AK, 1968-72 (EAD); public affairs officer, Cherry Hill, NJ, 1972-75 (Category H); senior unit chaplain, Niagara Falls IAP, NY, 1975-77 (Category A); base Protestant chaplain, Hill AFB, UT, 1977-80 (EAD), IMA chaplain, Travis AFB, CA, 1980-82 (Category B); senior unit chaplain, Travis AFB, CA, 1982-85 (Category A), chief, Recruitment and Ecclesiastical Relations Div., ARPC/HC, 1985-89 (EAD/265), senior unit chaplain, Peterson AFB, CO, 1990-92 (Category A); assumed present assignment October 1992.

Decorations: Meritorious Service Medal with 3 OLCs, AF Commendation Medal w/2 OLCs, AF Achievement Medal, Reserve Forces Medal w/HGD, National Defense Service Medal w/BS, AF Outstanding Unit Award w/3 OLCs, AF Organizational Excellence Award, Longevity Service Award Ribbon w/Silver OLC, Outstanding Marksmanship Ribbon, Overseas Short Tour Ribbon and Training Ribbon.

Assigned IMA to the Director, Chaplain Individual Reserve Programs HQ, Air Reserve Personnel Center Served as clergy, American Baptist Churches, USA Pastored Bethany Baptist Church, Colorado Springs, CO. Married Hazel Vaflor and they have three children.

DELBERT C. PARTIN, born Oct. 18, 1912, King, Knox County, KY to Henry C and Bertha Partin. He was valedictorian of his high school class at Campbellsville, KY in 1932; graduated from Eastern Kentucky State, 1936, from Southern Baptist Seminary, Louisville, KY, 1939 and ordained that spring after a call to Pastor Williams Memorial Church, Ravenna, KY.

Commissioned a chaplain in 1940 and assigned to the 149th Inf., 38th Div. (named Avengers of Bataan in 1945). Separated from service in 1945 and recalled the following July with a regular commission and assigned to the USAAF.

Several bases and two tours to Japan, later, Chaplain, Lt. Col. Partin was retired from Fort Lee, VA. He moved with his family to Maitland, FL where he has served several churches as interim pastor. Duties have included: bases in Mississippi, Louisiana, Hawaii, New Guinea, Philippines, South Carolina, California, Florida and Virginia as well as two tours to Occupied Japan.

Awarded the Bronze Star during the liberation of Bataan, PI and AF Commendation upon retirement

Delbert and Lois Darnell were married Jan. 11, 1939, and have one daughter, one grandson and one granddaughter

SHIMON PASKOW, Colonel, born in 1932 in Newark, NJ. Graduated Yeshiva High School; received the BA degree from Brooklyn College and the "Amit" Certificate of World Jewish Culture from the Hebrew Univ. in Jerusalem; I received a MA degree in 1959; ordained Rabbi by the Hebrew Union College-Jewish Institute of Religion in New York and awarded a fellowship for the year 1959-60. Taught at the Hebrew Union College-Jewish Institute of Religion in Cincinnati, OH.

Entered the US Army in June 1960 and served as a Jewish chaplain in France and Germany. Was honored by the commanding general of the 4th Log. Cmd and the National Jewish Welfare Board for his outstanding work Rabbi Paskow was promoted to the rank of colonel in the USAR in 1985 A graduate of the Army's Command and General Staff College; was deputy command chaplain in Alaska, Reserve Jewish chaplain for Tripler Army Medical Center in Hawaii. In October 1993 he was decorated by the US Army with the Meritorious Service Award.

From 1965-69 served as associate Rabbi of the Valley Jewish Community Center and Temple (Adat Ari El); has been sponsored by the B'nai B'rith Anti-Defamation League and the National Conference of Christians and Jews as a speaker representing the Jewish faith and is listed in various Who's Who directories.

Served on the faculties of Hebrew Union College-Jewish Institute of Religion; the Univ. of Judaism and Brandeis Bardin; member of the Central Conference of American Rabbis, the Rabbinical Assembly, The Board of Rabbis of Southern California, MCA, Assoc of Jewish Chaplains, Society of Biblical Literature and the American Jewish Historical Society and is also an active member of the American Friends of the Hebrew Univ. In May 1993 he was presented with the Torch of Learning Award by the American Friends of the Hebrew Univ. in recognition of his commitment to youth, education, Israel and the Jewish people.

He was one of the first activists instrumental in generating interest in the plight of the Russian Jewry and creating committees in their behalf. He is an honorary member of the Board of Trustees of the Southern California Council for Soviet Jews. In recognition of his many contributions, Rabbi Paskow has received two honorary doctorate degrees; one from the Hebrew Union College-Jewish Institute of Religion and Jewish Theological Seminary of America

Has served as chairman of campaigns for the United Jewish Welfare Fund and State of Israel Bonds. For a decade, he served on the Board of Directors of the Gregor Mendel Botanic Foundation, Inc., of the Great Conejo Valley, CA. Since 1970 he has been the volunteer Jewish chaplain with the Ventura School of the California Youth Authority in Camarillo, CA. He was also an active member of the Institutional Review Board of the Los Robles Regional Medical Center in Thousand Oaks, CA.

Met Miss Carol Bauman while overseas and shortly afterward they were married. Rabbi and Mrs. Paskow have one child, Michele, who was ordained a Rabbi by the Hebrew Union College in 1991. They are the proud grandparents of Aaron Daniel and Jonathan Jay Cohen.

S. JACK PAYNE, Lieutenant Colonel, born April 2, 1930, in Homer, GA Attended Mercer Univ., Yale Divinity School, Oxford Univ. (three years research).

Joined the USAF Oct. 16, 1960, and was discharged Oct. 31, 1987.

He continues to speak in World Mission Conferences across the country under sponsorship of his denomination. Payne has two children.

ERNEST BRIAN PECK, Lieutenant Colonel, born June 17, 1932, Sweetwater, TN Attended elementary and high school in Marshall County, AL; Snead Junior College, Boaz, AL; received associate degree in 1956, Birmingham-Southern College, Birmingham, AL, AB degree in sociology, 1958, graduated Candler School of Theology, Emory Univ., Atlanta, GA, BD degree, 1962.

Enlisted in the Alabama NG, 1949; the USAF in 1950; the USAR in 1955 Reserve Commission 2nd lieutenant, March 11, 1961; Reserve Commission 1st lieutenant, May 29, 1962; US Army Chaplain, July 4, 1962; RA, July 1970 Stationed at Lackland AFB, TX; Keesler AFB, MS, Maxwell AFB, AL; Japan.

Served as chaplain from 1962-80 at Fort Slocum, NY; Fort Rucker, AL; Schwaebish Hall, Germany; Dachau, Germany, Fort Bliss, TX; RVN, Fort Hamilton, NY, Fort Sill, OK, Seoul Korea; Fort Shafter and Schofield Barracks, HI; Presidio of San Francisco, CA.

Memorable experiences include the May 1969 action on Fire Spt. Base, his family's first travel outside the Continentel US to West Germany in 1964, service as the staging area chaplain at Tyndall AFB during the Cuban Missile Crisis in 1962; his retirement ceremony at the Presidio of San Francisco in 1980.

Awarded the Legion of Merit, Silver Star Medal, Bronze Star Medal, Meritorious Service Medal, Air Medal, Joint Service Commendation Medal, Army Commendation Medal (three OLCs), Good Conduct Medal, National Defense Service Medal (OLC), Korean Service Medal, Vietnam Service Medal (three campaigns), UN Service Medal, RVN Campaign Medal, Meritorious Unit Commendation, Vietnam Cross of Gallantry with palm, Vietnam Civil Actions Honor Medal.

Served as local church pastor from 1954-62 and again from 1980-86. Employed as director of Emergency Services, Madison County Chapter and the American Red Cross for six years.

Retired from the US Army July 1, 1980, from the North Alabama Conference of the United Methodist Church, June 1986 and from the American Red Cross December 1990.

Married Marzena Ann Hallmark, Nov. 5, 1954. They have two children and three grandchildren.

MERLE F. (FENTON) PEDIGO, Lieutenant Colonel, USAF (RET), born a twin on July 27, 1919. Attended public schools and two years of college in Cookeville, TN; received BA degree from Carson-Newman College, Jefferson City, TN in 1941; received the Th.M. degree from Southern Baptist Theological Seminary, Louisville, KY in May of 1944 and was pastor of Riverside Baptist Church from 1944-53.

Sworn into the USAFR April 6, 1953, and entered active duty July 4 of that year at Scott AFB, IL Subsequently served at Ladd AFB, AK; Robins AFB, GA where he served as wing chaplain with the 4137 Strategic Wing (SAC) and assistant chaplain with the 2853 Air Base Wing; group chaplain, 513 Cbt. Spt. Gp., RAF Mildenhall, England Assigned as division chaplain, 33rd AD, Fort Lee, VA; to the 3750 Air Base Gp., Sheppard AFB, TX in July 1969 where he served a second tour until Aug 1, 1973 with an unaccompanied tour to Ubon, Thailand with the 8th Cbt. Spt. Gp. (the Wolf Pack) in between.

Commissioned a regular officer in the Regular Air Force April 23, 1962, he served in numerous capacities including guard house chaplain, religious education, counseling, and pastoral duties, and occasionally flying missions with flight crews. In Alaska, he served as vice-chairman of the mid-night Sun Chapter of the Boy Scouts of America

Retired from Sheppard AFB and the USAF Aug. 1, 1973. Awarded the Commendation Medal with two OLCs, Meritorious Service Medal and the Bronze Star.

Chaplain Pedigo is married to the former Frances Ivalene (Wiggins) Pedigo They have two sons and four grandchildren

KENNETH DANIEL PERKINS, Commander, Chaplain Corps, USN (RET), born Aug. 11, 1908, Himrod, NY. Graduated high school in 1925; St. Stephens College in 1929 (BA); Berkeley Divinity School at Yale in 1932 (M.Div.); summer school in Social Work, Cincinnati, OH, 1930; 1935-36 graduate study at Univ. of London as Watson Fellow of Berkeley Div. School.

Ordained deacon June 18, 1932, at Cathedral of St. John the Divine, NY City; ordained priest Feb. 3, 1933, at St. Andrew's Cathedral, Honolulu, HI and made honorary canon of St. Andrew's Oct. 25, 1992.

From 1932-72 he was teacher of English and Sacred Studies at Iolani School, Honolulu; assistant at St. Andrew's Cathedral, Honolulu; vicar of Holy Apostles Church, Hilo, HI; appointed by Governor Poindexter to board dealing with conscientious objectors, chaplain, USN; rector of St. George's Church, Pearl Harbor, HI and rector emeritus in 1973

Reported for active duty at Pearl Harbor with duty assignments 1941-62 to Midway Islands; Johnston Island; Palmyra Island, 84th Naval Construction Bn (New Guinea, Brisbane, Australia); NTC, Sampson, NY; Naval Amphibious Training Base, Fort Pierce, FL; USS *Augusta* (CA-31), Atlantic Fleet; Naval Hosp., Corona, CA Served as senior chaplain, assistant district chaplain and senior chaplain at Pearl Harbor, San Francisco, CA; USS Kearsarge, Pacific Fleet; Naval Stations, San Diego, CA; Marine Corps Air Station, El Toro, CA with additional duty on Staff, Commanding General, AIRFMFPAC. Retired voluntarily June 1, 1962. He visited many countries and islands while on active duty.

Awarded the Distinguished Service Cross of the Diocese of Hawaii in 1964, American Defense w/star, American Theater, Asiatic Pacific w/2 stars, WWII Victory, National Defense and China Service Medal (extended).

Historiographer and archivist of the Episcopal Diocese of Hawaii, 1967-92. In retirement, a volunteer tutor in Hawaii Literacy and chairman of that group for several years. Served on Board of Directors of their 350 unit condominium for some years. Member of local and national historical societies; Hilo Rotary Club 1939-41.

Married Ruth Kirkpatrick of Ontario, Canada Jan 8, 1949.

EUGENE S. PETERSON, Colonel, born May 29, 1937, in Jackson, MN, graduated from Augsburg College (1959) and Theological Seminary (1962) and was

ordained a Lutheran pastor Served churches in Duluth and Cass Lake, MN. Received his M.Div. from Luther Seminary and MA from Long Island Univ. Commissioned a 2nd lieutenant, staff specialist April 20, 1961, he served in XIV Corps, USAR and as a chaplain in the 47th Inf. Div., Minnesota NG, before ordered to active duty with the 2nd Armd Div, Fort Hood, TX, June 1, 1966.

Other assignments include: 269th Cbt. Avn. Bn., Cu Chi, Vietnam; Fort Lewis, WA, 7th RRFS, Udorn, Thailand; Fort Hood, TX; Chaplain School, Fort Hamilton, NY; 37th Transportation Gp, Kaiserslautern, Germany; Staff, USACHCS, Fort Wadsworth, NY and Fort Monmouth, NJ; division chaplain, 2AD, Fort Hood, TX; and ARPERCEN, St Louis, MO from which he retired as a colonel, July 30, 1989.

Recalled to ARPERCEN for Operation Desert Storm. Awarded three Army Commendation and three Meritorious Service Medals, Air Medal, Bronze Star and Legion of Merit.

Married Sheila Bluhm, deceased in 1989; they had three daughters. He served a church in Bandera, TX until September 1993. He and his wife, Paula Craven-Peterson, reside in Seguin, TX and Jackson, MN while he completes a Ph.D They have four grandchildren.

JACK H. PHILLABAUM, born 1929 in Wabash, IN Enlisted in the Navy 1947. He was a member of the Navy's elite Underwater Demolition Teams Two and Four, 1960 commissioned naval chaplain with the longest enlisted service of any military chaplain and the only one qualified as a UDT member. Returned to civilian pastorate after the Bay of Pigs in 1963, having served Marine Corps and fleet assignments.

Transferred June 1, 1967, from the Naval Res Chaplaincy to the US Army Chaplaincy until retiring in 1975, having served in the Continental US, Vietnam, Korea and Europe Among his awards are the Bronze Star, Meritorious Service Medal, and the Army Commendation Medal.

Ministered to students at Univ of Louisville, Ball State Univ, and Ohio State Univ with churches in Indiana, Ohio, Kentucky, Virginia, New Mexico, Wyoming and Colorado Has BA from Univ. of Maryland; BA, M.Ed USC; M.Div., Louisville Presby. Theological Seminary, and D Min, San Francisco Presby. Theo. Seminary.

Married to Cassandra Britton, Bethesda, MD and has three children, Mark, Carla and Paul.

DONALD F. PHILLIPS, *No bio submitted, only photos*

CHARLES P. PICKENS, Chaplain, Presbyterian Church, U.S.A. He was born June 26, 1926 in Canadian, TX. and enlisted in the U.S. Navy in June, 1944, serving during World War II and the Korean War, 1950-1952 He served at the V A. Hospital, Sepulveda, CA for 17 years

His memorable experiences include ministering to veteran patients and federal prisoners and working with chaplains of Protestant, Jewish and Catholic faith groups.

Education includes a B.A, North Texas University; B.D., University of Dubuque Theological Seminary; D Min. Fuller Theological Seminary.

His civilian employment has included the M D C., V.A. Hosp., retired, 1991; part-time Federal Prison Chaplain Metropolitan Detention Center-Los Angeles, 1993 to date.

He has been married to Neysa M. for 41 years, and they currently live in Encino, CA. They have two children and two grandchildren.

JUDITH ANN CRAIG PIPER, the daughter of the late Col. Edward W Craig and Esther McCrady Craig, born in Newcastle, WY and was raised on US Army posts around the world following WWII.

A 1962 graduate of the Emanuel Lutheran School of Nursing, Portland, OR, she joined the US Army Nurse Corps under "Operation Nightingale," the first Army nurse recruitment effort for the Vietnam War and served with the MEDEVAC unit at Brooke Army Medical Center, Fort Sam Houston, TX, 1963-1965.

Graduating cum laude with the M.Div. degree from San Francisco Theo Seminary in 1978, she was the first woman to be ordained at the First Presbyterian Church of Berkeley, CA and is a member of the Presbytery of San Francisco, UP (USA).

Chaplain Piper received her commission in the US Army Chaplain Corps at the 6th Army HQ, Presidio of San Francisco, June 1980, serving as the first woman chaplain in the California NG until entering active duty from 1981-1984.

Following Chaplain School at Fort Monmouth, NJ, Chaplain (Captain) Piper was the first woman chaplain to be assigned to the 7th Inf Div. at Fort Ord, CA Completed her active duty tour as the first woman chaplain in the worldwide health services command stationed at Walter Reed Army Med. Ctr., Washington, DC.

Chaplain Piper has been a hospital chaplain with the Department of Veterans Affairs for the past 10 years. She is at present the senior Protestant chaplain, Washington, DC, VAMC. She is a life member of the MCA.

Married to Daniel G. Piper, Ph.D, and they have three children Mark, Mary-Esther and Rosanna, and one grandchild, Kevin.

GOLDWIN SMITH POLLARD, 1st Lieutenant, born in New Braintree, MA, Nov. 27, 1920. Received a BA from Amherst; Oberlin GST BD, T.C Columbia Ed.D, ordained New Braintree (MA) Congregational Church July 11, 1948, Joined the USAAC Aug. 20, 1942, and was stationed at Chanute Field, IL; Fort Bragg, NC; Germany; Fort Totten, NY. Served with 940th FA Bn., 933rd FA Bn.; 526th AAA Bn. (120mm)

Memorable experience was nine days after the 940th FA BN hit the line and the Germans in the Ruhr Pocket gave up. He fought during the Korean War in New York City with the 526th AAA Bn. Discharged from active duty May 14, 1952, as 1st lieutenant and from the Reserves Nov. 26, 1980, as colonel.

Married Mary Ellsberg Benson in 1949; she passed away in 1978. Remarried Rita DeSanto Barbera in 1984. He has two children and three grandchildren.

Pastor and director of the Staff, Mt. Desert, ME, 1948-50; Christian educator, 1952-71; chaplain, 1971-1985; and parish associate at Langhorne (PA) Presbyterian Church, 1988-present

LORRAINE K. POTTER, Colonel, born in Providence, RI. She graduated from Pilgrim High School, Warwick, RI; received a BA degree from Keuka College, Keuka Park, NY, M.Div. degree from Colgate-Rochester Divinity School, Rochester, NY, MA degree in personnel management from Central Michigan Univ., Mount Pleasant, MI in 1980. The American Baptist Churches, USA, presented her with the degree of Doctor of Humane Letters

She was the first woman ordained by the American Baptist Churches of Rhode Island in June 1971 Following ordination, she served as chaplain at Yale-New Haven Hosp., New Haven, CT, receiving additional training and certification as supervisor in Clinical Pastoral Education.

On Sept. 27, 1972, Chaplain Potter was commissioned at Bolling AFB, DC as the first woman chaplain in the USAF. Assignments included Wilford Hall USAF Medical Center, TX; Osan AB, Korea; Pease AFB, NH; Andrews AFB, MD; ASTRA officer, Office of the Chief of Chaplains, Bolling AFB, DC, Lindsey AS, Weisbaden, Germany; a second tour at Wilford Hall USAF Medical Center, ATC Command Chaplains Office, Randolph AFB, TX; and England AFB, LA. Chaplain Potter currently serves as chief, Plans and Programs, Office of the Chief of Chaplains, HQ, USAF, Bolling AFB, DC.

Awards and decorations include the Meritorious Service Medal w/3 OLCs, the AF Commendation Medal w/OLC, the Outstanding Unit Award w/OLC, the AF Organizational Excellence Award and the National Defense Medal w/Bronze Star. She completed Air Command and Staff College and Air War College.

Promoted to colonel Dec 1, 1992, becoming the first woman chaplain in the Dept. of Defense to obtain that grade; a life member of the MCA, having joined in the mid-70s, presently serves on the Executive Committee and is the national vice president.

She is married to Chaplain (Colonel) Robert "Rocky" Saunders, US Army, retired

GLENN R. PRATT, Lieutenant Colonel, born Dec. 28, 1925 in Watertown, NY Received a BA from Union College, BD, Th M Princeton Seminary, STD Temple Univ., grad. study, Princeton Univ., Yale Univ.

Joined the US Army, April 17, 1951, stationed at Eustis, FECOM, Devens, Drum, Bragg, Vint Hill Farms Station, Fort Buchanan PR, Fort Jackson, Fort Slocum, Fort Hamilton, Fort Wadsworth, Fort Pickett and Fort Lee Served with 187th Abn RTC, 278th Inf. RCT, ASA, Army Chaplain's School, 56th Station Hosp.

Memorable Experience broke back and neck in parachute jump with the 187th Abn. RCT in the Korean War and was evacuated to the US with full recovery after years of therapy Also memorable was serving in the revolution in the Dominican Republican in 1965 and the evacuation of civilians

Discharged as lieutenant colonel and is now in Retired Reserves.

Married Marion Burton and has four children and seven grandchildren. He was professor of phil. and rel. studies, VCU, Richmond, VA and retired Dec. 28, 1985.

BEN S. PRICE, Colonel, US Army (RET), born in Paris, TX Nov. 30, 1920 Served as an officer with the 1st Cav Div during WWII in the Philippines, and took part in the Japanese landing after the signing of the treaty aboard the battleship *Missouri.*

Upon discharge he attended East Texas State Univ. graduating in 1947 then attended Southwestern Baptist Theological Seminary earning his degree in 1950 and was subsequently ordained into the ministry serving a civilian church in Virginia. During the course of his career he also earned an MBA from Syracuse Univ., NY and graduated from the United States War College in 1969

As an Army chaplain he served at England Center, Fort Belvoir, VA, 402nd QMBN, Korea, 8044th Army Unit, Tokyo, Japan, USDB, New Cumberland, PA, USAG Kaiserslautern, USAREUR, instructor USACHS, Fort Hamilton, Div. Chaplain 2nd Inf. Div., Korea, director of assignments and Career Management, Office of the Chief-of-Chaplains, Washington, DC, HQ II Field Forces, Vietnam, post chaplain, Fort Knox, KY, staff chaplain, HQ TRADOC.

Service awards are the Legion of Merit, Bronze Star w/V Device w/2 OLCs, Air Medal Meritorious Service Medal, Army Commendation Medal w/OLC, American Campaign Medal, Asiatic-Pacific Campaign Medal, WWII Victory Medal, National Defense Service Medal w/OLC, Korean Service Medal w/3 Bronze Service Stars, UN Service Medal, Philippine Liberation Ribbon, Philippine Presidential Unit Citation Badge, Vietnam Service Medal w/4 Bronze Service Stars, Vietnam Campaign Medal w/60 device, Vietnam Cross of Gallantry w/Palm Unit, Vietnam Armed Force Honor Medal first class.

Upon retirement Chaplain Price did a year of graduate study at the Univ. of Louisville Medical Center earning accreditation as a marriage and family therapist. Currently, he serves as a chaplain of the Soldiers' and Airmens' home in Washington, DC.

MARCUS FLOYD PRICE SR., Lieutenant Colonel, is a native of Wrightsville, GA and was ordained by the Brown Memorial Baptist Church of Wrightsville, GA. He is a 30 year veteran of the USAF and saw combat with the infantry in the South Pacific in WWII. Awarded Combat Infantry Badge, Battle Stars, Silver Star on Peleliu Island (Bloody-Nose Ridge), AF Commendation Medal and others.

The Price family traveled extensively while serving in the military. They lived in many different states, including Hawaii and Alaska. While living in Anchorage, Reverend Price pastored, named and constituted (from a mission) the First Baptist Church of Eagle River, one of Alaska's full-time growing Southern Baptist churches cooperating with the Southern Baptist Convention.

He holds a BA in Bible theology; doctorate in Christian counseling, honorary doctor of law degree from the Augusta Law School in Georgia and is a graduate of the USAF Chaplain Staff College, Montgomery, AL. He is ecclesiastically endorsed by the Chaplain's Commission of the Southern Baptist Convention, a 32nd degree Scottish Rite Mason, a Master Mason, a former member of the executive committee of the Georgia Baptist Convention. Member of Lions Club, VFW, American Legion, Georgia Sheriff's Association and 30 years Chaplain Masonic Lodge

Retired after 30 years US Army and USAF; 19 years with CAP, seven years Georgia State Defense Force (Military Div.); 45 years Southern Baptist minister

Mrs. Price is the former Esther Harrison of Harrison, GA They have two children, Marcus Price Jr. and Bonnie Price Odom, and three grandchildren Jennifer, Marcus III and Nicky, all of Swainsboro

R. EUGENE PRICE, Lieutenant Commander, born on Aug. 4, 1929, in Hickory, NC, the second of three sons of Earl R and Desola (Deal) Price. He holds degrees from Anderson C , BS (1952); Anderson School of Theology, M.Div. (1957); and Sonoma State Univ , MA in counseling (1976) Post-graduate work was completed at California Graduate School of Family Psychology plus an 18-month internship in psychology and pastoral care at Ross Hosp. (psychiatry), Kentfield, CA.

Entered the USNR Aug. 17, 1959. Active duty assignments included Chaplains School, Newport, RI; 1st Marine Div., Camp Pendleton; 3rd Marine Div , Okinawa, NTC, San Diego; Destroyer Sqdn 36, Norfolk; Submarine Base, Groton, CT; and Marine Corps Base, Camp Pendleton Also, he was regimental chaplain, 23rd Marines, 4th Marine Div., Alameda, executive officer and training officer for I Marine Amphibious Force (Religion), San Francisco. He retired from the Navy on June 1, 1981, lieutenant commander. His civilian pastorates were in Ames, IA; Madera, CA and Oakland, CA.

Since February 1993 he has been staff chaplain (SBC) at the Fort Miley DVA Medical Center, San Francisco. As an associate life member of the Veterans of the Battle of the Bulge, he serves as chaplain for the Northern California Chapter. Other memberships include the Assoc of Mental Health Clergy and life memberships in MCA, TROA and AMVETS.

Most memorable experiences are serving as battalion chaplain, 2nd Bn., 3rd Marines, Far East in 1960-61, and as squadron chaplain on the USS *Laffey* (DD-721) Goodwill Tour to East African nations in 1965.

Married to the former Carol Ann Hays of Petaluma, CA They have one son, two daughters, and two granddaughters.

RAYMOND PRITZ, Colonel, born Jan 20, 1920, in Corona, NY. Received the BA from The King's College, Th.B, Eastern Baptist Theological Seminary, MA, Univ. of Pennsylvania

Joined the USAF, March 19, 1953. Stationed at Pope AFB, NC; Chicksands RAF; Wright-Patterson AFB, OH; Freising AB, Germany; Walker AFB, New Mexico, Lackland AFB, TX; Maxwell AFB, AL; Torrejon AB, Spain; HQ USAF/HC, DC; MacDill AFB, FL; Andrews AFB, DC. Discharged Jan 31, 1980, as colonel.

His memorable experiences include the four years in the USAF Chaplain School, three years in Chief of AF Chaplains office (Director of Ecclesiastical and Public Relations).

Married June 20, 1944 to Grace Eileen Castor. They had five sons and 17 grandchildren.

Civilian pastor, Waterloo, IA; Richmond, VA; Tampa, FL. Retired Feb 1, 1980.

RALPH H. PUGH, Colonel, USA (RET), born Dec 5, 1913, in Williamstown, WV. Attended high school in 1930; business college, 1931; Alderson-Broaddus College, BA, 1937; Crozer Sem., 1940, M Th; Stetson Univ., MA, history, Phi Alpha Theta 1968.

Entered active duty on March 4, 1941, and retired Aug 31, 1966. Received his RA commission in January 1942 and spent the next three years with the 94th Inf. Div. A few of his many post assignments were: West Point, NY; Fort Belvoir, VA; Fort Benning, GA; three years Occupation of Japan; 24th Inf. Div., (Europe 1958-60); Com-Z 1960-61, and his association with the US Army Chaplains' School as student, instructor, director of resident instruction, deputy commandant and finally, 17th commandant of the school. His last assignment was that of command chaplain, HQ US Army, Pacific, 1965-66, stationed in Honolulu, HI Retired Aug. 31, 1966, as permanent colonel, RA.

One of his most cherished memories of the war was the compliment paid him by his Arty. Gen. Louis J. Fortier, who told him, "Chaplain, you could command a battery."

Chaplain Pugh is a life member of TROA and the Chaplains' Association; also, of the Retired Chaplains of Orlando; member of Phi Alpha Theta; the Retired Teachers Association of Florida and Volusia County; The Retired Officers of Volusia County, FL; American Baptist Convention and the Ministers' Council of American Baptists.

He is a member of Upland Baptist Church, Upland, PA and was ordained in November 1939 by Immanuel Baptist Church, Chester, PA.

Married to Elizabeth, June 1, 1937 They have five children, 13 grandchildren and three great-grandchildren He pastored civilian churches prior to entering the Army. Employed as high school teacher from 1968-1976.

WALTER E. RACKER (WALLY), CH, Lieutenant Colonel, USAF, CAP, born June 10, 1920, in Wallingford, CT. Received BA from Baker (UMC), 1952; MST, Phillips Seminary, Enid, OK, 1965; postgraduate studies for MA in psychology (rehabilitation) SIU, Carbondale, IL; certificate in advanced clinical pastoral education, Anna State Hosp., Anna, IL. He was ordained in the Cong. Church (UCC) and later orders were recognized by UMC.

Served as the Chief of Chaplains for the Oklahoma CAP Wing WWII veteran (South Pacific) US Army Infantry, later USAAC then USAF He is chaplain-pilot with rank of lieutenant colonel, Oklahoma Wing (CAP). Discharged December 1948.

Made honorary "OKIE" by governor of Oklahoma for work with juvenile delinquents Associate director of Greater St. Paul, MN Council of Churches as Director of Chaplain Services Started the Police Chaplain Program and worked with Vice President Hubert Humphrey and the State Mental Retarded (Children) Association as well as a lot other programs

Served for five years as the Ecumenical chaplain for three Roman Catholic Hospitals and was the first Protestant Chaplain in history to be paid by the Catholic Church; was Sioux City Police Chaplain, served the AA (14 groups); was director of TV ministries for the four TV stations, served two Presbyterian Churches of the Winnebago and Omaha Reservations on Saturday and Sunday; was the AA counselor in Nebraska for the Bureau of Indian Affairs Hosp at Winnebago.

Has held International Healing Seminars at ORU with Tommy Tyson (UMC) and Dr Francis McNutt (last one was nationally televised). Life member of the VFW (for the past three years has been commander of local VFW Post), DAV, Masonic Lodge, Eastern Star, Scottish Rites and Shriners

Owner of a dairy farm in Wisconsin and has a beef ranch in Kansas Retired July 1, 1983; still serves as CAP chaplain and pilot; for the past eight years he has been supplying an open country church.

Married to the former Bethel Warren (SPFD Teacher, RN); they have three children and seven grandchildren.

KENNETH C. RAMSEY, Lieutenant Colonel, born in Somerville, NJ. He graduated from St. Petersburg High School, St. Petersburg, FL, received a BA degree from National College, Kansas City, MO, and a MDiv degree from Methodist Theological School in Ohio, Delaware, Ohio.is a life member of the MCA having joined in the late 70s.

Completed Squadron Officers School, commissioned in March 1968 and first duty assignment was at Altus AFB, OK. Succeeding assignments were to Ubon Royal Thai Airfield, Griffiss AFB, NY; Westover AFB, MA; Rhine Main AB, Germany, Patrick AFB, FL; RAF Lakenheath, U.K., Lackland AFB, TX and Williams AFB, AZ.

Awards include the Meritorious Service Medal w/3 OLCs, AF Commendation Medal w/3 OLCs, AF Outstanding Unit Award w/valour device, National Defense Service Medal, Vietnam Service Medal, RVN Gallantry Cross with device and RVN Campaign Medal.

Married to Shirley Louise Corder and they have two children, Lori and Sarah. Since retiring from active duty in August 1991, he has been serving as associate pastor, First United Methodist Church, Pompano Beach, FL

JACK C. RANDLES, Colonel, US Army (RET), born in Atlanta, GA in 1925, the son of the late E.E and Mary Cusick Randles.

Served as an infantryman in the 66th Inf. Div. during WWII Entered the Army Chaplaincy in June 1952 and served 17 months in Korea (March 1953-July 1954). Returned to the civilian pastorate during the period of July 1955-March 1960, at which time he returned to the Army Chaplaincy and served with the Americal Div. in Vietnam, July 1968-69.

Completed the basic and career courses at the US Army Chaplain School, the Armed Forces Staff College (1968) and the Army War College (CSI) (1971) Some of his assignments were brigade chaplain, 3rd Armd Div., brigade deputy and command chaplain, USA Training Center, Fort Knox, assistant division chaplain, Vietnam, Plans and Programs, USARPAC, deputy staff chaplain, TRADOC, post chaplain, Forts Belvoir and Knox, and deputy command chaplain, Forces Command.

Received 22 awards and decorations to include the Legion of Merit w/OLC, Meritorious Service, Bronze Star w/2 OLC, Air Medal, Army Commendation Medal, Purple Heart and the Combat Infantryman Badge. Chaplain Randles retired in October 1980 in the grade of colonel and was the last chaplain to serve on active duty who had participated in combat in WWII, Korean Campaign and Vietnam.

He presently lives in Fallston, MD, and does interim pastoral work. Married his wife Dorothy in 1946 and they have two adult children, Jill and Scott, both of whom live in Maryland

JAMES M. REAVES, Lieutenant Colonel, born July 3, 1920 in Lumberton, NC. Received a BS USNA, 1943; M.Div. VTS (Alex VA) M Ed., Univ. of Arizona

Joined the USA (Chap) January 1957. Joined the USN 1942-1946 Stationed at Fort Leonard Wood, MO, Fort Benning, GA; Fort Huachuca, AZ; USS *Concord*, USS *Duluth*; France; Germany; Korea, and Vietnam. Retired August 1972 as lieutenant colonel.

Memorable experiences include visiting hospitals and orphanages in Vietnam and Korea; visiting Hiroshima after bomb drop. Such a devastating result of modern warfare made him realize that the greatest needs of mankind are spiritual, and thus led him to consider the ordained ministry as a possible vocation.

Married Louise Henshaw Jan. 17, 1944, and has four children and three grandchildren. Held the position as rector of All Saints of the Desert, Sun City, AZ from 1976 to retirement in December 1985

CHARLES D. REED, Lieutenant Colonel, born in Newell, WV, Feb. 25, 1912. Attended Asbury College, Wilmore, KY, AB; Asbury Theological Seminary, Wilmore, KY, BD

Joined the Army, May 9, 1942, and served with the 116th Inf. Regt., 29th Inf. Div., 145th Inf. Regt., 37th Inf

Div His memorable experiences include: D-day, Second Wave; State Staff Chaplain, Ohio NG.

Awarded the Purple Heart w/OLC, Silver Star and Army Commendation Medal. Discharged Jan 11, 1969, as lieutenant colonel.

Married to Adaleen Witt and they have three children and six grandchildren He was minister of United Methodist, West Ohio Conference. Retired June 1977.

HAROLD L. REINHARDT,
Lieutenant Colonel, born Feb. 16, 1926, New Orleans, LA, the son of Rev Harry and Edna Reinhardt. Attended St John's College, Winfield, KS, graduated (BA) Concordia Seminary, St. Louis, MO, 1949; ordained and installed pastor of Trinity Lutheran Church, Monroe, LA, August 1949.

Began his Army ministry June 1953. Service included Camp Polk, LA; Korea; Japan; Fort Lewis, WA; Orleans, France, Fort Leonard Wood, MO; Vietnam; Fort Jackson, SC and Madigan Army Medical Center, Tacoma, WA. Army schooling included a year's training in Clinical Pastoral Education, Medical College of Virginia in Richmond.

Retired July 1973 after 20 years active service Honors include Legion of Merit, Bronze Star and Commendation Medal.

Received an MA in social sciences from Pacific Lutheran Univ., Tacoma, WA, 1974. Was director on the Council on Aging, a Lutheran social services program, 1974-1990 This information service for the elderly included publishing a newspaper and producing two TV programs each month for seniors Recognized in 1989 by the community as an "Outstanding Senior of the Year" for service to seniors. Since retirement in February 1990, Chaplain Reinhardt keeps active at church and volunteers for the Red Cross.

Married Dorothy Jahn, August 1949 and they have three children

JAMES EDWARD REITER,
Captain, born March 10, 1945, in Greensburg, PA, the son of Raymond and Betty Reiter. Graduate of Immaculate Conception School, Greensburg Central High School, Univ of Pittsburgh with BS, Duquesne Univ. with MS in education, attended Holy Apostles College and Seminary, Cromwell, CT and ordained priest April 22, 1990, in Mississauga, Ontario

Served on active duty with the USAF from 1965-68, and in the USAFR from 1968-88 as a chapel manager, retiring as a senior master sergeant in 1988 Joined the CAP in 1971 and is currently a CAP chaplain, serving in the grade of captain.

Served as administrator of Sts Peter and Paul Ukranian Catholic Church from 1990-92 He is now a supply priest for the Byzantine rite parishes in western Pennsylvania. Activities include membership in CAP (chaplain, captain), AF Sergeants Assoc , VFW, (life member and chaplain), American Legion, Loyal Order of Moose, Moose Legion, Lions Clubs, Knights of Columbus (4th degree) and is a life member of the MCA.

WILLIAM ALEXANDER RENNIE,
Lieutenant Commander, born in North Andover, MS, Feb. 16, 1916. Received BA from High Point College, NC; M.Ed from Boston Univ ; M Div from Yale and STM from Harvard.

Joined the USN May 23, 1943, and served with Gro-Pac 6 Tinian, Marianas, USS *Mindoro* (CVE-120); USN Base Key West, FL; Med. Bn , USMC, Korea; USS *Gen. T.M. Randall* (TAP-115); Sub Base, Pearl Harbor; USS *Fulton,* CG Trng. Station, Groton, CT. Discharged July 1, 1965, as lieutenant commander.

Married Bethel M Cate and they have four children and eight grandchildren.

Vice president for Endicott Col , Beverly, MA He retired July 1, 1981.

ARNOLD E. RESNICOFF,
Captain, born in Washington, DC. Earned a bachelor's degree, Dartmouth College and three master's degrees in international relations, Salve Regina Univ., strategic studies and national security affairs, Naval War College; Rabbinics, Jewish Theological Seminary of America, where he was later ordained

Received four academic prizes in the fields of homiletics, writing and rabbinic service; was the President's Honor Graduate for his Naval War College class, and later created and taught the Naval War College elective "Faith and Force Religion, War and Peace."

Began drilling with the enlisted naval reserves in 1963, switched to NROTC at Dartmouth College; duty in the Mekong Delta onboard USS *Hunterdon County* (LST-838); served with Naval Security Group and Naval Intelligence units operating out of Rota, Spain, before leaving active duty to enter seminary

Delivered the closing prayer at the 1982 dedication of the Vietnam Veterans Memorial; was present in Beirut, Lebanon, during the October 1983 truck-bomb attack and his written report was read aloud by President Ronald Reagan to the 20,000 attendees of the "Baptist Fundamentalism '84," Washington, DC, convention Was on the Navy Chief of Chaplains "Blue Ribbon Committee" that recommended the change in the Jewish chaplain insignia to Hebrew letters; was the driving force behind military Holocaust observances now scheduled annually as part of the National "Days of Remembrance" initiative, served as the Navy representative to the DOD Days of Remembrance Committee and delivered the closing prayer at the 1987 national ceremony in the Capital rotunda. He led Yom Kippur services in Iceland during the US-USSR pre-summit talks, and, while attached to the US Sixth Fleet, helped establish the Haifa, Israel, USO. In 1995 he coordinated the implementation of "J-MIL," the new world-wide internet resource service for all active duty Jewish military personnel.

His work in interfaith affairs has been recognized in many ways including a 1990 book on Christian religious education, "*Teaching for Christian Hearts, Souls, and Minds,*" dedicated in his honor.

Military assignments as a chaplain have included tours of duty with Commander Fleet Activities Yokosuka (Japan), Naval Station Norfolk, Commander Sixth Fleet, the Naval Chaplains School, the Chief of Naval Education and Training, and NTC Orlando

Military awards include four Meritorious Service Medals, two Naval Commendation Medals and the Combat Action Ribbon He is the recipient of numerous civilian honors including the 1991 Moment Magazine International Community Service Award, the Chapel of Four Chaplains "Hall of Heroes Gold Medallion," for his work with the wounded and dying in Beirut

In 1994 the Chaplain Arnold E. Resnicoff Scholarship Fund was established in his honor at the Jewish Theological Seminary of America to help rabbinical students who plan to serve as chaplains with the U.S. military. He is command chaplain for the Naval Submarine Base, New London and group chaplain for Commander Submarine Gp. TWO.

JERRY L. RHYNE,
Colonel, born Feb. 7, 1937, in Chester, IL Received M.Div. He joined the USAF November 1969 and was stationed at Seymour-Johnson AFB, Ubon Royal Thai AFB; Vandenburg AFB, CA, Oslo, Norway, HQ USAF Chief of Chaplains Office, DC; Military Airlift Cmd., Command Chaplain's Office, Bitburg AB, Germany; Offutt AFB, NE; Director of Pastoral Care, Wilford Hall Medical Center.

Was first division chief of Readiness and Reserve Div in the office of the Chief of Chaplains. Awarded the Legion of Merit, Meritorious Service Medal, four OLCs and AF Commendation Medal Retired Sept 1, 1992, as colonel.

Married Rev. Marion L Rhyne and they have two children and one grandchild. He is co-pastor with his wife at Boger and plans to retire Sept. 1, 1999.

ALBERT DEARDORFF RICE,
Lieutenant Colonel, born Sept 29, 1921, in Columbia, SC. Received AoG Central Bible College; Bob Jones Univ.

Joined the US Army April 10, 1954; attended US Army Chaplain School, Fort Hood, TX; Kaiserslautern, W Germany; Baumholder, W. Germany, Fort Myer, VA, Fort Meade, MD, Fort Knox, KY; Fort Eustis, VA, Sandia (Army) Base, NM; Fort Bliss, TX; Fort Irwin, CA; Camp Roberts, CA.

Served with 1st AD, 2nd AD, 4th AD, 45th AAA (Sep) Bn , 80th Div. Res., 11th SF Res. A memorable experience was serving with the 11th Special Forces

(Reserve) in "backup" to active duty unit during the Cuban Missile Crisis.

Divorced, he has two children and two grandchildren. He has held positions with Assemblies of God Church until retirement Sept. 30, 1986.

RICHARD W. RICKER, Captain, born Sept. 12, 1915, in Hudson, MA. Received BA from Nebraska Wesleyan Univ., 1939; Garret Seminary, MD, 1942; Naval PG School, Union Seminary, 1948-49.

Joined the USN July 1942 and attended Chaplains School, Norfolk, VA, July 1942; NTS Great Lakes, October 1942-June 1943; USS *Biloxi,* June 1943-March 1945; Naval Base, Norfolk, April 1945-December 1945; NAS Brunswick December 1945-July 1946.

Fleet activities: Yokosuka, Japan, 1946-48; Naval Post Graduate School, Union Seminary, 1948-49; NAS Norfolk, VA, 1949-51; instructor, Navy Chaplain's School, 1951-52; 1st Marine Air Ground Task Force, 1952-55; District Chaplain's Office, 9th ND, 1955-58; USS *Saratoga* (CVA-60), 1958-60; Force Chaplain, Naval Air Atlantic, 1950-52; District Chaplain, 4th ND, 1952-55; Detached Duty 8th ND 1955-70; Patuxent River NAS, 1970-71.

Memorable experience was treating wounded during Battle of Wotje (Marshalls) Christmas in 1944.

Retired as captain April 1, 1971. He was president of MCA 1972-74.

Married Isabelle B. King and they have two children and two grandchildren. Held position as associate editor, *The Upper Room,* until retirement Jan. 1, 1980.

ELDIN RICKS, Lieutenant Colonel, born March 26, 1916 in Rexburg, ID. Received BS from Brigham Young Univ.; MA, Univ. Southern California; Ph.D, Dropsie Univ., Philadelphia, PA.

Joined the service as chaplain in 1943; attended Army Chaplain School and enrolled in the school's extension reading program. Has also been enrolled in Chaplain Branch training courses in USAR schools for several years. Achieved the rank of lieutenant colonel.

Memorable experiences include the private interview with Pope Pius XII and R&R in Israel.

Married Irene Hailes and they have four children and 20 grandchildren.

Over the years he has served as a college student body president, chairman of a county civic improvement association and as a university department chairman. Retired from the position of bishop in the Mormon Church and as professor of Religion at the Brigham Young Univ., June 30, 1976. He died of a sudden heart attack Sept. 7, 1992.

FRANK C. RILEY SR., Colonel, born Dec. 31, 1916, in Augusta, GA. Received AB from Furman Univ., 1940 and B.Div., Southern Baptist Theological Seminary, 1949.

Entered service from Georgia as first lieutenant, March 1945. Served in Philippines and Korea, 1945-47; Chaplain School, Fort Devens, 1945; Philippines and Korea, 1945-47. Returned to Korea, 1950-51; Fort Lewis, WA, 1951-53; Trieste, 1953; Italy, 1954; Austria, 1955; Fort Devens, 1956-59; Adv. Ch. School, 1958; Germany, 1960-63; Fort Campbell, KY, 1963-65; Vietnam, 1965-66, and White Sands Missile Range; Las Cruces, NM, August 1966.

Returned to Vietnam as USARV command chaplain in 1972. Completed three years, six months tour in Panama Canal Zone as staff chaplain, 193rd Inf. Bde. (CZ) and command chaplain, USSOUTHCOM. He has visited Greece, Turkey, France, Belgium, Palestine and Egypt.

Received Bronze Star Medal w/V for Valor (Korea), Air Medal and Bronze Star (Vietnam), Legion of Merit, White Sands Missile Range, Meritorious Service Medal and upon retirement in December 1976, he received the Legion of Merit w/OLC. Retired Dec. 31, 1976, as colonel. Raised as Master Mason, Branford Lodge #130, Branford, FL, 1943.

Married to Etta Lee Riley and they have four sons, three grandsons and one granddaughter.

RALPH E. RIVERS, Major, born Feb. 17, 1940, in the Methodist Parsonage at Lake Panasoffkee, FL.

Attended public schools and graduated from Coral Gables Senior High School, Coral Gables, FL. Received BA degree from Mercer Univ., Macon, GA and a M.Div. degree from Emory Univ., Atlanta, GA, and Post Graduate studies at Emory Univ. Clinical pastoral education was received at Fort Gordon Army Post, Fort Gordon, GA. He is a graduate of the CAP Southeast Region Chaplain's Staff College and the Southeast Region Staff College.

Has served CAP in a variety of positions as squadron chaplain, lecturer at squadron leadership schools, Corporate Learning Course, Wing Chapel leader and Region Chaplin Staff College devotional speaker.

He is an ordained deacon and elder in the United Methodist Church and currently serving as senior pastor of First United Methodist Church, Okeechobee, FL.

His CAP awards and decorations include the Meritorious Service Award, Commander's Commendation Award, Unit Citation Award, Charles E. "Church" Yeager Aerospace Education Achievement Award and other service and training awards.

Married the former Sharon Anne Sebekow Miller of Oxford, FL. They have three children: Robin Cash, Ken Miller and Jason Miller, and three grandchildren.

ALLA WINSTON ROBERTSON, Commander, born Dec. 25, 1919, in Celina, TX. Retired March 31, 1970. During WWII he served as a chaplain's yeoman aboard the USS *Hermitage* (AP-54). In 1944 and 1945 he attended Texas Christian Univ., in the Navy V-12 (Pre-Theological) program and received his BA degree. He is a graduate of Southwestern Baptist Theological Seminary. Completed the Eleventh Institute of Correctional Administration, George Washington Univ. and graduate work at East Texas State Univ. and Univ. of Virginia.

Assignments: Chaplain's School, Newport, RI; 2nd Marine Div. FMFLANT 1st Tank Bn., 1st Marine Div. FMFPAC (Korea); NAS, Pensacola, FL; USS *Valley Forge* (CVS-45); USNTC, Great Lakes, IL; USS *Rochester* (CA-124); USNTC, Bainbridge, MD; MSTSLANT (AFLOAT); assistant district chaplain, 5th Naval District; regimental chaplain, 1st Marine Div., FMFPAC (RVN; HQ and Service Bn., FMFLANT.

Awarded the Bronze Star w/Combat "V", Navy Commendation Medal w/Combat V, Combat Action Ribbon, Good Conduct Medal, American Campaign Medal, EAME Campaign Medal, Asiatic-Pacific Campaign Medal, WWII Victory Medal, National Defense Medal w/Bronze Star, Korean Service Medal w/2 stars, National Defense Medal w/Bronze Star, Korean Service Medal w/2 stars, Korean Presidential Unit Citation, Vietnam Service Medal w/Bronze Star and FMF Combat Operations Insignia, Vietnamese Cross of Gallantry w/ palms and the Vietnamese Campaign Medal.

Chaplain Robertson is retired from Texas Department of Corrections and has served as pastor of four Southern Baptist Churches and currently serving as a volunteer chaplain at the Dallas Fort Worth, TX, International Airport.

Married Mary Jo Boykin, March 3, 1945; they have two daughters and four grandchildren.

RICHARD E. ROBINSON, Colonel, born Aug. 22, 1917, Pittsburgh, PA. Graduate of Waynesburg College, Western Theological Seminary, and Univ. of Pittsburgh (MEd) and ordained an evangelist by Pittsburgh Presbytery, June 1955.

Served in US Armed Forces 29 years, 1941-70. In 1956 resigned LTC USAF commission to be recommissioned chaplain (captain) US Army with WWII combat duty as B-17 pilot in ETO.

Other significant assignments as inspector general, Tactical Air Command; Berlin Airlift pilot and maintenance officer; Air Depot Procurement and supply officer; and as chaplain with Antilles Cmd., XII Corps; US Army Test and Evaluation Command Chaplain; I Corps Chaplain.

Retired from Fort Benning to accept call as assistant pastor, National Presbyterian Church, Washington, DC for a couple of years. Continues to service, since then, as supply pastor, nursing home and hospital chaplain, and, presently, as parish associate in Mission Presbytery, San Antonio, TX.

EDWIN WILLIAM ROGERS, Captain, born June 13, 1922, in Sumter, SC. Received M.Div. Duke Divinity School; D.Min., McCormick Theological Presbyterian Seminary, Chicago, IL.

Joined the Navy Nov. 2, 1942. Put the USS *Mobile*

(CL-63) in and out of commission. Served with the Pacific Theatre and earned 13 Battle Stars. Memorable experience: became Navy chaplain, Dec. 21, 1954, Chm., Palmetto Chapter, MCA 1987 (SC). Discharged as captain Jan. 2, 1946

Married Margaret Davis Rogers and they have four children and eight grandchildren. He held positions as United Methodist Minister. Retired Sept. 30, 1982. Total Service Enl , Supply Corps, USNR and as chaplain 38 years, three months, 11 days.

ROBERT F. ROLF, Lieutenant Colonel, born July 14, 1915, in Gaylord, MN. Attended Concordia College, St Paul; Concordia Seminary, St. Louis, MO, C.W R.U., Cleveland, OH.

Joined the USAR Sept. 13, 1943. Military locations and stations: Camp Adair, OR, North Africa, Italy; Fort Eustice, VA. Served with 362nd Inf. Regt , 91st Div., 43rd Div. Arty., Germany. Discharged as lieutenant colonel, July 10, 1953. Retired July 14, 1975.

During a pause in the artillery fire, both enemy and friendly, it was possible to gain access along a precipitous road to a village high in the Apennine Mountains of Italy. There, a squad of soldiers was ordered to hold the fort. It was Christmas Eve and the cave beneath the rubble reminded them of another cave in Bethlehem.

The soldiers asked, "When are we going to get out of this place?" His realistic response was, "I don't know " "I do know that no matter how dreary, lonely, dangerous this place is, the truth and message is as true, real and consequential as it has ever been or ever will be. For unto you is born in the city of David a Savior, who is Christ the Lord " Luke 2, 11.

Married Ruth C Schmidt Sept. 13, 1947 They have three children and six grandchildren. Held positions at St. Mark, Cleveland; Gethsemane, Fort Wayne, Our Redeemer, Cincinnati, OH Retired July 14, 1975

REV. LOWELL A. RONNE, Colonel, born in Weeping Water, NE, Nov. 24, 1920. On Dec 7, 1941 he married Cora Miller in Sacramento, CA. Subsequently, he was drafted into the US Air Corps. During WWII he served with the Materiel Air Service Command as a logistics officer. He was on duty at Naha Air Depot, Okinawa, when Japan surrendered

Subsequently, graduated from Seattle Pacific Univ., 1948, from Asbury Seminary, 1952 and ordained June 1952 a Free Methodist minister Commissioned chaplain in the USAF March 1954 serving at AF bases in Wyoming, Aviano, Italy; Spokane, WA; Wakkanai, Japan, San Angelo, TX; Yokota, Japan, Dayton, OH. April 1974, Col Ronne retired at March AFB, CA

He served as associate pastor of the Arcade Wesleyan Church, Sacramento, CA. until full retirement in 1986. Married to Cora B. of Winnsboro, LA and they have one child.

BENJAMIN ROSAYN, Major, born Oct. 13, 1921, in New York City. Attended Yeshiva Univ. and ordained Rabbi and B.R E. and M.R.E.; Augusta Law School, LL.D, Philathea College, D.D.

Joined the USAR October 1962. Stationed at Tyndall AFB, Panama City, FL. Served with all personnel at TAFB and also Fort Rucker, AL.

Memorable experiences: At TAFB Hosp., an airman near death from bacterial infection and after his next of kin came, they all prayed together and he recovered. His Polish Catholic colonel invited and honored him (a CCAR Rabbi) as homily-giver at local Holy Name Society. Discharged as major in May 1966.

Married to Davida Goaali Rosayn and they have two children, Barry Benjamin and Brock F.). They also have five grandchildren.

Held positions as Federal Sector Arbitrator-Adjudicator; Community Relations Board; and Boca Raton YMCA Board, Florida Atlantic Univ., forum moderator; St. Vincent de Paul College-Seminary at Boynton Beach, professor OTI. He retired June 1994 and received a Certificate of Appreciation from MCA.

ROBERT N. RULEMAN, Commander, born Sept. 20, 1918, in Eagle Grove, IA. He received a BA from Morningside College, Sioux City, IA; M.Div. from Garret Biblical Institute, Evanston, IL.

Joined the US Navy, June 25, 1943. Military locations and stations: 92nd CB, Tinian; 1st Marine Div , Korea. Served with the USS *Helena,* 1st Marine Air Wing, 3rd Marine Div , NAS Midway Island. Retired as commander July 31, 1963

Married to Freda A Hall and they have three children and eight grandchildren

Held positions as United Methodist pastor Iowa churches Vol chaplain Iowa State Patrol 1984; Vol Chap., FBI

BRUCE A. RUMSCH, Commander, born April 26, 1952, in Springfield, IL. Attended Concordia College and Seminary, Fort Wayne, IN (1974-78).

Joined the USN, June 3, 1982. All of his service has been in the Naval Reserve, except for the four month activation for Operation Desert Storm in 1991. Units served have been MAFREL 322, Spokane, WA; MAFREL 422, Tacoma, WA; NAS 4089, NAS Whidbey Island, VMAQ 4, NAS Whidbey Island, and 6th Engr. Spt Bn., Portland, OR

Memorable experience· His reserve unit was mobilized for Operation Desert Storm and he spent four months at MCB Camp Lejeune, NC.

Ordination was in June 1978, in the Lutheran Church-Missouri Synod. Civilian parishes served have been Lutheran Church, Missouri Synod congregations in Chula Vista, CA, Osburn and Mullan, ID; Oak Harbor, WA; and Hillsboro, OR.

Married Carol M Schroeder June 29, 1974, and have two children, Becky and Charlotte.

WILLIAM G. RUPRACHT, born April 18, 1945, in West Monroe, NY. Graduated from North Greenville Junior College, Carson Newman College, New Orleans Baptist Theological Seminary and Doctorate from San Francisco Theological Seminary.

He is Chief of Chaplains at the Tuscaloosa VA Medical Center and also serves as the senior individual mobilization augmentee to the command chaplain for the Air Force Materiel Cmd. at Wright-Patterson, OH. Professional military education includes Squadron Officer School, Air Command and Staff College and Air War College.

Some of awards that he is most proud of consists of Empire State Farmer; Outstanding Young Preacher; Vietnam Era Presidential Certificate for Outstanding Community Achievement, Outstanding Officer Individual Mobilization Augmentee of the Year, National Association of Social Workers Public Citizen of the Year; and two time recipient of Four Chaplain's Legion of Honor

Chaplain Rupracht has a daughter, Kimberly Dawn, and they live in Tuscaloosa, AL.

WILLIAM A. RUSHFORD, Major, HQ, 164th Engr Cbt. Gp., North Dakota ARNG has for a period of over 20 years distinguished himself, the US Army and the ARNG of North Dakota by his outstanding record of civilian and military service.

Enlisted in the US Army on March 7, 1943. After completion of basic training at Camp Roberts, CA, he saw service with Co. B, 111th Inf. Div. with tours of duty at Camp Stoneman, CA; Hawaii; Eniwetok in the Marshall Islands; and Guam in the Mariana Islands of the Pacific Theater of operations. He returned stateside in July 1945 and was released from active duty at Fort Leavenworth, KS on Dec. 9, 1945

While on active duty in the Pacific Theater he was awarded the Combat Infantry Badge and the Good Conduct Medal. He was promoted to the grade of sergeant prior to his discharge in 1945

Chaplain Rushford is a graduate of Saint Thomas Seminary where he received his priesthood and BA degree. Prior to receiving his degree he attended Crosier Seminary for three years.

In addition to his civilian degree he is a graduate of the Chaplain Officers Basic Course, US Army Chaplain School, Fort Hamilton, NY. By 1970 he had qualified himself for promotion to major by completion of the Chaplain Officer Academic Course.

Throughout his career in the NG, Chaplain Rushford has demonstrated a high spirit of dedication in improving the chaplain's services and moral support to all members of the NG. Even with his many demands as a priest he found time to keep up on the latest information available to chaplains by attendance at conferences and seminars in various parts of the US. As a staff officer he made himself available at any time to counsel and assist commanders with troop morale

Prior to his retirement in 1978 he was awarded the Meritorious Service Medal for his military leadership and spiritual guidance to all regardless of creed.

Because of his outstanding achievements and distinguished services rendered to his state, nation, and the North Dakota NG, Chaplain (Major) William A. Rushford was awarded the Legion of Merit of the State of North Dakota

MICHAEL A. RUSNOCK, Colonel (06) born Nov. 9, 1923, in McAdoo, PA. Received BA, MT St. Mary' College, Emmitsburg, MD 1945; Th.M, Princeton, NJ, 1974. Ordination: RC Priest, Baltimore, MD, 1948. US Army Command and General Staff College, Levenworth, KS 1963. Joined the US Army Sept 8, 1952.

Military locations and stations: Korea, Bronze Star Medal, 1952; Atlanta, GA, 1954; Hawaii, 1957; Fort Irwin, CA 1959; W Germany, 1963; Fort Benning, GA, 1966; Thailand, CM, 1967; Fort Leonard Wood, 1968; 1st Cav. Div. Ch., Legion of Merit and Air 1969 VN. FORCECOM Atlanta, GA, 1972, secretary, US Army Chaplain School, Fort Hamilton, NY Legion of Merit with OLC. Retired in 1972. Retired as colonel (06) October 1972. Memorable experiences: curator and emeritus, US Army Chaplain School, Fort Monmouth, NJ 1980-1985. GS II. Founder, US Army Chaplain Museum Association, 1985.

Civilian employment assistant and director, Reigner Reading Room, Religious Education Research Department, Princeton Seminary, Princeton, NJ 1974-1979 Consultant, Davis and Associates, Management Development for AT&T, 1988

Past member American Museum Assoc., American Assoc of State and Local History, charter member, Da Nang Vietnam Ch. MCA 1989; Sec New York Ch. MCA, 1971, member MCA from 1954, National Committee and life member MCA.

Married Joan E. Kist March 17, 1973, in nuptial mass in Princeton Univ. Chapel with dispensation from Pope Paul VI. They have no children.

KHOURIYE BARBARA ANN GASPAR SAHADY, born Nov. 14, 1956, in Cincinnati, OH. Graduated from North College Hill High School, OH in 1972 and completed an associate degree in science, majoring in dental hygiene, in June 1977

From 1980-86 she lived and worked in Zurich, Switzerland, as a dental hygienist, then back-packed around the world; in September 1987 she studied at the Univ of Cincinnati; in September 1988 she continued her studies at St Vladimir's Orthodox Theological Seminary in Crestwood, NY, where she met her husband, Fr. Mark Sahady.

MARK WILLIAM SAHADY, Captain, born Nov. 25, 1959, and is a native of Jefferson and Republic, PA. Graduated from Brownsville Area High School, Brownsville, PA, 1977. Completed a bachelor of music degree in music education from Westminster Choir College in Princeton, NJ.

Taught seventh grade in Elizabeth, NJ, while leading conferences and workshops in church music and doing missionary work in the USA, Dominican Republic and Haiti.

Moved to Ambridge, PA where he was the minister of music and the youth coordinator at Holy Ghost Russian Orthodox Church, directed the Community Chorus and a substitute teacher in the Public School System

In September 1986 Fr. Mark went to St. Vladimir's Orthodox Theological Seminary in Crestwood, NY (Yonkers), where he graduated in May of 1989 with a M.Div. and a MA in liturgical music. Commissioned in the USAFR on April 5, 1988, as a 2nd lieutenant, a 1st lieutenant in March 1990 and a captain in March 1994. Trained at Maxwell AFB in Montgomery, AL, Lackland AFB, San Antonio, TX, Vandenburg AFB, Lompoc, CA; McGuire AFB, NJ. Active duty July 25, 1994, to Offutt AFB, NE.

He has been very active in ecumenical and interfaith work. He met his wife Barbara while both were studying at St. Vladimir's Seminary in September 1988.

PHILIP G. SALOIS, 1st Lieutenant, born Nov. 22, 1948, Woonsocket, RI. Attended St. John's Seminary College in Camarillo, CA, received BA degree from Providence College, RI; M.Div. degree from Weston School of Theology, Cambridge, MA; professed religious of the missionaries of Our Lady of La Salette and ordained a priest June 9, 1984.

Associate pastor of Blessed Kateri Tekakwitha National Indian Parish, Lakeside, CA, 1984-86; transferred to Attleboro, MA in 1986 to become the administrator of La Salette Shrine until 1989 Worked at Boston VA Medical Center as a staff chaplain. In 1990 worked as a readjustment counselor on the Providence VAMC Post-Traumatic Stress Disorder Clinical Team (PCT)

March 1969, drafted into the US Army; received basic infantry training and AIT at Fort Ord, CA, September 1969, served as infantryman with Co. A, 3rd Bn., 7th Inf. of the 199th Light Inf. Bde.; stationed in Bien Hoa, Xuan Loc, Ham Tan and Tanh Linh in War Zone D in the 3rd Field Force

Returned to Vietnam June in 1990 as part of a psychological study to assess the therapeutic value of revisiting one's battlefield. Father Salois was the first Combat Veteran turned priest to celebrate Mass in the Cathedral of Saigon (Ho Chi Minh City).

Among his military decorations are the Silver Star, Combat Infantry Badge, Air Medal, Good Conduct Medal, Army Commendation Medal w/2 OLCs, Army Achievement Medal w/2 OLCs, Vietnam Service Medal, Vietnam Campaign Medal, Army Service Ribbon and National Defense Service Medal.

He is the founder and president of the National Conference of Vietnam Veteran Ministers, the first and current national chaplain for Vietnam Veterans of America, the department chaplain (holding that position for three years) for the American Legion, Massachusetts Dept., the state chaplain for Massachusetts State Council, Vietnam Veterans of America (life member), American Legion, VFW, AMVETS Catholic War Veterans of the US (founded the only CWV Post in Attleboro, MA, the John F. Kennedy Post #109), VietNOW, MCA, National Assoc. of VA Chaplains, National Assoc. of Catholic VA Chaplains, life member of the Knights of Columbus, 3rd and 4th Degree.

Received a commission in the USAR as a 1st lieutenant in March 1990 and currently serves as hospital chaplain for the 455th Field Hosp. Unit in Providence, RI.

Among his civilian awards are the Celtic Cross Award, Catholic War Veterans highest national award for outstanding work among Veterans deserving of national recognition. He is also the fourth recipient to receive Vietnam Veterans of America's highest national award, the Commendation Medal, for similar recognition.

WILLIAM H. SANFORD, Lieutenant, born April 11, 1932, Port Republic, NJ. Graduate of Atlantic City, NJ High School; Mississippi College with a BS in chemistry, 1956; M.Div at Asbury Theology Seminary in 1967; and all but dissertation, completed D.Min. San Francisco Theological Seminary.

Served CAP as a visiting clergy to the Gulfport, MS, Composite Sqdn. and received his chaplain's commission Jan. 1, 1982. Served as Mississippi Gp. 2 chaplain for two years, a short time as Natchez, MS Composite Sqdn. chaplain; one year as deputy wing chaplain in Mississippi, 6 3/4 years as Mississippi Wing Chaplain and one year as vice commander, before becoming director of personnel CAP for the Southeast Region Recommissioned a chaplain in 1994 and is serving the Baton Rouge (LA) Cadet Sqdn.

Graduate of CAP's Sqdn. Leadership School, Corporate Learning Course, SE Region Chaplain Staff College, SE Region Staff College, SW Region Chaplain Staff College and National Staff College (staff chaplain 1994-95). Also a graduate of USAF Squadron Officer School and Air Command and Staff College

Served as CAP Deputy National Director of Chaplain Recruitment and Retention. Additionally, he teaches CAP radio communications and has served as chaplain at many group, wing and region cadet encampments He was the senior International Air Cadet Exchange escort in Israel in 1990 and project officer of the Mississippi Wing's hosting of the National Cadet League of Canada's IACE members in 1991 and an escort at the USAF Christian Leadership Conference at Lake Junaluska.

An advanced ground and instrument instructor for pilots, an FAA aviation counselor, a private pilot. a CAP pilot, Search and Rescue mission observer, a counter-narcotics mission observer, he holds an extra class amateur radio license and is a volunteer examiner for the FCC in amateur radio.

Received six Wing, two Southeast Region, and one National Commanders Commendation Awards, five Meritorious Service Awards (including two by National Commander) and an Exceptional Service Award

Retired from the Mississippi Conference of the United Methodist Church in 1990 after 31 years of service Served the USAF at Sampson AFB, completed aviation cadet preflight training at Lackland, 1953, basic pilot training, Columbus AFB (MS) Class 54-I and attended Advanced Pilot Training Vance AFB. Other assignments included: Tierra Amarilla AFB, and welfare specialist at HQ Sqdn. 34 ADD, Kirtland AFB. Received his honorable discharge Dec 10, 1954

Past president of the Kemper County, Jackson County and Greater Gulf Coast Interdenominational Ministerial Associations as well as chairing many United Methodist District Committees, and several years as director of United Methodist youth ministries in various counties He was service unit director for the Salvation Army for Mississippi and Louisiana 1986-89.

He has two sons and one daughter

DALE M. SAWYER, Lieutenant Colonel, born March 20, 1930, in Lancaster, CA. Attended Molalla, OR High School, Northwest Christian College (BTH), Drake Univ. (M Div.)

Joined the USAF November 1964 Stationed at Duluth AB, MN, Yokota AB, Japan, Richards-Gebaur AFB, MO; Sondrestrom AB, Greenland; McClellan AFB, CA, Kingsley Field, OR, Hahn AB, Germany and Indian Springs AFB, NV. Counseled first POW released from North Vietnam; spoke at the Danish/American Festival in Denmark in 1974; conducted services on *President Cleveland* on the Pacific Discharged Nov. 1, 1984, as lieutenant colonel.

Married Joyce Mae Nelson Aug. 22, 1953, Bellingham, WA and has five children and five grandchildren. Adopted Japanese son, Richard Toshio, in 1969 who died of cancer in 1976 at Mather AFB Hosp They adopted a Korean son, David Dae Kyo, in 1978 while Sawyer was stationed at Kingsley Field in Klamath Falls, OR, he is currently a student at TCU in Fort Worth. David was married to Seongae Gregory in March 1994.

Their son Daniel is a major in the USAF stationed at Andrews AFB. Daughter Rhonda lives with her family in Pittsburgh, PA where her husband Mark is in Christian radio. Diane lives with her husband in Grass Valley, CA. Sawyer is pastor at Aloha Christian Church, chaplain, NW Hosp.

PAUL G. SCHADE, Colonel, born Sept 26, 1913, in Cincinnati, OH Received BA, 1935 Univ. of Rochester, NY, Phi Beta Kappa; BD, 1938, Colgate-Rochester Divinity School, Rochester, NY; MA, 1949, Yale Univ, New Haven, CT (American Church History), M.Div., 1972, Colgate-Rochester Divinity School, D.Min., 1975, Andover Newton Theological School, Newton Centre, MA.

Joined the USAF in 1943. Military locations and stations: 2nd AF, Oregon, 36th Ftr. Wing, Nebraska; 2nd AF, Nebraska, Texas and Kansas, 330th BG, Kansas and Guam, 40th BG., Saipan and California, New York ANG; 106th BG. and 22nd AB Gp., California; 35th Ftr. Interceptor Gp., Japan, Air Trng Cmd. and Crew Trng., Nevada; Ballistic Missile Div., California, USAF, Europe and Germany; Log. Cmd., Ohio, SAC and TAC, Idaho; 2nd AF, Central USA; 5th AF, Japan, Korea and Okinawa, HQ USAF, Washington, DC.

Awarded two Legion of Merit Awards, one w/ OLC, Commendation Ribbon, and 12 lesser awards. Last assignment with the Chief of AF Chaplains as chief of the Professional Div Discharged Oct 1, 1973.

Married Dorothy Flannery and they have three children and six grandchildren.

Pastorate positions in Meriden, Monroe and Norwalk, CT, chaplain, Undercliff Tuberculosis Sanitarium, Meriden, CT; pastoral counselor, Middletown, MA. Retired 1985.

SIGMUND C. SCHADE was born Jan. 23, 1923 in Gera, Germany He received an AA from Yuba College, Marysville, CA in 1943, a BA from Westmont College, Santa Barbara, CA in 1948, BD from San Francisco Theological Seminary, San Anselmo, CA in 1958 and a Ph.D. in Christian Ethics at the California Graduate School of Theology, Glendale, CA in 1976.

He joined the U.S. Navy on Feb. 1, 1943 and served until Feb. 1, 1946 and he also served from June 15, 1964-Oct 1, 1984. His duties and stations included. enlisted service from 1943-1946 as a Signalman 1/c He was commissioned as a Naval Reserve Chaplain in 1962 and as a Chaplain was stationed at Treasure Island; Newport, RI; with the 2nd Bn. 8th MAR; Military Sea Transportation Service; U.S. Naval Station, Long Beach, CA; USS *Annapolis*; AGMRI; Phibgrp 11, MAG 24 Chaplain, Kaneohe, Hawaii; Schools Command, NTC, San Diego; RTC, San Diego; USS Iwo Jima (LPH2), ADDU Amphib. Grp.; Iceland Defense Force, and COMSERVGRU ONE.

He married Martha Currier on July 6, 1946, they have three daughters and four grandchildren

Awards: Asiatic-Pacific with four stars, Philippine Liberation with one star, World War II Victory Medal, American Area Medal, Good Conduct Medal, Vietnam Medal with five stars, Vietnam Campaign Medal, American Defense Medal, Sea Service Medal, Unit Commendation Medal and Combine Forces Commendation Medal

He retired from the military on Oct. 1, 1984. Since then he has served as Associate Pastor at the First United Methodist Church, Yuba, CA from October 1984- -June 1986 and he was Senior Pastor, Salem United Methodist Church, Lodi, CA from June 1986-June 1990. He retired from the pastorate in 1990

ROMAN JOSEPH SCHAEFER, Colonel, born Feb. 14, 1916, Nicollet, MN. Graduated Trinity High School, New Ulm, in 1932, Nazarath Hall 1932-36; St. Paul Seminary 1936-42, ordained at St. Paul Cathedral June 6, 1942. Served at St Agnes Parish in St Paul and St. Aloysius in Olivia until he entered the USAAF March 21, 1944 at Fort Snelling, St. Paul and attended Harvard Chaplain School, Boston, MA, 1944

Served in 2nd AF in Boise, ID, Lincoln, NE; Great Bend, KS; Albuquerque and Roswell, NM Went overseas to Germany 1946-50. Returned to San Bernadino, CA and March AB at Riverside, CA. During the Korean War at Yokuta, Japan and later at Sidi Slimane in French Morocco, Africa, 1952-53.

Then with SAC at Rapid City, Ellsworth AB 1953-54. From there to NE Air Command at radar sites Frobisher Bay, Resolution Island, Hopedale Cartright and St Anthony, Newfoundland, at Pepperall AFB, HQ NEAC, 1955-56. Returned to Walker AFB, Roswell, NM 1956-59 From there went to England at Mildenhall AFB 1959-62 Returned to Dover AFB, DE, 1962-63 and Sheppard AFB, Wichita Falls, Texas Air Trng. Cmd

Then to Anderson AFB in Guam during Vietnam War 1963-64. Returned to the US flying around the world via C-141 transport through Philippines, India, Arabia, Spain, Rome, Italy and was stationed at Vandenberg AF Missile Base near Santa Barbara, CA until retirement in 1969 as a colonel USAF.

Returned to New Ulm Diocese, assigned to St. Andrew's Church at Fairfax until Jan. 28, 1981, then to St. Augustine Church, St Paul He is a member of the American Legion Post, Fairfax and Post 8459 VFW at Fairfax since retirement from the AF Has been Minn. Dept. Chaplain VFW since 1974 and was elected the national chaplain of the VFW at the national meeting last August in Chicago, IL. Elected charter president of the Fairfax Lions Club in 1975, chaplain of the Knights of Columbus, 1969-81. He is a member of the Catholic Aid Society and Catholic Order of Foresters at Nicollet, MN

As national chaplain, he attended council meetings at HQ VFW in Kansas City, MO and the Annual Washington Conference in 1981 Met with President and Mrs. Ronald Reagen, Senator Rudy Boschwitz, Senator Oberstar, Rep. Vin Weber and attended the Senator Caucus for Veterans Affairs in Congress The term of office included conduct of the 82nd National Meeting of the Foreign Wars in Philadelphia August 14-20.

Conducted several overseas travel tours to Europe visiting in Germany, Ireland, France, Spain, Egypt, Syria, Jordan and Israel. Rewarding pilgrimages of faith to Lourdes and Fatima, to the Vatican with audiences of the Pope at St Peters in Rome.

GREG T. SCHLUTER, Major, born Dec. 19, 1960, New Orleans, LA Joined the chaplaincy after 10 years of international ministry. He has been a member of the MCA for two years; an alumnus of Oral Roberts Univ., Tulsa, OK; International Seminary, Plymouth, FL, where he earned the Th.D. degree summa cum laude and is endorsed by Chaplaincy Full Gospel Churches.

Duty assignments include: wing chaplain, Tinker AFB, OK, squadron chaplain, Corpus Christi Composite Sqdn, NAS Corpus Christi, TX; and visiting clergy. Qualified aerial observer, radio operator and mission chaplain and has served in these capacities on Search and Rescue (SAR) missions and exercises. Graduated from the Chaplain Region Staff College

Civilian ministry experience includes 10 years of missionary work in Central America, the Caribbean and Europe. Served as the civilian pastor of a US Army congregation near Bremen, Germany He is now pastor of Christ the Redeemer Church, Corpus Christi, TX He resides with his wife Susan and daughter Michelle

JOHN PETER SCHMELING, born in Beach, ND, Oct 31, 1938. Graduated from Dickinson State College in 1961; Wartburg Theological Seminary and ordained in the Lutheran Church in 1968; earned Ph.D from Indiana State Univ. in 1977.

Commissioned in the USAR, Oct. 13, 1965; served with the 604th MP, the 337th Gen. Hosp and served as Command Staff chaplain for the 70th Div. (TRAINING) and the 416th Engr. Cmd.

During Desert Storm he was the senior engineer

chaplain in the theater After the war he became the Chaplain Theater Redeployment-Reunion Program Chief. The RRP Teams under his direction provided classes to 70% of the soldiers leaving the gulf. He was awarded the Bronze Star for action in combat

Served as professor of religion and history, director of the Vincennes Univ. Prison Program, chair of the Social Science Div and vice president and dean of the faculty until retiring in 1989. He also has 12 years parish experience and does international consulting.

THOMAS A. SCHULTZ was born July 14, 1935 in Pleasant Hill, OH. He received a BS in Education from Ashland University in Ashland, OH in 1958, a M. Ed. from Wittenberg College in Springfield, OH in 1963, a M Div. from Hamma School of Theology, Springfield, OH in 1967, a M Div. from Ashland Theological Seminary, Ashland, OH in 1973, a M. A. from Talbot Theological Seminary in LaMirada, CA in 1977, a Ph.D. from California Graduate School of Theology in Glendale, CA in 1978 and a D. Min. from Fuller Theological Seminary in Pasadena, CA in 1981.

He served in the Army from August 1954 - July 1956 with the 4th Infantry Division and was on inactive status from July 1956 - July 1962. He was a SP4 (E-4). He was commissioned as a Navy Chaplain on April 1, 1969. He had the following duty stations: NAS Whidbey Island, Oak Harbor, WA, MAG 15 1st MAW, Iwakuni, Japan, Vietnam, NAVSTA Long Beach, CA; USS Camden (AOE-2), Bremerton, WA; DUINS, USC, Los Angeles, CA, Station Chaplain, MCAS (H) Tustin, CA, NMCB-40, Port Hueneme, CA, Advanced Course, Navy Chaplain School, Newport, RI, US Naval Home, Gulfport, MS; and DIR CREDO, NTS, Great Lakes, IL. He retired from the Navy in September 1988 as a Commander.

Awards: Navy Commendation Medal with two stars, Meritorious Unit Commendation, Navy "E" Ribbon, Army Good Conduct Medal, Navy Expeditionary Medal, Army of Occupation Medal, National Defense Service Medal with one Bronze Star, Vietnam Service Medal with USMC Device, 17 Campaign stars, Sea Service Ribbon, Republic of Vietnam Campaign Medal with device, Republic of Vietnam Civil Actions Unit Citation, Navy Expert Pistol Medal, and Navy Expert Rifle Medal.

His post active duty activities include volunteer police chaplain and a public schools senior high school counselor.

His memorable experiences include: serving in Vietnam, serving with the Seabees going from island to island. It was an outstanding privilege to serve God and our country with the greatest people in the world.

He married Patricia Jane Preston on June 18, 1954. They have three children: Stephen Thomas, Mark Allen and Timothy Joe.

DAVID P. SCHUSTER, Captain, born in Chicago, IL, March 25, 1934. Graduated from Elmhurst College, 1957; Dubuque Theological Seminary, 1961; ordained a minister in the Presbyterian Church, USA and commissioned a lieutenant (jg), Chaplain Corps, USNR, May 1, 1961

Began active duty Sept. 3, 1961 Following Chaplain School, Newport, RI, he reported to the National Naval Medical Center, Bethesda, MD. Subsequent assignments included: Military Sea Transportation Service, Pacific, 1962-64, USMC Mountain Warfare Training Center, Bridgeport, CA, 1964-66, during which he was augmented into the regular Navy; Commander Middle East Force, Bahrain, 1966-68; NTC Great Lakes, 1968-70; USS Guadalcanal (LPH-7), 1970-72, NAS Brunswick, ME, 1972-75, including advanced training at the Marriage Council of Philadelphia, February 1974, 3rd Marine Div., FMFPAC, Okinawa, Japan, 1976; NAS South Weymouth, MA, 1977-80, Chaplain School Advanced Course, Newport, RI, August, 1980-June 1981; NAS Barbers Point, HI, 1981-85; NAVSTA Treasure Island/NAVBASE, San Francisco, CA, 1985-88; and Naval Amphibious Base, Coronado, CA, 1988-91.

October 1991 he retired as captain, CHC, USN and resides in Colorado Springs, CO, where he is a member of Pueblo Presbytery. Awarded the Meritorious Service Medal, National Defense Service Medal, Sea Service Deployment Ribbon with Bronze Star and the Navy Expert Pistol Shot Medal.

He and Barbara Ann Salvatori were married Aug. 10, 1957, and have two children and four grandchildren.

ROBERT M. SCHWYHART, Captain, born in Tama County, IA, Jan. 3, 1908. Graduated from Northern Iowa Univ. (BA), Southern Baptist Theological Seminary (Th.M), received doctorate (DD) from American Baptist Seminary of West; ordained by Southern Iowa Baptist Association in 1934; commissioned a lieutenant (jg) in Chaplain Corps, USN Aug 16, 1937. Served thereafter on active duty for 31 years, retiring July 1, 1968, as captain.

Active duty assignments: three ships, USS Wyoming, USS Nevada, USS Vincennes. overseas at naval station, Guantanamo Bay, Cuba; Pacific Fleet as assistant fleet chaplain and as fleet chaplain. NAS. Alameda, CA and Pensacola, FL; Staff, Naval Air Trng Cmd.; NTC, Great Lakes, IL; 1st Marine Div. in Korea, 12th Naval District; OIC Navy Chaplain School; Office of Chief of Chaplains.

Received 12 awards and decorations including Bronze Star w/Combat "V," and Navy Commendation Medal

First chaplain to receive four Chaplains Awards; first chaplain to receive Chaplain of Year Award, American Baptist Convention.

Memorable experiences include combat in Pacific, Battle of Midway; Battle of Savo Island during which his ship USS Vincennes was sunk, with US Marines in Korea as division chaplain, 1st Marine Div

Married Elizabeth Neyman May 21, 1935 They have two daughters and two grandchildren.

Held positions with staff American Baptist Churches 1968-83 Pastor at Broadway Baptist Church, Denver, CO, 1984-85

JAMES RALPH SCOBEY, Lieutenant Colonel, born April 1, 1922, in Newbern, TN Received BA and M.Div. Pastorates prior to chaplaincy: First Cumberland Presbyterian Church, Lexington, TN; Morning Sun Cumberland Presbyterian Church, Cordova, TN. Post Retirement: pastor, Calvary Cumberland Presbyterian Church, Jackson, TN; chaplain, Farmington State Hosp., Farmington, MO (13 years). Member of Missouri Presbytery, Cumberland Presbyterian Church; MCA (life member), Masonic Lodge; Board of Directors, Mineral Area Hospice, Park Hills, MO; past member, Presbyterian Council for Chaplains and Military Personnel

Entered USAF, Oct. 23, 1951. Attended Chaplains School, Fort Slocum, NY, 1951; Tyndall AFB, FL, 1951-53, 1807th AACS Wing, Germany, 1953-56, McDill AFB, FL, 1956-60; Shemya AS, AK, 1960-61; Grand Forks AFB, ND, 1961-64; Clark AFB, Philippines, 1964-66; Richards-Gebaur AFB, MO, 1966-70 (retirement). Discharged March 31, 1970.

Served with US Army, 100th Inf. Div., HQ Co., 399th Regt., Dec. 1, 1942-Feb 2, 1946; ETO Oct. 6, 1944-Jan. 28, 1946; USAR, Feb. 2, 1946-Feb. 1, 1949.

Awarded the Bronze Star Medal, Good Conduct Medal, Meritorious Unit Emblem, American Campaign Medal, European Campaign Medal w/2 stars, WWII Victory Medal, Army of Occupation Medal w/Germany Clasp, Expert Infantryman Badge, Combat Infantry Badge and Commendation Medal w/OLC.

Married Darlis Rebecca Edwards and has two children and four grandchildren Retired April 1, 1970.

MARLIN D. SEIDERS, Captain 06, born Jan. 9, 1927, in Middletown, PA. Received BA; M.Div; M.Th; MA; DD Commissioned a lieutenant (jg) in the USN Chaplain Corps. April 14, 1951, and assigned to the NTC, Bainbridge, MD. Escort Destroyer Sqdn SIX; NTC, San Diego, Harvard Univ. in 1957; 3rd Marine Div.

Stationed in USS Prairie (AD-15), Naval Hosp, St. Albans; Naval Station, Pearl Harbor; NAS, Lemoore, assistant division chaplain, 3rd Marine Div ; NTC, San Diego; Naval Base, Guantanamo Bay; Naval War College; force chaplain, Naval Air Force, Pacific; senior chaplain, Fleet Support Office, Athens, Greece; fleet chaplain, Commander in Chief, US Naval Forces Europe; and Fleet Chaplain, US Atlantic Fleet; special assistant to USN Surgeon General.

All of his experiences were memorable including being national president of MCA 1984-86.

Married to Nancy Jean Deimler, Ph.D They have one son and one grandchild

Held position of associate pastor, Covenent UMC, Lebanon, PA. Retired July 1, 1991

EDWARD W. SENSENBRENNER, Colonel, born Jan 6, 1932, in Los Angeles, CA, the son of Maynard E. and Mildred H. Sensenbrenner. Grew up in Columbus, OH and graduated from Columbus West High School, where he was elected president of his senior class. He earned two degrees from the Ohio State Univ.; a BS, summa cum laude in 1954 and a MBA in 1955.

On June 10, 1955, he was commissioned a 2nd lieutenant in the US Army Transportation Corps, having completed the ROTC program at Ohio State. In August 1955, he entered active duty as 2nd lieutenant; completed the US Army Transportation Officer Basic Course at Fort Eustis, VA and was assigned to the Port of Whittier, AK At the Port of Whittier, he served as company executive officer, Port S-2, port statistician and assistant port comptroller.

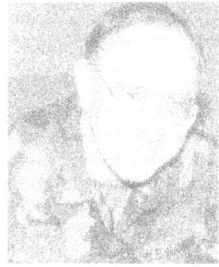 

After completing active duty in August 1957, he went to work in industrial relations for Pittsburgh Plate Glass Co., until he was called to seminary in 1959 Graduated from Pittsburgh (Presbyterian) Theological Seminary with a MD magna cum laude in 1962 and was ordained in the Presbyterian Church, USA, in June 1962

Still active in Transportation Corps, he had been promoted to captain while in Seminary. After ordination he transferred to the Chaplain Corps and became an Army chaplain. Major assignments in the USAR were as senior hosp chaplain for the 2291st US Army Hosp. (1,000 bed) and as staff chaplain for the HQ of the 83rd USAR Cmd. Chaplain Sensenbrenner served two assignments, totaling 15 years, as the staff chaplain for the HQ, 83d ARCOM, making him perhaps the longest-serving ARCOM chaplain in the USAR.

A graduate of the Transportation School Officer Basic Course, the Chaplain Officer Basic and Career Courses and the Command and General Staff College.

Received the Legion of Merit, Meritorious Service Medal w/OLC, Army Reserve Components Achievement Medal w/2 OLCs, the Armed Forces Reserve Medal, Overseas Service Ribbon and the Army Service Ribbon. Retired from the US Army in 1989 with 34 years of service to his country.

Served three pastorates in the Presbyterian Church in Ohio. Currently he is pastor of the First Presbyterian Church of Troy, OH, where he has served for 23 years. He is married to Lois (Farrand) and they have five children and two grandchildren.

MORTON SHALOWITZ, Colonel, born on Dec. 27, 1923, in Chicago, IL. Graduated Roosevelt High School, Herzl Junior College, Central YMCA College with a BA degree (1945), all in Chicago, IL. Attended one year post-graduate work at the Univ. of Chicago (1946) Ordained Rabbi at the Hebrew Theological College with a BHL (1949) in Chicago.

Served as Rabbi at Minot Hebrew Congregation, Minot, ND (1950-52); (Associate Rabbi) Kehilath Israel Synagogue, Kansas City, MO (1954-57), Rabbi at Heska Amuna Congregation, Knoxville, TN (1957-62), Congregation Yehudah Moshe, north Miami, FL (1962-63); Temple Beth Israel, Fond du Lac, WI (1963-91), retired 1992

Entered the US Army Chaplaincy (ORC) at Minot, ND as a 1st lieutenant Serving on active duty in the Korean War (1952-54) with service in Seoul, Korea Graduated the US Army Chaplain Basic and Officers Career Courses; US Army Command and General Staff College, Air War College, National Defense Univ.

Industrial College of the Armed Forces. Retired as colonel in 1983 after 30 years service in the USAR

Life member of MCA, American Legion, VFW, Jewish Veterans of America, ROA, National Association of Uniformed Services.

Awarded the Korean Service Medal, UN Service Medal, National Defense Service Medal, ROK Presidential Unit Citation, Army Reserve Medal w/cluster, and Meritorious Service Medal. Built first Synagogue in Korean history dedicated by Gen Maxwell D. Taylor, May 2, 1954.

JAMES E. SHAW, Colonel, born in Boone, IA, Sept. 28, 1928, graduated from Iowa State Univ. (1950), was drafted, went through OCS, and served as 2nd lieutenant during Korean conflict Attended Concordia Theological Seminary, Springfield, IL, ordained June 14, 1959, and entered the Army chaplaincy.

Military assignments included. Office, Chief of Army Chaplains (1962-64); Americal Division, staff chaplain, Vietnam (1969-70); post chaplain, Fort Ord, CA (1973-77); VII Corps Chaplain, Stuttgart, Germany (1979-81), 6th US Army Chaplain, San Francisco, CA (1981-83)

Retired as colonel, June 30, 1983, to become endorsing agent, Lutheran Church, Missouri Synod Awards include Doctor of Divinity, Martin of Tours (2), Legion of Merit (2), Bronze Star, Meritorious Service Medal (2) and Air Medal (2).

Chaplain and Mrs. (Joanne) Shaw have four children and six grandchildren. President of National MCA (1986-88). Retired in Lago Vista, TX (1994)

KATHERINE A. SHINDEL, Lieutenant Colonel, born in Alton, MI and is the senior chaplain, 355th Wing, Davis-Monthan AFB, Tucson, AZ She leads a staff of five chaplains, five enlisted chaplain service support personnel, and a secretary in providing for the free exercise of religion of Wing and HQ 12th AF personnel and their families

Commissioned a chaplain in March 1980, served as a Protestant chaplain, a senior Protestant chaplain, a senior chaplain and a course director at the USAF Chaplain School.

Education: 1967, BA, psychology, Albion College, MI, 1973, M Div., Union Theological Seminary, NY; 1984, Squadron Officer School, Maxwell AFB, AL (Correspondence); 1986 Air Command and Staff College, Maxwell AFB, AL (Seminar); 1994 Air War College, Maxwell AFB, AL (Seminar).

Assignments as Protestant chaplain: 1980-82, Bolling AFB, Washington, DC; 1982-85, Yokota AB, Japan; 1985-88, Luke AFB, AZ; 1988-89 Senior chaplain at Comiso AS, Italy; 1989-92, course director, USAF Chaplain School, Maxwell AFB, AL; 1992-94, senior Protestant chaplain, Davis-Monthan AFB, AZ; 1994-present, senior chaplain, Davis-Monthan AFB, AZ.

Received the Meritorious Service Medal w/2 OLCs, AF Commendation Medal w/OLC, Outstanding Unit Award, Overseas Long and Short Tour Ribbons

She was first woman senior chaplain to serve at an overseas base (Comiso AS, Italy 1988-89) and first

woman to serve on the faculty of the USAF Chaplain School (1989-92)

JOSEPH C. SIDES, Colonel, born Dec 8, 1908, Corydon, KY Attended high school, Columbia, MO, Univ. of Missouri, BS in public administration; Chicago Theological Seminary, BD, completed June 1933 At age 18 received Local Preachers License, dated Dec. 2, 1926, from the Annual Conference of the Methodist Episcopal Church, South. Pastor, 1927-30, of Ashland Circuit; pastor, Washburn Congregational Church of Half Day, IL; 1937-38, pastor, Homewood Community Church, Homewood, IL.

Military service: ROTC first two years of college. Army Reserve Commission Aug. 20, 1930. Active duty with Civilian Conservation Corps 1933-37; regular commission October 1938. From Ocober 1938-August 1948: Fort Brown, TX; Fort Riley, KS; Borinquen Field, Puerto Rico; Langley Field, VA; HQ 2nd AF, Colorado Springs, CO, Guam, Staff Chaplain of the 20th AF, Rome-Georgia Biggs AFB, El Paso, TX, Greenville, SC, School, Chicago, IL.

From September 1948-November 1966: Biloxi AFB, Biloxi, MS; School, Maxwell AFB, AL, Fontainbleau, France, Chateauroux, France; Mitchell AFB, NY, Iceland, McChord AFB, WA; MacDill AFB, Tampa, FL; Elgin AFB, FL. He was promoted to colonel while in Iceland Retired November 1968

Author of book *"Fort Brown Historical,"* published in 1942 At Fort Brown he was in the cavalry, assigned his own horse and accompanied the men on maneuvers via horseback. Creditable statement of service for pay purposes 37 years, 28 days. Total active service 34 years, four months, 10 days.

State chaplain for the Florida AF Assoc. for many years Received the "Jimmy Doolittle Fellow" Award in 1989. Now at age 85 is "Honorary" Chaplain After 1968 retirement, he was pastor of Thonotosassa United Methodist Church, Thonotosassa, FL, for nine years.

Married to Dorothea Campbell, 1937-1970 (deceased) to Mildred Logan, 1972 to present. They have four children and two grandchildren

MARTINUS E. SILSETH, Colonel, born Aug. 29, 1925, in Litchfield, MN. Received BA from Univ. of Minnesota and M.Th., Luther Seminary. Drafted into the Army Dec. 1, 1943, took basic at Fort Benning and specialized training at Camp Polk.

August 1944, went to England with 97th Sig. Bn., September 1946 assigned to 97th Sig Bn, ETO; took part in Occupation of Germany (especially at Bamberg) Received three Battle Stars for Ardennes, Rhineland and Central Europe.

Completed Univ. of Minnesota in 1948 and commissioned in ROTC, completed Luther Seminary, St. Paul, in 1952 and commissioned in Army Chaplaincy. Served in Korea from 1952-54 and received three Battle Stars. Served in Japan until 1955 in various units, and in the Army Reserves from 1955-78 generally in 452nd Gen. Hosp., Milwaukee. Service 1952 to date has been in Army Chaplaincy, 1943 to date in Army and received appropriate ribbons and Legion of Merit.

Memorable experiences: Battle of the Bulge, crossing Rhine; helping city of Bamberg in Germany; Korean orphanage projects and the blanket projects in US for Korean orphans, operation Christmas Star Left the service August 1985 as colonel

Married Vera and they have three children and seven grandchildren. Held position as director church relations - Lutheran Social Services. Retired February 1989. Chaplain for TROA, MOWW, Constabulary (National) American Legion and VFW

SAMUEL M. SILVER, born June 7, 1912, in Wilmington, DE. Attended Univ of Delaware and Hebrew Union College. Joined the Army; stationed at Camp Breckinridge, Fort Rucker and Hawaii; served with 98th Inf Div. in the Philippines.

Served with the 98th Inf. Div. in Kentucky, Alabama, Tennessee maneuvers, and Hawaii. Transferred out of of the division and served with the HQ Base on Leyte in the Philippines. Served for four years; along with his men, he marched and in Hawaii did jungle training.

At one point he heard that men over 38 could be released if they could get defense work. He got in touch with defense plants in the US and was successful in getting some superannuated GIs out of uniform and back into civilian life Discharged in 1946 as captain.

Served as rabbi in Cleveland, OH and in Stamford, CT. He is now the rabbi of Temple Sinai, Delray Beach In uniform from 1942-46, he is listed in *Who's Who in the US*.

He was president of the Jewish Chaplains Association of the US and was national chaplain of the JWV of the US. Married and has five children and 11 grandchildren.

MATTHEW H. SIMON, Captain, born Aug. 6, 1932. Received masters in political science and Hebrew Literature; Doctorate in Humane Letters. Joined the USN in 1958 and stationed in Japan, California and Washington, DC.

Served with COMNAVFORJAPAN, 23rd Marines, Santa Monica, CA, 3rd ANGLICO, Long Beach and Naval Hosp., Bethesda, MD Discharged in 1986 as captain.

Married Sara Rubinow Simon and they have three children and three grandchildren

He has held positions as rabbi

JOHN WHITON SIMONS, Colonel, born June 2, 1931, in Melrose, MA. Received BA in history at Drury College, Springfield, MO; M.Div., Bexley Hall Episcopal Seminary, Gambier, OH

Joined the Army/National Guard, January 1952. Stationed in Fort Eustis, Germany; Ohio and Missouri. Served as MP, 107th ACR; HQ STARC, Ohio. Memorable experience was as senior staff chaplain at Kent State 1970. Discharged June 2, 1991, as colonel

Civilian employment as rector, 1959-70, Church of St Philip the Apostle, Cleveland, OH; rector, 1970-86, Grace Episcopal Church, Willoughby, OH; associate rector, 1986-91, Trinity Episcopal Church, Columbus, OH; interim vicar, 1991-92, Pershore Abbey, Pershore, Worcester, England; interim rector, 1994-St. John's Episcopal Church, Henderson, NC He retired June 2, 1991.

Married to Nancy Pyle Simons and they have four children and four grandchildren.

JOHN W. SIMPSON, Colonel, born in Forbes, WA, Nov. 22, 1930 Graduated from Northwest College in 1953, Seattle Pacific Univ in 1956 and Golden Gate Baptist Theological Seminary in 1961. While in college and seminary, he served in the NG and USAR. Ordained in the Assemblies of God, he entered active duty in June 1962 from a church in San Francisco.

Served garrisons at Fort Ord, Lewis and in Panama, the 9th Cav on the North Korean border, 2nd Armd. Div duty at Fort Hood and Army advisors in 102 locations in southern most Vietnam. Served in administrative positions in Fort Lewis, Germany and Fort Ord and retired as a colonel in 1981.

Awarded the Legion of Merit, Bronze Star, Meritorious Service (2) and Army Commendation (3) medals. Served as a volunteer probation counselor the past nine years. Married to Katherine Gayle and has two children and one grandchild.

BERNARD SYLVESTER SIPPEL, Lieutenant Colonel, born April 13, 1939, in Fon du Lac, WI. He received a M.Div. Joined the Wisconsin NG Jan. 29, 1968, and served all 20 years in the NG of Wisconsin with the 128th Inf , 32nd Bde , 57th FA

Served on riot control at the State Capitol and the Univ. of Madison during the Vietnam period. Also served during two fire department strikes in the city of Milwaukee in the late 70s Discharged April 13, 1988, as lieutenant colonel. Bernard is a Catholic priest and presently in the inactive reserve.

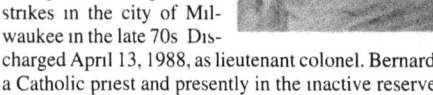

CLARENCE P. SMALES, Lieutenant Colonel, born June 4, 1906, Jackson, OH. Graduated from Otterbein College in 1928 and ordained same year. Smales pastored several churches in Ohio before moving his family to California in 1936. In 1941 he joined the USAAC as chaplain, 1st lieutenant. He was the first Assembly of God minister to enter the Air Force.

While stationed in California, he was a traveling chaplain serving radar sights along the California and Oregon coasts His motto was "Have Bible, Will Preach." Stationed at several Stateside bases and also in Iceland, Newfoundland and Goose Bay, Labrador. In Goose Bay, he often went by dog sled. His last engagement was France Retired to Lakewood, CA, where he served as a chaplain for the VA Hosp and filled in for absent ministers at several churches.

Smales passed away Dec. 22, 1992, and is survived by his wife of 68 years, Helen, four children, 11 grandchildren, 26 great-grandchildren and two great-great-grandchildren.

ELDON ROBERT SMITH JR., Lieutenant Colonel, temporarily residing in Louisville, KY, born in New Albany, IN, adopted Texas as home state after assignments in Amarillo, Fort Worth and San Antonio. Asbury College conferred the BA degree in 1957, followed in 1952 by the BD degree and the M.Div. degree by Emory Univ., Atlanta, GA. Graduate courses at Princeton Univ. and Univ. of Texas.

Military service began in 1945 as a draftee into the US Army, continuing in the USAAC, the USAAF and the USAF until August 1987 with an 11 year break for education along with civilian ministry. Exceptional assignments include: Berlin, Germany, Paris, France; Ontario, Canada, Suffolk, England; Tokyo, Japan.

Memorable experiences include conducting Christmas services on Wake Island and Easter services in New Orleans for the ROTC National Convocation. The most unexpected honor was receipt of the Honor Graduate, Advanced Course, USAF Chaplain School, June 19, 1964, award. The commandant said, "This pen set may some day sit on the Chief of Chaplain's desk." Mandatory retirement came on Aug. 1, 1987, with 31 years of active service, seven years of inactive reserve, and the grade of lieutenant colonel.

Married to Norma Jean Gilland in 1950, the Smiths have one child, Eldon Robert Smith III, a captain, USAF, missile officer. Serving civilian churches from 1987-93 in the South Indiana Conference of The United Methodist Church, a second retirement was precipitated by cardiac deficiencies. Triple by-pass surgery in 1994 has restored vitality and hope for a long life.

JAMES HENDERSON SMITH, Colonel, born June 23, 1918, in Charleston, WV, the son of John and Almeda Smith

Education was accomplished in the public schools of Huntington, WV; BA degree from Alderson-Broaddus College, Philippi, WV; BD degree was granted by the Central Baptist Theological Seminary, Kansas City, KS He served Baptist and Presbyterian Churches in Kansas, Wyoming and Nebraska.

Military service began in 1949 with the Wyoming ARNG and continued with the Nebraska ARNG, from which he entered upon active duty at Fort Leonard Wood, MO, in 1952. Active duty assignments were in Missouri, Korea and Illinois. Upon release from active duty, he was assigned to the Kansas Military District. In

1958 he was assigned to HQ, 89th Div., USAR, in Wichita, KS.

Military education includes Chaplain Basic, Chaplain Advanced Courses, Command and General Staff College, Industrial College of the Armed Forces, and numerous chaplain annual training conferences. Retired as colonel in 1978 with the rank of colonel.

Civilian activities include church teaching and preaching. Memberships are held in MCA, TROA, ROA, MOWW and Lions Club. He is currently a retired Presbyterian clergyman residing in Wichita, KS.

MEREDITH P. SMITH, Colonel, born Dec. 18, 1913, in Wilmerding, PA. Received AB, Asbury College, M Div. and M Th., Boston Univ., MA, Boston, Doctor of Div., Asbury College.

Joined the USAAF in November 1942. Military locations and stations: Fort Douglas, UT; Camp Cook, CA; Mitchell Field, NY; Chatteauroux, France; Ethan Allan, VT; Kirtland, NM; Ankara, Turkey; Ellington, TX; Clark, Philippines; McGuire, NJ; Elmendorf, AK; Andrews AFB, Washington, DC.

Units served with were 5th Armd Div; 3rd Inf. Div.; base chaplain, Kirtland AFB, EASTAF, MAC; command chaplain, Unified Command, AK; SAF Systems Cmd. Memorable experience was landing at Normandy.

Awarded ETO Ribbon with five campaign stars, Army Commendation Medal, Air Force Commendation Medal w/2 OLCs, United Command Commendation Medal (Alaska) and Legion of Merit. Retired as colonel in July 1974.

Married to Leda Yarnell and they have three children and seven grandchildren. After retirement from the Air Force, he pastored churches in New Hampshire, Massachusetts and Utah; Salem United Methodist Church and Gettysburg for 15 years.

RALPH LINDON SMITH JR., Colonel, born on Dec. 24, 1928, in Bellflower, IL. At Bellflower High School, he excelled in athletics, oratory and music and served as president for the Class of 1946. Following a BS Education degree from Illinois State Univ. in 1950, his plans to teach and coach were cut short by the Korean War where he served as a Navy reservist briefly before entering the Army in 1951.

Basic training and Leadership School at Fort Leonard Wood, MO, led to Infantry Office Candidate School at Fort Benning, GA in 1952 with commissioning on August 1 as a 2nd lieutenant, Inf. After Airborne and Jumpmaster Schools, his first duty was with the 503rd Abn. Inf. Regt., 11th Abn. Div., Fort Campbell, KY. The highlight of that duty was service as a platoon leader during Operation Warmwind in Alaska in December 1952.

After a brief stint as a squad tactics instructor, Lt. Smith was ordered to Japan (Eta Jima Specialist School) and then to Korea where he served twice on Outpost Harry (Iron Triangle) with Co C, 23rd Inf. Regt., 2nd Inf Div. After the Armistice in July, 1953, Smith served as Special Services Officer for the 23rd Inf. Regt until an early release from active duty in November 1953.

Following completion of graduate school at the Univ of Arizona in Tucson (M. Education, 1955), he taught health and physical education and coached freshman basketball at Tucson High for six years. At the same time, he was active with the 4150th Tucson USAR School, completing six years of Basic and Advanced Artillery and Ranger School in 1960 with promotion to captain.

Graduation from seminary at Perkins School of Theology, Southern Methodist Univ., (BD, 1964) and ordination as elder in Methodist Church led to a branch transfer to the Chaplain Corps. Duty with Army Reserve units in the Dallas area paralleled local church pastorates from 1964-79. Service as staff chaplain with the 94th Gen. Hosp., Mesquite, TX, led to a year of clinical pastoral education and service as director of Chaplaincy Services at Irving Healthcare System in 1980. His final four years of reserve duty were with the MEDDAC, Fort Leavenworth, KS where he retired in March 1988 with 36 years of service.

Chaplain Smith is active in many national, state and community organizations including MOWW (chaplain general, 1989-94); SAR (Texas Society chaplain, 1988-95); Irving Noon-Day Lions Club; VFW; ROA; fellow, College of Chaplains, clinical member, ACPE; American Legion; and TROA. He was inducted into the Officer Candidate School Hall of Fame at Fort Benning, GA in February 1990. He is a life member of MCA and served as founding president of Metroplex Chapter (Dallas-Fort Worth) in 1975. He served two terms on the Executive Committee and continues to serve the Metroplex Chapter as historian.

Decorations. Bronze Star, Meritorious Service, Army Commendation w/OLC, National Defense Service, Korean Service w/Bronze Star, Armed Forces Reserve w/2 10 year Devices, Army Reserve Components Achievement w/2 OLCs, NCO Professional Development Ribbon, Army Service Ribbon, United Nations, Combat Infantry Badge, Parachutist Badge, Ranger Tab and Korean Presidential Unit Citation Ribbon.

Chaplain Smith's wife is Alice. They have three children and five grandchildren and have resided in Irving, TX since 1974.

RODERIC LEE SMITH, Captain, born Aug. 6, 1900, Lincoln, NE. Pastor 1926-42 of churches in Pittsburgh, PA and Buffalo, NY. Graduate of Monmouth College, Monmouth, IL (AB, 1923); Pittsburgh Theological Seminary, Pittsburgh, PA (Th.B, 1926); ordained a minister in the United Presbyterian Church of North America in May 1926; (DD, 1941) from Monmouth College.

Active duty as Navy chaplain since April 1942 when commissioned in the grade of lieutenant, Chaplain Corps, USNR. Transferred to regular Navy in August 1946. Reported to Commander MSTS on Oct 9, 1959, as staff chaplain. A clergyman of the United Presbyterian Church of the USA, he was academy chaplain, USCG Academy, New London, CT, prior to his present duty.

Naval service (1942-62): sr. chaplain, NAS, Glenview, IL; Pacific combat service as chaplain of the USS Cabot; sr. chaplain, Naval Hosp., Great Lakes, IL; force chaplain on the staff of the Commander, Amphibious Force, Atlantic Fleet; assistant district chaplain for Naval Reserve in the 9th Naval District, Great Lakes, IL; sr. chaplain, USS Midway; chaplain, USMC, Camp Lejeune, NC, chaplain, USCG Academy, New London, CT; senior chaplain, Commander, MSTS, Washington, DC, when retired due to age.

Promoted to captain in the Chaplain Corps, USN, July 1, 1956; retired in 1962 and called as assistant in the National Presbyterian Church, Washington, DC until September 1970. Served as assistant in the Warner Memorial Presbyterian Church, Kensington, MD, 1970-78. Finally, chaplain-in-residence, Vinson Hall, McLean, VA until 1989.

Married to Carol Davidson of Stanwood, IA, and they have two children, Lt Roderic Lee Smith Jr., USNR and Mrs. Marcia Smith Voors; one grandson, three granddaughters. Wife Carol died in 1973. In 1976 he was united in marriage to Lois Faust, Bethesda, MD and acquired three stepchildren: Robert Faust, Lynne Cross and Meredith Bennett, and six grandchildren.

SAMUEL SOBEL, Captain, USN, (RET), born in Greensboro, NC, July 14, 1916. He was educated at Gratz College (Teachers Diploma); Yeshiva College, BA, Columbia Univ., MA; Hebrew Union College-Jewish Institute of Religion, MAHL, DD (honorary); Jackson College, Ed.D; Norfolk State Univ., MSW; and a year's postgraduate study at Union Theological Seminary in New York.

In 1946 he became the first chaplain of the Jewish faith to be appointed to the Regular Navy, and later, the first person of that faith to devote a full 30 year career in the naval chaplaincy.

Among his military awards are Purple Heart and Bronze Star Medal for service in the Korean War, Armed Forces Expeditionary Medal for Lebanon, the Vietnam Service Medal, Legion of Merit for his work as the executive director of the Secretary of Defense Armed Forces Chaplains Board and a Gold Star in lieu of a second Legion of Merit for his accomplishments as the chaplain. USMC.

Served as adjunct professor on the faculties of George Washington Univ., Old Dominion Univ., Tidewater Community College, and was president of the Eastern Virginia Philosophical Society, Norfolk Civitan Club, and the Tidewater Board of Rabbis.

His publications include *A Treasury of Jewish Sea Stories, Intrepid Sailor* (Commodore Uriah Levy, for whom the Norfolk Naval Station's Jewish Chapel is named), selected prayers for Jewish Patients (JWB), and *Sing and Be Joyful* (US Government Printing Office).

Married to Selma Frances Salzberg and they live in Norfolk near their children and grandchildren.

Continuing his interest in pastoral ministry, he is rabbi of Kempsville Conservative Synagogue and serves as chaplain in the Veterans Affairs Medical Center at nearby Hampton.

WAYNE E. SOLIDAY, Colonel (06), born April 14, 1916, in Johnstown, PA. Attended college at Bible Institute of Pennsylvania, Wheaton College, Eastern Baptist Seminary, Temple Univ. and several military schools.

Joined the US Army July 14, 1943, as 1st lieutenant. Served with 94th MGT Bn. and 328th Inf. Regt.; Infantry Center, Fort Benning, GA; 60th Gen. Depot and 7th Inf. Regt., (Korea); Air Defense Cmd., 102nd Regt., 43rd Div., 11th Regt., 5th Div., USA Chaplain Board and USA Chaplain School, Fort Slocum, NY; SACOM,

Munich; USAMTC, Fort Sam Houston; staff chaplain, MDW, Washington, DC. Received campaign ribbons and various service ribbons including the Army Commendation w/cluster, Purple Heart, Bronze Star w/V and Legion of Merit.

Memorable exeriences: receiving custody of captured Chief-of-Chaplains, German army, Gen. Dohrman; and being selected as chaplain and participant in the state funeral ceremonies, Washington, DC for Gen Dwight D Eisenhower.

Ordained Baptist minister Nov. 12, 1942 Pastored churches in Pennsylvania, Virginia, Maryland and Arizona. Presently chaplain of Sun Health Hospice, Sun City, AZ. Life member TROA, DAV, MOPH, MCA, MOWW, VFW, ROA. Board member of Youth for Christ, San Antonio, TX; Conservative Baptist Foreign Missionary Society, Baptist Foundation/Retirement Center, Phoenix, AZ.

Married to Hazel Search Hartzell July 3, 1937 They have three children, eight grandchildren and two great-grandchildren.

JOHN WILLIAM SPARKS, Colonel, born Jan. 9, 1911, Rocky, Washita County, OK. Received BA, Bethel College, McKenzie, TN; M.Div., Vanderbilt Divinity

School, Nashville, TN; Honorary DD, Bethel College 1954, "For outstanding service to his church, his country and to higher education".

Entered Army Nov. 7, 1942, assigned to US Army Chaplain School, Harvard Univ., Cambridge, MA. Assigned to 475th Truck Regt. until October 1943. At that time assigned to Railway Bn., Anchorage, AK, serving troops who operated and maintained Alaska Railroad Spent several months on Adak Island in the Aleutians and followed that with duty as a roving chaplain which entailed visiting smaller isolated groups such as weather stations and camps having no permanently assigned chaplain.

In 1947 he returned to duty with an engineer test unit at Yuma, AZ After one year he was sent to duty at the Port of Bremerhaven, Germany In 1948 he was assigned regimental chaplain with the 351st Inf., Trieste, Italy (TRUST Cmd.). In 1953 he attended the Advanced Course of Chaplain School, Fort Slocum, NY. At the end of the course he went to Korea, then to Japan as post chaplain at Camp Zama.

In 1955 assigned to staff and faculty of Chaplain School, Fort Slocum. During his four years there he served as director, non-resident training, senior instructor, director of instruction and assistant commandant. In 1960 he went to Frankfurt, Germany, where he served as supervisory chaplain for Northern Area Cmd. (NACOM). His last assignment was to HQ 4th Army, Fort Sam Houston, TX, where he retired in May 1966 with rank of colonel He received the Legion of Merit Award upon his retirement

Shortly after retirement he was elected moderator of the general assembly of the Cumberland Presbyterian Church in Memphis, TN. After that term of office ended he became pastor of a church in Bertram, TX. After two years he went to Memphis, TN where he served with the Board of Finance at denominational headquarters. He also served part-time on the faculty of Memphis Theological Seminary.

Married Jacqueline Hays in 1936 and had two children, Alice and Jon. His wife Jacqueline passed away in 1980 at Memphis. He remarried in 1988 to Ingrid Padial, a Spanish instructor at Univ. of Memphis. She is now instructor at Univ. of Tennessee, Martin, where they now make their home.

JAMES S. SPEESE, Lieutenant Colonel, USAFR, born Nov. 24, 1911, Harrisburg, PA. Graduated from Gordon College, Gordon Divinity School, Univ. of New Hampshire Graduate studies at Michigan State, Marquette Univ., Burton Seminary and Northern Illinois Univ. Received a BA, MA, BD, Th.M., Th.D. and ordained in 1943 Pastored churches in New England, Wisconsin, Michigan, Ohio, Illinois and Missouri, 1941-76 Served 28 years, 1943-71 in active and reserve duty, USAFR He headed the Department of History and Political Science, College of Emporia, KS, 1968-71. adj. professor, Florida Southern College, Orlando Campus, 1977-93

Received 17 Freedoms Foundations Awards, including two principal awards 1972, 1974, (Awards 1970-93). MCA member since 1987, president Spaceport Ch 1988. Chaplain Central Florida Chapters of ROA, TROA, AFA, MOWW, Florida State AFA, Florida State ROA, Region VI MOWW, Department N Florida MOWW.

Married to Mary Florence Giddings, 1943. They have children Carolyn, James and Shelley.

ARNOLD P. SPOHN, Lieutenant Commander, born in Spring City, PA in 1917 After studies at Muhlenberg College and the Lutheran Seminary in Philadelphia, he served as assistant pastor at Grace Lutheran Church in Lancaster, PA.

Joined the Navy in 1944 with tours of duty as follows: USS *Hinsdale*, USS *Tanner*; USS *Block Island*; and the USS *La Salle*. Overseas tours of duty were Naval Construction Bn., Guam; Marine duty during the war in Korea; Kwajalein Naval Base in the Marshall Islands; Naval Communications Station, Oahu, HI. Stateside duty was at Little Creek, VA, NAS, Oceana, VA; Naval Station, Washington, DC, Sandia Base, Albuquerque, NM; and the Marine Corps Air Station, Beaufort, SC.

Participated in the last two battles of WWII; Iwo Jima and Okinawa (where his ship was completely disabled by a Japanese kamikaze airplane on Easter morning 1945). In 1948 and 1949 he volunteered to meet weekly with the Japanese war crimes prisoners for 18 months on the island of Guam.

He and his wife, Eleanor, reside in Blue Bell, PA Son Paul lives in New Jersey with his wife and two sons.

MURRAY STADTMAUER, Lieutenant Colonel, born in Brooklyn, NY in 1930. Graduated from the Erna Michael College of Yeshiva Univ with a Hebrew Teacher's Diploma (1950) and from Yeshiva College with BA (1951). Ordained as rabbi (1955) at the Jewish Theological Seminary (New York City), from which he received an honorary DD (1980); he also has five earned master's degrees.

Entered active duty in 1955, serving two years at Fort Chaffee, AR Remained active in the Army Reserve with different units in the NYC area, retiring as lieutenant colonel (1990).

Most startling experience occurred during his first six months of active duty, when he appeared as an expert witness at a court-martial of a young recruit in defiance of a regimental commander. When the recruit was found not guilty, the commander retaliated by arranging for an adverse officer efficiency report to be prepared on Chaplain Stadtmauer. The report was later ruled to be "manifestly inappropriate" by the Office of the Adjutant General, Washington, DC, and ordered withdrawn.

Chaplain Stadtmauer is the rabbi of the Jewish Center of Bayside Hills, NYC, and a part-time chaplain at the Brooklyn, VA Medical Center

IRA CARROLL STARLING JR., Captain, born Nov. 27, 1939, in West Palm Beach, FL. Received an AB from Duke Univ in 1962 and M.Div. from Drew Univ. in 1966.

Joined the USN July 6, 1967, with assignments from 1967-92: NAS, Memphis, TN; 1st Mar. Div., Fleet Mar. Force, Vietnam; NAS, Ellyson Field, FL; USNA, MD; USS *Independence*, Norfolk, VA; USN Security Gp. Activity, Edzell, Scotland; Naval Chaplains School, Newport; instructor, Newport; 1st MAW, Iwakuni, Japan; Marien Corps Development and Education Cmd., Quantico, VA; Naval District, Washington, DC; Chaplain Resource Board, Norfolk, and from October 1992 to present, Naval Base, Norfolk.

Awarded Meritorious Service Medal (Gold Star in lieu of third award), Navy Commendation Medal, Navy Achievement Medal w/Combat "V", Combat Action Ribbon, Vietnamese Campaign Medal, Vietnamese Service Medal and National Defense Medal. Left the service Oct. 1, 1994, as captain.

Married to Maren Carlson and they have three children and one grandchild Ph.D. candidate, Old Dominion Univ., Norfolk, VA. Retired Oct. 1, 1994.

LEONARD F. STEGMAN, Colonel, born in Offerle, KS on May 31, 1917. Ordained June 23, 1943, at St Mary's Church, Marathon, WI. Served in specialized assignments through the mid-western states, entered active duty in April 1950 and served until May 31, 1977

Served in both the Korean and Vietnam wars, and had many assignments at every level of the Army, ending up with assignments as staff chaplain of the 3rd Inf Div., US Army Air Defense Cmd , US Army Vietnam, 3rd US Army, HQ FORSCOM and US Army Materiel Cmd Graduated from the Army Command and Staff College, Army War College, Preacher's Institute of Catholic Univ. and won two master's degrees from George Washington Univ.

Retired in the grade of colonel. His many awards and decorations include two Silver Stars, Purple Heart, three Legion of Merit and Bronze Star.

VERNON E. STENBERG, Captain, CHC, USNR (Ret), born Nov. 1, 1927, to Casper and Blanche (Hanson) Stenberg. After three honorable discharges, a release from active duty, and being placed on the active retired

list he received a Certificate of Retirement from the Navy on Nov. 1, 1987

Regular Navy enlisted duty followed high school in Jewell, IA. Reserve enlisted duty was served during college years. A line ensign commission was received following graduation from St. Olaf College, Northfield, MN in 1952.

Twelve years active duty in the Chaplain Corps as a reserve on active duty came after graduation from Luther Theological Seminary, St. Paul, MN in 1956.

First duty in the Navy was on a small seaplane tender supporting commander Middle East Force in the Persian Gulf. Last duty was with Naval Forces Central Cmd whose responsibility included the Persian Gulf.

On extended active duty from 1956-68, he served in 11 different commands. From 1968-86 he served in nine organized reserve assignments. These included command of 1 MAFREL 220, staff chaplain 4th Marine Air Wing and the reserve unit supporting Naval Forces Central Cmd. He had 32 active duty for training assignments including duty with Marines, Submarine Force, hospital duty, sea duty, Marine air and a number of advanced training courses.

Medals include the Navy Commendation, Meritorious Unit Commendation, Armed Forces Reserve Medal w/Hour Glass Device, National Defense Service Medal w/Bronze Star and WWII Victory Medal.

Memorable duty was five weeks in the Persian Gulf area during the Iran-Iraq War

During reserve years and following, he has served seven different congregations as pastor or interim pastor. He is a life member of MCA, TROA, and member of ROA, VFW and American Legion.

Married to Barbara Joan (McGee) June 10, 1956 They have two sons and two daughters and reside in the foothills of the Sierra Mountains near Placerville, CA.

EDWARD A. STERLING, Lieutenant Colonel, born March 10, 1921, in Grandfield, OK. Received BS, Texas A&M, 1942; M.Div , Episcopal Theological Seminary of Southwest, 1957; prior service May 17, 1942-Dec 7, 1953

Joined the Army (Chaplaincy) Jan 2, 1959. Stationed at Fort Leonard Wood, MO; Korea, Fort Ord, CA; Vietnam; Fort Dix, NJ; Fort Riley, KS; Germany; Fort Lewis, WA. Served with 85th Inf Div., Italy, WWII; US Army Trng. Ctr , 1st Cav. Div., 138th Engr. Bde., 7th Engr Bde. All elements of chaplaincy service, especially worship services with troops in the field was memorable. Discharged June 30, 1975, as lieutenant colonel. Married Margaret M. (Taylor) in 1951 They have four children and seven grandchildren. He held positions A supply priest and Vicar of Mission. Retired June 30, 1975.

LELAND ROBERT STEVENS, Colonel, born on July 1, 1929, Minneapolis, MN. Attended schools in Minnesota and California, preparatory studies at Concordia College, St. Paul, MN and California Concordia College, Oakland, CA. Graduated from Concordia Seminary, St. Louis, MO in 1953 with BA degree and Theological Diploma

Served internship at St Paul's Evangelical Lutheran Church, Bronx, NY. Ordained into the Holy Ministry July 6, 1953, and reported for active duty as a military chaplain in the USAF at Ent AFB, CO

Received MA from Syracuse Univ., 1968 through the AF's Institute of Technology; M.Div from Concordia Seminary, St Louis, 1983; in 1987 Saint Louis Univ awarded him the Ph.D. in American Studies. Retired from the AF chaplaincy in 1973 in the rank of colonel, his last assignment as a staff chaplain of the Systems Cmd., Andrews AFB, Washington, DC

Was the first chaplain to be assigned to the radar sites of the Pine Tree Line, 1954-55; was chaplain to fighter squadrons and wings at Niagara Falls, NY, Itazuke AB, Japan and Holloman AFB, NM, began staff chaplain duties as director of the Alaskan Cmd. Chaplain Program.

Decorations include the Army Commendation Ribbon, AF Commendation w/cluster, Joint Services Commendation Ribbon and the Meritorious Service Ribbon w/cluster.

Served as pastor in Bowie, MD and Alamogordo, NM, was executive director of the *Lutheran Witness,* began service in 1984 as pastor of Shepherd of the Hills Lutheran Church, Ruidoso, NM; retired on July 1, 1990.

Served as circuit counselor, member of the board of directors, chairman of the Synod's Armed Forces Commission, and as member of the Division of Service to Military Personnel, Lutheran Council in the USA. In retirement he has been appointed counselor of the Pecos Circuit, Rocky Mountain District

He has written for the Synod's *Life/Light* Bible series, prepared student material for the second part of *Exodus,* served as vacancy pastor at Trinity Lutheran Church, Alamogordo, and Grace Lutheran Church, Hobbs, NM, and is on the adjunct faculties of Central Texas College and Park College, Holloman AFB Extension Center.

Married Meta Adele Asendorf June 15, 1952, and they have three children

THOMAS L. STRAYHAND, Major, born March 27, 1920, in Newnan, GA. Received BA, Paine College, Augusta, GA; M.Div , Gammon Seminary, Atlanta GA, Chaplains Courses, Fort Slocum, NY; attemded seminars, workshops and counseling refresher courses, while at Fort Benning, GA and Oakland Army Bases

Enlisted in the USAAF August 1942-45 and served in Army Chaplains 1952-69. Stationed at Camp Breckenridge, KY; Korea; Fort Sill; Germany; Fort Benning, GA; Vietnam, Oakland, CA Served with training regiments: infantry regiments, artillery group; engineers and overseas placement centers

Memorable experience was conducting Christmas Eve service in Korea 1966 and spending the rest of the night counseling service men who had received "Dear John letters" from home and sentiment on Christmas was too much for them. Left the service as major Nov. 1, 1969.

Married and has two children Pastor, 1948-52, 1969-86. Retired in 1986

ROBERT C. STROUD, born June 4, 1954, at Oceanside, CA. Received BA in history from Univ. of Washington, 1977, BA in journalism, Univ of Washington, 1977; M Div , Luther Theological Seminary, St. Paul, MN, 1981, M.Th., Jesuit School of Theology at Berkeley, 1984.

Commissioned as chaplain in the USAFR in 1983. In 1986 he completed a five and one-half year pastorate at Ascension Lutheran Church in Citrus Heights, CA and entered active duty. Due to base closures and related circumstances, his first eight years of active duty service involved six separate assignments.

Assignments included the 12th USAF Contingency Hosp., Mather AFB, CA (AFRES), Reese AFB, TX; Taegue AB, ROK; RAF Greenham Common, UK, RAF Alconbury, UK, and AF Institute of Technology studies at the Univ. of Puget Sound. Currently assigned to the Resource Div , USAF Chaplain Service Institute, Maxwell AFB, AL.

Awards include the Meritorious Service Medal, AF Commendation Medal w/3 OLCs, AF Achievement Medal, Army Achievement Medal, SWA Service Medal, National Defense Medal and the Outstanding Unit Award w/4 OLCs. He is a graduate of Squadron Officer School.

During assignments in the UK, in recognition for outstanding performance of his duties as a chaplain, he served as an escort officer for the Soviet Intermediate Nuclear Forces Treaty verification team. In the aftermath of the Gulf War, he accompanied the 39th Special Operations Wing in their support of Operation Provide Comfort

Married on July 17, 1976, to Delores Ciganik. They have three children: Aaron, Kristen and Lucas.

WALTON GARRETT SUGG JR., Colonel, born Oct. 3, 1910, in Tarboro, NC. Received AB from Davidson College and BD from Union Theology Seminary

Joined the US Army May 15, 1941 Served at Camp Callan, CA; 98th and 24th Inf. Div , San Francisco POE Discharged as colonel, Sept. 30, 1969.

He held positions in civilian pastorates in Texas and Alabama. He is a life member of MCA. Married to Frances Miller Sept. 10, 1937 They have three children and eight grandchildren.

LESLIE J. SUMMERS JR., 1st Lieutenant, born March 12, 1965, in South Bend, IN Received BA from Texas Christian Univ., 1987 and M Div from Brite Divinity School, 1990.

Joined the USAFR March 22, 1989. Stationed Eacker AFB, Blytheville, AR; Scott AFB, IL; Offutt AFB, NE. Served with 55th WG/HC, 97th WG/HC, 132 FW/HC (ANG).

Memorable experiences: working mobility during Desert Shield/Storm; working around various aircraft (KC 135, EC 135, B52, F16, C9).

Married July 11, 1993, to Rev. Jacquelyn S. Meece. He is pastor of Woodward Christian Church

FREDRICK D. SUNDLOFF, Lieutenant Colonel, born Nov. 23, 1927, in South Bend, IN. Attended Moody Bible Institute, Chicago; Univ of Illinois; Princeton Theological Seminary, M Div., American Univ , Washington, DC

Joined the USAF, May 30, 1952. Stationed at Lowry AFB, Denver, CO, 1952-54; French Indo-China (TDY), 1954-54; (Tourane and Haiphong during battle of Dien Bien Phu), Iwo Jima, base chaplain, 1954-55; 1254th Air Transport Gp., Special Missions, (AF One); Washington National Airport, Washington, DC, 1955-58

Overseas to Furstenfeldbruck AFB, Munich, Germany, 1958-J58; Bushy Park AFB, London, England,

1958-61; Williams AFB, AZ, 1961-63, American Univ. (AFIT) Washington, DC, 1963-64; Air Univ., Maxwell AFB, AL, chaplain to students, 1964-66; Misawa AFB, Japan, base chaplain, 1966-68; Andrews AFB, Washington, DC, 1968-72

Retired after 20 years. Received Meritorious Service Medal, senior Protestant chaplain

Married Dorislee Nicholls and they have six children and three grandchildren. Dorislee was the MCA secretary and editor of the MCA Magazine with Ch. Wm. Austil, March 1955-57 He was pastor of Palmdale Presbyterian Church Melbourne, FL for 18 years Retired March 1, 1992.

VERNON SWIM,
Colonel, graduated from Bethany Nazarene College (BA) 1957, Nazarene Theological Seminary (M.Div.) 1961, and Chapman College (MA) 1973. Served as a Church of the Nazarene Army chaplain 1962-86 at Presidio of San Francisco.

Overseas with 1st Cav. Div., Korea; 5th Inf Div, Fort Carson; 98th Gen. Hosp., Germany; 18th MP Bde., Vietnam, Graduate School in Marriage and Family Therapy, Chapman College; Fort Lee, VA; Staff, Army Chaplain School, Fort Hamilton, NY; director, Religious Retreat House, Berchtesgaden, Germany; Chief Dept. of Ministry, Walter Reed, installation chaplain, Redstone Arsenal.

Awarded the Legion of Merit, Bronze Star, Meritorious Service and Army Commendation Medals.

Retired as colonel in 1986 to become director of pastoral care, Memorial Hosp., Colorado Springs. Married to Shirley Schreuder, a former Army nurse. They have two children: Bradley, a 1992 West Point graduate, and Verna, a 1994 graduate of Baylor Univ.

ROBERT PRESTON TAYLOR,
Major General, born April 11, 1909, in Henderson, TX. Received his BA degree in 1933 from Baylor Univ., Th.M in 1936 from Southwestern Baptist Theological Seminary, Th.D from Southwestern Baptist Theological Seminary in 1939; holds four honorary degrees and is a graduate of the Air War College, June 1953, Maxwell AFB, AL.

Entered military service in September 1940, first assignment as post chaplain, Barksdale Field, LA. In April 1941 he was assigned regimental chaplain of the 31st Inf Philippine Div.

With the declaration of war Dec. 7, 1941, his division was transferred to the front lines of Bataan. Following the surrender of American forces he participated in the "Death March", and was a prisoner-of-war for three and one-half years during which time he ministered to 10,000 patients in Bilibid and Cabanatuan prison hospitals. Wounded in the sinking of one or two prisoners ships sunk beneath him by American forces with a loss of over 1,000 lives. Caught smuggling food and medicine to the patients in the hospital, he was put in solitary confinement in a small tiger cage too small to lie or stand for 14 weeks. Released for Christian burial, he was nursed back to health by fellow POWs.

Upon his release he has held assignments as wing chaplain, Mather AFB, CA; deputy chaplain, Air Trng Cmd.; deputy chaplain, Air Material Cmd., National CAP Chaplain, Washington, DC, staff chaplain, HQ Air Univ., Maxwell AFB, AL; Chief of Personnel Div, Office of the Chief of Chaplains, Washington, DC; deputy chief of chaplains, and retired as major general, chief of chaplains, USAF, in August 1966

Decorations include the Silver Star, Bronze Star, Presidential Unit Citation w/2 OLCs, the Philippine Presidential Unit Citation and the POW Medal. His non-military awards include the "Hall of Heroes" Award from the Chapel of Four Chaplains in Philadelphia, PA and the Gourgus Medal of the Supreme Council Scottish Rite on Jan 9, 1976. On June 2, 1965, he received the "Distinguished Alumnus Award" from Southwestern Baptist Theological Seminary "

Married to the former Mildred Good of Carrollton, TX; they have one son, R.P. Taylor Jr., and two great-grandchildren. They live in Arlington, TX

RODNEY THAINE TAYLOR,
Colonel, born May 7, 1909, in Yellow Springs, OH. Received a AB, Th.B, M.Div. and DD.

Joined the Army July 1941; stationed in the USA; Trinidad, BWI; England; France. Served with 121st Engrs., 29th Div., Trinidad Sector and Base Command, chaplain, France; Northern District, chaplain.

He met many wonderful human beings and very few of the other kind. Discharged as colonel Oct 3, 1945, and retired from the Reserves Feb 28, 1969.

Married and has three children, seven grandchildren and two great-grandchildren.

January 3, 1946, called to become minister of historic Falling Springs Presbyterian Church; organized in 1734 while George Washington was three years old. Also was close to two women's colleges, the Hymns sure sounded pretty. Remained minister for 24 years until Jan 28, 1970

DAVID M. TERRINONI,
Captain, born in Cleveland, March 17, 1957. Married Victoria Lynn Malo, Oct 2, 1982, and they have two children, Marissa and Alanna Received AA degree, William R. Harper College, Palatine, IL, 1978; BS, Western Illinois Univ., 1981; M.Div., McCormick Theological Seminary, Chicago, 1990. Graduated USAF Chaplain School, 1991 and ordained to ministry Presbyterian Church (USA), 1990

From 1987-89 he was seminary assistant pastor at Presbyterian Church, Palatine, IL; intern minister 3rd Presbyterian Church, Rockford, IL; night chaplain, Rockford (IL), Memorial Hosp, interim associate pastor, First Presbyterian Church, Sterling, IL; member Middle East Task Force Blackhawk Presbytery, Oregon, IL; member Sem. Governance Reorganization Task Force, Chicago; M.Div. rep. Sem. Common Council, Chicago.

Awarded Commendation Medal (AF), National Defense Service Medal and Longevity Ribbon. Entered active duy service at Robins AFB, GA, 1992 to present.

Other activities include Boy Scouts of America; Middle Georgia Special Olympics Council; Board of Directors, Presbyterian Nursery School, Sterling, 1990-92; Chaplain USAFR, 1991-92 Recipient of James W Angell Award for preaching McCormick Theological Seminary, Samuel Robinson Award, Outstanding Chaplain Candidate Award, USAFR. He is member of MCA and National Eagle Scout Assoc.

STEVEN E. THOMAS,
Commander, earned his BA degree from Univ. of Illinois, Urbana, 1974. Graduated Concordia Theological Seminary, Fort Wayne, 1978 with M.Div. He was commissioned a TSP ensign in 1977.

Called to active duty in 1980, Navy Chaplaincy, USS America (CV-66); transferred to staff naval hospital, Portsmouth, VA; 1984 called to Immanuel Lutheran Church, Sheboygan, WI. Served as a Reserve chaplain with the NMCB 25 and in 1989, became CO, NR4 MEFREL 713. Recalled in 1991 for Desert Storm and deployed with the Marines, 3rd LSB and 9th Motors out of Okinawa, served on Operation Provide Comfort and is currently on Reserve Staff 2nd Fleet.

In 1993 he accepted a chaplain position at Fox Lake Correctional Institution, Waupun, WI. Cmdr Thomas and wife Donna have two daughters, Rebecca and Stephanie.

Among his many awards are the Navy Achievement, Navy Expeditionary, Armed Forces Expeditionary, Fleet Marine Force, SWA and National Defense

WILLIAM E. THOMPSON JR.,
Colonel, born Dec. 22, 1930, in Norfolk, VA. Received BA, Th M, D.Min. Attended Wake Forest College, Southern Baptist Theological Seminary, American Baptist Seminary of the West, chaplain intern at St. Elizabeth Hosp., Washington, DC.

Joined the Navy April 16, 1967; served with 3rd Marine Div. in Vietnam and stationed at Naval Hosp, Portsmouth, VA

Memorable experience was serving with Marines, Navy and Army Reserve. Was staff chaplain with Army Reserve units: 311th COSCOM and 349th Gen. Hosp. Discharged as lieutenant, Navy, June 27, 1970, and retired as Army Colonel Dec. 31, 1990

Married Betty Louise Smith and they have three children and three grandchildren. Held the position as director, Chaplain Service, San Diego, CA. He is still working at the VA Medical Center.

HENRY B. THORSEN,
Major, born Jan. 29, 1928, in Pensacola, FL. He did four years post graduation work, Seminary, St. Mary's, Baltimore.

Joined the Air Force in November, 1962 and stationed at Scott AFB, IL; Naha, Okinawa; Lackland AFB, San Antonio; Ankara, Turkey; Saudia Arabia; Barksdale AFB, Shreveport, LA, Utipao Thailand; Keesler AFB, Biloxi, MS, Berlin; and Fort Walton Beach, FL. Discharged November 1982 as major.

He is a Catholic priest and held position with Diocese of Birmingham, AL. Retired from Birmingham Diocese February 1993, lives alone and does relief work out of his home

ANDREW J. TIBUS,
Lieutenant Colonel, born July 21, 1936, McKees Rocks, PA Received BA degree in philosophy, St. Vincent College, Latrobe, PA, 1958; M Th degree, St. Vincent Seminary in 1962; and ordained a priest in 1962 for the Diocese of Pittsburgh.

Served as pastor to churches in Pittsburgh, PA; Bridgeport, WV; New York, NY; chaplaincy duty at Bellevue Hosp.; Episcopal Church Center, New York, NY, and USNR chaplain from 1967-73 at McKeesport and Neville Island, PA and New York, NY. Achieved a M Div. from General Theological Seminary, New York, NY in 1971 and advanced master's specialist degree in Marriage and Family Life Therapy from St Mary's Univ., San Antonio, TX, 1981

Entered the USAF Chaplain Service in 1973 and assigned to the 7th Cbt. Spt. Gp., Carswell AFB, TX, 1973-75; the 3rd Cbt. Spt Gp., Clark AB, P.I., 197-76, 323rd Air Base Wing, Mather AFB, CA, 1976-78; 3700 AB Gp., Lackland AFB, TX, 1978-83; HQ, USAF Europe, Ramstein AB, Germany, 1973-87; Goodfellow AFB, TX, 1987-89; senior chaplain at Eglin AFB, FL, 1989 until he completed his military chaplaincy career on May 1, 1993.

From 1993-94, he served as interim assistant, St. Luke's Episcopal Church, Alexandria, VA On Aug. 1, 1994, he assumed the position of interim vicar, Episcopal Church of the Messiah, Chancellor, VA Currently a doctoral candidate in the Pastoral Counseling program, Loyola College, Columbia, MD. He continues professional development through theological studies at the Virginia Theological Seminary, Alexandria, VA.

Married to the former Karen L. Becze of Pittsburgh, PA. Their three children are Jennifer, Jonathan and Jeannie. They reside in Vienna, VA.

WILLIAM L. TOLAND JR., Colonel (06) born April 12, 1928 in Macomb, IL. Received an MA from Bradley Univ.; BS from Western Illinois Univ., Bexley Hall-Seminary.

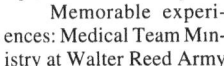

Joined the Army, Sept. 11, 1957, and stationed at Fort Leavenworth, Fort Hamilton, Fort Sill and Fort Leonard Wood Served with 687 S&S Bn., 303rd Ord Gp., 102nd Gen. Hosp

Memorable experiences: Medical Team Ministry at Walter Reed Army Hosp. and MEDAC at Fort Leonard Wood and Fort Sill.

Discharged as colonel (06) April 12, 1988. Received USAR Achievement, Army Commendation and Meritorious Service Married to Rosemary K. Gahwiler. Employed as social worker for Department for Children and Family Services

WILLIAM L. TRAVERS, Colonel, O. Carm., born March 10, 1918, Brooklyn, NY. Ordained a Catholic priest at Catholic Univ in Washington, DC, Feb. 3, 1945, and taught high school classes in New York and Los Angeles, CA for four years On April 28, 1949, he joined the USAF at Hamilton AFB, San Rafael, CA

Sent to Korea in 1950 and became the Catholic chaplain for the 49th Ftr Wing until May 1952. He flew many combat missions, both in T-33s and B-29s, and was promoted to captain. Assigned to the 7330th Flying Trng. Wing at Furstenfeldbruck AB in Germany. The Wing was assigned the job of training NATO and the new Luftwaffe pilots to fly jets and he received permission to go through the jet course

He holds 17 medals including the Legion of Merit, Bronze Star and the Soldiers Medal for heroism in saving two Army soldiers who had been trapped for several hours in an overturned cannon in the area of Furstenfeldbruck.

Served in London and Madrid and several bases in the US. Final assignment was as staff chaplain for 22nd AF, Military Airlift Cmd. at Travis AFB, CA. Retired in the grade of colonel on May 1, 1971.

After retirement he served the Catholic parish in Vacaville, CA and in 1978 was asked to come to Bonn, Germany as the pastor of the American Embassy Catholic parish. Retired from that position in 1995.

JACK EVANS TRETHEWEY, Lieutenant Commander, born Nov. 16, 1923, in Ironwood, MI. Received AB, Augustana College, Rock Island, IL, 1950; M.Div., Lutheran School of Theology at Chicago, 1954 CPE Augustana Hosp., Iowa Lutheran Hosp.

Joined the USNR Feb 15, 1943 (AS, SV, V6, USNR), commissioned May 19, 1958, as lieutenant (jg) CHC, USNR Date of rank: Nov. 22, 1956. Stationed in European and Asiatic Theaters of Operation. Served with 2nd Marine Div., FMF, Camp Lejeune, NC, 1960-62; Deployed with SOLANT AMITY II, a goodwill cruise to the South Atlantic and Indian Ocean aboard USS LST-1175 in 1961; USN hospital, Camp Lejeune, NC, 1962-64, Ready Reserve, 1958-60; 1964-76. Commander, LST Group 28 Staff aboard USS LST-229 and USS LST-491

As an enlisted man, he was given the opportunity to conduct a Divine Service at sea by James W. Knox, CO of the USS LST-491, a dedicated Christian leader. He believes it was the Lord's leading him to become a Navy chaplain.

Married Donna J. Joneson on Dec. 27, 1949, they have three children Sue, Thomas and Erik and two grandchildren, Brittany and Kyle Trethewey. Held positions as parish pastor, 12 years, VA chaplain, 23 years; Retired Chief, Chaplain Service, VAMC, Salisbury, NC, 1988

ROSS H. TROWER, Rear Admiral, born in St Louis, MO, Feb 22, 1922. Prepared for ministry in the Lutheran Church at Carthage College, then at Carthage, IL, now at Kenosha, WI, and the Lutheran School of Theology at Chicago (Maywood). Ordained by the Illinois Synod of the United Lutheran Church in America on Feb. 21, 1945, and commissioned in the Chaplains Corps of the USNR on the same date. He came to active duty on March 26, 1945, and in June 1947 he achieved a commission in the Regular Navy.

During more than 38 years of continuous active duty as a chaplain, Chaplain Trower served afloat and ashore and with Marines in combat both in Korea and in Vietnam. He was a "plankowner" of the USS *Canberra* and the USS *Kitty Hawk.* He was the Pacific Fleet Chaplain and director of the Chaplains School in Newport, RI, before becoming the 15th Chief of Chaplains of the Navy from 1979-83. He was placed on the retired list with the grade of rear admiral on Aug. 1, 1983. Among a number of personal awards, his highest decoration is the Distinguished Service Medal of the Navy.

During an assignment under instruction at Harvard in 1953-54, Chaplain Trower earned the Master of Theology degree In the late 80s he studied at the Lutheran School of Theology at Chicago and was awarded the degree of Doctor of Ministry in 1990. His alma mater, Carthage, conferred upon him the honorary degree of Doctor of Divinity in 1977.

Chaplain Trower married the former Margaret E. Doering of Vandalia, IL They have four children: David, Martha (now Edmonds), Paul and John, and four grandchildren. Since 1984 he has served as an associate pastor of St. Mark's Lutheran Church in Springfield, VA. The Trowers reside in Springfield, located in Fairfax County of northern Virginia.

WALLACE B. TURNER, Captain, USN, (Ret), born April 11, 1936, Pontiac, MI. Commissioned in the Navy Ensign Program in 1959 at Concordia Seminary St. Louis, MO. Graduated, ordained, by the Lutheran Church-Missouri Synod, and went to Chaplain's School in 1962. Served as a reserve chaplain in Tacoma, WA while in the parish ministry and called to active duty in November 1965. Ten years were served with the Marines at Camp Pendleton; El Toro; Vietnam, Kaneohe, HI; and San Diego, CA.

In 1972 he attended Postgraduate School at Claremont, CA and in 1978 awarded a D.Min from Claremont School of Theology. Navy tours have included Navy Hosp., Camp Pendleton; NTC Great Lakes, Naval Chaplains School, Newport; USS *Kitty Hawk* in the Iranian crisis; Naval Station Pearl Harbor; COMNAVAIR PAC Chaplain and COMNAVSURF PAC in San Diego

Awarded Legion of Merit, two Meritorious Service Medals, three Navy Commendation Medals w/ Combat V, Combat Action and various other campaign and service medals from Vietnam conflict and duty in the Indian Ocean.

Beverly Bogart became his bride in Cedar Rapids, IA on June 18, 1960; they have two sons, a daughter (deceased); and two grandchildren. Turner serves as part-time assistant pastor of Pilgrim Lutheran Church in Chula Vista, CA.

MARTELL HERMAN TWITCHELL, Captain, born April 25, 1907, Kosciusko, MS. Received a BA and BD degree from Divinity School, Duke Univ., Durham, NC; Millsaps College, Jackson, MS

Joined the USN in 1937 and his military stations from 1938-60 include: USS *Portland*; US Submarine Base, Pearl Harbor, NAS Pensacola, FL; Navy Preflight School, Athens, GA; USS *New Mexico*; Naval Receiving Station, Bremerton, WA; NOB Kodiak, AK with ADDU District Chaplain, 17th Naval District; MCAS El Toro, Santa Ana, CA, senior chaplain; force chaplain, Fleet Marine Force Pacific, staff of CG, Honolulu; NAS Jacksonville, FL, NTC Great Lakes,

IL, senior chaplain, with additional duty as district chaplain, 9th Naval District; Staff Hdg., with ADDU, senior chaplain, MCAS, El Toro. Left the service June 30, 1960, as captain, USN.

Memorable experience was when a Japanese torpedo struck and blew up a jeep carrier, the USS *Lipscomb Bay,* 500 yards off his ship's starboard bow.

Served as pastor, minister of visitation, associate minister and pastor. Retired from the pastorate June 30, 1971 Some of his activities include East Bay Chapter ROA; life member, MCA; volunteer chaplain at Prather Mem. Methodist Home, Alameda, 16 years.

Married Mamie Vivian Varner, June 26, 1934, and they have three children and 12 grandchildren.

DANIEL J. TYLER, Lieutenant Colonel, born Nov. 27, 1953. He is President of International Seminary and has been active in ministry since 1968, having served in virtually every major position in the local church. Served as vice-president of International Seminary in Plymouth for 17 years before being named president in 1988. He travels extensively, having visited all 50 states in America, and having made numerous mission trips to foreign countries including Israel, Austria, Belize, Jamaica, Honduras, Paraguay, Argentina, Brazil, Haiti, and Yucatan (Mexico).

Attended a number of schools including Southeastern Bible College, the US Army Chaplain School, Troy State Univ. and Alabama Aviation and Technical College. Received AA and BS from Rollins College, bachelor of religious education degree from International Seminary, MA in Biblical studies degree from Liberty Christian College and D Min degree from North Florida Baptist Theological Seminary.

Served as a chapel activities and religious education specialist with the 46th Engr Cbt. Unit and presently serves as a chaplain with the rank of lieutenant colonel, deputy wing chaplain, Florida Wing in the USAF Auxiliary, CAP. He is a law enforcement chaplain, serving in both the city of Apopka Police Dept. and the FBI. Also serves as official ecclesiastical endorsing agent for military chaplains, listed with the National Conference on Ministry to the Armed Forces. He is a member of the MCA, the International Conference of Police Chaplains and Sertoma International.

Received numerous military, civic and religious awards including the Key to the city of Apopka; membership in the Holy Orthodox Order of St. Gregory the Illuminator; Certificate of Appreciation, Chief of Chaplains Office, USN; Commendation for Outstanding Duty; Award of Appreciation, Apopka Police Department; Certificate of Appreciation; Outstanding Chaplain of the Year Award; Gill Robb Wilson Award and the Southeast Region Commander's Commendation, USAF Auxiliary, CAP. Married April 21, 1979 and has two children.

ORVIL T. UNGER, Colonel, born Aug. 22, 1912, in Camden (Ray County), MO. Received an AB and Th.M Joined the USAF November 1942.

Stationed in CBI, Korea, Philippines, Thule and England. Served with ATC, ADC, SAC, 75 ADW, 3rd AF Attained the rank of colonel (06).

Awarded 11 medals, awards, decorations and ribbons. Founded Rocky Mountain and Space Port Chapters, MCA and is life member #224.

Married to Marie Toloso Unger and has two children, six grandchildren, three great-grandchildren.

Held position as coal miner, farmer, and pastor Retired Sept. 1, 1972.

DAVID R. VAN HORN, Colonel, born in Plainfield, NJ. Received a BA degree from Missouri Valley College, MO, in 1977 (Cum Laude) and a M.Div. from St. Paul School of Theology, MO in 1977. Graduated from the CAP National Staff College, Maxwell AFB, AL and was named the Unit Chaplain of the Year by CAP in 1987 Became a member of the MCA in 1982

An ordained minister of the Christian Church in May 1977 and is presently serving two United Churches of Christ in the Arrow Rock, MO area. Served on active duty during 1970-72 in the US Army as a school trained chaplain's assistant and received the Army Commendation Medal along with the Good Conduct Medal and National Defense Medal. He has served three different squadrons, deputy Missouri Wing chaplain, North Central Region chaplain, deputy chief of chaplains and was appointed as CAP chief of chaplains and promoted to the grade of colonel in November 1993

Awards include the CAP Exceptional Service Award (one Bronze Clasp), CAP Meritorious Award (five clasps), CAP Commander's Commendation Award (nine Bronze Clasps), Unit Meritorious Award (five clasps) the Gill Robb Wilson Award (CAP highest training award), the Aerospace Award, and other service and training awards.

Married to Marlene Cooper and has two daughters, Jennifer and Tosha, who live at home, attending high school and grade school respectively.

RICHARD F. VAUGHAN, Lieutenant Colonel, born Oct. 19, 1918, in Chicago, IL. Post graduate, received MA in 1975, graduate of Air War College. Joined the USAF October 1961. Began serving as an AF chaplain in 1961 at Amarillo AFB and joined the CAP, working with that organization for more than 20 years.

When the Amarillo base closed, he was teaching in an Amarillo High School Even though he was an auxiliary, he was allowed to live on the base during the summer months. Since he was a CAP chaplain, he was permitted to wear the CAP uniform and rank. He also helped out at Altus AFB, Perrin AFB and Ellington AFB. Left the service in 1978 as lieutenant colonel.

Since leaving the AF he was a pastor at St. Joseph's Parish and Blessed Sacrament Parish in Amarillo. In July of 1993 he resigned his parish and took over the Mission Office for the Amarillo Diocese. He also serves as vicar of clergy.

FRANK O. VAVRIN, Lieutenant Colonel, born Racine WI, in 1920. Received AB Carthage College (Kenosha, WI), 1942; BD Northwestern Lutheran Seminary, Minneapolis, 1945, pastor, Santurce, Puerto Rico, 1945-1947.

Commissioned March 13, 1950; Chaplain Course summer of 1950; called to active duty Dec. 10, 1950. Service included: 188th Abn Inf. Regt , (11th Abn Div.), Fort Campbell, KY, 1951-53; I Corps Arty., (Korea), 1953-55

Served with various units: 82nd Abn. Div., Fort Bragg, NC, 1955-60; Berlin Brigade (Germany), 1960-63; 34th Gen. Hosp (Orleans, France), 1963-64; 79th Ord. Bn., (with them to Vietnam), 1964, 173rd Abn. Bde (Vietnam) 1964-65; Military Police School Staff (Fort Gordon, CA), 1965-67; 97th Gen. Hosp., Frankfurt, 1967-69.

Attended US Army Chaplain School, parachute training to include Jump Master Qualification Special Warfare. Principal achievements: master parachutist with 125 jumps. Served three times as stockade chaplain; two tours as hospital chaplain; eight years as airborne chaplain.

Special experiences being in Berlin at the beginning of the erection of the wall, the busiest time of their lives; being in France at the time of turbulence of France in Algeria (they knew some French military and civilians involved in this); Korea with 30 church services every week for a year and a half (five every Sunday); Vietnam.

Among happiest thoughts are the number of former assistants who have become pastors. He is deeply honored that he was part of their lives.

Being a troop chaplain for all of his 20 years compels him to thank heartily the US Army Chaplaincy. He never wanted to be anything more than a pastor and, God bless em, that is the way it turned out. Most of the work, as other chaplains can appreciate, was seven-days-per-week. Since retiring, he served at the VA, Helena, MT 1971-73 Returned to the parish, 1973-80. Retired again.

Active since the "retirement" in community theater, TV and radio commercial work, recording for the blind. Senior tennis. Eager now to see what the future holds. So much to see and do.

Married to Jean Neal. They have three children, (two deceased), two grandchildren, and one great-grandchild.

JOHN F. WAKEFIELD, Colonel, a life member of the MCA, born Aug. 13, 1920, in Pineville, LA, the son of the Rev and Mrs. James E Wakefield. He is a graduate of Baylor University (BA), Waco, TX and the New Orleans Baptist Theological Seminary (Th.M).

His military career began in 1937 when he joined the Louisiana National Guard as a private in Co. B, 106th QM Co. Called to active duty as a sergeant when the guard mobilized in 1940. He served in the Persian Gulf Command from 1942-44, returning to CONUS to attend Officer's Candidate School at Fort Benning, GA and was commissioned a 2nd lieutenant infantry in 1945. Discharged in October 1945, he joined the Reserves. In 1952 he was called to active duty and changed branches from infantry to chaplaincy and assigned to Korea from 1953-54.

During his tour in Korea, he was appointed as chaplain in the Regular Army. The first two tours in Germany began in January 1959 and included duty at the Tank Training Center, Vilseck, and with Special Troops as USAEUR HQ in Heidelburg. Returning in 1967, he served as sub-district chaplain in Munich and as division chaplain of the 4th Armd Div., Goeppingen. From Germany, he was assigned to the 24th Corps HQ in Da Nang, Vietnam as Deputy Corps chaplain. Stateside duty included: Fort Rucker, AL; Fort Bliss, TX; Fort Meyer, VA; Vint Hill Farms Station (ASA), VA; and Fort Polk, LA. He was post chaplain at Fort Polk when he retired July 31, 1974, with 36 years, ten months total service.

Decorations include the Legion of Merit w/2 OLCs, the Bronze Star w/2 OLCs, the Army Meritorious Service Medal and 21 citations for WWII, the Korean War and Vietnam. He retired as colonel in the regular Army.

Pastored the Wildwood Baptist Church in a resort-retirement community north of Beaumont, TX for seven years where he currently resides.

Married Grace Gayer in 1947. They have five children and 15 grandchildren.

BRUCE C. WAKEMAN, Major, born April 15, 1955, Bryn Mawr, PA. Received BA from Whitwork College, Spokane 1977, M Div. from Pacific School of Religion, Berkeley, CA in 1980.

Joined the Army NG, March 1974; Washington NG, company clerk and chaplain assistant HHC, 161st Inf. (Mech), Spokane, WA; Army Reserve, chaplain assistant, HHC, 41st Truck Bde., Tigard, OR; Army Reserve, chaplain assistant, 352nd Evac Hosp. (SMBL), Oakland Army Base, CA; Active Army, chaplain, HHB 3rd Bn., 6th FA. (MLRS), 1985-86, Fort Riley, KS; Active Army, chaplain, HHC 5th Bn., 16th Inf., 1987-88, Fort Riley, KS.

Other military schools and training: Fort Dix, NJ, Fort Wadsworth, NY, Fort Hamilton, NY; Camp Riley, OR, Yakima Firing Center, WA, Fort Monmouth, NJ, New Braunfells, TX; Fort Sam Houston, San Antonio, TX, Germany-Holland (REFORGER 86), Fort Lewis, WA; Fort Gordon, GA; Fitzsimmons Army Medical Center, Aurora, CO. Continuing his military service in Army as IMA.

Memorable experiences: extremes of heat and cold, lack of sleep, righteousness and immorality; a few good field services (Easter 1987); tent stove troubles; jeep stuck in the mud and many others.

Married Frances Ann Whitfield of Bakersfield, CA on Nov. 29, 1980, Harrington, WA. They have two children Elizabeth and Derek.

Presently pastor for retirement home ministry in Spokane; president of local chapter of American Family Association; taking CGSC courses, business selling ferns in summer.

ALEXANDER CROSSFIELD WALKER JR., Lieutenant Colonel, born March 25, 1917, in Alfonso, VA. Received BA from University of Richmond in 1939; Th.M, SBTS, 1942; Th.M Union, Richmond, 1951. Joined as chaplain in 1943 and attended Chaplain School in January 1944.

Stationed with 134th Inf., 35th Inf. Div. Served as 134th Inf. Regt. as chaplain. Participated in combat in Europe, July 1944-45; occupation of Japan, 1947-48, post chaplain, Camp Gordon; assistant post chaplain, Fort Richardson, AK; Head State Chaplain, Virginia NG. Retired as lieutenant colonel in 1977 with 30 years.

Married Margaret Cooksey Walker and they have five children and 10 grandchildren.

Held positions at Amissville Field, 1942-43; Rhoadesville, VA, 1955-60; 1984, Forest Grove Baptist Church.

CONRAD N. WALKER, born in Herrick, IL, March 2, 1932. Attended grade schools in Illinois; graduated from Grant Community High School in Fox Lake, IL in 1951, where he excelled in student leadership and athletics. Graduated from the University of Washington in Seattle, WA, in 1955. After four years of study, he graduated from Lutheran Seminary, St Paul, MN, and was ordained a pastor of the Evangelical Lutheran Church on April 5, 1959.

He was called as pastor of Shiloh Lutheran Church in Elmore, MN, 1959-62. In September 1962, he was called to enter active duty as a US Army chaplain. While in seminary and as a parish pastor, he served in the USAR and the Minnesota NG.

Pastor Walker served at Fort Campbell, KY, 101st Abn Div.; South Vietnam, 173rd Abn. Bde.; Fort Benning, GA, Student Bde. (Airborne, Ranger, Pathfinder School), Fort Hamilton, NY; Advanced Student, Thailand, USARSUPTHAI and Special Forces; Fort Leavenworth, KS, Command and General Staff College, Fort Hood, TX, 1st Cav. Div. chaplain; Carlisle Barracks, PA, post chaplain; US Forces Korea, 8th US Army; command chaplain UN Command/Combined Forces Command; Fort Sill, OK, post chaplain, Kaiserslautern, Germany, 21st Spt. Cmd., command chaplain, 5th Army chaplain at Fort Sam Houston, TX and is presently senior pastor at MacArthur Park Ev. Lutheran Church in San Antonio, TX.

Awarded the Silver Star, Bronze Star with V, Legion of Merit, and Purple Heart for his pastoral mission under hostile conditions in South Vietnam.

Spent many years as an outstanding athlete and played guard for the University of Washington Huskies. He had opportunities to play professional football and box professionally upon graduation, but followed the call to enter seminary to further prepare to be a pastor. He was a heavyweight boxer for nine years, holding titles in the Midwest and on the West Coast. He coached boxing throughout his Army 'calling.' Pastor Walker is a master parachutist, having made over 1,000 jumps with "The Troops," to include one combat jump.

Pastor Walker and his wife Ann are the parents of five young adults. Beverly, Miriam, Randall, Timothy and Gracia, three of whom are serving in the US Military with distinction. They have six granddaughters and six grandsons - Praise God!

PAUL R. WALKER, Colonel, born Nov. 26, 1910, in Mason City, NE. Graduated from the University of Nebraska in 1932 and received degrees from Clark University, Worcester, MA and Andover Newton Theological School.

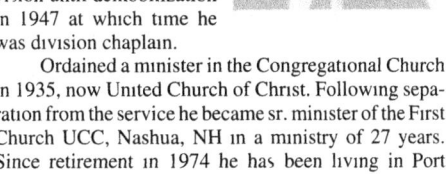

Commissioned a 1st lieutenant in the US Army Chaplain Corps in June of 1942. He joined the 104th Inf. Div. before its activation and served with the division until demobilization in 1947 at which time he was division chaplain.

Ordained a minister in the Congregational Church in 1935, now United Church of Christ. Following separation from the service he became sr. minister of the First Church UCC, Nashua, NH in a ministry of 27 years. Since retirement in 1974 he has been living in Port Hueneme, CA.

Married first to Lula Rumery and second to Gloria Oren. He has two children, five grandchildren and six great-grandchildren.

LOUIE WILLIAM WALTER, Colonel, born Sept 19, 1920, Little Rock, AR. Graduated from Little Rock High School. Earned a BS degree and a MS degree at the University of Arkansas and later earned a Ph.D degree at the University of Texas. Service began in March 1943 as a Signal Corps officer, and he became a chaplain in June 1956.

A graduate of the USA Chaplain School basic and advanced courses, he completed the Command and General Staff Course at Fort Leavenworth. Chaplain Walter has served with the 1st, 2nd, 4th, 5th and 7th Inf. Divs. and has been stationed at Forts Knox, Lewis, Bragg, Hood and Lee and in Germany, France and Korea (three times).

Memorable assignments include: director CDC Chaplain Agency, and staff chaplain UNC-Eighth Army in Korea. Retired from AD Aug. 31, 1974, as colonel (06). Received the Legion of Merit and OLC. He is a life member of MCA since 1974.

Married over 50 years to Mary Elizabeth Heath; they have two children. Civilian employment: University professor and chairman, Dept. of Business Adm.; Pan American University, Brownsville, TX.

JAMES ARTHUR WALTHER, born April 3, 1918, in Upper St. Clair, PA. Received AB, Grove City College; STB, Pittsburgh Theological Seminary, Th.D, Victoria University, Toronto.

Joined the USNR April 27, 1943. Military locations and stations. Chaplains School, Williamsburg; Office, 14th Naval District; Naval Hospital, Pearl Harbor, USS *Proteus*, Naval Hospital, Millington. Served with Marine Corps Reserve, Pittsburgh.

His memorable experience was being present in Tokyo Bay when the Japanese surrender was signed. He achieved the rank of commander and retired April 27, 1973. Held positions as assistant pastor, Concord Presbyterian Church, Pittsburgh; pastor, Edinboro, PA Presbyterian Church; associate professor classical languages, Grove City College; professor of Biblical Literature and Exegesis, Pittsburgh Theological Seminary; founding writer, Kerygma Program; author, editor and lecturer.

Married to Janet S. and they have two children and one grandchild. Retired June 30, 1983.

WAYNE R. WARD, born Nov. 7, 1934, in Kansas City, KS. Received BS, Kansas University, 1956; M.Div, Iliff School of Theology, 1962; graduate study, Texas Christian University, 1969-71; ordained, Greater Area Christian Churches (Disc. of Christ), May 1962.

Joined the US Army Aug. 6, 1956; commissioned on Jan. 3, 1961. Stationed at Fort Carson, CO; Fort Riley, KS; RVN, Fort Bliss, TX. Served with 9th Inf. Div., 62nd Maint. Bn., Air Defense School Support Command.

Memorable experiences: working with the RCath French Orphanage at Ba Ngoi, RVN in 1967; working on

MEDCAP operations at Binh Hung Island, RVN, 1967; preaching at re-opening of John Wesley Methodist meeting place at Edgewood Arsenal, MD in July 1983. Discharged as colonel (served E1-E5, 01-06), Dec. 6, 1989.

Married Jan C. Spurlin, Fort Lupton, CO, Sept. 4, 1960. They have three children and one grandchild.

Held position at Christian Church pastorates at Elkhart, IA; Dublin, TX, Pueblo, CO. Retired from Disciples of Christ pastorate Sept. 1, 1994.

CLIFFORD T. WEATHERS, Colonel, born in Augusta, GA. An ordained elder in the North Georgia Annual Conference of the United Methodist Church. Received BA degree from Asbury College and M.Div. from Candler School of Theology, Emory University. Served as pastor of four small churches and was honored as the North Georgia Conference Town and Country Preacher of the Year during his middle year in seminary.

Entered active duty as a chaplain in the US Army, serving for 30 years. Initial assignments included troop duty with the XVIII Abn. Corps Arty., Fort Bragg; 11th Armd. Cav. Regt. in Germany; Vietnam; Okinawa, and Germany. In CONUS, he served on the staff of HQ 5th Army and as command chaplain, Military Dist. of Washington and twice on the staff of the Army Chief of Chaplains in the Pentagon.

Awarded the Legion of Merit (4), Bronze Star, Meritorious Service Medal, Joint Service Commendation Medal, Army Commendation Medal w/OLC, Vietnam Service Medal, National Defense Service Medal, Vietnam Civic Action Honor Medal, Vietnam Campaign Medal w/4 Bronze Stars and the Presidential Unit Citation.

Currently the coordinator for the National Conference on Ministry to the Armed Forces. Married to the former Marjorie Jean Jennings They are the parents of three sons. He has been a member of the MCA for more than 20 years and presently serves on the Executive Committee as trustee.

HARRY WARDEN WEBSTER, Lieutenant Colonel, born Stockton, CA, Sept. 14, 1908. Attended College of Pacific, Asbury College, Asbury Theological Seminary, New College, Edinburgh. Pastorates: Christian and Missionary Alliance Churches in Livermore, Long Beach, and Lafayette, CA and International Protestant Church, Saigon, Vietnam.

Army assignments. 43rd Inf. Div., New Guinea and Luzon; occupation duty in Germany and Japan; Korea. Post chaplain at Forts: Worden, Hood, Chaffee and Mason.

Received the Bronze Star w/OLC Retired in grade of lieutenant colonel, Oct. 31, 1961. His wife of 63 years, Katherine died in 1993. They had four children, four grandchildren and two great-grandchildren. In 1994 he married Jeanette Allen and now resides at Town and Country Manor, Santa Ana, CA. He is the author of three books: *The Road Less Travelled By, Sawdust Trail Chaplain,* and *Ambassador for Christ Without Portfolio,* all autobiographical. Life member MCA.

NORRIS M. WEBSTER, born May 14, 1931, in Roanoke, VA. Received a BA, DB, M.Div. Joined the US Army April 25, 1962

As a military chaplain from 1962-88, he served in various units and locations: the US Army Trng. Ctr, Fort Knox, KY; Nuremberg, Germany; Fort Bragg, NC; Vietnam; Fort Knox, KY; Brooklyn, NY; Fort Campbell, KY, Burtonwood, England, Karlsruhe, GE, Presidio of San Francisco, CA; command chaplain, HQ, US Army Recruiting Command, Fort Sheridan, Evanston, IL; staff chaplain, Combined Field Army, South Korea; post chaplain, HQ, US Army Trng. Ctr. and Fort Jackson, SC

The military is the greatest mission field on earth Every day is Sunday in combat! It was a most exciting and rewarding career. Discharged as colonel July 1988

Married Dr. Lois P Webster, Ph D. They have three children and two grandchildren. Held positions as interim pastor, ABC, in Pennsylvania and New York.

PATRICK CLARENCE WEDEKING, born Dec. 4, 1951, in Topeka, KS. Received BA from St. Thomas Seminary, 1981, Denver, CO; M.Div from Holy Apostles Seminary, 1988, Cromwell, CT. Ordained a Catholic priest for Diocese of Gallup, May 14, 1988. Assistant pastor at Immaculate Conception, 1988-90, Cuba, MN; assistant pastor, Immaculate Heart of Mary, 1990-91, Page, AZ; pastor, Santo Nino, Aragon, NM, 1991-present

USAF military service (enlisted) from 1970-83 includes Lackland AFB; England, AFB, Hahn, AFB, Forbes ANGB Achieved rank of staff sergeant and was discharged from Active USAF, November 1976 and ANG, January 1984

Chaplain military service in USAFR: Commissioned March 1991, served with 9018th ARS (ARPC/HC), Denver, CO and 833rd CSG/HC & 49th FW, Holloman AFB, NM. Achieved the rank of captain, March 8, 1995. Awarded the AF Outstanding Unit Award, AF Good Conduct Medal, Air Reserve Forces Meritorious Service Medal, National Defense Service Medal, AF Longevity Service Award Ribbon w/2 devices, AF Training Ribbon, w/device.

THOMAS EDWARD WEIR, Lieutenant Commander, born April 6, 1925, in Washington, NC. Received BS, University of South Carolina, 1945; BD, Emory University, 1954; Ph D., University of Edinburg, Scotland, 1945.

Joined the USN July 1, 1943 Participated in four tours each, destroyers and Marines. Memorable experience was beating Denny Kinlaw, Jim Kelly and Frank Garrett, 1967-1975, on all points but one. Achieved the rank of lieutenant commander. Retired June 1, 1975.

Married to Rebekah Kennedy Turner; they have two children and two grandchildren. Held positions as national director, Masonic Service Assoc. Hospital Visitation Program; National Chaplain, Knights Templar.

WILLIS WARREN WESSMAN, born Oct. 18, 1920, in Cokato, MN, served USN, 1944-1946. Graduated from Augsburg College, Minneapolis, MN, 1948; Bethel Theological Seminary, St. Paul, MN, 1950; ordained; endorsed Baptist General Conference Army chaplain; commissioned 1950.

Active duty, Camp Atterbury, IN, February 1951, 7th Cav, Korea, July 1951, Camp Crawford, Hokkaido, Japan; 313th Signal Bn., Fort Meade, MD; 3rd Armd. Cav., Bindlach, Germany (commissioned Regular Army chaplain, 1956); post chaplain, Fort McNair, Washington, DC; Fort Riley, KS; staff chaplain, 25th Inf. Div., Schofield Barracks, HI; 6th Army, Presidio of San Francisco; Cam Ranh Bay, Vietnam, US Disciplinary Barracks, Fort Leavenworth, KS

Retired in 1979 as colonel Graduated from C&GSC. Awarded the Legion of Merit, Bronze Star, Meritorious Service and Army Commendation Medals

Following retirement, was interim pastor at Baptist Church and chaplain at nursing home until 1985 in Red Wing, MN. Married to Dolores Poole and has two children and three grandchildren.

DAVID E. WHITE, Rear Admiral, born Nov. 26, 1938, in Amsterdam, NY. Received BA degree from Hope College majoring in chemistry and mathematics, received M.Div. degree, 1963, from New Brunswick Theological Seminary; ordained minister of the Reformed Church in America and served three years as associate pastor of the DeWitt Reformed Church on the lower east side in NYC. Awarded a DD degree, 1991, Hope College.

Commissioned in the USNR in 1963; reported for active duty in 1966 to Destroyer Div. 142. Subsequent tours included the Naval Hospital, Newport; Landing Ship Sqdn. 3 and Naval Station Guam. Received MS degree in management from the Naval Postgraduate School, Monterey, CA, 1973 and served on staff of the Chief of Chaplains as Head, Procurement and Personnel Branch until 1977

Two year tour as sr chaplain aboard USS *Nimitz*; assigned to NAS, Jacksonville, FL, then served as brigade chaplain, 1st Mar. Bde, FMF for two years. In 1984 assigned as executive assistant to the Chief of Chaplains and 1985-88 served as fleet chaplain, US Pacific Fleet. Deputy Chief of Chaplains 1988-91, when appointed chief of chaplains.

Awards include the Defense Superior Service, Legion of Merit, Meritorious Service, Navy Commendation, National Defense Medals and the Sea Service Deployment Ribbon.

Married to Mary Lenore Fryling of Newark, NY June 23, 1962, and has three children: Amy, Claudia and David.

JOHN B. WHITE, Lieutenant Colonel, born March 18, 1929, Harlingen, TX Served the US Army Chaplains Corps for 26 years from the commissioning date as 1st lieutenant Dec. 7, 1959. Called to active duty Nov 1, 1961; Fort Benning, GA with the HHC 291st Engr. Bn., serving as chaplain during the Berlin Crisis. Assigned to the 3rd Bde. and trained young recruits in basic combat training at Fort Bliss, TX.

Served overseas in Thailand with the 809th Engr. Bn.; Sakhon Nahkon; Nahkon Phenom Royal Thai

AFB. Returning to the States and assigned as OCS chaplain at the Artillery Bowl Chapel, Fort Sill, OK.

Began a civilian ministry in Burkburnett, TX and service to the HHC 980th Engr. Bn. in Wichita Falls, TX; called to a Fort Worth Church, he began service with a Dallas, TX higher HQ of the 493rd Engr. Gp.

Serving the Trng. Bde. in Stillwater, OK and held four worship services at week-end drills in company units in Ponca City, Enid, and Shawnee, OK which were members of the 95th Training Div.

Chaplain White retired in 1985. Married to the late Jean Smith a classmate at Texas Christian University where he received the BA and M.Div. degrees.

Served as president of the Metroplex Chapter of the MCA; life member of National MCA.

Retired from the Army and from his denomination. He is an active representative for American National Life Insurance Co. and has a large debit. Remarried to Betty H. Carey and lives in Arlington, TX.

ROBERT MERIWETHER WHITE, Lieutenant Colonel, born Dec. 14, 1927, in Waxahachie, TX. Received bachelor of business administration 1949; BD, 1952; M.Div., 1975;

Joined the USAF, Aug. 21, 1953. Stationed at Wichita Falls, TX; Shepherd AFB; High Wycomb AFS, England; Suffolk County, NY. Served with 6147th TCG 1953-54 Korea; Hamilton AFB, San Francisco, CA; Reese AFB, Lubbock, TX; Wright Patterson AFB, Dayton, OH; Clark AFB, P.I.; Scott AFB, IL; Travis AFB, CA.

Memorable experience was flight line evacuation ministry and experiences in Philippines and Scott AFB. Discharged as lieutenant colonel, Aug. 31, 1973.

Married to Rona Frances Duckworth and they had one son. He passed away Jan. 26, 1995.

ARTHUR JOHN WIENANDT, Major, born Jan. 21, 1948, in Ontonagon, MI. Received BA, M.Div., M.Ed.

Joined the National Guard, June 4, 1982, and served with 1/108th Armd. Cav. Sqd., Senatobia, MS and the 2/114th FA, Starkville, MS. Active duty Nov. 20, 1987, with 92nd Engr. Bn. (Cbt.) (H), Fort Stewart, GA and SWA; 509th Sig. Bn., Camp Darby, Italy; 8th Spt. Gp., Camp Darby and 16th CSG, Hanau, France.

His memorable experience was the six months spent in Desert Storm. Retired as major Dec. 1, 1993.

Married Mary E. and they have two children. He has held positions as teacher, counselor, pastor in Mississippi.

JAMES EDWARD WILLIAMS, Captain, born July 22, 1947, in Warren, OH. Received BS in education from Edinboro University of Pennsylvania; M.Div. from Methodist Theological School in Ohio.

Joined the USAF Sept. 17, 1986. Stationed in Loring AFB, ME, 1986-90. Served with RAF Alconbury, 1990-93; Seymour Johnson AFB, NC, 1993. Served in Turkey during the Gulf War and presently serving in Cuba with Joint Task Force 1994 at Guantanamo Bay.

Married to Jo-Ann Gural and they have two sons, Bruce and Paul. Was United Methodist Pastor in Western Pennsylvania for 14 years prior to service.

ROBERT W. WILLIAMS, Lieutenant Colonel, born Feb. 18, 1921, in Des Moines, IA. Received AB, Illinois College; M.Div., Brite Div. School (TCU); Div. School, University of Chicago).

Joined the Army, Feb. 18, 1945. Stationed in Philippines, Japan, Korea, Hawaii, Germany and Vietnam. Served with Military Army Command, 11th Abn. Div., 101st Abn. Div.

Memorable experience was conducting six services per Sunday from Da Nang to Quang Tri; also memorable was traveling by Army Otter, light plane aircraft, 1965-66. Achieved the rank of lieutenant colonel and was retired Feb. 29, 1968.

Married Mary Louise Hudson in Harrison, AR, Aug. 22, 1940. They have two daughters, one son and eight grandchildren. He held positions two located, nine interim pastorates.

CHARLES F. WILLS, Colonel, a long-time member of the MCA, was born in Avalon, NJ. He holds a BS degree from Wheaton College, IL and the bachelor of divinity and MTH degrees from Eastern Baptist Theological Seminary, Philadelphia, PA. He also is a graduate of the resident course of the Air War College, Maxwell AFB, AL.

Entered the US Army from the Reserve in November 1941. Served with the first US Inf. Div. in the Tunisian and Sicilian campaign and was wounded in action in the latter. Integrated into the Regular Army in 1946. In 1949 he was selected as one of the 166 Regular Army chaplains to be transferred to the Regular Air Force as cadre for the chaplaincy of that service.

Served in various commands of the USAF, Stateside and in Japan and Hawaii. He concluded his Air Force career as command chaplain of AF Logistics Command, retiring in 1967. Among his decorations are the Legion of Merit, Purple Heart and Bronze Star.

Following his military career he was executive secretary of Chaplaincy Services of the American Baptist Churches, Valley Forge, PA and ecclesiastical endorser for that denomination 1969-78. His last staff position was as associate secretary of the Baptist World Alliance 1978-80 although he continued as a member of its commission on Doctrine and Interchurch Cooperation until 1990.

Married to the former Charlotte Emily Robson. They have four children, two daughters and two sons, both of whom have had careers in the Air Force. They have nine grandchildren and, thus far, three great-grandchildren.

GLORIA D. WILSON, Captain, Rev. Gloria D. Wilson, outreach minister of St. Paul AME Church of Berkeley was promoted to the rank of captain in the USAR, and assigned as the first female chaplain at Letterman Army Medical Center, Presidio of San Francisco, CA. Capt. Wilson is also a staff chaplain at Veterans Administration Medical Center in Palo Alto and Menlo Park. She is currently assigned to MEDCOM at Fort Sam Houston, TX.

Rev. Wilson received her M.Div. from San Francisco Theological Seminary, and has completed clinical pastoral education courses at Stanford University Medical Center. She most recently completed a master of science in counseling, with a focus on marriage, family and children, and a couseling certificate at California State University in Hayward.

Rev. Wilson is married to Paul Wilson Sr. and they have two sons, Paul Jr. who is a personality at Oakland Childrens' Fairyland, and MaShon who is an active preschooler.

MELVIN E. WITT, Colonel, graduated from Concordia Seminary, St. Louis, MO, in 1952. Volunteered for the USAF and served at Sewart AFB, TN; Niigata AB, Japan; Castle AFB, CA; Wheelus AB, Libya; Lackland AFB, TX; Grant Heights Housing Area, Japan; Maxwell AFB, AL; Tactical Air Cmd. Chaplain's Office, Langley AFB, VA; MACV Cmd. Chaplain's Office, Vietnam and SAC Chaplain's Office, Offutt AFB, NE. A 1967 graduate of the Air War College (Maxwell AFB, AL), and also completed 24-hours of graduate studies at two universities.

Retired from Offutt AFB in December 1972 with the rank of colonel and was appointed director of World Relief for the Lutheran Church-Missouri Synod, St. Louis, MO, visiting more than 30-foreign countries. Retired from full-time ministry in 1989; served World Relief part-time until June 1993.

From 1992-94, he served as interim pastor of Lutheran Church of the Resurrection (1,800 members) in suburban St. Louis. In October of 1994, he was appointed as the interim executive director of the Council of Lutheran Churches of Greater St. Louis.

His 10 military awards include the Bronze Star and Joint Service Commendation Medals. Honorary degrees: Doctor of Letters from St. John's College (1985), Winfield, KS and Concordia Teacher's College (1986), Seward, NE. Married to Alice Fredricksen Trout and has three children and two grandchildren. He and Alice reside in St. Louis, MO.

HARRY CLINTON WOOD, Captain, born in Trenton, NJ, Aug. 29, 1908 Graduated from Maryville College in 1933; Princeton Theological Seminary in 1936; ordained a Presbyterian minister and served as a civilian parish minister in West Virginia from 1936-39.

On Sept. 1, 1939, he was commissioned a lieutenant (jg) in the Chaplain Corps USN and ordered to active duty aboard the USS *Maryland*. He was aboard when the Japanese attacked Pearl Harbor, Dec 7, 1941. In 1944 he relieved the 4th Mar. Div chaplain in the midst of the Saipan-Tinian campaign and continued with them through the invasion of Iwo Jima for which he was awarded the Bronze Star with Combat V and a citation for services under fire.

His career as a chaplain in the USN continued after the war, with duty aboard USS *Missouri* and USS *Wasp*, a year of graduate study at Union Theological Seminary, NYC, NAS Corpus Christi, TX; NAS Norfolk, VA and then several administrative positions as staff chaplain with COMSTS, PRNC, Washington, DC and CINCNELM in London, England and finally, district chaplain, 3rd Naval District in NYC where he requested retirement in order to assume a civilian position as executive secretary of the Department of Chaplains and Service Personnel of the Presbyterian Church, USA.

JOHN O. WOODS, Colonel, born Sept. 20, 1907, Laramie, WY, son of the late Rev. and Mrs. Oscar Woods. Attended schools in Nebraska, Iowa, West Virginia and Pennsylvania Graduated from Elderton, PA High School, 1924, AB, Thiel College 1928; DD, 1954 and MST, Chicago Lutheran Theological Seminary, 1931 Served as pastor St. Paul's Lutheran Church, Coudersport, PA, 1931-35.

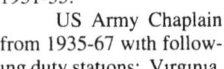

US Army Chaplain from 1935-67 with following duty stations: Virginia, CCC Camps; Carlisle Barracks, PA; 80th Inf. Div. and four battles in ETO, post chaplain, Fort Lee, VA; post chaplain Frankfurt A/M Germany, 2nd Army Chaplain, Fort Meade, MD; senior chaplain, Korea, XVIII Abn. chaplain; Fort Bragg, NC (90 plus military jumps); senior chaplain in European Theatre, Heidelburg, Germany; post chaplain, Valley Forge US Army Hospital. Retired Oct 1, 1967, and lives at St Paul's Retirement Community, Greenville, PA with wife Arlene.

Member of Holy Trinity Lutheran Church and chaplain of Post 140 American Legion, member of VFW, chaplain, 80th Div. Veterans Assoc. and chaplain, PA NW Charter Ret. Officers Assoc ; member and past president Greenville Kiwanis Club and supply pastor of the NW Synod of the Evangelical Lutheran Church of America.

He has two sons LCDR John P Woods, USN (RET). Benicia, CA and Lt Col. Harman O. Woods, on active duty at US Army, St. Louis, MO. His daughter, Virginia, (Mrs. Thomas Hajewski) is an instructor of German at Edinboro University of Pennsylvania. He also has two granddaughters and two grandsons.

R. B. WOODS JR., Colonel, born March 16, 1921, in Rio, IL. Received a BA, BD, MS, M.Div, and Dr. degrees.

Joined the USAF in August 1945. He spent 15 years overseas and 15 years in the States. His last assignment. PACAF as command chaplain

Received two Legion of Merits. He retired in September 1975 as colonel

Married Justine Woods and they have three children and six grandchildren. He pastored two civilian churches.

GEORGE A. WRIGHT, July of 1994 Chaplain George Arthur Wright was awarded a Certificate of Appreciation for 50 years' dedicated service to the Department of the Navy and Veterans Affairs

A native of Johnstown, PA, he began his 32-year Navy career in 1942 following college, seminary and two years pastoral experience near Mt. Pleasant, PA

His diverse assignments as Atlantic Fleet Chaplain, Fleet Chaplain Europe, Force Chaplain Japan, Amphibious Force Chaplain Pacific, District Chaplain, 5th, 3rd and 12th Naval Districts, and combat duty afloat during WWII (USS *Yorktown*) and Korea (USS *St Paul*), plus duty with "Airdales" (Alaska and California), "SeaBees" (Aleutians, Antarctica), "Submariners" (Panama), "Coastguardsmen" (Atlantic) and "Recruits" (MD) enabled him to claim the world as his parish

After retirement from the Navy in July of 1974, he began his ministry to the VA Medical Center, Palo Alto, CA, on a part-time basis until a cardiac by-pass in 1988 caused him to switch to "fee basis" employment.

Born in Salix, PA Oct. 18, 1913, Chaplain Wright has a number of "firsts" to his credit, beginning with his initial assignment to Sitka, AK. Shortly thereafter when he augmented from Reserve to Regular Navy status, he became the first and only USN chaplain from the former Evangelical Church before its merger with the United Brethren and Methodist churches.

In 1964 he was commended for being the first to organize and conduct Navy sponsored professional seminars for senior command and staff officers in the Norfolk, VA area, dealing with problems caused by alcohol and drug abuse. Shortly thereafter the program was extended to include the Navy's civilian components, the first official Directives on Alcohol and Drug Abuse, and the establishment of rehabilitation facilities

As Fleet Chaplain Atlantic he traveled great distances to support chaplains serving from Iceland to Antarctica. As Fleet Chaplain Europe, with the approval of the Holy Fathers governing the monasteries of the Holy Land of Mt Athos, Greece, he joined with his chaplains in a pilgrimage to the world's only theocracy. In England he was invited to preach at the British Naval Academy, and to preach at Babworth Church during the 350th anniversary of the Pilgrim's Fathers' sailing for the New World.

Right after the cessation of Japanese hostilities and prior to the signing of the formal peace treaty on board *Missouri*, he was catapulted from the *Yorktown* in a TBM to land between bomb craters (!) at JAB, Atsugi where he and a war correspondent caught a train to the Japanese Naval Base at Yokosuka to join *Yorktown's* Marine landing contingent quartered at the base hospital.

While on duty in the Canal Zone, he served as interim pastor of the Union Church, Gamboa, CZ, and again in England, as charter member and one of the founding fathers of The American Church in London. As their first interim pastor he was invited back in July of 1994 for the 25th anniversary.

He has been married to Helen Locke of Glen Ellyn, IL for 57 years, they make their home in Los Altos, CA. They have four children, eight grandchildren and three great-grandchildren.

KARL A. WUEST, Colonel, grew up in a devout Roman Catholic home in Cincinnati, OH He attended seminary at St. Charles Seminary, Carthagena, OH, a seminary of the Society of Precious Blood.

Ordained as a Precious Blood priest, he was an assistant pastor at St. Boniface Church in Piqua, OH. After Pearl Harbor, he accepted a commission as a chaplain in the US Army.

Served overseas during WWII in the Italian campaign. Chaplain Wuest served 27 months on active duty and then completed his career in the Army Reserve.

He served parishes in Ohio and retired to his Seminary, which is now a Precious Blood Retirement Home. He passed away in July 1993 and is buried in the cemetery of his beloved St. Charles Seminary. He authored the book, *They Told It To The Chaplain* (Vantage Press, New York), describing his WWII experiences.

EDWARD G. WULFEKUEHLER JR., Colonel, a native of St. Louis, MO. Received his BA degree in English Literature from Drury College where he was elected to Omicron Delta Kappa, Honorary Academic, Athletic and Activities Fraternity. Earned his M.Div. in 1953 and D.Min. in 1977 from Pacific School of Religion, Berkeley, CA. Ordained in the Congregational Church (now UCC) in June 1953, he was commissioned that year as a Reserve Forces Chaplain.

He has held pastorates in Missouri, Oregon, Virginia and California. Since retiring in 1989, he has been a certified interim minister and most recently returned from two years service at historic St. John's Presbyterian Church in downtown Wellington, New Zealand. The New Zealand Returned Servicemen's Association conferred upon him an honorary lifetime membership in 1993.

Civilian activities and recognition include the J.C.'s Distinguished Service Award, DeMolay Legion of Honor; president of local ministeriums and councils of churches; board member of Planned Parenthood, Alcohol and Drug Abuse Councils; College President Advisory Committee and Hillah Temple Shrine Chaplain.

His military career of 34 years included three active duty tours. Air Force 1955-58; Army 1962-65 and as reserve advisor to the Army Chief of Chaplains, 1980-84. Promoted to colonel in 1976 and served as 63rd Army Reserve Command Chaplain, 1976-80.

Military decorations include the Legion of Merit, Meritorious Service Medal w/2 OLCs and the Army Commendation Medal. He is a life member of the MCA, the ROA and the Emerson Foundation of MCA.

Dr Wulfekuehler has three grown children, Deborah, David and Christopher, and seven grandchildren. He lives with his wife Shirley near Jefferson City, MO.

CHRISTOPHER BREESE YOUNG, Commander, born in Syracuse, NY, Oct 12, 1929 Graduated from Florida State University in 1954 and from the School of Theology, Sewanee, TN June 3, 1957. Ordained an Episcopal priest in Winter Park, FL, 1957, and served as rector of St. Richard's Episcopal Church in that city until entering the Navy in 1960. He remained on active duty until retirement in July 1986 as a commander.

His Navy career included a variety of shore stations, overseas duties including Operation DEEPFREEZE 52, Antarctica for 13 months, staff commander, Middle East Force out of Bahrain; two deployments in Vietnam where he was awarded the Bronze Star Medal w/Combat V. He served at all three Navy boot camps: the Coast Guard on Governors Island, NY; the Marine Corps at 29 Palms, CA; Cherry Point, NC. His 15 medals and awards include the Navy and the Coast Guard Commendation Medals.

Young's final assignment was as chaplain at the Naval Station, Pearl Harbor, Hawaii His ministry has continued unabated since retirement from active duty serving central Florida missions, parishes and helping at the Recruit Training Command, Orlando, FL.

LESLIE F. ZIMMERMAN, Colonel, born and educated in Washington state Graduated from Spokane University 1931 with BA degree. Graduate study at numerous colleges with special studies in the field of psychology, pastoral counseling and personnel management. Graduate degrees: M.Div. and DD. Special training in the fields of Marriage Counseling and Vocational Rehabilitation. Married in 1928 to Mary (Kaye) Bradeen and has four married daughters

Ordained to the Ministry in the Christian Church in 1931 with pastorates in Dayton, WA and Seattle, WA. Commissioned as a military chaplain in 1937 with 26 years of service; served with the US Army in 1941; with the Air Force thereafter.

In 1941 assigned to Air Force units in Manila, Philippine Islands where he underwent the siege of Manila, the Defense of Bataan, the Death March, a hell ship trip from the Philippines to Japan. Liberated after 42 months.

In spite of disease, malnutrition and several hospitalizations totaling over 21 months, he became the highest ranking colonel in the Chaplaincy of the Air Force before his retirement in 1963 for physical disability.

Spent 10 years on the executive staff of Goodwill Industries of Orange County, retired at the age of 65 and moved to Desert Hot Springs After a heart attack in 1980, he moved from the desert to Claremont (Claremont Manor) in 1980. He has been involved in manor activities as editor and associate editor of *Manor Items*, served on the Religious Activities Committee and several short term activities.

Served as an elder and adult Bible class teacher, First Christian Church (Disciples of Christ) and on the Board of the Pomona Valley Community Services and the Retired Senior Volunteer Program.

He is a member of the University Club and recently withdrew, for health reasons, as a member of Kiwanis Club of Claremont He is now in his third thousand public addresses.

VASTEN E. ZUMWALT (BUD), Lieutenant Colonel, born Feb. 4, 1929, at Leachville, AR A graduate of Arkansas State University and Southern Baptist Theological Seminary He did graduate work at University of Missouri and San Francisco Theological Seminary, CA. Pastored Calvary Baptist Church, Dexter, MO and First Baptist Church, Memphis, MO before entering the USAF

Served at Keesler AFB, MS, RAF Alconbury, England, Kirtland AFB, NM, Korat AB, Thailand; Tinker AFB, OK, Radar Sites McChord AFB, WA; Pease AFB, NH; Shu Lin Kou AB, Taiwan, Clark AB, P I., Mather AFB, CA, Iraklion AB Crete, Greece; England AFB, LA. Served in enlisted status for three years in US Army 1946-1949

Decorations include the Bronze Star, Meritorious Service Medal, AF Commendation, AF Outstanding Unit Award, Army Good Conduct Medal, WWII Victory Medal, the National Defense Service, Vietnam Gallantry Cross w/device and the RVN Campaign

Memorable experiences: the enriching fellowship with chaplains, chapel personnel and lay persons; coffee with the Archbishop of Crete; baptizing airmen in Mediterranean Sea

Retired from the USAF chaplaincy April 1, 1986, with the rank of lieutenant colonel having served 25 years

Married Betty Jen Overfelt of Moberly, MO, Feb. 10, 1954. They have three children and two grandchildren.

He has pastored the Community Church of Sunsites, Pearce, AZ, lived in Colorado Springs, CO, before coming to Sun City, Las Vegas where he presently pastors Grand Vista Baptist Church. He resides in Las Vegas, NV.

Chaplain Herbert Cleveland with President and Barbara Bush in prayer at the White House.

INDEX

Editor's Note: This index does not include the biography section since they already appear in alphabetical order.

-A-
Ableson, Bradford 22, 23
Al Jubail, Saudi Arabia 39
Albuquerque 18
Ambrose, George 24
Anderson, Alister C. 27
Andrews, Howard A. 19
Annapolis 18
Appel, Alva R 16, 19
Appel, Wilma J. 19
Arlington Cemetery Amphitheater Rotunda Museum 16
Arlington National Cemetery 11, 16
Atlanta 18
Atlantic Beach, FL 17
Axton, John Thomas 8

-B-
Baker, Alan T. 23
Baltimore, MD 8, 14, 18
Baylor University 14
Bennett, Ivan 10
Bentley, F.E. 33
Bershon, Richard Y. 25
Bethesda, MD 11
Bezanson, Ronald Scott 24, 25
Bishop Brent 8
Bishop, Edwin L. 32
Black, Jim 9
Blair, M Douglas 19
Boggs, Jay 17
Bolling Air Force Base 11
Boston, MA 18
Bowers, Ted 39
Brasted, Alva 8
Brent, Charles H 18
Briggs, Ellis O. 28
Brown, Charlie E. 10

-C-
Cape May, NJ 11, 14, 18
Carlisle 18
Castellani, John 37
Chambers, S. David 12, 13, 14, 18, 19
Chicago, IL 8, 11, 18
Christmas Island 32
Cincinnati, OH 8, 18
Clark, Mark 9
Cleveland, Herbert B. 12, 14, 17, 18, 19, 36
Cleveland, OH 8, 18
Clinton, Hillary Rodham 17
College Park, MD 13, 18
Collins, John A 11
Colorado Springs, CO 13, 18
Conte, James W. 19
Craven, John H 6, 28, 35
Cua Viet River 25

-D-
Daley, Virgil Welden 33
Dallas, TX 11
Dando, G. William 14, 15, 17, 19
Daniell, R.D. 26, 29, 38
Darlington, Henry 18
Day, Clayton E. 37, 40
Deblieux, Earl V 23
Devik, Rudolf 19
Dover, DE 14
Drury, Clifford M. 8

-E-
Ebner, Frank H. 12, 13, 18
Edwards Jr., C W. 32
Eglin AFB, FL 23
Ellens, J Harold 19
Ellison III, E.D. "Doc" 17
Elson, Edward L.R. 18
Emery, Bill 14
Emery, William F. 11, 13, 18
Erdman, Pardee 10, 18
Ernstmeyer, Milton S. 18
Esterbrook, Edmund P 8
Everett, David 30

-F-
Fort Hood, TX 32
Fort Meyers, VA 18
Fort Slocum 18
Fort Snelling, MN 12
Fountain, David B. 38
Fourth Marine Division Cemetery 6
Ft. Bragg, NC 35
Ft Campbell, KY 35

-G-
Garner, James 26
Gibson, Ellen Elvira 17
Glenn, Leslie 18
Goodyear, Augustus 10
Graham, Billy 37, 38, 40
Grannini, L P. 9
Graves, Samuel 38
Green, Philip L 18
Griepp, Frank R. 24, 34
Guantanamo Bay 23, 24
Gulf War 22, 23

-H-
Halley, Michael D. 19, 38, 39
Hampton, VA 14, 18
Harmon, James 37
Herrstrom, Bruce 36
Hessian, Patrick J 11
Holland, David John 22
Holt, Harry 31
Hope, Bob 10
Hue Phu Bai 37, 40
Hughes, William 18
Huntington Sheraton Palace Hotel 9
Hyatt, Will 10

-I-
Island, Christmas 20
Iwo Jima 6

-J-
Jacksonville, FL 18
Jay, M.H. 36
Johnson, President Lyndon 31
Justus, Karl B. 9, 10, 13, 18

-K-
Kammerer, Colonel 29
Kelley, Edward J. 17
Keyser, Charles L. 38
Kindley AFB, Bermuda 37
Kingsley, E. James 10, 11, 19
Knight, Cecil J. 19
Knight, JoAnn 17
Kobrinetz, Simeon 18
Korea 22
Korn, Bertram 10, 11
Koschny, William S. 19

-L-
La Rochelle, France 38
Laird, Melvin 10
Lauer, James P. 17
LeMaitre, Leo J. 28
Long Binh 38
Louisville, KY 8, 18
Luffman, Elden 25, 36, 37
Lyons Jr., Arthur E. 22

-M-
Maase, Robert 20, 32
Magee Jr., John Gillespie 30
Magnum, Cyril 9
Martin, James B. 19
Martin, Jerry L. 39
Marty, Dr Martin 14
McCallum, Arlington A. 18
McCoy, Michael L. 17
McDonald, James 37
McNabb, Talmadge Ford 31
McPherson, Everett A. 29
McPherson, Raymond G. 29
Mehring, R.A. 34
Mekong Delta, Vietnam 24
Middleton, Osburn J. 37
Miller, Harry Rhodes 19
Moore, Withers M. 19
Mulligan, Edward B. 19
Murphy, Charlie 10

-N-
Nashville, TN 12, 18
New York, NY 8, 18
Newport, RI 18
Newsom, Ernest B. 17, 19
Noll, Frank H 19
Northrop, Clyde 29
Nunn, Sam 17

-O-
O'Connor, John J. 19
Offutt AFB, NE 23

-P-
Parker, Ray 10
Parrot's Beak 25
Pasadena, CA 9, 18
Patton, General George 8
Payne, S.J 37
Pepple, Robert H. 19
Persian Gulf 22
Peterson, Ted 9
Philadelphia, PA 18
Pittsburgh Theological Seminary 14
Poling, Daniel A 18
Pollard, Rita DeSanto 19
Pope Paul VI 37
Port of Al Jubayl 22
Potter, Lorraine K. 17, 18

-Q-
Quang Tri City 29

-R-
Renne, Eric S. 17
Resor, Stanley R. 10
Reynolds, Fred C. 18
Rice, Robert 9
Ricker, Richard W 18
Riverdale, MD 11
Ryan, Patrick J 9, 11, 18

-S-
Salisbury, Stanton W. 18
Sampson, Francis L. 10
San Francisco, CA 9, 18
Sanford, William H. 19
Santa Monica, CA 18
Saudi Arabia 22, 23
Sawyer, D.M. 34
Schade, Sigmund 32, 37
Schultz, Thomas A. 32, 34
Scott, Simon H 11, 13, 18
Seager, Alfred R. 13
Seattle, WA 18
Seiders, Marlin D. 11, 13, 17, 18
Seifried, Kenneth 17
Seoul, Korea 31
Shaw, James E. 11, 12, 13, 18
Sheehy, Maurice S. 18
Sherman House 10
Smith, James Roy 11, 18
Smith, Ralph 19
Snyder, Howard E. 18
Song Be City 24
SS Dorchester 8
St Paul, MN 36
St. Francis Hotel 9
St Louis, MO 8, 18
Stearns, Gustav 18
Stegman, Leonard F. 18
Stevenson, Neil M. 11
Stillwell, Richard 37
Stirling, Al 25
Synan, Edward A. 19

-T-
Tacoma, WA 11, 12, 18
Tampa, FL 13
Tan Son Nhut 37
Taylor, Maxwell D. 28
Thomas, Hazel 39
Thomas, John M. 18
Thompson, Jean W. 19
Thompson, Mark R. 12, 13, 19
Tomb of the Unknown Soldier 16

-U-
Ujonbu, Korea 31
USNS Geiger 26
USS Coral Sea 38
USS Iwo Jima 32, 37
USS Proteus 14
USS Puget Sound 38, 39

-V-
Varvin, Frank O. 35
Vietnam 24, 25, 27, 30, 37

-W-
Wakefield, John F. 35, 36
Walker, "Connie" 33
Walker, Robert T. 37
Walter Reed Army Medical Center 39
Washington, DC 8, 9, 12, 13, 18
Washington Navy Yard 19
Weathers, Clifford 17
West Nottingham Academy 14
West Point 18
White, David E. 17
White, R.J. 9
White, Robert M. 18
Williams, Richard 35
Winter Park 18
Wright, John 39
Wulfekuehler Jr., Edward G. 19

-Y-
Yates, Julian 8
Ylvisaker, Nils 8, 18
Yongpyoug, Korea 34

-Z-
Zeis, Melvin 37
Zellerback, James D. 9

Chaplain Alister Anderson celebrating Holy Communion for the troops of the 25th Infantry Division in the Iron Triangle, Vietnam in November 1967. (Courtesy of Fr. Alister C. Anderson)

www.ingramcontent.com/pod-product-compliance
Lightning Source LLC
Chambersburg PA
CBHW081921180426
43200CB00032B/2904